METAPHYSICS OF THE PROFANE

ERIC JACOBSON

$M^{ETAPHYSICS}$ OF THE P_{ROFANE}

The Political Theology of Walter Benjamin and Gershom Scholem

COLUMBIA UNIVERSITY PRESS   NEW YORK

Columbia University Press

Publishers Since 1893

New York Chichester, West Sussex

Library of Congress Cataloging-in-Publication Data

Jacobson, Eric.

   Metaphysics of the profane : the political theology of Walter Benjamin and
Gershom Scholem / Eric Jacobson.

    p.   cm.

   Includes bibliographical references and index.

   ISBN 0–231–12656–5 (cloth : alk. paper)—ISBN 0–231–12657–3 (pbk. : alk. paper)

    1. Benjamin, Walter, 1892–1940—Contributions in political theology.   2. Scholem,
Gershom Gerhard, 1897—Contributions in political theology.   3. Political theology.
4. Messiah—Judaism.   5. Judaism and politics.   6. Language—Philosophy.
7. Justice (Jewish theology)   I. Title.

B3209.B584 J33 2003

261.7'092—dc

2002031455

Columbia University Press books are printed on permanent and durable acid-free paper.

Printed in the United States of America

c 10 9 8 7 6 5 4 3 2 1

p 10 9 8 7 6 5 4 3 2 1

FÜR MISAKO

CONTENTS

PREFACE

Many new materials are presented here for the first time in English, including previously untranslated selections from Gershom Scholem's journals and letters, the early writings of Walter Benjamin, and unpublished material from the Scholem Archive in Jerusalem. A short note on the use of the German in this work is therefore due. Each citation is given in translation, followed by the original that Columbia University Press has kindly allowed me to include in the notes to the chapter. In the case of Benjamin, several works from the early period are now available in English, and I have sought to refer to these translations whenever possible. Nevertheless, I have chosen to modify them to better serve this study. On occasion, reference is given but the translations will strongly diverge.

I would like to thank Suhrkamp Verlag for kind permission to reproduce Walter Benjamin's "Theologisch-Politisches Fragment," from *Gesammelte Schriften* II:203—204, "Notizen zu einer Arbeit über die Kategorie der Gerechtigkeit," and Gershom Scholem's "Der Bolschewismus," from Gershom Scholem, *Tagebücher* I:401–402 and II:556–558, and "Thesen über den Begriff der Gerechtigkeit" (Scholem arc. 1599/277.34) from the Gerschom Scholem Archive in Jerusalem. Many thanks to Rafi

Weiser, Department of Manuscripts, the National and University Library in Jerusalem, for permission to reproduce Scholem's Hebrew rendition of Benjamin's "On Language As Such and the Language of Man." Chapter 1 has appeared in a modified form under the title "Understanding Walter Benjamin's *Theological-Political Fragment*" in *Jewish Studies Quarterly* 8, no. 3 (2001): 205–247. An abbreviated version of chapter 2 appeared in Italian as "Anarchismo e traditione ebraica: Gershom Scholem" in Amedeo Bertolo, ed., *L'anarchico e l'ebreo*, pp. 55–75 (Milan: Elèuthera, 2001).

In preparing this work, there are several individuals to whom I am most grateful. I would like to thank Dietrich Böhler, Peter Carrier, Werner Konitzer, Michael Löwy, Christopher Powers, Andrea Garetto, Martin Schmidt, Kelly Ann Stoner, and Jürgen Thaler for their comments on the first stages of this project as well as Anson Rabinbach and Gary Smith for their criticism. Thanks to the Visiting Research Fellows program at the Hebrew University and staff at the National and University Library in Jerusalem, in particular the Gershom Scholem Archive and Library, I was able to consult the Scholem Archives in 1998. Giulio Busi, Johanna Hoornweg, and Claudia Ulbrich are gratefully acknowledged for their efforts in the work being awarded a Tibertius prize by the Senate of Berlin's Department of Culture in 2000. In preparation of the manuscript for publication, I am very grateful to Wendy Lochner and Susan Pensak at Columbia University Press for their tireless efforts as well as Frank Böhling, Harry Fox, Sander Gilman, Julie Kelley, Josephine Rodigues, Samira Teuteberg, and Myrna Weissman for their help and good advice. Most of all, I am grateful to Joseph Dan for his guidance through every phase of this work. Despite this support, any remaining errors are my own.

METAPHYSICS OF THE PROFANE

INTRODUCTION

What began with a visit to Berlin, one rainy summer a few years after the fall of the wall, burgeoned into the following study of the intellectual partnership of Walter Benjamin and Gershom Scholem, which I wrote over a period of nine years at the Free University of Berlin. *Metaphysics of the Profane: The Political Theology of Walter Benjamin and Gershom Scholem* concerns an early phase in the thinking of both authors, bound in many ways to the period surrounding the First World War. Their friendship could have begun as early as the fall of 1913, when Scholem's Zionist youth group, Jung Juda, met the Sprechsaal der Jugend, which was formed under the influence of the anarchist pedagogue Gustav Wyneken.[1] Benjamin had been chosen that evening by Wyneken's group to speak on the question of Zionism.[2] Yet the first encounter between the two actually took place on July 16, 1915, in the library of the University of Berlin.[3] Following this initial meeting, their friendship was to span twenty-five years, until Benjamin's suicide in 1940 while fleeing the Nazis.

The most intensive phase of this intellectual partnership began in 1915 and probably reached a peak during the highly creative but also isolated period of the authors' residence in the town of Muri, Switzerland in 1918. It most definitely culminates in 1923 with Scholem's departure for Palestine. Other than two brief encounters in

Paris in the 1930s, the authors were never to meet again. Following Scholem's departure, the discussion takes the form of letters—those best preserved date from the years 1933 to 1940—that Scholem published with great satisfaction toward the end of his life.[4] On account of Scholem's efforts we are able to examine this late period with relative ease. Yet the early years, which were undoubtedly seminal for the later exchange, remain largely unknown. Recent publications of Scholem's journals and letters in German have made a record of these discussions available to the public for the first time.[5] Other early manuscripts in Scholem's hand have yet to see the light of day. The nature of these highly theoretical discussions has also contributed to the fact that this formative period remains for the most part unexplored. Benjamin's and Scholem's ideas, which I have here characterized as an early political theology, are the focus of this study.

Politics were clearly a main issue of debate. The beginning of their relationship, in marked contrast to its development, was constituted by a shared interest in politics, with the activities of the young Scholem a central topic. This was perhaps the period in Scholem's life when he was most politically engaged, attending clandestine meetings with his brother Werner (later USPD-Faction representative with Luxemburg and Liebknecht to the Reichstag)[6] and campaigning with the Jung Juda against the First World War, for which he was thrown out of the *Gymnasium* a year before graduation.[7] Passionately stating the case for a socialism with an "anarchist streak,"[8] Scholem developed a penchant for revolutionary and utopian political theory that was to have a considerable influence on Benjamin, carving the contours of an intellectual exchange that spanned their entire friendship.

Scholem's magnum opus, *Major Trends in Jewish Mysticism*, begins with a dedication to Walter Benjamin as the genial metaphysician, critic, and scholar. Yet more than simply a eulogy for a friend, these three dimensions of Benjamin were to have an influence on Scholem extending far beyond the "friendship of a lifetime," as he puts it in the English version. Indeed friendship is, to the best of our knowledge, that which one experiences in a lifetime, yet the tenor, focus, and, to a great degree, content of the early period of intellectual exchange and mutual influence was to penetrate far into the recesses of Scholem's late work, many years after Benjamin's death. The nature of these early influences can be said to have shaped the very basis and structure of his conception of Judaism. More than a friendship, the relationship between the authors can rightly be termed an intellectual partnership, one that was essential for Scholem's work as a whole. But what does this say about the legacy of the genial metaphysician, critic, and scholar? What is thus an appropriate measure to evaluate the lasting significance of Benjamin thought? If we consider the reception of Benjamin's work, where Theodor Adorno has long been considered the most important successor, it was actually Scholem who was the first to extend Benjamin's philosophical tradition to his own thought, indeed remaining closer in many ways to the early categorical analysis. In this respect the Marxist reception of Benjamin's work in the 1970s was incorrect where it sought to paint Scholem as a conservative. It failed to see Scholem's critique of Bolshevism, as well as his friend's turn to Marxism in the later years, as a product of his early "metaphysical anarchism," which the authors indeed developed together. In this sense the need for a reappraisal of Scholem's work is overdue. I have therefore sought to make Benjamin's influence on Scholem's work one of the key aspects of this book, beginning with the early period and extending into Scholem's late studies on Kabbalah. It would also have been a task of great worth to extend the early political theology to Benjamin's more mature writings, particularly with regard to a messianic understanding of history. Yet this question, in its own magnitude and complexity, and necessarily predicated on a firm conception of the early period, will have to be reserved for a future project.

Despite these initial words, the reader will find the personal anecdotes of the authors reduced to a minimum in the following study, not because they fail to make good reading—they often do—but because they tend to substitute for a project establishing the main currents of their thought. I have therefore sought to restrict the narrative aspect of this study to the chronology of the exchange and to the social and historical conditions that affected them rather than focusing on biographical events themselves.[9] The aim of this book is to provide a close reading of the authors, seeking to reconstitute the character and verve of their early political theology. To that end I have sought to explain their theory in an exegetical manner, favoring speculative commentary over personal association.[10] Nevertheless, I do not think that it can be emphasized enough how thoroughly unique this partnership was in relation to its historical moment—a moment that would conclude with the campaign to exterminate German and European Jewry. As with every other aspect of German-Jewish culture, the Shoah has also fundamentally altered the nature and meaning of this partnership, placing

Benjamin and Scholem squarely within a generation that culminates centuries of German-Jewish culture. I have here tried to give the English-speaking reader insight into the intellectual atmosphere that gave rise to these ideas, from contemporary political and theological thinking in figures like Franz Rosenzweig, Ernst Bloch, and Gustav Landauer to influences such as Franz Joseph Molitor, Samson Raphael Hirsch, and Søren Kierkegaard.

One of the central problems facing this book is Benjamin's early relationship to Judaism. In his late *Passagen Werk* Benjamin explained his stance toward theology using the metaphor of ink and a blotter, suggesting that theology permeates all aspects of his thought. During his interaction with Scholem in the early years these thoughts become more concerned with articulating a distinctly Jewish dimension, albeit a Judaism unique to what he himself had experienced. His experience in this regard, no less than Scholem's, was one to which all German Jews were subjected: either convert and thus abandon Judaism, assimilate and abandon the question, or turn to Zionism and seek an *Erneuerung des Judentums,* a "rejuvenation of Judaism" in the words of Martin Buber. "The problem of Jewish spirit," he writes to Buber in a letter from November 1915, "is one of the most central and consistent objects of my thought."[11] Yet, unwilling to be subjected to the terms constructed by any of these positions, Benjamin sought to forge his own path to an understanding of Judaism. If his goal was to be able one day to call his thinking a "philosophy of Judaism," as Scholem reports, a study of the theological dimension of Benjamin's thought would also need to evaluate the degree to which this was achieved. However, if this proves difficult, because of Benjamin's rather modest knowledge of Judaism and classical Jewish literature, we must then evaluate his legacy in Scholem, on whom the statement made a lasting impression.[12] In this respect I think it is necessary to try to dispel a misconception some have associated with such a project—an illusion that no doubt has much to do with the tremendous interest in the study of Judaism in Germany today. Clearly the wish to repair an intellectual tradition so utterly destroyed over a half century ago cannot be restored by overcompensation, in which a German Jew is made to appear to have been more concerned with Judaism than he or she truly was. Instead, a careful evaluation is needed, whereby the one does not rule out the other. I did not see any reason to portray Benjamin as having been more occupied with Judaism than he was, nor the opposite, for that matter. At best I would only hope to have followed a course laid out by Scholem many years before: not seek to apply Judaism to Benjamin but rather Benjamin to Judaism.

The title of this study should also be qualified by a few remarks. I have taken to the term *metaphysics* to highlight the basic nature of the thinking addressed in this study: it is a highly speculative philosophy of fundamental questions regarding politics and theology, drawing on a near scholastic aptitude for categorical analysis and Talmudic rigor within a conception of divine continuity of meaning. In this way it is in fact a philosophy of divine as well as profane questions. "Metaphysics," Scholem once remarks in his Swiss notebook, "is a legitimate theory in the subjunctive form. This is the best definition I have found so far; it says everything."[13] The tenor of this discussion is indeed abstract, speculative, subjunctive, and, in the case of Benjamin, even to the furthest possibilities of German grammar. Yet although the methodology is metaphysical, the subject matter is not solely ethereal. The emphasis of the authors is, in fact, distinctly oriented toward worldly affairs, not merely in the sense of somehow "secularizing" theological notions to take on profane meanings but also in advocating qualified restraint with regard to the divine realm while searching for its link to the profane.[14] Rather than a metaphysics of divine realms, the early political theology is concerned with the profane and consciously addresses itself to it. One might indeed want to question the use of the term *metaphysics* here, where the word *speculation* might suffice, not to speak of the broader meaning of the use of such categories as messianism or justice. But in this regard I did not make it my task to draw normative conclusions from the authors' dialogue, nor have I sought to preform a critique of their ideas. The focus of this study is to seek an accurate presentation of the authors' views, to make them accessible to the general public and ultimately susceptible to criticism.

The use of the term *political theology* also requires some explanation. It stems from a desire for a concise phrase to serve as an umbrella for subject matter related to messianism, speculations on divine language and on justice. It goes without saying that the use of the term here has nothing to do with Nazi theorist Carl Schmitt's use of it in the title of a publication in 1923, after the period in question.[15] In contrast to Schmitt, who spuriously claimed to have invented the term,[16] the view presented here is that political theology begins with the Torah and the political and religious structure of the Israelites, their classes of priests and judges, the divine ordination of kings—in short, everything that led Josephus to coin the term *theocracy* to capture the meaning of their social and religious organization.[17] It is in a biblical sense that political theology is used here.

This work is divided into three parts that reflect the main areas of discussion: messianism, language, and justice. Part 1 is perhaps the most accessible to readers familiar with Benjamin's early writings, for it attempts to frame the context of the discussion on messianism within the early work and the categories he himself establishes in the period. This is followed by a broader portrayal of Scholem: the categories of his theological politics and the metamorphosis this politics undergoes. The discussion then turns to the linguistic aspect of the authors' exchange, examining the proposals of Benjamin's early essay from 1916, "On Language As Such and the Language of Man," in light of the history of linguistic speculation in Judaism. Benjamin's proposals on language and its relationship to Judaic linguistics becomes a formidable influence in Scholem's first studies of Jewish mysticism. It is an influence, however, that Scholem is unable to fully explore until his late essay of the 1970s, "The Name of God and the Linguistic Theory of the Kabbalah," where he applies Benjamin's linguistic speculations to the history of the Kabbalah and Judaism. The reader will now hopefully be steeped in the perspectives and terminology of the authors for part 3, on justice. It focuses on their idea of divine justice, first formulated through Benjamin's critique of the notions of original responsibility, the highest good, law, and right, followed by Scholem's application of the categories to the Torah and particularly to the prophets. It is here in part 3 that we see political theology come to fruition as a metaphysical tradition.

I would like to begin here with a more comprehensive overview of the chapters. Part 1 focuses on Benjamin's early concept of the messianic in history. According to Benjamin, the advent of Messiah is clearly juxtaposed to the course of history shaped by the mighty and powerful. The Messiah disrupts history and is determined to usher into worldly affairs a transformative age. The first question we are faced with is whether this world to come is seen by Benjamin as a consequence of the Messiah's arrival or of a world fermented by humanity but consummated by the Messiah. In other words, does the Messiah bring on redemption or is the arrival of the Messiah, after the initiation of human activity, the a posteriori signal that redemption has come? This question, which is just as essential for revolutionaries contemplating revolution (in place of the Messiah) as it is for the messianic idea in Judaism, is taken up through an analysis of one of Benjamin's early texts, the "Theological-Political Fragment."[18] The categories that Benjamin uses to construct the fragment form the basis of the discussion here as well as the political and theological structure of the book in its entirety. One of the categories that consistently reappears in Benjamin's early thinking is the need for a rigorous partition between the divine and profane. While the divine is enveloped in absolute terms, he directs his attention to the profane, speculating on the meaning of the division and opening up the realm to human activity. After situating the discussion in the division of the divine and profane and then introducing a messianic rupture of these two spheres, the question turns to the role of humanity in the messianic drama. Benjamin seeks to define a dimension of human activity capable of reaching the divine in representative form. This largely unintentional activity requires the kind of devotion he discovers in the hero of tragic drama. In seeking to understand the relationship between the fate of the hero and his or her devotion, the notions of fate and character come into play, with Benjamin drafting a short essay of the same title a few years later. Two theological categories featured in the fragment are discussed here: that of the *restitutio in integrum*, meaning the messianic promise of the restoration of things to their original state, and immortality as the guaranteed condition of humanity in a messianic age. I propose the necessity of these categories, along with the concept of theocracy, for any messianic theory.

The discussion on nihilism, which concludes the first chapter on messianism, makes the transition to a more narrative phase in this study, bringing together Benjamin's movement toward abstract, political speculation with the historical moment in which he is writing. Benjamin's early political activities in the German student movement and the influence of anarchist theory are put aside in favor of a retreat from politics. It is arguable whether Benjamin is ever truly political in a practical sense, but his advocacy of a nihilism in conclusion to the fragment has as much to do with the collapse of historical politics following the outbreak of the First World War as with a renewed and intensified commitment to an abstract political theory, governed not by history but by a philosophy of right.[19] In this he affirms the role of theology in framing the contours of political analysis. Nihilism, as a "world politics," contends Benjamin, is also articulated as an affirmative, political idea by Scholem in this period. In Scholem's case nihilism is preceded by a more traditional political notion of anarchism that he defines in opposition to his brother, Werner Scholem, an avowed independent socialist and later member of the Reichstag. Scholem can be seen here in the broader context of young, German-speaking Jews at this time who discover a hidden affinity between Judaism and a utopian, revolutionary consciousness centering around figures such as Martin Buber and Gustav Landauer. Scholem grasps this utopian dimension and seeks to steer it further toward a political conception of Judaism, one able to see the biblical notion of Zion not simply as a metaphorical covenant but as a living obligation and historical goal. Whether Zion should be interpreted as a metaphor or as a program is the focus of a debate between the two authors, and it is also the center of Scholem's early anarchist Zionism, which I discuss at length here. By the latter part of the war Scholem's activist front begins to retreat into the background, as a more pensive and, in some ways, critical approach to the potential for immanent transformation emerges. This occurs while Scholem joined up with Benjamin in an intensive phase of intellectual exchange in Muri, Switzerland in 1918.

In the remaining sections of part 1, we leave Benjamin behind on the shores of Europe and embark on a narrow journey in search of an overview of Scholem's theological politics. We begin with Scholem's research into the messianism of Sabbatai Zvi in his essay "Redemption Through Sin" (1936), followed by a synopsis of his later political reflections, which I have termed a critical anarchism. Here a new perspective on the early political theology is introduced: anarchism comes to describe elements within Judaism rather than a more general political practice or theory. Cataclysmic tendencies in Jewish messianism are understood by Scholem to be anarchic forces that yield new historical forms through their destructive activities. Drawing on this notion, we are able to see how Scholem begins to evaluate radical changes in religious law and observance as anarchic elements within Judaism. His use of anarchism as a critical category gives rise to a notion of Judaism beyond worldly confines, inexhaustible and constantly reinventing itself in the face of new traditions and historical constraints. Finally, in his later years, Scholem turns to a critical form of religious anarchism, claiming that anarchism is the only position that makes religious sense.

The second tier of this early political theology is the conception of language, which likewise constitutes part 2 of this study. Turning back to 1916 and his early essay, "On Language As Such and the Language of Man," we find Benjamin employing the story of creation to construct a philosophy of language based on a concept of innate meaning. In his analysis language is not the *means* to expression but *is* the expression of all things and ideas. Here the content of a thing is not expressed *through* language but *in* it. In this way creation is key to Benjamin's theory, and, by painting the broader context of linguistic speculation in Judaism, particularly in Genesis and midrashic literature, Benjamin's categories emerge as part of this tradition.

With Benjamin's supposition that the essence of a being or an idea is its language, we are immediately confronted by the problem of linguistic expression. Benjamin formulates the question in the following way: if a thing or idea *is* its language, then what is the meaning of a metaphor? And, when referring to the divine, what else are we to find in language other than a metaphor? In questioning the idea of representation, Benjamin seeks to inquire into an existence beyond the possibility of expression, here meaning the existence of the divine within language. He attempts to address this problem in the story of creation: God expressed His inner substance to create humanity, and ultimately the universe, "in His image," but He Himself remains incommunicable, inaudible, and untranslatable. The act of creation is performed linguistically and therefore suggests to Benjamin the existence of a divine language distinct from our own. He then turns to the names given by Adam to the animals and asks, How could Adam have known the names of the created beings unless they somehow communicated themselves to him? The name thus becomes the focal point of speculation as to the linguistic expression of an object, the expression of its "substance of the intellect." With the idea that the animals somehow expressed themselves to Adam in such a way that he was able to recognize and therefore give them their names, Benjamin considers the magic defined in the relationship between an object and its name in the context of revelation, a transmission of this "substance" from the divine to the profane. A magical transition from the inexpressible to finite expression must take place here as well, he adds, supporting the observation with another passage from Genesis on the creation of Adam. Benjamin, in his reading, plays down the physical aspects of the transition of the spirit of life, God's spirit, to Adam, thus deliberately steering his interpretation away from Hamann and other linguistic thinkers who emphasize an incarnation theory in the word of God forming the flesh of the son—in other words, a Christian linguistic theory. The relationship between the expression of the named and the namer is brought fully into theological focus, with the problem for Adam of knowledge in God succeeding the act of naming.

Benjamin seeks here to address the finite nature of the human word in relation to the infinite nature of God's. This linguistic transition from God
to Adam, from a creating word to a naming one, and, ultimately, after the
expulsion from paradise, from divine language to the profane, is examined
by Benjamin in the concept of translation. In all forms of expression he
seeks to define a continuous transporting of one language into another,
from written to acoustic, from animate to inanimate, from profane to divine. In the expulsion from paradise the expression of this translation was
lost. What emerges in its place is a language of "damaged immediacy," as
Benjamin writes, examined here in the confusion between sign and symbol. In the breakdown of an immediate relationship between a name and
the thing that is named, a multiplicity of words abound for the same object, just as a multiplicity of languages exist for the same expression.

Profane language emerges from paradise damaged. Yet human language is not without any reference to its predecessor, claims Benjamin, seeing within humanity a residue of the creating word of God. This creating
word is preserved in profane expression in the language of judgment—the
dimension of justice in the profane. Judgment is deemed the ray of hope
through which a redeemed language of pure immediacy will once again be
established, while immediacy harkens back to a pure linguistic state in the
garden of Eden. The "irony" of the fall to which Benjamin refers at the end
of this episode is that the expulsion from paradise was not the birthplace of
good and evil but an example of how God administers divine justice; the
existence of the two in the form of the fruit of the tree precedes the forbidden act. Thus the lesson that this passage carries for Benjamin is one of the
"mythical origins of law." This is expanded in part 3.

At this point I turn from a close analysis of Benjamin's early philosophy of language to explain the discussion in the context of possible influences. The newly published materials from Scholem reveal a tremendous
debt to the Christian Kabbalist Franz Joseph Molitor and his book *Philosophy of History; or, On Tradition* (1827), whose critical influence on Scholem began to take effect around the time of the authors' intensive discussions on language. Indeed, if Benjamin sought a concise source for
many of the ideas that he presents in his essay, he would have had only to
turn to Molitor to obtain a clear and sophisticated understanding of Jewish linguistic theory. In Scholem's enthusiastic reference to Molitor's work
as "a true ideology of Zionism" he was to link himself in no uncertain
terms to a conviction that Molitor shared: the notion of Hebrew as the di-

vine language. It appears that Molitor and Scholem diverge at this point from Benjamin, who suggests in its place a theory of translation.

Benjamin's orientation to a philosophy of language, which is supported by some of the main elements of classical, Jewish linguistic speculation, was a great impetus for Scholem and his early research into the Kabbalah. He wanted, in fact, to write his doctoral dissertation in 1921 on linguistic mysticism based largely on his discussions with Benjamin. But after some initial scholarly research in the vast, unchartered waters of the history of the Kabbalah, he was forced to change course. After fifty years of a tireless quest, Scholem was finally able to return to his youthful pursuit in the 1973 essay "The Name of God and the Linguistic Theory of the Kabbalah." This essay is the subject of the remaining sections in part 2.

Perhaps the center of Scholem's essay, and that which marks his attempt to apply the early political theology of language to the history of the Kabbalah, is the assertion that linguistic speculation is metaphysical speculation, seen here as reflection on the meaning and truth of the Torah. Consequently, a metaphysical approach to creation is also the starting point of Scholem's study. The categories of his analysis begin, first of all, with the acoustic dimension of God's pronunciation, that is, "Let there be light," and light occurs. Here expression is viewed in much the same way that it was by Benjamin: substance is manifested *in* language and not *through* it, where language is more than simply a medium of expression. We see Scholem presenting a similar problem to that which we saw in Benjamin: how does a symbol express the inexpressible? Scholem links the "magic" of the symbol, in its ability to articulate the unpronounceable, to Benjamin's "linguistic mysticism," as he calls it, thereby paving the way for a broad study of mystical linguistics in terms first drawn up by Benjamin. In addition, Scholem establishes three points with which he seeks to define Jewish linguistic theory. First, that creation and revelation are linguistic expressions of God's infinite nature that confront the profane in the limited form of a symbol. Second, the name of God is the metaphysical origin of language, from which everything else emerged. Third, the theory of the name is located in the magic of its expression in the profane and its link to the human word. These three stipulations mark the focus of Scholem's analysis. The remaining chapter follows Scholem's journey through the history of Jewish linguistic thought, seeking to expose the ways in which his methodology is indebted to the early linguistic theory. The idea of the creating word of God and His unpronounceable name returns in Scholem's late essay to the paradox already posed by Benjamin, in which the name that God used to name Himself, the name with which He is addressed, is no longer expressible or pronounceable. It is a name that creates meaning but is itself meaningless. For Scholem this paradox typifies the power of the divine. He draws a distinction between the unpronounceable name and God's creating word, providing the groundwork for the discussion of the hidden, divine combinations of the letters of a creating language.

Postbiblical linguistic thinking in Judaism abounds in the possibilities of discovering elements of this creating language, even if only in the limited sense of a symbol. If the Torah acted as the blueprint for the story of creation, which one of the earliest commentaries on Genesis, *Bereshit Rabbah*, suggests, then the discovery of this language must consist of deciphering a code concealed in the words of the Torah. Naturally, we encounter a problem with the physical aspects of creation when viewing words as the building blocks of the world, as Benjamin's notion of the spirit or breath of God comes into focus. The letters themselves, the smallest particles of the word, turn to figurative atoms under a linguistic microscope. Their combinations, as the book *Sefer Yetzirah* proposes, is the key to their power. This tradition, continuing in medieval Spain, Scholem pursues in the writings of Nachmanides, Moses de Leon and Joseph Gikatilla, medieval thinkers who are speculative grammarians of the divine name, searching for the structure and meaning of the divine in symbolic form. Scholem introduces figures such as Isaac the Blind from Provence and contrasts him to Schlegel's proposal that philosophers are grammarians of reason. But unlike philologists, who view the written form as a secondary or mediated representation of true language, the Kabbalists see the written as the "true representation" of its secrets, says Scholem, situating Benjamin chiefly among them. In Scholem's essay we witness a transition from early rabbinic thought to medieval microlinguistic speculation where the metaphysics of language are based on the secret dimensions of its atomic parts. Scholem considers the contributions of the Iyyun circle to linguistic speculation in the Kabbalah, followed by a theory of a historical Torah that reveals a new meaning in every age. He then seeks to expose the metaphysical orientation of Jacob Ha-Kohen of the thirteenth century and Israel Sarug of the seventeenth century, linking them implicitly to Benjamin's speculations of a paradisiacal language. Scholem returns here to the question whether Hebrew itself was the divine language, enabling a distinction between the views of the Kabbalists and Benjamin.

The microlinguistic theory of the thirteenth-century Kabbalist Abraham Abulafia and his "science of prophecy" takes on a central role in Scholem's essay. We see here how Abulafia shares Benjamin's conception of linguistic intelligence, which the former perceives not only in Hebrew as the divine language but also in every translated language. The divine name and the pursuit of knowledge remains at the core of the analysis, as well as a theory of linguistic magic. In short, we are able to detect quite a few of Benjamin's categories in Scholem's portrayal of Abulafia. The final section of part 2 reviews Scholem's own conclusions concerning a Judaic philosophy of language, drawing on the early categories in the late research and suggesting a linguistic tradition to which Benjamin belongs.

Part 3 concerns the idea of justice, the third dimension of this early political theology. By the very suggestion that justice is the substance of redemption, it can no longer be viewed as part of the profane. Thus the very first proposal in Scholem's and Benjamin's conception is the necessity to ascribe justice to the realm of the divine and construct in its place a notion of judgment in the profane. In a redemptive conception of justice we discover early references imbued with new meaning. The judging word, which we encountered in Benjamin's linguistic theory in part 2, is explored here in great detail, along with notions of the mystical origins of law, fate, and responsibility. The relationship between character and fate initially encountered in the first section on messianism is here coupled with the problem of the origins of evil. I begin this chapter with a comparison of Kierkegaard's notion of responsibility to that of Benjamin's, seeking to explain how the origins of evil in the first encounter with sin undergoes a radical reinterpretation in Benjamin's metaphysics of Genesis. Similar to Kierkegaard, a new ethics is proposed on the basis of the actions of the individual and not on original sin. Yet rather than an original sin transferred to individual sin, Benjamin seeks to overturn the notion of sin altogether, substituting it its place a redemptive pursuit of responsibility. In contrast to the universalization of suffering proposed by Kierkegaard, Benjamin seeks the universalization of the Jew.

Ideas of distributive justice, virtue, and the material and spiritual restitution in the just state are the categories that emerge from the early discussions with Scholem concerning a Judaic conception of justice. Scholem's journals again play an important role in reconstructing the early debate as well as presenting us with a hitherto unknown text by Benjamin entitled "Notes to a Study on the Category of Justice," presented here in

English for the first time. In addition to exploring terms that belong to a restitutio in integrum of the 1921 fragment, these notes also constitute a precursor to the concept of justice in his "Critique of Violence." Benjamin differentiates ethical, worldly activity once again from the category of justice, focusing here on the difference between the terms *mishpat* and *tzedek,* which he formulates in Hebrew script. One of Scholem's manuscripts from the archive in Jerusalem entitled "Thesen über den Begriff der Gerechtigkeit" (Theses on the Concept of Justice) appears to be a direct commentary on Benjamin's notes on justice, with the first few theses attempting to pinpoint the sources of Benjamin's text. Scholem reflects on the idea of distributive justice and comes to the conclusion that it must point to something beyond the mere universalization of goods, be it material goods or "the highest good." Echoing Benjamin's terminology, he attempts to distinguish justice from virtue, moving to a discussion of the morphology of the word *tzedek* from a perspective enriched by the categories of the divine and profane. Violence is then the focus of his inquiry into virtue and righteousness.

In another of the newly released archival manuscripts presented here in English for the first time, Scholem seeks to contextualize the discussion on justice in the language of the prophets, drawing on the story of Jonah as well as the groundwork of divine justice in prophecy as a whole. Once again, the distinction between justice and judgment takes center stage through the terms *mishpat* and *tzedek*. The postponement of judgment in the story of Jonah—more specifically, the postponement of the *execution* of judgment—is suggested as an indicator of the meaning of divine justice as a whole. If justice in Jonah's prophecy is exhibited in the postponement of the execution of judgment, then justice on earth would be the permanent suspension of the Last Judgment, Scholem concludes. Here, he introduces the concept of the *tzadik*, the righteous figure, who represents the "being of justice."

The concept of justice in the early political theology draws on the distinction between the divine and profane, situating the idea of justice solely in the realm of the former. Prophecy, in this respect, is an attempt to articulate the terms of a divine conception of justice. And yet this distinction immediately calls into question the demands of justice in the profane world. Indeed, the culmination of the First World War disrupts the decisive political nihilism that Scholem and Benjamin had constructed during their isolated existence in Muri, Switzerland. In this period of critical reflection on practical politics a debate ensued on the meaning and importance of the Bolshevik revolution. Scholem's thoughts from the period are preserved in a handwritten manuscript from 1918 bearing the title "The Bolshevik Revolution," presented here in English. In his late recollections of the debate he writes that he defended the principle of revolutionary dictatorship, if this meant the dictatorship of the impoverished and not necessarily the proletariat.[20] Scholem's sympathies, according to his late reflections, lay with the social revolutionaries against the Bolsheviks. Yet in this early manuscript Scholem was more inclined to entertain the messianic qualities of a Bolshevik movement that imparted a "magic" to its ranks in the notion of a "dictatorship of poverty" and linked to the messianic idea. But as a historical force promising future justice, Scholem already suggests in 1918, Bolshevism proves unable to judge its own actions in the present. The dictatorship of poverty, he writes, is constituted to end in blood.

The idea of the justified use of violence becomes one of the key components of this political theology, and, with the preceding debate on divine and prophetic justice in mind, we can now turn our attention to one of the most celebrated essays among Benjamin's early writings, the "Critique of Violence" of 1921. In many ways it presents itself as the most political of the early pieces, making explicit claims with regard to the question of justified violence in the hands of the state, the police, and the judicial system in contrast to the counterinstitutions of strikes and antiwar pacifism. However, the proposals with which Benjamin concludes his critique have little to do with practical political activity. In one sense we see him defending the anarchist-pacifist challenge to the monopoly of state violence. The true basis of violence, he argues, is divine violence, which God manifests in the world. He defines here the worldly counterforce to an arbitrary or "mythical" violence as a "politics of pure means." By this Benjamin points to the friendly exchange between individuals as a basis for a new politics, itself formed from a "culture of the heart." What begins with a rather political thesis turns to theological speculation on divine violence and a messianic community of freely acting individuals. The "Critique of Violence" also seems to have had a considerable impact on Scholem, as the latter part of his "Theses on the Concept of Justice" reveals. Scholem here seeks to bring together his analysis of justice in the form of divine postponement with several of Benjamin's ideas.

In the last section of the final chapter on justice, we turn to the impact of the early political theology on the mature Scholem, moving into the late

1950s to consider what effect these early speculations on justice may have had on Scholem's later conception of the righteous figure. In the manuscript on Jonah and in the "Theses on the Concept of Justice" we witnessed a growing interest in the role of the worldly just, focusing on the linguistic relationship between justice, charity, and righteousness. This takes its cue from the focus on virtue, *mishpat,* and the righteous individual in Benjamin's "Notes to a Study on the Category of Justice" and "Critique of Violence," presenting many of the categories again with renewed vigor in an essay for the *Eranos Jahrbuch* in 1958 on "The Teachings on the 'Just' in Jewish Mysticism." Here Scholem divides the figure of righteousness into three types, through which many of the early categories are expressed. These are the righteous, the pious, and the scholar—*tzadik, Chasid,* and *talmid chakham.* The final few pages explore Scholem's personal link to the meaning embedded in names and the anarchic, collectivist, even comical eruption of justice in the world in the form of the righteous figure. It is clear, from the perspective established in this chapter, that the characteristics Scholem finds in the righteous are also those of the Messiah.

The focus of this study can be summarized as an attempt to reconstruct the early discussion of the authors in the framework of an intellectual partnership, seeking to emphasize the mutual effect that each had on the other regarding the body of ideas I have termed a political theology. It is also a study of the lasting influence that this early political and theological speculation was to have on Scholem. Many new materials are presented here for the first time in English, including parts of Scholem's journals and letters, unpublished material from the Scholem Archive in Jerusalem, as well as untranslated early texts by Benjamin. Should this study make a contribution to the understanding of the foundations of Scholem's pioneering research into Jewish mysticism and messianism, or the Judaic and theological underpinnings of Benjamin's thought, the author would be most gratified.

PART I

Messianism

Die Geschichte ist der Kampf zwischen den Begeisterten und den Trägen, den Zukünftigen und den Vergangenen, den Freien und Unfreien. Die Unfreien werden stets den Kanon ihrer Gesetze uns vorweisen können. Wir aber werden das Gesetz, unter dem wir stehen, noch nicht nennen können. Daß es Pflicht ist, fühlen wir.

History is the battle between the fervent and the yoke, between those of the future and of the past, between the free and unfree. The unfree are perpetually able to present to us the canon of their laws. Yet we are not able to name the law under which we stand. We feel this to be an obligation.
—Benjamin on Gerhart Hauptmann (1913)

CHAPTER 1

THE MESSIANIC IDEA IN WALTER BENJAMIN'S EARLY WRITINGS

In the early writings of Walter Benjamin, history is an unending battle between past and future, between the right of law and the right to establish law, between the history of the conquered and that of the conqueror in which both past and present are governed by laws not their own. Accompanying a history of legal tyranny and subjugation, Benjamin submits there is a past containing its own living law, a law insurmountable by worldly dictates, pertaining to historical occurrences and their hidden structure, that he seeks to defend in this early formulation on the work of Gerhard Hauptmann.[1] To reveal this obligation is apparently beyond the capacity of the critic in 1913. Yet, after a lengthy period of theological and political reflection, the main currents of this law reemerge as a philosophy of history in the terse and rather thesislike "Theological-Political Fragment" of 1921.[2]

This fragment begins where most tractates on history conclude. Yet here the end of history is neither one formed by an outburst of cumulative reason nor the might of a worldly empire whose sovereignty rests on the shoulders of the defeated but by the Messiah who completes all historical occurrence and repatriates the downtrodden. It points to the conclusion of a temporal and spatial plane, meaning both an end to past and future as well as the division of this world from the next. The end of history connotes a messianic understanding of the unfolding of worldly events whose approach is juxtaposed to the empty resolution of history—represented by the history of the worldly victorious. This messianic understanding, termed mystical in Benjamin's text, strives to reveal an abstract representation of the divine kingdom in theological terms, or utopia in its anarchist counterpart. The question of human agency is at the center of his analysis concerning the relationship between the divine and profane worlds. The mediating tension between the two is understood as giving rise to a dynamic in which an event in one realm is shown to have an effect in the other. This dynamic is then characterized in the form of a messianic drama, where the nature and actions of the individual takes shape with the decline of all spatial and temporal parameters. The focus of the tragic hero is thus the redemptive act, viewed as worldly activity that inadvertently establishes the conditions of eternity and, therefore, redemption.

Before presenting an in-depth account of the elements that constitute this messianic conception of history, let us turn briefly to the text and the controversy that surrounds it. The following is a new translation and a complete reproduction:

THEOLOGICAL-POLITICAL FRAGMENT

First the Messiah completes all historical occurrence, whose relation to the messianic (in this sense) he himself first redeems, completes, and creates. Therefore nothing historical can intend to refer to the messianic from itself out of itself. For this reason, the kingdom of God is not the telos of the historical dynamic; it cannot be set toward a goal. Historically seen, it is not a goal but an end. Thus the order of the profane cannot be built on the idea of the kingdom of God; theocracy, therefore, has no political but only religious significance. To have repudiated the political meaning of theocracy with all intensity is the greatest service of Bloch's *Spirit of Utopia*.

The order of the profane has to be established on the idea of happiness. The relation of this order to the messianic is one of the essential elements in the teachings of historical philosophy. It is the precondition of a mystical conception of history, whose problem permits itself to be represented in an image. If one directional arrow marks the goal in which the dynamic of the profane takes effect, and another the direction of messianic intensity, then clearly the pursuit of happiness of free humanity strives away from every messianic direction. But just as a force is capable, through its direction, of promoting another in the opposite direction, so too is the profane order of the profane in the coming of the messianic kingdom. The profane, therefore, is not a category of the kingdom but a category—that is, one of the most appropriate—of its most quiet nearing. For in happiness everything earthly strives for its decline, and only in happiness is the decline determined to find it. While clearly the unmediated messianic intensity of the heart, of the inner, individual person, passes through tragedy, in the sense of suffering. To the spiritual *restitutio in integrum,* which introduces immortality, corresponds a worldliness that ushers in the eternity of the decline and the rhythm of this eternal passing away, passing away in its totality— worldliness passing away in its spatial but also temporal totality—the rhythm of messianic nature is happiness. For the messianic is nature in its eternal and total transience.

To strive for this, even for those stages of humanity that are nature, is the task of world politics whose method is called nihilism.[3]

THEOLOGISCH-POLITISCHES FRAGMENT

Erst der Messias selbst vollendet alles historisches Geschehen, und zwar in dem Sinne, daß er dessen Beziehung auf das Messianische selbst erst erlöst, vollendet, schafft. Darum kann nichts Historisches von sich aus sich auf Messianisches beziehen wollen. Darum ist das Reich Gottes nicht das Telos der historischen Dynamis; es kann nicht zum Ziel gesetzt werden. Historisch gesehen ist es nicht Ziel, sondern Ende. Darum kann die Ordnung des Profanen nicht am Gedanken des Gottesreiches aufgebaut werden, darum hat die Theokratie keinen politischen sondern allein einen religiösen Sinn. Die politische Bedeutung der Theokratie mit aller Intensität geleugnet zu haben ist das größte Verdienst von Blochs »Geist der Utopie«.

Die Ordnung des Profanen hat sich aufzurichten an der Idee des Glücks. Die Beziehung dieser Ordnung auf das Messianische ist eines der wesentlichen Lehrstücke der Geschichtsphilosophie. Und zwar ist von ihr aus eine mystische Geschichtsauffassung bedingt, deren Problem in einem Bilde sich darlegen läßt. Wenn eine Pfeilrichtung das Ziel, in welchem die Dynamis des Profanen wirkt, bezeichnet, eine andere die Richtung der messianischen Intensität, so strebt freilich das Glückssuchen der freien Menschheit von jener messianischen Richtung fort, aber wie eine Kraft durch ihren Weg eine andere auf entgegengesetzt gerichtetem Wege zu befördern vermag, so auch die profane Ordnung des Profanen das Kommen des messianischen Reiches. Das Profane also ist zwar keine Kategorie des Reichs, aber eine Kategorie, und zwar der zutreffendsten eine, seines leisesten Nahens. Denn im Glück aber erstrebt alles Irdische seinen Untergang, nur im Glück ist ihm der Untergang zu finden bestimmt.— Während freilich die unmittelbare messianische Intensität des Herzens, des innern einzelnen Menschen durch Unglück, im Sinne des Leidens hindurchgeht. Der geistlichen restitutio in integrum, welche in die Unsterblichkeit einführt, entspricht eine weltliche, die in die Ewigkeit eines Unterganges führt und der Rhythmus dieses ewig vergehenden, in seiner Totalität vergehenden, in seiner räumlichen, aber auch zeitlichen Totalität vergehenden Weltlichen, der Rhythmus der messianischen Natur, ist Glück. Denn messianisch ist die Natur aus ihrer ewigen und totalen Vergängnis.

Diese zu erstreben, auch für diejenigen Stufen des Menschen, welche Natur sind, ist die Aufgabe der Weltpolitik, deren Methode Nihilismus zu heißen hat.   (II:203)

Benjamin's "Theological-Political Fragment" presents a discrete framework to evaluate his early thinking on history and redemption in the context of the early writings.[4] In 1920–1921, the years during which this sketch of a theological politics is supposed to have been written,[5] the gaping wounds of the carnivorious First World War had yet to heal, followed by the eruption of the short-lived revolutions and general strikes in Munich and Berlin. The array of support for the war, from Social Democrats to the intellectual and political leadership of the Jewish community, most notably Martin Buber, contributed to an atmosphere of despair concerning notions of allegiance, moral fortitude, and political agency.[6] The growing influence of Soviet Marxism after the Russian Revolution also added to a state of confusion regarding ends and means.

Most readers are inclined to interpret historical events as having had a considerable effect on Benjamin's political writings.[7] The fragment seems no less the case. The curious oddity of this minuscule text, however, is that naming this period has proven highly contentious. The fragment was given its title by Adorno in the first edition of Benjamin's writings in 1955 and has retained a place of controversy ever since. According to Adorno, he and his wife met Benjamin for the last time at the end of 1937/1938 in San Remo, Italy. Benjamin reportedly read them the text aloud, referring to it on that occasion as the "Newest of the New." Adorno dated the text 1937 accordingly.[8] Yet Scholem believed something quite different:

> I rest assured that these pages were written in 1920–1921 in conjunction with the *Critique of Violence* and did not entertain a relationship with Marxism at the time. It exhibits a metaphysical anarchism that corresponded to the author's ideas before 1924. Adorno dates the text from 1937. My response is that the date is a jest, to see if Adorno would mistake a mystical-anarchist text for a recently composed Marxist one. Benjamin, by the way, engaged from time to time in such experiments.[9]

Beyond a commitment to historical accuracy, Scholem's skepticism about the dating of the text had much, apparently, to do with an eager audience that sought to believe in the unbroken passage of the messianic idea to Marxism. Scholem, however, saw the text as being rather characteristic of an earlier period where Benjamin's inclination toward articulating a "philosophy of Judaism"[10] and a metaphysical anarchism loomed large upon his intellectual horizon. If one is to consider some of the formative literature of the early period, namely, Ernst Bloch's *Spirit of Utopia* (1919) and Franz Rosenzweig's *Star of Redemption* (1921), in relationship to the fragment, it does appear possible to place the text in the context of the early writings.[11] In this respect the focus of the following chapter is to rework the "Theological-Political Fragment" back into the fabric of the early years, allowing the central categories of Benjamin's early political theology to come to the fore. These terms and categories will then serve as points of reference for further speculation, beginning with the concept of redemption in the idea of the Messiah.

The Messianic State: Does the Messiah Initiate or Consummate?

> *It is therefore as the Baal Shem says, that the Messiah is capable of coming only after all the guests are seated at the table. This table is, first, the table of labor, and only then the table of the Lord—the organization of the earth possesses its own unmediated effect and unmediated, deductive metaphysics in the secrets of the kingdom.*
> —Ernst Bloch, *Spirit of Utopia* [12]

The Messiah consummating the messianic process as a conceptual tradition can be seen in many different sources, periods, and schools of thought in Judaism.[13] Whether in *Sefer Zerubbabel*, which features a Messiah consummating redemption in an ultimate battle,[14] or in the "Treatise on the Left Emanation" of Jacob Ha'Kohen, in which the Messiah is featured as a warrior set to extinguish the satanic embodiment of evil, the Messiah stands alone in the task of redemption. In both apocalyptic dramas the Messiah enters as hero, Satan naturally as his opponent, and history the stage upon which the plot unfolds.[15] No particular role is attributed to humanity in these two early narratives of redemptive activity. In either form the Messiah "completes all historical occurrence" in solo. His actions are not dependent on worldly activity but concentrated purely on conquering evil.

We witness a radical transformation of this idea in the sixteenth century with the emergence of Lurianic Kabbalah. The notion of the consummation of redemption takes on an entirely new meaning in this school of thought, one in which humanity now plays a very active role in its own redemption—even, one might say, in the redemption of God.[16] The necessity of collective participation in redemption through worldly activity is indeed the hallmark of this new theory. The central position played by the Messiah in the first two narratives becomes all but secondary here. What is important in Lurianic theory is the role of humanity in initiating the messianic age. The standard dimensions of Jewish messianism—a Messiah without features, yet one preforming distinct, predesignated historical acts—are naturally not lost here. Yet the role of human agency takes on new importance, heralding a revolutionary interpretation of redemption that has profoundly influenced the messianic idea in Judaism up to the present.

I present this summary of two particular stands of messianic thinking, along with the opening allusion to the Baal Shem found in Bloch's *Spirit of Utopia*, to illustrate a central problem of the messianic idea with which the fragment begins: whether redemption is initiated prior to or only after the arrival of the Messiah. This difference is clearly essential to a messianic conception of history, for, in the latter, redemption is inaugurated by the Messiah alone, in whose hands all historical responsibility therefore rests. In the former, however, redemption is induced by the redemptive acts of the individual in the world. This distinction goes back to a conversation between the two authors on the immediacy of the messianic idea. Scholem makes a note of it in his journal entry for November 3, 1917:

> The greatest portrait [*Bild*] of history, upon which the infinitely deep connection of history to religion and ethics is based, has been discovered in the concept of the messianic kingdom. Walter once said, "The messianic kingdom is always present." This perspective is very true—but only in a sphere that I believe no one has reached since the prophets.[17]

In the opening lines of the fragment, however, the role of the Messiah is emphasized, whereas in Scholem's recollections, if the messianic kingdom is already present, there would no longer be a need for the arrival of the Messiah or, indeed, if such a need still existed, then merely in the role of a final confirmation. Thus the presence of the kingdom supports the first proposition, that redemption is dependent upon the redemptive acts of the individual in the world. The fragment, however, is more complex, and a participatory interpretation of redemption is soon its focus. Nevertheless, what is certain and relevant for the interpretation here is that both positions on the messianic idea are addressed by Benjamin. We shall see how they remain largely unresolved in his thought.

The order of redemption is therefore undoubtedly central to Benjamin's messianic idea. Yet whatever one might think of the author's early ambition to construct a philosophy of Judaism as Scholem reports, it is incumbent upon us to evaluate Benjamin's thinking within the context of Judaism, if for no other reason than the statement that the profane cannot be established upon the kingdom of God, severing the link between worldly affairs and theocracy. With regard to the idea of redemption in Judaism, which always takes place upon the stage of history and in a collective sphere before the community, offering little by way of individual salvation, we are compelled to distinguish Benjamin's ideas from those of Christian theocracy and Messianism.[18] There are no references in the fragment, nor in the early writing, to a second messianic event linked to a first, to Jesus as the Messiah and the son of God, nor to any of the elements that constitute the basic tenets of Christian faith and distinguish it from Judaism.[19] Belief in the authenticity of the Messiah as a means of individual ascension or salvation is not the focus of Benjamin's messianism but rather the final conclusion of worldly suffering in a collective and permanent end of history. Thus, with the notion of the Messiah as consummator, expressed in the statement "First the Messiah completes all historical occurrence," we turn our attention to theoretical components of Benjamin's messianism in the context of Jewish tradition.[20]

Focusing now more specifically on Benjamin's notion of completion, we see the Messiah's actions directed to a final conclusion of history, in which the last remnants of bad actions are made good again. This is what is meant by the idea of all historical past being redeemed—the divine reparation of all actions in the world that went awry. These past events are historical, for they were formed in the world. Rather than being forgotten, they are returned to their original state of wholeness.[21]

In this way the idea of redemption ending historical time, since predicated by history itself, can be understood within the broader notion of historical completion. The end of historical time, however, is not to be confused with the end of history. History's completion is here expressed not as "a goal but an end."[22] While time generates various irreconcilable moments in history, redemption is its only complete and thus true end, rather than a goal set for it as a telos in history. Seen from a negative perspective, neither an earthly kingdom of God, nor the worker's state, nor bourgeois democracy can be pronounced as the end of a historical telos for Benjamin. Only an understanding approaching history as events that face their end, unmitigated by any external worldly preconditions, reflects a messianic conception, in his view. An end that is placed in relationship to the creative act is an end that harbors no worldly telos, no self-generation, no intention, no motor of history—it is merely the inverse of beginning. Toward creation it appears messianic, for it alone completes creation. A determinate end, which is understood in relation to creation and constituted as messianic, is therefore an end in redemption.[23] In a conversation with Benjamin on the subject, Scholem recalls in his journal, "The new heaven is heaven without a night. The new creation is time, as Walter says, which rises [erhebt sich] at the end of time."[24] When "beginning" can no longer remain indeterminate and, to be beginning, is distinguished from the moment in which it is no longer development but standstill, in which everything related to the state of "beginning" returns to itself, only then is there a "completion of work" in the sense of conclusion.[25] Everything that is incomplete when redemption commences, springing forth from creation but still hanging onto its beginning, is returned back into itself.[26]

A model to conceptualize the notion of a redemptive end in relation to creation can be found in the *Star of Redemption* in the idea of the work of art.[27] In the profane world only the work of art is able to approximate a closed, finished state of completion and therefore to grasp the principle of end in its necessity and categorical integrity. End is categorical and historical, but as it reaches the aesthetic realm it achieves the possibility to arrive as such and be complete. Through its inherent transformative dynamic the work of art in the profane realm is given to comprehend the redemptive category of what Rosenzweig calls "das Fertigwerden," "to become finished." By this he seeks to show how the end of history can be understood in relation to a work of art. It occurs. Its self-differentiation appears no longer at the beginning but at the same time always contains the meaning of coming to a complete and final condition.[28] Bloch also conceives of an end in relation to creation, such that a full and complete end in the *Spirit of Utopia* is situated within worldly time, between past and future: "In this way, the world has a beginning as well as an end in time," he writes, "as it is only conceivable as a process, for only history forms the [most] appropriate and essential method of world-knowledge."[29] Bloch emphasizes the lasting aspect of historical occurrence, the notion of which itself necessitates a concept of history.[30]

Of interest here is not historical occurrence itself, locked in the mortality of passing away, but clearly an approach to history and the historical events of the powerful. These can never be the "telos" of the dynamic of history, says Benjamin, which themselves can never lead to the "kingdom of God." Such a conception of history, needless to say its application, is precisely at odds with the view presented in the fragment. Here "the Kingdom of God . . . cannot be set toward a goal," just as the notion of justice. which, in being relegated to the divine, also cannot be intentional.[31] The kingdom of God is not an aim of the worldly realm because it is not an act but a state; if it can be sought, it surely cannot be targeted. Thus as a state of being and not as a goal, it is possible for a full and complete end to be reached. For this reason, everything that pertains to history cannot be paralleled by the ahistorical, i.e., that which is beyond the realm of worldly events. The order of the profane and worldly experience cannot be structured on events in the divine world, events with which no notion of time can be associated. Since no distinction between thought and action extends to the divine, no historical occurrence can likewise be established on the idea of the kingdom of God as an aspect of progress. With this distinction the divine and profane realms are initially determined to be discrete and radically separate entities.

Thus Benjamin's opening remarks concern the role of the Messiah in fermenting the end of history. Whether the role of the Messiah is to consummate a new dimension or to conclude this historical process, messianism is situated both in an ongoing tension in his own work and in Judaism as a whole. This discussion is then transferred to the debate on human agency, as we shall see shortly. The focus so far has been the relevance of Benjamin's comments on the meaning of the Messiah and the messianic event. Now, if only the Messiah "completes all historical occurrence," such that the end of history is predicated exclusively on messianic arrival, a question naturally arises as to the state of the messianic event. This is juxtaposed to the fact that, as we read, the order of the profane cannot be built upon the concept of a kingdom of God. This means that a worldly determination of the notion of redemptive praxis has no place in the schema of a divine kingdom, a state in which God is the ultimate measure of all being. To be sure, the profane is not completely independent of the divine; a link between the two realms is indeed elaborated at a later point. For the moment, the profane is a condition and the construction of agency in this world. Agency, in other words, is here conceived independently of the idea of a divine kingdom, for while agency has a practical, almost visceral meaning, the kingdom of God does not. It is most clearly not political. Moreover, this distinction is quite apparent if one considers the problem of revelation: for revelation without divine intention contravenes the first postulate of the theory of attributes, that God is all-knowing, which situates the divine realm far from sensory experience. Therefore, the construction of worldly agency must be kept critically separate from what the telos of history would inevitably bring under the dictates of the notion of progress. This does not imply a disengagement from history; it only calls for categorical independence in the construction of an approach to politics.

It is for this reason that theocracy has no *political* meaning.[32] Theocracy constitutes the ideal of a divine world, which, in contrast to the world of the living, can only remain a categorical reflection. As such, it cannot be a fulfillment of politics, which stands antithetical to theology, or one that is void of historical agency. Only in the realm of a categorical absolute can a theocratic state be postulated, says Benjamin. This realm would take its independence from theology, which stands free to conceive of the constitution of the world from the perspective of its hidden messianic dimension. Such an approach is therefore presupposed by a methodology of historical understanding beyond history, a historical philosophy that postulates a messianic dimension of history through the prism of its redemptive end. This concept of history connotes the formulation of a non-historically determined dynamic, independent of any teleological prescription or any precise unyielding development but nevertheless imbued with the necessary contours of being, i.e., a beginning and an end. Agency is a moment of intervention into this dynamic that is ultimately capable of canceling this division and allowing the end to rectify the beginning.

Theocracy as politics has therefore to be seen as something extraneous to Benjamin's analysis: the political categories of theology, if not to fall into falsehood, must remain absolute. Rather than as a political notion, theocracy is to be understood as a divine category that is only meaningfully contemplated in the context of the Messiah. This would appear to lead us to the "great service" of Bloch's *Spirit of Utopia* that Benjamin praises in the fragment as a "repudiation" of theocratic politics. With such a definitive statement, any reader would find it hard to believe that no clear discussion of theocracy as such is to be found in the *Spirit of Utopia*, leading some to interpret Benjamin's comments as a disguised critique of Zionism via Bloch.[33] However, if a critique of Zionism can be found in the *Spirit of Utopia*, it would express the very opposite: condemnation not of theocratic zealotry but the aspirations of the parvenu. In his chapter on the Jews Bloch criticizes Zionism for denying the "power of being chosen" and seeking the assimilation of the Jews into a balkanized national state, no different from the rest.[34]

By the time Benjamin read the *Spirit of Utopia*, his views on Zionism were surely well formed. In this sense it is true that little seems to have changed in terms of his clear rejection of "practical" Zionism in 1912, where he expresses his lifelong conviction, however much at times distraught, that Judaism has found its home in European culture.[35] Although Zionism does not speak to him, he says, "I perceive Judaism to be at my core."[36] He defines three forms of "Zionist Judaism": Palestine-Zionism, what he labels practical Zionism elsewhere, German Zionism, which he sees as assimilationist ("they propagate Palestine and drink like Germans"), and cultural Zionism, which he says has "Jewish" value in every place and thing.[37] He identifies with this last position, referring to it again in this period as a *Zionismus des Geistes,* a "Zionism of the spirit" and a "Jewish-spiritual project."[38] His later decision to learn Hebrew, even acquiring a stipend through the first president of the Hebrew University, Yehuda Magnes (which he later spurned to the embarrassment of Scholem), actually does not deny his earlier views.[39] Scholem, however, fundamentally disagreed with Benjamin's rejection of a political role for Zionism and later in life may have even seen Benjamin's isolated and ultimately devastated European existence as a model for a form of Jewish alienation that he bitterly deemed self-imposed.[40]

Yet in itself, without any further indication in this regard, the introduction of the concept of theocracy here cannot be taken as a hidden critique of Zionism, which, as a religious or potentially theocratic movement, is largely a phenomenon of the last few decades. Nor can it be understood merely as a statement on the necessity of pure thought. The search for a messianic conception of history gives rise to a more fundamental problem: no discussion of political theology is complete without a concept of theocracy, not only in the accidental sense of the contemporary resurgence of theocracy the world over but for reasons inherent to the messianic idea itself. As in other religious movements with a political dimension, theocracy has therefore to be seen as an essential component of Jewish messianism. It is the notion of a state that is executed in law but grounded in the covenant with God, existing as a form of rule but also as a means of organization. Josephus, who is believed to have first coined the phrase in relation to other Greek terms describing political forms (democracy, oligarchy, hierarchy), sought a term to capture not only the form of religious structure of the Israelites but one that would articulate the nature of their social organization.[41]

Some may argue that the Torah proscribes a covenant with God that supersedes legal obligation, as do the prophets who limit the power of kings, yet a conception of messianism without the restoration or completion of the Davidic dynasty is hardly possible. Even if the postbiblical ideas of theocracy, beginning with Talmudic and Midrashic traditions, do not always strictly emphasize the house of David reconquering the kingdom, it is difficult to conceive of Judaic redemption outside of a monarchical structure and a centralized, political theocracy.[42] In Benjamin's fragment the question of theocracy can also be read in terms of a "political" structure carried over into a "religious" domain. If it is to remain an element of political theology, then the category of theocracy implicitly poses the question: Can there be a conception of messianism without theocracy; i.e., is there such a thing as a theocracy that is truly utopian, free from domination and hierarchy? An anarchist kingdom of God?[43]

THE DIVISION OF THE HOLY AND PROFANE

As in the fragment, Benjamin creates a juxtaposition of the divine and profane in his essay on Hölderlin. The issue at hand is immortality: "The heavenly ones have become signs of infinite life, which, however, is limited by it."[44] Immortality, in this passage, is the yearning of the profane and a mark of the divine. Why, one might ask, does Benjamin reinstitute a radical partition between the divine and profane centuries after philosophy asserted its collapse? An answer to this question first requires an understanding of the nature of the dichotomy. Where the juxtaposition is dualistic, there can be no ultimate unity of the holy and profane in redemption; where it is dialectical, it is capable of being messianic.[45] If the dualistic realms of heaven and earth would seek the neutralization of messianic tendencies, then to postulate a final abrogation of all previously necessary divisions could therefore be seen as integral to a dialectical theology. Rosenzweig's understanding of this division is essential to his own notion of its ultimate negation not as a destruction but as a final reunification of "the kingdom of God and the kingdom of the world."[46] He links the two realms en route to redemption, in which revelation is directed solely toward humanity, having no existence in-itself but purely for-itself.[47] Redemption is here the completion of the world through its fulfillment in the world. Unlike creation, which occurs spatially, and revelation, which occurs temporally, redemption ends both spatial and temporal parameters. It cannot therefore merely exist but rather must come into being through its own link to the world. This portal, through which redemption makes its entrance and is therefore perceivable in the world, is achieved through human activity. For Rosenzweig, this activity is die Nächstenliebe—the principle to "love thy neighbor."[48]

A similar division between the divine and profane can also be found in Bloch, where history is conceived in its final abrogation through the rejoining of the worldly and heavenly realms.[49] In Bloch the holy represents "a supra-worldly sphere, a utopian reality or a not-yet-established but fully functioning reality of the idea . . . a supra-sensory, supra-empirical world" that exists for the "utopian-absolute subject" in contrast to a "sensory" and "sub-empirical world."[50] The world above represents the 'not-yet-existing' and in this sense fully reflects the abstract, not-yet-attainable conception of the divine in Benjamin. The world above, which, although mediated by the profane, is seen from its end in redemption and therefore is expressed only as a "kingdom-in-between" (GdU:430). Its categorical integrity of being "above" and not "below" is metaphorical and can immediately be disputed, for it does not exist for us in our worldly selves but is intended to serve as a realm of ideas. What is not under question is the firm separation between theology as a form of critical understanding and politics in its materialist realization. Thus the use of the concept of kingdom can never be understood as the will to establish God's kingdom on earth. The question therefore turns to the perception of the divine in the profane.

We have thus far seen a bifurcated conception of history, resting on a conception of temporal and spatial existence. This conception, polarized by the tension between a profane world and a messianic one, Benjamin describes as "one of the essential elements in the teachings of historical philosophy," which is the precondition of "a mystical conception of history, whose problem permits itself to be represented in an image." We begin therefore with a positive statement on mysticism representing a historical philosophy contingent upon the tension between agency and the messianic and revealing a messianic index within profane activity. This mystical conception can only be represented in an image, which permits its representation insofar as the falsehood of images itself is retained. Just as no idol is permitted by God to stand before Him, the divine kingdom is not to be revealed through imitation, through words or symbols that allow passage into the divine realm through mere mimicry.[51] However, although the image is an impoverished representation, it is the only form able to capture this messianic understanding. In "The Life of Students" we also see a reference to the conception of history as only understandable and possible as "an image of the highest, metaphysical state."[52] In this sense the representation of a messianic history is mediated by the image-seeking divine representation.[53] The image is like a mirror: it presents metaphysical truth within history but only in an inverted form. It is captured by a weak, profane capacity but is able, nevertheless, to express a fragment of the divine in "dissonance." We see this elsewhere in the essay on Hölderlin with regard to metaphysical truth locked within the image:

> The dissonance of the image, which, given the most radical emphasis, suggests a tonal dissonance, has the function of making the inherent intellectual ordering of joy in time perceptible, audible, in the chain of an infinitely extended event corresponding to the infinite possibilities of rhyme. Thus, the dissonance in the image of the true . . . evokes the ability to be stridden upon as the unifying relation of the orders, just as "opportunity" signified the intellectual-temporal identity (the truth) of the situation. Within the poetic structure, these dissonances bring into relief the temporal identity inherent in every spatial relation and hence the absolutely determining nature of intellectual existence within the identical extension.[54]

In the excerpt above we read of an image that resonates with sound, associated here with verse and rhyme. Dissonance arises out of a harmonic image of truth in its externalized expression, carrying with it a divine purpose: revelation concerning the underlying structure of time so that time no longer appears as a lineal string of barbarism but rather as a table of events that are bound to redemption, the "temporal order of happiness." It is here that we can see his discussion with Scholem playing a role in the notion of historical events being countable without necessarily numerically ordered.[55] In this text dissonance of the image reveals its identity as truth in spatial existence, determining itself and nature in the context of the underlying identity of time. In this imagery, the concept of words being read as images is akin to the notion of image in Jewish scholarship, which often must contend with the problem of Hebrew being the language of both God and humanity. Here time is measured not in terms of past events, nor simply in a negative relationship of the present to the future, but from the point of perfection to the past, the present being just a moment in between.

The theological problem of the image is already present in Genesis where we find humanity created in the image of God, not however in his essence, which is pure truth.[56] If the notion of the image is to be seen as speculation on Benjamin's part concerning the perception of the truth of God in the profane, he would indeed be touching on a central concern of theology, needless to say a fundamental problem in Jewish theology, in regard to the corporeality of truth.[57] Accordingly, a discussion of the importance of the representation of God and His image are present in both the *Star of Redemption* and *Spirit of Utopia*.[58] But perhaps the best known treatment of this problem is be found in Maimonides' *Guide of the Perplexed*.[59]

The division of form from content here is paralleled by a discussion of myth and divine manifestation in the context of justice, where revelation upsets the order of mythical forces.[60] The purity of the divine, and the "damaged immediacy" (II:153) of its worldly perception, as Benjamin suggests, appears in many ways to be what Rosenzweig had in mind when he referred to the question of whether God, and more specifically God's countenance, or *Antlitz*, can be expressed in an image:

> We speak in images. But the images are not arbitrary. There are essential images and coincidental ones. The irreversibility of the truth can only be enunciated in the image of a living being. For among the living, an Above and a Below are already designated by nature prior to all theory or regulation.[61]

Rosenzweig concludes that in order for an image to exist a division between projection and reception must be presupposed, i.e., projection from up high, perception from below. The compelling truth of the image expresses itself in its existence but only by the fact that it is necessarily received by the living. The image here mediates the pure truth of God, and while the divine requires no mediation, truth capable of expression by the living is the earthly side of God's countenance.[62] In reception, and in the capability for apprehension, the means is created by which we are able to see the truth of God—His true history, so to speak, in the apprehension of the revealed image, which is indeed beyond worldly life and what Rosenzweig calls "the view on high of the redeemed world-above."[63] In the fragment the image appears to have a distinctly "mystical" task in history—mystical for it seeks an unseen realm in the profane, placed there by divine providence. The divine plan governs the terms of the beginning and the means of the end. It is a measure of God's truth and therefore finds its profane expression in a limited form, in the idea of an image.

THE MESSIANIC INTENSITY OF HAPPINESS

The concept of happiness is the basis of Benjamin's thinking on messianic agency. As part of the preformation of the messianic age in the world, its pursuit is constituted by a worldliness and thereby introduces a counter-force into redemption.[64] Like the juxtaposition of profane and holy, the two concepts of happiness are postulated in opposition to each other. Happiness that runs against the direction of redemption is a countermessianic force.[65] The difference between the two forms of happiness may also lie in the difference between happiness itself and its pursuit, where the latter could take the form of an overdetermined and misguided will. It must be said, however, that the *Glückssuchen* (search for happiness) to which Benjamin refers is somewhat different categorically, although perhaps not conceptually, from the *Streben nach Glück*, which is generally associated with the pursuit of happiness. However, that the category of happiness takes up the position uniquely reserved for the ultimate counterforce suggests a more integral role for a negative happiness in Benjamin's conception of redemption. But how, one might ask, could the "pursuit of happiness of free humanity" be seen as representing the Antichrist of the messianic dialectic? In this sense we find Benjamin seeking to uncover an inherent structure that emits redemptive forces in *this* world, leading to the next. As he writes in this text: "But just as a force is capable, through its direction, of promoting another in the opposite direction, so too is the profane order of the profane in the coming of the messianic kingdom."

Like an object that is circumscribed by everything it is not and is therefore able to generate its opposite, which already exists implicitly within itself by moving fully through itself, so is the "profane order of the profane" conceived as praxis in the world, capable of forwarding the coming of the messianic kingdom. In this sense both the terms *Reich Gottes* (kingdom of God) and *des messianischen Reiches* (the messianic kingdom) are bound to the notion of an image. They are only approximations as a result of the impoverishment of expression and not solely because the telos of the dynamic of history has no goal that we can name. Language, in its own internal exile of "damaged immediacy," is constitutionally unable to fully convey the messianic age or assist as a means of its coming, save for a realm of language preserved for the pure "judging word," which itself must be renewed by the age in which it finds its true meaning.[66] The concept of the profane order of the profane points therefore to worldly realms, not the least of which is language. Profane is repeated here twice to emphasize the context of this order: it is based on the living, sensuous conditions of the world and its juxtaposition to the divine kingdom. While praxis as form is agency, the body that it structures is the profane, worldly pursuit of proprietary and consumptive happiness, existing in fundamental opposition to the next world. But in being by its nature the opposite and by standing in direct relationship to the messianic, it acts to forward the conditions by which a redemptive age could be ushered in. Therefore, the profane order of the profane stands in distinct relation to the idea of evil.[67]

Although the category of negative happiness stands in relation to redemption, its relationship is not necessarily dependent. It is, indeed, postulated with a degree of independence, suggesting an evil that would bear no necessary, causal connection to the nature of God.[68] "Free humanity" is a distinctly negative freedom that seeks those aspects of the world in conflict with the course of redemption. In generating further degrees of self-alienation, this "seeking" releases its opposite. Perhaps this form of happiness is hedonistic, in some manner a bourgeois conception of history that finds its end in consumption. In either case the profane unleashes within itself, i.e., within the world, those elements of freedom that would contravene the course of redemption, thus representing the principle of evil. Yet, through this relationship of juxtaposition, the evil element stands as the opposite of redemption and therefore partly as grounds for its existence. Under these presuppositions evil becomes all but necessary in the coming of the messianic age. Such reasoning, which aims to reveal the world as it is and separate it from the concept of the next world or the world as it should exist, is the work of Benjamin's historical philosophy, whose aim is not to justify or prescribe a predetermined goal in its development but to understand a messianic dynamic of the world in its unfolding.[69]

All events in this world have a relationship both to the profane and to the coming of redemption. Activity in *this* world, which may appear commonplace and *ungesegnet*, i.e. profane, is simultaneously the essential cornerstone "from which the *next* world is itself built" (SdE§328). Worldly affairs are conducted with a force that entails the introduction of a realm of sanctity into the world of things.[70] The search for happiness of free humanity appears to be directed in the opposite direction to that of the divine. In actuality, however, the gravitational force of motion toward the earth is the same force that lays the foundation for its worldly abrogation, its "decline toward eternity," says Rosenzweig, overcoming a division that "penetrates the whole of life."[71]

The idea of an eternal passing away becomes an essential moment in the effect the profane has on the divine. Happiness is here the force pointing the way, as Benjamin writes in the fragment: "For in happiness everything earthly strives for its decline and only in happiness is the decline determined to find it." The idea of happiness, upon which the order of the profane is established, corresponds to everything earthly, which is by nature everything belonging to the profane in the process of passing. It strives for its own abrogation, as does nature, and only in happiness, in the formation of the limits of agency and evil, is this passing away constituted to find the last and true prefiguring of messianic redemption. The unmediated messianic "intensity" of this act, which is paralleled by the spirit of revolutionary transformation, seizing each person and stirring a longing for a totally different world, a redeemed world, is forced into a state of unhappiness, not unlike the idea of the Messiah the Sabbatians ascribed to their anointed one. "When the Messiah is fighting evil at its core," writes Joseph Dan on perhaps the most dynamic messiah of the last three hundred years, Sabbatai Zvi, "his external melancholy is the result; when he approaches the divine world with the redeemed sparks, he is exalted, happy, in a state of enlightenment."[72] Since the early Christians attributed great meaning to the suffering of Isaiah's Israelite, the category has remained one of the cardinal signs of messianic activity.[73] *Unglück* (unhappiness/tragedy), in this case, however, is not merely a state but an event, or an event that opens up a state in its relationship to the tragic hero and is perhaps best understood here as tragedy rather than the more inconsequential misfortune. In the case of Zvi it is the moment when he is engaged in the ultimate form of Lurianic redemption of the divine sparks, which are inaccessible to the normative and collective activities of redemption. Melancholia is the condition that sets in. But *Unglück* has another, more important meaning for Benjamin, one that links him to the concept of antiquity in his time: the hero of Greek tragic drama and his *Untergang* (decline).

The direction of all human activity toward the transformation of the profane is the condition in which everything worldly can take its leave; a condition, for example, that forms the cornerstone of redemption in Rosenzweig's system.[74] In Benjamin it is clear that the world must pass away, but its passing can only be achieved through happiness. This happiness is at

once constituted to be worldly and at the same time messianic, in the sense
of being directed toward messianic activity. In this respect the focus of this
development, which is based on happiness, turns to the motor of redemption. Benjamin's response to the question of agency concerns the problematic unity of the collective and individual in what he calls the striving of the
inner solitary person who passes through "tragedy, in the sense of suffering," which is here understood not merely as misfortune or subjective unhappiness but rather tragedy. Similarly, in "The Life of Students" Benjamin
speaks of original "striving of the solitary individual" that has been replaced
by a more narrowly defined, pedestrian form of social service.[75] That figure,
embodying the "unmediated messianic intensity of the heart," the passionate intensity of the solitary individual, suggests another distinct figure of ancient literature, distinct in this case from the Messiah, which requires that
we turn our attention briefly to Athens rather than Jerusalem. Interest in the
idea of the tragic hero was common among several literary, political and
theologically oriented German-speaking Jews in the period preceding and
following the First World War.[76] Rosenzweig, Bloch, Lukács, and Benjamin
were all concerned with the relationship between tragedy and the messianic
structure of the solitary individual, but at the same time the inner quality of
every individual who passes through a predetermined series of historical
events was seen in light of the suffering Messiah.[77] The connection to the
characterless Messiah and the messianic, anticipatory activity of the single
person in his or her relation to the world lies within the concept of the decline of the hero.

TRAGIC DEVOTION

Nietzsche's contribution to the understanding of this figure of ancient literature was sure to have influenced the concept of tragedy in Benjamin's
period. In *The Birth of Tragedy* Greek drama is characterized as presenting
a concept of individuation in which the hero determines his existence by
acquiring knowledge of himself, understood as tragic knowledge. Tragic
knowledge, in fact, is deemed a relative of the fall from grace. The tragic
hero of Greek mythology is said to be the "Aryan" brother of the "Semitic"
tree of knowledge. The tragic hero suffers in his acquisition or transmission of knowledge and undergoes a form of punishment. Through this act
he has not only determined his existence, in the sense of existing spatially

as well as temporally, but has also reached into the heavens as a mortal, thus transgressing the division between the divine and earthly worlds. This transgression, which is deemed a demonic force, imparts at the same time immortality.[78] Nietzsche, for his part, ultimately rejects the tragic hero, symbolized in Socrates' death, with its moral calling and dialectical optimism. Benjamin introduces the figure of the Messiah at this juncture.[79]

Rosenzweig's notion of the tragic hero and Benjamin's clearly converge in the later *Trauerspiel* book.[80] A short presentation of Rosenzweig's concept at this point may assist us in forming a better picture of Benjamin's own approach.[81] Rosenzweig presents his idea of tragedy in the context of character:

> Tragedy readily creates the impression that the demise of the individual necessarily restores some kind of equilibrium to things. But this impression is based only on the contradiction between the tragic character and the dramatic argument. As a work of art, the drama needs both halves of this contradiction in order to survive, but the actual tragic element is thereby obscured. The hero as such has to decline, only because his decline makes possible his ultimate heroization, namely, the most isolated "selfication" of his self. He yearns for the solitude of his decline, because there is no greater solitude than this. Accordingly, the hero does not actually die after all. Death only cuts him off, as it were, from the temporal features of individuality. Character solidified in the heroic self is immortal.[82]

The necessity of the fall of the individual was a predetermined given of classical drama, which sought to restore a sense of balance to the natural world, writes Rosenzweig. But in the constitution of the hero's character within the unfolding of his fate, we witness a profound break with the tragic element altogether. Although the hero must fall or "go under," he achieves the highest state of heroism and the self-definition of his own character. This is then defined as immortality. There is no greater isolation than this going under, that is, achieving an afterlife in this world, as there is no commonality between mortals and gods. He shares commonality with neither the divine nor the profane, which therefore forms one aspect of his suffering. In this sense the hero does not actually perish in his fall, or at least a part of him lives on, i.e., his character, which is only able to arrive at immortality through a confrontation with fate, with the "temporality of individuality," and with the nature of passing away. Indeed, the tragic hero wins his own character both in its "temporal and spatial totality," as expressed in the fragment, and thereby marks his end in worldly affairs. The individualistic aspects of the self, his personality, are determined by this tragic confrontation such that character becomes immortal as the individual passes away into the undifferentiated nature of good and evil.[83]

The first appearance of Benjamin's formulations of the categories of tragedy and obligation, fate and character occurs in the summer of 1916, directly preceding his essay on language.[84] "To obtain a deeper understanding of the tragic," writes Benjamin, in a piece entitled "Language in *Trauerspiel* and Tragedy," "we should perhaps look not just at art but also at history."[85] Here the concept of tragedy is already transposed to the realm of historical transformation. The individual stands at the center of this process:

> At specific and crucial points in its trajectory, historical time passes over into tragic time; such points occur in the actions of great individuals. There is an essential connection between the ideas of greatness in history and those in tragedy—although the two are not identical.[86]

Rather than being a static and closed "kingdom" of art, tragedy forges a point of transition in history. Time is clearly differentiated from history in its ability to go beyond tragedy in the actions of "great people." These individuals then form a shared character in the collective effect of their actions, not in mythic, archetypical forms that are unintentionally filled with real individuals but rather in collective, empirical transformations that are transtemporal. In history messianic significance is attributed to time, remaining "infinite in every direction and unfulfilled at every moment." He continues:

> For empirical events time is nothing but a form, but, what is more important, as a form it is unfulfilled. The event does not fulfill the formal nature of the time in which it takes place. For we should not think of time as merely the measure that records the duration of a mechanical change. Although such time is indeed a relatively empty form, to think of its being filled makes no sense.[87]

As a mere device for counting empirical events in their passing, time remains empty and unfulfilled, for the "determining force of historical time" is neither fully collected nor fully contained by the events themselves.[88] Historical time may be countable, he tells Scholem once, but not necessarily numbered.[89] In an early text Scholem composed for Benjamin as a birthday gift in July 1918, entitled "Ninety-five Theses on Judaism and Zionism," he captures the relevance of this notion for their early discourse. Thesis 84 reads: "The concept of time in Judaism is the eternal now."[90] In Benjamin's text he refers to an event that is "perfect in historical terms" and quantitatively indeterminate in what is truly a different idea of time: "This idea of fulfilled time is the dominant historical idea of the bible; it is the idea of messianic time."[91]

Messianic time is conceived not as individual but collective time. This determination, we are told, differentiates "tragic time from messianic time," posing the same problem as the difference between individual and godly fulfillment of time.[92] In tragedy the hero dies, for "no one can live in fulfilled time."[93] The hero "dies of immortality," which Benjamin here describes as "the origins of the tragic hero" and "tragic responsibility," where hubris forms the "true expression of responsibility" of the hero.[94] Hebbel's notion of "individuation as original sin," with which Benjamin here confers, conceives of evil in the fall from grace, where knowledge served to differentiate Adam and ultimately cause his suffering.[95] Only in his decline does the hero discover his responsibility and, for this reason, departs in his own "going under." This *Untergang*—a decline of the individual in confrontation with fate—appears to be out of the hero's control at first glance and therefore takes the paradoxical form of his "complete passivity." Benjamin continues in the same strain:

> For often the fateful climax of the hero's time is fulfilled during moments of utter tranquillity—during his sleep, as it were. And in the same way the meaning of the fulfilled time of a tragic fate emerges in the great moments of passivity: in the tragic decision, the retarding moment, and in the catastrophe.[96]

In tragic drama actual tragedy occurs when the hero meets his fate, which has already been decided for him. Unable to know or to understand this decision, he appears vain and passive, despite all his efforts. His death, however, is not actually passive; seen religiously, courage is the measure of his devotion. Here the passive moment does not alter the rather active conception of the hero's passing.[97] Elsewhere Benjamin writes that "courage is the devotion to the danger that threatens the world." He continues:

> Courage is the sensibility of the individual who subjects himself to danger, in order that, through his death, this danger will become that of the world and, at the same time, overcome. The greatness of danger emerges from the courageous—only by striking him, through his utter dedication to it, does danger strike the world. In his death, however, danger is overcome; it reaches the world and no longer threatens it.[98]

The devotion of the individual to the world, despite its continuous threat, inhabits the same paradoxical realm as the tragic hero. Only in passing away is tragic fate overcome. Scholem picks up on this theme in his journals from August 1918–1919, drawing out the distinctly messianic connotations of the elimination of tragic death.[99] He formulates here both the end of fate through death and the entrance of messianic time:

> The idea of the historical death of all beings in messianic time eliminates fate. Isaiah 65, 19–24 speaks clearly of the fatelessness [*Schicksalslosigkeit*] of this order. The transformation of space [*Landschaft*] to the site (historical site) [*Schauplatz*] means redemption in Judaism. . . . And *for this reason,* the idea of messianic death is understood at its core to be redemption.[100]

This portrayal of historical death ties in well with the courage of the tragic hero that Benjamin describes. Benjamin's hero takes on the dangers of the world, eliminating his fate, and yet perishes in the process. Scholem's historical death is deemed messianic, for it eliminates fate. The link between immortality and redemption is therefore also present in this passage, and the concept of a messianic site, or *Schauplatz*—the scene and historical site of messianic transformation in the world—is brought to the fore. On the previous page he identifies *Schauplatz* as Benjamin's term for the "site of historical occurrence" (tag II:344). It appears that the authors had an extensive dialogue regarding the theme of tragic death as well as the idea of the end of history presupposing the start of messianic time.

Turning back now to Benjamin's problem of tragedy and its relationship to redemption, we find him wrestling with the distance between dramatic form and historical transformation. In the passage above he addresses the paradox of the tragic hero who finds his passing accidentally. It is, in part, because of the paradox imbedded in the dramatic form that the dramatic powers of tragedy have slowly come unwound. The "temporal character" of tragedy, meaning the fate of the tragic hero in relation to the messianic act that takes place in history, "is shaped and exhausted in its dramatic form."[101] So, too, is the role of death as a dramatic device in the Trauerspiel: "The law governing a higher life prevails in the limited realm of earthly existence and all performances, until death puts an end to the act, so as to repeat the same act, albeit on a grander scale, in another world."[102] Trauerspiel is only able to present the law of a higher, eternal life—and thereby of good messianic "living"—in the limited sense of the earthly realm. Death puts an end to its unfolding in the profane so that it may repeat itself in a higher form. But the Trauerspiel cannot put on this eternal performance before God and the angels alone, for it is not the "image of a higher existence but only one of two mirror-images, and its continuation is not less schematic than itself. The dead become ghosts."[103]

Drama does not actually fulfill time, however much it has been able to reflect the idea of redemption. The Trauerspiel is no divine image; the dead are merely ghosts, not the reincarnated sages whose reappearance is perhaps the most important sign of the beginning of messianic time. "The idea of [the] resolution," of Trauerspiel in this otherworldly sense, no longer lies "within the realm of drama itself."[104] For Benjamin, the final distinction between Trauerspiel and tragedy therefore lies merely in a metaphorical realm, for while the dramatic rite is closed in itself and can make no transition to that which is beyond itself—the *Untergang* (decline) of the individual in his or her messianic act is a part of the filled-time of redemption (II:134). Trauerspiel itself may still find a redemptive place in music, he concludes, pointing to this sense of place as a "feeling" in the text "Language in *Trauerspiel* and Tragedy." Yet in order to transcend its limitations Trauerspiel is forced to leave the realm of performance and be understood as transformative rather than merely descriptive, not simply to "pass away" as a fallen historical occurrence but to unleash the conditions of immortality: "The performance must find redemption, and for Trauerspiel that redemptive mystery is music—the rebirth of the feelings in a supra-sensuous nature."[105]

Thus the tragic model of human devotion is left behind in the sphere of Trauerspiel, while the meaning of the hero confronting fate is carried over further into speculation concerning the inner constitution of the individual. In Benjamin's piece from 1919 on "Fate and Character,"[106] he begins with the question of whether the character of a given individual can be known in terms of its relationship to worldly events, as in the case of the fate of the tragic hero (II:171). If the response to particular events can be understood, then, as with the dramatic form, the fate of the individual may also be understood. In the ability to view character and fate as intimately intertwined and not limited merely to the body, as is the case with character predictions drawn from horoscope and astrology, says Benjamin, "the possibility of making a prediction of fate rationally comprehensible" would be at hand.[107] It would also be possible to speak of a core of character, which, if not completely predictable, he writes, would be knowable to the degree that the external world is knowable. Character is not formed simply by will alone, for humanity and world here are mutually transformative and self-mediating. Following Nietzsche's principle that character entails an eternally recurring experience, Benjamin's concludes that if the character of an individual is constant, so is his fate.

This first conclusion is then juxtaposed to the necessity of maintaining the spheres of both categories separate, so as not to usurp "the authority of higher spheres and concepts."[108] In this sense Benjamin likens character to ethics and fate to religion. In these realms, where an erroneous concept has been lodged, exposition and repudiation are necessary: "This fallacy arises, as regards to the concept of fate, through association with that of guilt. Thus, to mention a typical case, fateful tragedy [*Unglück*], seen as the response of God or the gods to the attribution of religious guilt [*Schuld*]."[109] *Schuld* (responsibility) here is understood as a form of guilt in which an eternal punishment is applied to an eternal crime. Fate is then associated with tragedy as punishment, as *Verschuldung*, i.e., to make one responsible for a crime. One example of this is Greek tragedy, another, Jewish "responsibility" for holy tragedy.[110] This erroneous concept, Benjamin concludes, has to be understood in part as related to an undeveloped concept of fate and responsibility: "In the classical Greek development of the idea of fate, the happiness granted to a person is not at all understood as a confirmation of an irresponsible wandering through life but as a temptation to the most grievous attribution of responsibility, hubris."[111] *Glück* (happiness) in this sense is not happiness bestowed in avoidance of responsibility, not aimless wandering, but rather

the quest for the most difficult responsibility of all: challenging the arbitrari-
ness of the gods and the course of history upon which they have decided.[112]
It is not imposed but chosen. The relationship between fate and happiness is
essential, for it is happiness that is able to be released "from the embroilment
of fate and from the web of one's own fate."[113] Happiness is therefore not
permanently in opposition to tragedy but rather something that is able to
point beyond the relationship between responsibility and tragedy toward a
messianic return to innocence. It is therefore a final category, one in which
the distinction between God and humanity loses clarity—what Benjamin
understands as the meaning of Hölderlin's *Schicksallos* (fateless). *Glück*
brings humanity out of the confrontation with fate as if returned to a state of
innocence in a release from the responsibility for sin. Rather than irrespon-
sibility, i.e., in the avoidance of sin, the natural state of happiness, freed from
a false application of sin, leads to the restitution of a returned enchantment
of humanity with nature and with its language.[114]

The Worldly Restitution of Immortality

As with the notion of happiness, Benjamin formulates two versions of immortality: in the form of the eternity of the messianic hero in his "going
under" and a bad infinity of empty time. In the individual's position to the
world, he or she is bound by the conditions of timelessness: time is boun-
tiful but meaningless in light of the eternal. It is only in the movement toward the first form of eternity that unfathomable death no longer remains
the medium through which all activity is measured. In "Metaphysics of
Youth" this is articulated with one foot resting on the Aristotelian proofs
of the eternity of the universe:

> With hopeless earnestness the question is posed: in what time does
> a person live? The thinkers have always known that a person does
> not live in any time at all. The immortality of thoughts and deeds
> banishes the individual to a timeless realm at whose heart an in-
> scrutable death lies in wait. Throughout life the emptiness of time
> surrounds the individual, but not immortality.[115]

We have seen that the character of the fallen hero becomes eternal in
the fragment as well as in the authors surrounding the fragment (such as

Bloch and Rosenzweig).[116] From this we have been able to deduce that, just as character becomes divorced from the organic, all human life seeks immortality through redemption. Moreover, just as the next world must indeed be constituted in direct contrast to this world, our natural world must be *vergänglich*, that is, able to pass away, as the eternal world must be *unvergänglich*, i.e., inorganic. This is the principle of their opposition, which we saw in the paired identity of the holy and profane structures. These tightly wound contraries correspond to the human and immortal worlds.

The divine inorganic is therefore the reference point for immortality. Death itself is a stranger to both God or gods; it defines a completely worldly condition in which nature is the atmosphere surrounding all living beings. God, however, is inorganic. As the source of nature, He is beyond *Vergänglichkeit*, i.e., the capacity to decline. If holy is the category of immortality, worldly is the essence of humanity. But rather than a determination of being, which takes center stage in Rosenzweig, the underlying notion of death in the fragment expresses an orientation far less existential and more metaphysical: all natural things die, and not merely in a final stage, but are in a constant state of decay, of passing.[117] However, with regard to the notion that the difference between the holy and profane is precisely immortality in the inability to be organic, Rosenzweig formulates a similar notion of the *Nichtsterbenkönnen* (immortality) of the individual.[118] This is the constitution of the fallen hero whose self as character becomes "unsterblich" (immortal).

How humans achieve immortality, which is a necessary condition for a redemptive age, is a central dimension of Benjamin's theology. He is apparently aware of this already in 1912 when he puts forward the question whether "religion guaranties us an eternity" and again in "Metaphysics of Youth," where he returns to eternity as a central category of religion.[119] Bloch also raises the question of the immortal elements of the body that separate themselves and become eternal through the organization of the earthly world, which contains within itself the germ cell of its completion and perfection. The focal point for this transition from the organic to the inorganic, and thereby the restitution of all past forms of life, both animate and inanimate, is the restitutio in integrum, from which Benjamin may take his cue. In the *Spirit of Utopia* we read:

> The life of the soul transcends the body. There is an innermost plasma of the soul, and the trans-physiological immortality is not

affected by the loss of the body. In order that the life of the soul transcends the abrogation of the world, it must be "finished" in the deepest sense of the word and its toes happily across the line of the landing point beyond. The core plasma of the soul must not to be marred by the abyss of eternal death and the goal of eternal life upon which the entire organization of the earthly world depends, the transcosmological immortality that is the only reality of the kingdom of the souls, the restitutio in integrum of the labyrinth of the world—this must not be lost to the mercy of Satan.[120]

Bloch's conception of a transcosmological immortality, with its spatial dimension, is implicit (or at least implicitly possible) within the constitution of the worldly sphere—the active restructuring of the profane within the context of the cohesive reality of the kingdom of the souls.[121] This he identifies with the restitutio in integrum. This term can also be considered in relation to that which he elsewhere articulates as "the absolute center of reality": "the birth and placement of all things and beings in their possession."[122] The restitutio in integrum finds one other expression in the *Spirit of Utopia,* in a passage where the "holy mother" Mary gently illuminates "the brothers" on the importance of earthly concerns.[123]

    In Benjamin we read of a *spiritual* restitutio in integrum that is represented by the worldliness of the profane. The addition of the word *spiritual* to this phrase indicates a marked contrast to the greater materialist meaning of Bloch's restitutio in integrum.[124] Rather than merely the return of all things to their original status of possession, Benjamin here emphasizes something other than a purely materialist component of the final return. If there is an impulse toward secularization in Benjamin, the emphasis here is on the opposite.[125] In turning back for a moment to "Metaphysics of Youth," we find an earlier elaboration of the relationship between eternity and the restoration of things:

> But in this, the birth of immortal time, time no longer occurs. The self experiences timelessness, all things are assembled in it. It lives all-powerful in distance; in distance (the diary's silence), the "I" experiences its own, pure time. In distance it gathers itself; no thing pushes its way into its immortal juxtaposition of events. Here it draws the strength to impinge on things, to absorb them, to misjudge its own fate.[126]

The "birth of immortal time" does not actually take place in time.[127] Timelessness, in this sense, is what lends a messianic element to the temporality of all past event. If there is to be an ingathering outside of the realm of time, it would be difficult to suppose this collection of objects is to have merely a physical, materialist meaning. The ingathering of the self (the individual or perhaps individuals) occurs at a distance from the divine kingdom; it does so as an experience of the divine from afar and is thus linked to the notion of image. This ingathering then takes the form of the medium with a divine quality, in which this newly constituted self creates a force that enables the experience of the things in pure time again, beyond fate as such. "No thing or human being," Benjamin writes in "The Religious Perspective of the New Youth," "should be discarded by the young, for in everything (in the advertisement board and the criminal) can the symbol or the holy take hold."[128] In Benjamin's hopeful conception of the religious conviction of the youth movement, the relation between things and people is spiritualized, such that word and deed are seen as one: "There are many things which these youths share with the first Christians, for whom the world appeared so overflowing with holiness it could emerge in everything, that, in their eyes, engaged the word and act."[129] In the experience of the early Christians, says Benjamin, a residue of the earliest notion of divine language was alive.[130] Such a language, in which word and deed were one and the same, is to be found in a linguistic conception of genesic creation, where the creation of things and people were both consecrated by a divine utterance, in which a divine insignia was transferred to all created beings. Therefore, even corrupt objects and human forms have a redeemable quality that compel their preservation. Here the ingathering in itself and a restitutio in integrum find some common ground if a spiritual (i.e., less secularizing) emphasis is added to the latter.

Bloch interprets immortality in terms of human history transcending history. Humanity does not pass into the divine to achieve immortality by dissolution but remains a "full house," solid and enlightened, as everything natural takes its course. In his concept of tragedy the hero achieves his own destiny in the very moment when he overcomes the determining force of fate. This is achieved by a tragic hero who overcomes his isolation and achieves his purpose in redemption. In this sense he posits a retreating God, essentially a secularized Lurianic *zimzum*, illustrated by the metaphor of God exiting the state of history.[131] God here is no longer the unmoved mover but merely a spectator: the inorganic is ultimately bound not to the gods but to science.[132] Only if humanity remains intact, while the rest of the world falls and passes away, can God return from exile to take up residence. The transmigration of the souls and its restitutio in integrum would then have a social, historical, cultural—in a word, a materialist meaning. Its distinctly "spiritual" dimension is lost.

Benjamin may have partially anticipated this discussion in his "Dialogue on the Religiosity Today" to the degree that he recognized religion as being based on "an inner striving toward unification with God."[133] Unlike Bloch, he introduces the social and historical, even material dimensions of a redemptive restitution without necessarily postulating the annihilation of the divine. Benjamin seeks to conceive of this restitution in a way that would not render the divine-profane structure completely arbitrary. For him it is precisely the negation of the profane rather than an inner abolition of the divine that opens the portal to redemption.

NIHILISM

> For the messianic is nature in its eternal and total transience. To strive for this, even for those stages of humanity that are nature, is the task of world politics whose method is called nihilism.

Vergängnis—here rendered as "transience"—is the force behind a dialectics of existence that is its "eternal state of decline": everything is in a state of passing, evolving, declining—the Heraclitian concept of time upon which the dialectic is based.[134] This also represents the internal process of nature. Nature in its *Vergehen* (passing away) is its rhythm, that is, the pace at which it generates negation.[135] The totality of nature, an outline thereof, is the knowledge of messianic redemption; it is a state of existence beyond the passing of nature. "The last center of the messianic idea is perhaps the transformation of nature into pure history," writes Scholem in his journal in a paragraph that makes explicit reference to Benjamin and the application of his categories regarding a messianic conception of history: "for messianic time has to be defined as time in which all occurrences are historical. The events of the natural world become historical in themselves and the countryside completely becomes a site [historical site] in the messianic kingdom. (The concept 'site' for the site of historical occurrence comes from Benjamin)."[136] In Scholem's formulation nature passes into history as a sign of the transformation of worldly, historical time to messianic time. Nature, in this sense, becomes messianic: it's eternal passing, in itself, rendered transformative rather than static. The decline of nature, however, must first take on the form of historical decline—passing and yet giving way to new dimensions rather than repetition, for repetition can also appear infinite where it is only a finite repetition of passing. Historical occurrence is worldly here and thus precisely necessary. Achieving a point beyond passing, i.e., a final and true form of immortality, is therefore messianic happiness. This concept of happiness is then the unity of the holy and profane. It is the conception of the transcendence of the division of theory and praxis, mental and manual labor, represented in a messianic nature, a redeemed creation, a return to origins: "To strive for this," which again suggests a unity in the concept of human agency, is defined as the task of world politics. To understand the rhythm of messianic nature leads to a striving. This striving is a praxis in itself. But just as it is a praxis of program, it is a praxis of nihilism, meaning a retreat from worldly participation in favor of an abstract and categorical realm of messianic reflection, embodied in a "mystical" understanding of history. If there is a historical program that could be said to follow this early political theology, it is perhaps best captured by the opening paragraph of "The Life of Students" where "the historical task is to expose this immanent state of perfection and make it absolute, to make it visible and dominant in the present."[137]

The worldly task is none other than to witness the immanent, temporal index of redemption in every moment of the present, under the strain of the catastrophe enveloping it. The search for happiness in a political form, which sees the unhindered development of each individual into a full human being, what Adorno characterized in Benjamin's thinking as his "salvation of the dead as the restitution of disfigured life,"[138] is unambiguously understood by the early Benjamin as an ethical form of anarchism:

> An exposition of this standpoint is one of the tasks of my moral philosophy, in which the term anarchism can surely be used. It calls for a theory that does not reject a moral right to violence in itself, but rather in every human institution, community or individuality that accords itself a monopoly of violence, or reserves the right to violence on principle, in general, or from some other perspective, instead of showing reverence for it as the providence of divine power, in specific cases as *absolute power*.[139]

Anarchism is defined here largely categorically, as an ethical program that rejects both the monopolization of the use of violence and the monopolization of the right to violence. Nevertheless, after a short career in the youth movement Benjamin was never to express his political convictions in an organized way. Despite his proximity to Spain and his repeated visits to Ibiza in the 1930s, he took no stand in relation to the most important anarchist movement in the twentieth century.[140] Nihilism in this text is therefore a form of "world politics" actually reserved from worldly affairs. It expresses a will for a transformed world, free from domination, a world understood in the messianic sense of redemption, yet only in abstraction.

In many ways this was a nihilism of circumstance, shared to a great degree by Scholem in their collective retreat to the countryside of Switzerland toward the end of the First World War. As we shall see in the next chapter on Scholem's theological politics and the role that nihilism comes to play, Benjamin's worldly political nihilism is an abstention from outward political activity in the hope of revealing a more authentic dimension of politics. In Benjamin's turn to nihilism he announces a worldly retreat—in Scholem's words at the time, an *Abschied*—from political engagement while preserving a political idea with the world as its subject. This is a politics that lives on in an unintentional aspect of humanity and, at the same time, in an abstract theory of worldly transformation.

CHAPTER 2

GERSHOM SCHOLEM'S THEOLOGICAL POLITICS

"At this hour, I no longer believe, as I once did," noted Gershom Scholem in a pivotal moment in his journals, "that I am the Messiah."[1] With this realization, the young man's query whether it was he whom God anointed to end human suffering was put to rest. Following the disillusionment that would have to accompany such thought, the groundwork for the task of worldly affairs is initiated, drawn not from a divine mandate but from profane, human reality. The Messiah, in being chosen to fulfill a prophecy announced long before his appearance, has himself little to choose from in matters concerning worldly redemption. But for the false messiah Gershom Scholem politics is born in the very moment in which his messiahship is revealed to him to be of the profane. Thus the task of uncovering the means of political agency in worldly affairs and distinguishing between categories of political thought is left for him to decipher. "There are only two grand political options," remarks Scholem, a few years after this fateful discovery, "anarchism and theocracy."[2] Anarchism, nihilism, Zionism, theocracy are indeed the categories that confront the curious reader of the early political and theological thought of Gershom Scholem. The ideas that prompted Scholem's radical decision to move to Palestine in 1923 and formed the basis of his later notions of politics is a treasure chest, rich for the political explorer.

With the recent publication of Scholem's journals and letters from this period, a thorough analysis is slowly being made possible.[3] The texts that have already appeared, however, are abundant in thoughts of a political nature and offer a fairly reliable first-hand account of a rather intimate collaboration with Benjamin in the years 1915 to 1919. A comprehensive understanding of Scholem in this period may therefore have the additional effect of helping us form a better picture of the conditions that shaped Benjamin and his early writings.

Scholem's theological politics began and ended with anarchism. There is therefore nothing more essential than an examination of this notion if we are to come to terms with Scholem's political and religious ideas and how these ideas came to inform and guide his research. For the purposes of such an analysis, I have divided Scholem's conception of anarchism into four categories: traditional, nihilistic, cataclysmic and critical. But like Scholem's own formulation of the messianic idea, whose conservative, restorative and utopian divisions are no doubt informed by an understanding of anarchism,[4] they are dependant on each other and thus weave themselves in and out of various states of his life, though always remaining integrated with his first traditional understanding. It also must be said that in every stage of formulation anarchism was never to be seen as a political substitute for dogma, and the variation the concept undergoes is testimony to this fact. This unyielding, transformative aspect is later taken up in its final conception as the hallmark of a critical religious anarchism and the epistemological orientation that accompanies it.

TRADITION AND ANARCHISM

Scholem's reflections concerning his early political convictions in *Walter Benjamin: The Story of a Friendship*, written many years after the fact, suggest a far more somber attitude, if not secondary interest, than the enthusiasm revealed by the journals and letters of the early period. As he recalled nearly sixty years later:

> In those days I read a great deal about socialism, historical materialism, and above all anarchism, with which I was most in sympathy. Nettlau's biography of Bakunin and the writings of Kropotkin and Elisé Reclus had made a profound impression upon me. In

1915, I began to read the works of Gustav Landauer, especially his *Aufruf zum Sozialismus* [Call to Socialism].[5]

The first discussion on anarchism took place in the context of an exchange of letters with his elder brother, Werner Scholem, who was already active in the German Social Democratic Party. The debate was to touch upon several points of conflict between anarchism and Marxism. Gershom Scholem writes with the news that he has read the 1891 Erfurt Program of the Social Democrats and agrees with its contents but refuses the label *Social Democrat* for the term *socialist*. The heart of his difference concerns the question of organization: "Organization is a murky sea," writes the younger brother, "in which flows the beautiful, wild current of the idea that the sea no longer releases. Organization is synonymous with death, not only among the social democrats, but with all the other -isms and -ists, although with the socialists in a particularly horrible way. They yearn for such beautiful things, and their goal is to liberate humanity, yet they force them into organizations. What irony!"[6] "Tell me then," writes Werner Scholem in reply, "what should the socialists do if not organize. . . . How can the party lead the political struggle . . . or perhaps it shouldn't lead any at all, so that the workers vote, man for man, for the center or the liberals?"[7]

In that the question for the younger Scholem concerns the freeing of the individual from the yoke of organization, a twofold relationship with traditional anarchism emerges. First, in a general sense, it expresses the imperfection of human organizations and the restriction of the individual within them, in relation to the perfection of divine laws and structural order of the divine world. This enables a traditional religious anarchic critique of worldly authority and its bodies. Second, a faith in divine socialism distinguishes itself from worldly socialism achieved through the formation of a party where party structure and discipline become the overriding factors in its vision of a new society. His was a moral and perhaps even spiritual opposition: "The flame of socialism, the flame of the divine will of the people, must not be robbed of its nourishment in sealing it off through organization."[8] Scholem's vision of a religious socialism, consisting of free associations of morally active individuals, is therefore more akin to the utopian frontrunners of anarchism such as Charles Fourier, Saint-Simon, and Robert Owen.[9] Scholem's views were also drawn in part from the fiery rhetoric of Michael Bakunin and his critique of the state.

"The organization of every so-called provisory and revolutionary political power," as expressed in a resolution of the International Congress of 1872, partly formulated by Bakunin, "in order to assist in destruction, can only be a new form of deception that is just as dangerous for the proletariat as all the current governments."[10] "The unavoidably revolutionary politics of the proletariat," continues Bakunin elsewhere,

> must have the destruction of the state as its immediate and solitary goal. . . . We will not accept a transitional form as revolutionary— neither national conventions nor constitutional assemblies nor provisional governments nor so-called revolutionary dictators— because we are convinced that the revolution is only just, honest and true in the hands of the masses. When the revolution is concentrated in the hands of a leading figure, it unhesitatingly and unavoidably becomes reactionary.[11]

Bakunin's banishment from the First International is put to Werner Scholem for an explanation in the first exchange of letters.

The essence of Scholem's challenge to his older brother's thoroughly worked out arguments concerns the Marxist view of good and evil. "I would very much like to know," writes the young challenger, "if you [Marxists] all hold morality to be something real, meaning a given, or something created. This is essential to understand both your [*eurer*] position on anarchism, as well as the basis, the inner basis of your [*eurer*] socialism."[12] With the debate on human nature and the origins of evil, Scholem draws here on the premises of the Russian natural scientist Peter Kropotkin and his book *Mutual Aid*.[13] Despite the fact that Kropotkin's work does not formulate an argument on the innate qualities of human nature, Scholem interprets him in this light, for, in his view, Kropotkin is "one who stands on the ethical side of anarchism and believes in morality."[14] He was to find an even more developed appeal to the ethical dimension of human nature in the work of the revolutionary anarchist-socialist Gustav Landauer, who was to play an important role in Scholem's development. In addition to his *Call to Socialism*, Scholem's journals reveal quite an extensive reading of Landauer's works.[15] His notes on Landauer reflect both criticism and praise; the imperative tone of Landauer's "Sind das Ketzergedanken" (Are these heretical thoughts?) found favor with the fiery young scholar, whereas the essay on Buber struck him as being largely rhetorical (tag I:181,126). He also alludes to differences with Landauer on Zionism based on his readings of the essays appearing in the influential collection *Vom Judentum* (On Judaism, 1913), published by the Bar Kochba circle in Prague. Scholem heard Landauer speak on at least three occasions, on romanticism, "The Problem of Democracy," and on socialism.[16] After one particular lecture he reports discussing with Landauer the question of Zion, stating that he "stands very close to Zionism."[17]

ZION: ANARCHIST PRAXIS OR METAPHOR?

Scholem's journals reveal quite a rhetorical penchant in the young scholar, one linked to a radical program in several different spheres of life. On January 4, 1915, he made the following entry:

> Our principle goal [is]: Revolution! Revolution everywhere! We don't want reforms or reshuffling, we want revolution or renewal, we want to incorporate revolution into our constitution. Outer and inner revolution . . . against the family, against the parental home. . . . But most of all, we want revolution in Judaism. We want to revolutionize Zionism and preach anarchism, which means the absence of domination [*Herrschaftslosigkeit*].[18]

Anarchism and Judaism were intimately intertwined in Scholem's conception of socialism. In this regard he was to form a very unique brand of Zionism that was linked to the cultural imperative articulated by Ahad Haam and whose collection of essays entitled *Am Scheidewege* (At Crossroads) were to have a lasting impact on both him and Benjamin.[19] Political Zionism, or what Benjamin once more aptly referred to as practical Zionism,[20] he rejected out of hand. The problematic relationship of the Jew and the world in *galut* or exile could neither be articulated by a single problem, such as the lack of political sovereignty, nor solved by the formula of a state. For the young Scholem, if a means existed to solve *the Jewish question*, "to solve . . . in fact all Jewish questions . . . means: to lead a holy life."[21] Scholem picks up the same strand of thought in a letter to a member of the Jung Juda two months later (October 1917): "We are Zionists, which means: we want more than merely a national Judaism which we see

as empty and schematic. . . . We, like Ahad Haam, want a Judaism with
Jewish content."[22] Zionism was not to be merely a Jewish state in the form
of an imperialist handmaiden as Herzl envisioned; "That, we reject." He
continues in the same passage of his journal:

> For we preach anarchism. That is, we don't want a state, but rather
> a free society. . . . We want to go to Palestine not to found a state—
> O you little Philistine—and wind up trading old chains for new
> ones. We want to go to Palestine out of a thirst for freedom and a
> longing for the future, for the future belongs to the Orient.[23]

A state, in fact, was very far from Scholem's idea. According to his vision,
a return to Zion was to be informed by "the most sublime anarchist teachings," which would transform and revolutionize the Orient.[24] Scholem's
emphasis on the term *Zion* over *Zionism* should not be overlooked. In his
letters and journal entries he appears to favor the former over the latter,
pointing to a rather unique approach to Judaism and Jewish culture, in
which Zion, Zionism, and Judaism were to be expressed as a unified
whole. In this sense no distinctions were drawn between Zion and Zionism and no impediment to the transformation of the biblical idea into political theory was envisioned. In Scholem's view the prophetic conception
of Zion and the return to Palestine in the twentieth century were conceived to be one and the same; the two were just as well expressed as one.
This conclusion was in fact to follow quite logically from his conception
of Judaism, for if the Torah is to be understood as the cornerstone of Judaism and the return to Zion as an integral part of the Torah, it was a for-
gone conclusion that a return to Zion should be synonymous with the will
toward a "Rejuvenation of Judaism" as such. "For us," he writes, "Zionism is Judaism."[25] Should biblical Zion and modern political Zionism be
understood as standing in direct historical relationship to one another, we
would also have to assume an unmediated interpretation of the Torah,
one founded on a belief in the divine origin of Scripture. As in the voice
of the prophets: "The Torah begins in Zion and the word of God in
Jerusalem" in Isaiah 2:3 and again in Micah 4:2—a phrase that forms a
very standard part of the liturgical procession in which the Torah is
read.[26] In a brisk exchange of letters with Siegfried Lehmann, one of the
influential figures in the Judische Volksheim, the Jewish Center (who

himself was strongly under the influence of Buber), Scholem passionately articulates his political thesis on Zion:

> The Torah . . . according to the words of the prophets—begins with Zion, which I understand inwardly [to mean]: that the inner point of the beginning of the Torah must be for Zion—*Zion is a religious symbol*—that Zion is the inner core of the Torah, both external and internal, and that whoever is a Zionist must strive for the Torah, not for experiences [*Erlebnissen*] but for life, and that the Zionist can only receive the word of God from Jerusalem.[27]

Although the premise of this view may have perhaps changed over the years, as we shall see in the later observations on epistemology, the unity of prophetic Zion and the movement in the twentieth century of the Jews to Palestine in this formulation remains part and parcel of the same political phenomenon. In a journal entry from March 1918 he notes: "In the most profoundly deep sense, I believe Zionism to be contained within the religion and legitimated only by it, and that my 'nationhood' is a religious concept: goy kadosh."[28] Many years later he was to write, "For me Zion was a symbol that linked our origin and our utopian goal in a religious rather than a geographical sense."[29] This notion of Zionism, therefore, naturally placed Scholem in a unique position vis-à-vis the Zionist movement. Should a prophetic Zion have been sought, the means to pursue it had been set out long before in orthodox Judaism through the study of the Torah. If, on the other hand, the ingathering of the exiles was to be seen in strategic or imperial terms, there could be little room for a biblically conceived Zion. That political Zionism was held to be an abomination of prophetic Zion by the orthodox was something Scholem was quite familiar with at the time. Such views were widely held in traditional religious branches of Judaism and similar to the orthodox Agudat Yisrael that was just forming in Berlin when Scholem became a principle member. Agudat Yisrael had just released its manifesto in which religious devotion and the study of the Torah were juxtaposed to the practical Zionists in a quasi parody of their recent declarations.[30]

In his autobiographical writings, we read that Zion was conceived as a religious symbol. It is therefore quite surprising to find that in his "Ninety-five Theses on Judaism and Zionism," written initially in July 1918 as a birthday gift to Benjamin that was never presented, we read under number

21 the supposition "Zion is no metaphor."[31] This statement opens a new dimension to the idea of Zion: that its literal interpretation transforms the notion of divine Scripture. But what is particularly interesting here is the degree to which Scholem's political notions take shape in the context of debate. In a letter to Max Fischer (author of *Heine, the German Jew*), whom he discovers is a convert to Christianity, Scholem lashes out, claiming his apostasy was undertaken in ignorance of Judaism. In attempting to draw this distinction, Scholem argues polemically that he

> must stand not with God, like yourself [Fischer], but with humanity. I am different from you particularly because for you, *civitas dei* is not only more important than *civitas humana*—it is of sole importance. For us . . . there is no other way to *civitas dei* than through *civitas humana*. This is through Zion.[32]

Zion is envisioned here as the outcome of a civitas humana in which a devotion to worldly affairs facilitates the realization of civitas dei. The favoring of the latter to the exclusion of the former, which is Scholem's assessment of Fisher's Christian division of heavenly and worldly, expresses Scholem's desire to distinguish between Judaism of the past and of the future, between the two poles dividing German Jewry: assimilation or Zionism. And this is where the debate with Benjamin comes into the picture. As we have seen in the previous chapter, Benjamin divides the notion of theocracy into the categories of the political and the theological. But only in the latter does theocracy have meaning. A political notion that has as its goal the establishment of a religious state, therefore, is for Benjamin simply a facade that throws the divine origin of Scripture into question. On August 24, 1916, Scholem writes in his journals:

> On the first evening we discussed whether Zion is a metaphor, which I affirmed—for only God is not—and Benjamin rejected. We arrived at the question by way of the prophets, as Benjamin argued against the metaphorical use of the prophets, should one accept the divine authority of the Bible.[33]

From the vantage point of Scholem's thoughts, we can now see to what degree Benjamin sought to distinguish his own views from Scholem's, which slowly began to emerge with friction. A few years later, in the intense period of collaboration in Bern, this friction turned to open conflict on several occasions.[34] Benjamin's notion of theocracy, a notion we have seen to be inherent in the messianic idea, is not metaphorical; in contrast to Scholem, it is articulated as a notion of Zion, discharged of its messianic power in history. Back in 1912, in his debate with Ludwig Strauss, he formlates the tenants of a spiritual Zionism that rejects Zionism "as it exists and only able to exist: with nationalism as its final value."[35] Although he also criticizes the meaning of a Zionism that remains "esoteric," he nevertheless suggests one that is perhaps a step beyond the profane. Indeed the negation of the metaphorical dimension and, at the same time, the rejection of a realization in any concrete sense presents us with a rather ambiguous concept. As a weak messianic force it may perhaps be inherent in history but remains unable to be actualized in the history of here and now. And this conception was not so much a difference articulated as a matter of principle but of interpretation,[36] for if Zion is to be understood merely as a metaphor, then the authority of Scripture is also thrown into question, in which theocracy might then have a political and not merely a theological form. In a note to himself from September 1917, a year after the discussions on Zionism above, Scholem is somewhat troubled:

> Is Walter Benjamin really a Zionist? Isn't there still a huge abyss between us? Isn't he also *for* the *central life* and not for *Zion*? Has he really come to the synthesis in himself, which is the true Zionist synthesis: invest in the measure of the teachings [*Lehre*]? He is a purely theoretical person.[37]

Scholem criticizes Benjamin's Zionism for being unable to place faith in the teachings, *die Lehre*—more precisely, divine Scripture, Torah. In this sense, his Zionism remains abstract and indeed esoteric. Unable to place oneself within the meaning of the Scripture, his conception of Judaism, from Scholem's point of view, would remain doomed to a fate expressed in the last part of "*Trauerspiel* and Tragedy" on the nature of Trauerspiel, which appears transformative but is only able to present the law of the divine world in a limited sense and is never able to reach it.[38] Judaism, through the prism of Zion, is subject to the same limitation, not only in its projection of the divine world, but of a praxis in this world that could lead the way.

A Programmatic Torah

Aharon Heller, a fellow member of the Jung Juda, writes to Scholem on the ninth of July 1917: "Our goal is the realization of Zionism = the realization of the Torah" along the lines of Exodus 19:6—"And you should become a land of priests and a holy people."[39] Heller's views on Torah and Zionism correspond to Scholem's own. But what is meant by Torah when not the five books of Moses, a divine book of teachings, or even the tradition of rabbinical Judaism? For Scholem Torah envelops a far broader collection of ideas and events:

> What is Torah? I understand it to be: 1) the principle by which the order of things are formed. Following the Judaic perspective that this is also the language of God, it is uniquely discernible in it being handing down to humanity . . . therefore 2) the Torah means an integral—the essence of the religious traditions of the Jews from the first days to the days of the Messiah—an integral by which Judaism, although not identical with the law of things, merges with it in an unusual way and with that which is expressed in a book, the Torah, as the word of God—the spoken essence of the intellect of the world.[40]

In contrast to the opening debate with Werner Scholem and the classical conception of anarchism in utopian form, a divine order of things formulated here explains in part the poverty of worldly organization. Knowledge of this order is possible through tradition, of which Torah is the center. Torah is not merely "teaching" or "law" but a reflection of the divine order, i.e., law and essence of the law, placed in the hands of humanity to understand—not so much a book of laws but the invariable order of the divine. It is, as in *Bereshit Rabbah*, a blueprint of the world used by God in creation as his construction plans. As such, the building blocks that formed its foundation must be linguistic. In the story of Genesis God articulated words, and these words took shape and formed things. These things were formed according to the structure of God's utterances, in which the formation of light was followed by the creation of the heavens through the separation of water, followed by the drying of the land, the emergence of grass, trees, and so on, all through speaking.[41]

God, surprisingly enough, turns out not to be the measure of this observation, not even the measure of the Torah. "For me," writes Scholem, "Zion is the center. . . . If God is [truly] the center of everything, I don't know but I don't believe it. God can only be recognized from the center."[42] God is rendered secondary in history or at least of secondary concern. History has an independent course, which, if determined by God, is certainly not steered by Him. In this view, history is not eternal but transitory. Here we are able to distinguish between two categories of the messianic idea and situate Scholem's early Zionist notions accordingly. The first would consist of a redemption occurring where and when history ends, namely, in the arrival of the Messiah. Human vocation might be reduced to a minimum in this plan. Once the Messiah appears, the work of redemption can begin with the participation of the living and the resurrected. A second perspective on the messianic idea is denoted by human activity and a commitment to worldly affairs before the arrival of the Messiah. In this view humanity is imbued with a power, perhaps even a theurgic power, that is capable of enacting redemption through its own agency in the world. In Scholem's conception of Zionism we face the following elements: a commitment to worldly affairs that, through its realization, ushers in a state of the divine and a Torah that explains Jewish practice as the movement toward Zion, where Zion is no longer a metaphor but an idea to be realized. With such a clear formulation one cannot help but notice a distinctly messianic quality to Scholem's thinking, despite the fact that Scholem was to argue passionately in his later years against just this form of mixing Zionism and messianism, pleading for a radical separation of the two in every sense and warning against the havoc that messianism has unleashed in Jewish history.[43] But if Zionism here implies a commitment to a civitas humana through which a civitas dei is possible, in which the realization of the Torah is not conceived to be a divine act but rather one that takes place in history, then it is difficult to conceive of Scholem's Zionism here as anything but messianic, leading to a civitas dei as theocracy.

Thus Scholem's early thought is fundamentally radical. It reveals an unmistakable longing for an origin and a purity of desire, boring its way through the early letters and journals and leading directly to Palestine. "Better to live eternally in exile and carry my sins alone," notes Scholem in a journal entry of 1917, "then to lead a hedonistic life in the land of Israel."[44] Everything in exile was merely preparation for a future life in Zion, devoted to the study of Judaism. The cadre in exile is to prepare for this transition. A "bettering of the heart," in the words of Ahad Haam, was to take a more radical form in the Jung Juda and to be applied to all aspects of Zionism, not the least of which "the sexual relations" of its members.[45] He continues in the same passage:

> We all must make sure that a bit of asceticism (in all things) is part of building what it is we want to build. Here in the military I have to be exposed in the most terrible way to what sexual impurity does to human beings. If we were to strive for the same basis of popular health as the Germans that I'm brought together with here, a healthy people, we would be lost. For every chance at sanctity is lost through obscenity. But if we want to be holy . . . we must commit ourselves to solitude. Every community that does not emerge from real solitude today is a swindle, for it has not yet overcome *Golus* [exile] and carries, moreover, its main poison in its heart.[46]

REVOLUTIONARY NIHILISM

Lying on a cot in the barracks reserved for the psychiatrically ill under a six-week observation period, Scholem wrote these lines in July 1917 in response to Heller's letter previously quoted while waiting for an exemption from military service.[47] These sentiments mark a definitive shift in Scholem's political thinking, moving from the early, more traditional anarchist notions and a corresponding idea of action to a more critical view toward outward activity that had already begun to take effect in Berlin. A propaganda campaign for Zion began to appear futile, the avocation of the cause of piousness vain. Scholem began to see a concentration of the self and the Jung Juda in a movement away from external activities as a necessary step. The juxtaposition of the sexuality of the Jung Juda to the goals of the movement suggest a radical turn inward in Scholem's thinking. Thus a distinct form of nihilism comes to the fore, which was to shape and form the previous conception of politics anew. In a phrase written many years later, to distinguish this form of political theology from its more destructive correlate, he termed it "nihilism of a quietistic nature."[48] I believe it is best understood here as an anarchist nihilism.

The first indication that the use of the term *nihilism* implies a with-drawal from politics occurs in the debate with Werner Scholem in 1914, where the term is used to illustrate his own absolute rejection of the war in contrast to the opportunism of the Social Democratics (B II:5). But it is not until 1917 that the initial conception of active politics was thrown into question, until then primarily focused on the introduction of his and Jung Juda's conception of Zionism into the youth movement. "We are all in agreement," writes Scholem to another member of the Jung Juda, "that we must abstain for the time being . . . from 'external work' in the sense of large gatherings and work internally."[49] It appears as if the Zionism of the Jung Juda had little success in winning over many to its demanding vision of Jewish renewal. Isolation was therefore the outcome in the substitution of *Außenarbeit* [external work] for inner teaching, as Scholem remarks in the letter to Heller quoted above. A community of Zionists of Scholem's nature must recognize the profound state of alienation in exile and form its activities with this in mind. Just as the Jew in Zion cannot be hypothesized from the Jew in exile, so too would a politics of the possible in *Golus* be, in his words, "poisoning the core of Zion." Thus Scholem was not to embark on a trail of pessimism or to resign from previously held views of an anarchist, utopian-socialist nature, nor was his nihilism a critique of everything in existence. It seems that his nihilism is best surmised as a politics in *Aufschub* (postponement).[50] Activism would be left to the preparation of the few as Jung Juda was poised to become a *Geheimbund* (clandestine organization).[51]

The move toward this nihilistic conception of politics was crystallized in an open letter to Siegfried Bernfeld, editor of the *Jerubbaal* (a journal of the Zionist youth movement) entitled "Abschied" (farewell/departure).[52] This period marks the height of Scholem's anarchist nihilism in Muri. Following the intense contact with Benjamin, Scholem embarked on a reevaluation of the youth movement from the distance of Switzerland and of the war. His belief that Benjamin also subscribed to the views articulated in this open letter to the Jewish youth movement and, as a consequence, his anticipation that Benjamin would articulate his own "Abschied" (which had de facto already taken place) in cosigning this letter suggests profound theoretical agreement between the two, which Scholem alludes to with such uniform clarity on rare occasion. Benjamin does take Scholem's "departure" from the Zionist movement as a decisive moment in their political theology. Regarding the open letter Scholem was preparing at the time, Benjamin writes, "With your exit from the Zionist organization, we will both be able to solidify the unity of our thought."[53] The subject and the tone of "Abschied" in many ways do tend to confirm the idea of a joint program, but there are also marked differences between the authors that are present in the text.[54] Nevertheless, an atmosphere of reflection on the metaphysics of politics and terms upon which community would be possible are the sentiments of this open letter. But the community desired by both the revolutionary socialist and the Zionist, Scholem concludes, is only possible through the very condition it seeks to overcome:

> Community demands solitude: not the possibility of together desiring the same but only that of common solitude establishes community. Zion, the source of our nationhood, is the common . . . solitude of all Jews. . . . As long as this center is not restored to radiant brightness, the order of our soul that honesty bids us to acknowledge must be anarchic. In *Galut* [exile], there can be no Jewish community valid before God. And if community among human beings is indeed the highest that can be demanded, what would be the sense of Zionism if it could be realized in *Galut*.[55]

In "Abschied" we witness a call for a disengagement from practical, worldly affairs, particularly from the movements that rattle the sabers of change but reveal themselves as idle chatter, no further along than where they began. For in exile there can be no true community.[56] What is held in common are not political goals but the alienation from their immediate realization. Necessary for this realization are not worldly organizations but rather the orientation of the individual to these goals that, we are told, are informed by anarchism in its utopian sense, until the restitution of the divine "order of the soul" supersedes this isolation, by which redemption is undoubtedly meant.[57] Thus silence (as opposed to idle chatter) is the element the youth movement needs in its quests for the reparation of the division between the word and its meaning, word and deed:

> Just as youth cannot be solitary, it cannot be silent. The silence in which word and deed unite is alien to it. . . . Those who are unable to be silent, however, also are unable to speak with each other in the final analysis. . . . [In chatter] all things mingle in an indiscriminate manner and are perverted: Zion to the state of the future, Judaism to spirit. . . . To restore language to youth: that is the task.[58]

Little can be more representative of a retreat from concrete political life than silence, nothing that connotes a greater sense of reflection without action. But out of this transitive moment of reflection in which politics can be thought anew, not based solely on general directions but on the understanding of the difference between essentials, youth will finally be able to return to language. For the strength of the youth movement is not determined by "its debut and its demands, but rather by the seclusion in which it takes up its task, and the greatness of the renunciation in which its fullness assumes form."[59] For such a youth movement would have Hebrew as its highest goal and "Zion would no longer be a symbolic metaphor."[60]

The "departure," however, turned out to be far greater than from the German Zionist youth movement. Scholem's open letter precipitated a crisis in the intellectual partnership. Indeed, several factors may have played a role in the mounting tension between authors, not the least of which had to have been Scholem's complicated relationship with Dora Benjamin and the seclusion of all three in Switzerland. By December 1918 a definitive rupture is detectable in the collective project. In a rather lengthy journal entry shortly before the new year, Scholem expresses deep frustration with the intellectual community and their metaphysical anarchism:

> Being together with Walter is not a lasting anarchist community, but one that is dominated by historical laws: only in revolutions might our relationship be realized. . . . In the end we simply have differing views on what abstention [*Verzicht*] means, which periodically renews and embodies the contradictions in our relationship. My idea of abstention is such that nothing is irrelevant in relation to it. For Walter and Dora, however, there are things from which they believe they have a right not to abstain. . . . I was wrong when I wrote . . . that I have a completely positive relationship with Walter. And this error has to be corrected now, even if it is going to create problems. Three years of this attempted and unrealized community has taught, instructed, challenged, and restricted me.[61]

Scholem comes to a turning point in his thinking after nearly three years of intensive exchange. The Swiss years had reached an end, as his "return to Germany" begins to appear immanent.[62] Rather than a break— there is no real indication of a collapse of their friendship—these moments suggest the pinnacle of their intellectual partnership. Apart from the per-

sonal strains of the three, a turning point was indeed engendered by differing views. Differences concerning the realization of the Zionist idea was
one, even if, as Scholem notes in his journal, he wasn't fully able to articulate this difference to the others;[63] a second was the notion of abstention,
integral to Scholem's revolutionary nihilism. Abstention was the term by
which he criticized the Zionist youth movement in his "Farewell" letter, as
we have seen. Now it is also a critique of Benjamin's nihilism.

Nihilism is thus an abstention from political engagement out of a desire for a new political idea. Although it rejects direct participation, it would
be wrong to assume a full rejection of politics as such. On the contrary, it
was born from considerations of an expressly political nature and is still undoubtedly entwined in a utopian anarchism of the earlier period. Yet in
contrast to Benjamin, Scholem appears here to be more consciously searching for a realm in which this abstract nihilism could find a political home.
Evidence for this can be found not only in his differing views on the realization of a spiritual Zionism but also by the fact that he continued to be
moved by the changes taking place around him. In a letter to Werner Kraft
from Bern, he articulates this enthusiasm for the events in Russia, which
were felt by many at the dawn of the revolution, not the least of which the
Russian anarchists abroad.[64] He writes, "In my life I have never seen such a
humanly gripping and honest collection of political writings as the documents of the maximalist [Bolshevik] revolution."[65] Yet this embrace is but-
tressed by a nihilism that can only to be transcended by redemption:

> The difference in my position to war and revolution is quite clear:
> although I do not take part in either, with the former, I distance
> myself, yet with the later, I observe. I bring this revolution, which
> without a doubt has historical legitimacy, into my visual hori-
> zon—not more but also not less. As long as the spiritual position
> of the new order of things is not completely impaired, it is my ob-
> ligation not to abandon a "well-meaning neutrality." For while the
> revolution, in which my *participation* would be important, is the
> theocratic revolution, which surely is not identical with this one
> (however much this revolution naturally has something messianic
> about it). I cannot do anything more.[66]

In his journal entry from October 13, 1918, he copies over this paragraph
from his letter to Werner Kraft and adds one final sentence, which I believe

is quite revealing of the moment: "The principle difference between social-ism and anarchism (the precursor of theocracy) is now clear."[67]

CATACLYSMIC ANARCHISM

The crucial moment in which Scholem would leave the shores of Europe behind for the "Orient of the future" finally arrived in 1923, bringing to an end a period embroiled in the causes and concerns of a Berliner youth culture. New problems, unanticipated from the distance of Jena, Münich, or Berlin, began to emerge: on Zion, the Hebrew language, the formation of a Jewish state, and Jewish-Arab co-existence.[68] So too with his conception of anarchism. If it was going to continue to be meaningful, anarchism could no longer be based solely on the events and thinkers of Europe and would have to undergo a transition to correspond to this new phase in his program of Jewish renewal.[69] This transition was no less radical then the former and Scholem's newfound conception was once again fundamentally at odds with the very formulations preceding it.

Although the terms *anarchism* and *nihilism* rarely appear in the years directly following Scholem's emigration, they were surely compelling forces in the subterranean grottoes of his research. With the publication of his 1936 Hebrew essay "Mitzvah haba'ah be'avarah" or "Redemption Through Sin," however, these categories resurface once again with renewed vigor as his interest in the messianic figure of Sabbatai Zvi[70] and the movement surrounding his pronouncement in 1666 to be the Messiah took definitive form.[71] Rather than the "well-meaning neutrality" we encountered in the previous section, anarchism comes to the fore as the most intense partiality, a nihilism of violent and destructive forces so extreme that they inevitably turn back on themselves. A messianic tendency is here expressed in its most apocalyptic form, in a vision of a "general upheaval and cataclysm" far removed from the weak messianic drive, lodged in the enlightenment idea of progress.[72] Destruction as an end in itself serves as the explanation for the conflagration that Sabbatai Zvi and his apostle, Nathan of Gaza, ignited in Jewish history, the embers of which still smolder in corners of the Jewish world.

In the early years of Scholem's emigration, a marked transition occurred in his conception of politics. But despite the fact that he borrowed quite heavily from these terms in his 1936 essay on the Sabbatian movement, Scholem failed to address them directly. It wasn't until a renascence of interest in the utopian dimension of religion and revolution that anarchism and nihilism were once again bought to the forefront of his thinking and categorically addressed. Thus a short historical detour is required. In his 1974 essay "Der Nihilismus als religiöses Phänomen" (Nihilism as a religious phenomenon), Scholem portrays the nihilist in a somewhat different light than we have seen so far. Here he is conceived as a Russian revolutionary, a "fundamental opponent to every form of authority, who cannot accept any principles based on belief, regardless of the attention which may surround such principles."[73] The nihilist takes the form of a modern rebel who rejects the contradictions of feudal and precapitalist Russian life and, as a consequence, becomes a legislator over his own norms and behavior. Nihilism—Scholem notes while drawing on Nietzsche's *Will to Power*—is the "most distressing of all guests," one that lies outside the doors of bourgeois society in wait, ready to launch itself upon the hypocrisy of its ways out of its own professed logic.[74] This feat was ascertained, first and foremost, by its implicit relationship to anarchism:

> The anarchists actively integrated this idea into their propaganda and became the classic representatives of nihilism in the consciousness of other circles, before Nietzsche—well beyond the political sphere and in consideration of the implications of the collapse of the handing down of authoritarian systems of value— recognized nihilism as the stony guest waiting at the door of our party.[75]

The withering of meaning of the authority structures that engulfed Russian nihilists at the end of the nineteenth century left little alternative, in their view, than to embark on a program of complete destruction. In this way the establishment of a connection between the nihilists and the revolutionary transformation sought by the anarchists was a natural development: if reconstruction was to take place, then the wreck of an edifice that masqueraded as a regime had to be fully pulled down. For this young generation nihilism meant "the destruction of all institutions, in order to discover what positive assets might withstand such destruction," with whom the sentiments of Bakunin's motto of destruction being a creative act were certain to reverberate.[76] The proximity of Kropotkin's formulation of the nihilist impulse to anarchism, notes Scholem, is based on the fact that both

movements advocate "the continuous struggle against tyrannical and hyp-
ocritical institutions for the freedom of the individual and support for the
free association of independent and mutually assisting communities."[77]
Both their radical critique of society and its authority structures facilitated
a unity of causes that extended inward through the purity and radical application of this critique to everyday life. The transition of the term *nihilism* from secular revolt to radical theology, according to Scholem, thus
followed a course that philosophically nihilistic movements had already set
into action: "The decline of the old authoritarian religious value systems
still based on revelation was declared a consequence of the collapse of the
religious world in connection to the religious and philosophically critical
movements that were nihilistic."[78] But how is this form of nihilism related
to the anarchist nihilism established in the last section? In this late essay Scholem differentiates between two forms of nihilistic revolt: a "quietistic nihilism" and a "nihilism of the deed." The former is distinguished from the
latter through the fact that it is "not institutions or even reality itself that it
seeks to negate or destroy in active opposition, but in contemplation and
from a metaphysical, Archimedean standpoint."[79]

If the conception of nihilism in the previous section referred to a retreat from worldly affairs into the realms of a "metaphysical anarchism,"
the term was now used to refer to a radically active and historical movement, ready to turn the world upside down. The principle that "the viola-
tion of the Torah could become its true fulfillment (bittulah shel torah
zehu kiyyumah)"[80] is deemed a hallmark of this active form of nihilism of
the deed, what Scholem understood as the "dialectical outgrowth" of the
solipsistic messianism inherent in Sabbatianism. "Just as a grain of wheat
must rot in the earth before it can sprout, so the deeds of the 'believers'
must be truly 'rotten' before they can germinate the redemption."[81] The
act of sinning became the very act that was to bring on the redemption, the
destruction of the existing order would bring on a new, just order. It was,
however, in the works of Nathan of Gaza that radical paradox was canon-
ized as the basis of Sabbatian theology. Contradiction became a "lasting
characteristic of the movement: following upon the initial paradox of an
apostate Messiah, paradox engendered paradox."[82]

The figure that Scholem attributes to having brought paradox to its
farthest extremes was the late Sabbatian Messiah Jacob Frank of Poland, an
even more radical "reincarnation" of Sabbatai Zvi a generation later. Advocating a nihilism and a "mystical theory of revolution" with "rare au-

thenticity," Frank's utopian vision was founded on the quest for "a life of anarchic liberty."[83] This mystical revolutionary idea carried with it a mission that extended beyond the demands of Lurianic Messianism, which requires the redemption of "sparks" and the congregation of the Jewish world before the dominion of exile for all peoples could be ended (j3:200). In Sabbatianism a universal dimension of the messianic task was revealed:

> [Frank] continuously repeats the two-fold principle of his teachings: the *removal* of all values, positive laws and religions in the name of the liberation of *life*. The way there is led through the abyss of destruction. A key term for Frank is the word *life*, through which his anarchist pathos expresses itself. Life for him is not the harmonious order of nature and its gentle laws—he is no advocate of a return to nature in the sense of Rousseau. . . . Life is freedom from constriction and law. The anarchic life is the object and content of his utopia that promises a primitive striving for a lawless notion of freedom and promiscuity for all beings. This anarchist life intoxicates the "big brother" and contains all of the positive tones and overtones for Frank that this concept otherwise has in religious tradition with an entirely different meaning. A hundred years before Bakunin Frank placed the redemptive power of destruction in the center of his utopia.[84]

Life was no longer to be governed by the rules of the past: what was once particularized was now made universal, what was once restricted was now permitted; everything that existed before was a prehistory of suffering, everything that existed now, the striving for "life."[85] A pure experience as such, unmediated by external authority, was the cardinal hymn of Frankist anarchism and what, in many ways, bares striking resemblance to more contemporary libertine figures. "To live is the rarest thing in the world," once wrote Oscar Wilde. "Most people exist, that is all. . . . For what man has sought for is, indeed, neither pain nor pleasure, but simply life."[86] Rather than the socialist individualism of Wilde, Scholem envisioned Frank in light of Michael Bakunin and the uproar he sought to instigate at every opportunity across Europe in the revolutions of 1848. The destructive nature of such uprisings were met with little remorse, for Bakunin's destructive rationale was equally drawn from an idea of negation, originating out of a notion of dialectical necessity. The conviction that revolution could only be created out of the ashes of the old were conclusions that led him to ferment uprisings everywhere he went, in the open and in secret societies. The affinity Scholem was to find in Frank's program of destruction, however, was distinctly more poignant, in the sense that Frankist nihilism was capable of being focused to a far greater extent than secular nihilism was ever able to achieve. In Jacob Frank's own words: "Whereever I go, everything will be destroyed. I must destroy and annihilate—what I build, will last for ever."[87] But this period of destruction has not yet reached its conclusion, as Scholem states, "In the meantime, the moment for construction has not yet arrived. The gravitation toward destruction, an original and authentic anarchism, takes hold at all levels of our existence."[88]

The anarchist idea is here identified with a religious yearning for freedom from law whose nihilist content is fully exposed years before Bakunin. Frank's mystical theory of the real, anarchist life necessitates the victory over every state and religion, where "the vision of nihilist redemption" is contained within "the overthrow of all laws and norms."[89] In a separate passage he formulates the Frankist conception of law: "This world is dominated by an 'unworthy law.' For this reason, the true task is to pave the way for an end to the authority of these laws—*all* laws of this world—which are the laws of death that impair the dignity of man."[90] Frankism, according to Scholem, sought the complete abrogation of everything in Judaism and, ultimately, the complete abrogation of the self, what he calls the "nothingness of religion" or "the nontheological."[91]

For the Sabbatian anarchists immanent revolution meant complete destruction. Theirs was a release from messianic expectation that had evolved not only from their own agitation but from generations of expectation whose hopes were dashed by the terrible irony of a Messiah whose greatest redemptive act consisted of converting to another religion. But rather than resignation the apostasy, conversion, and "descent" of the Messiah gave a whole new dimension to the messianic idea, which, instead of provoking a retreat into disarray, was greeted with a doctrine and, later, the practice of "contradictory acts."[92] Those who in every outward manner suggested the most devout practice of Jewish tradition had, through Sabbatianism, "begun to embark on a radically new inner life of their own" in which the apparently most observant were often the most radical believers in a new era ushered in by Sabbatai Zvi.

Anarchism here, just as in the traditional conception with which this chapter begins, is wedded to the "desire for total liberation," where destruction is conceived of as a catalyzing force.[93] Paralleling other revolutionary movements, Sabbatians too "desired to prolong the novel sensation of living in a 'restored world' by developing attitudes and institutions that seemed commensurate with a new divine order."[94] But this very act of forming new ritual and structure, even a new Torah, meant destroying the ritual and structure of an old Torah, and this triggered in Scholem a fearful moment in his conception of the revolutionary idea. A common feature in all individuals is the dimension of nihilism, he writes, "the instincts of anarchy and lawlessness that lie deeply buried in every human soul."[95] In the case of Frank these tendencies were responsible for an outburst that sought the destruction of Judaism[96] as such: "Traditionally Judaism had always sought to suppress such impulses, but now that they were allowed to emerge in the revolutionary exhilaration brought on by the experience of redemption and its freedom, they burst forth more violently than ever."[97] Repression was the critical force that maintained rabbinic Judaism as a cohesive and viable tradition, concludes Scholem. Judaism, perhaps like all other religions, continually provides new avenues for heretical elements that derive from the inherent paradox of religion: the construction and destruction of religious institutions and organization. A prime avenue to the destruction of such institutions is the phenomenon of mysticism, which inherently questions the divine right of all authority.[98] So long as tradition exists, it will be necessary for it to provide "vents" leading outside itself, whose variability is dependent on the norms that govern it just as much as the age in which these impulses emerge.[99] The outcome of this conflict determines how the messianic idea is to be reinterpreted in a given age, based on its own internal ventilation and the period in which it takes shape. A nihilistic outcome of this conflict thus stands in explicit relationship to repression: "As long as no affirmative means was available through which a messianic revolt could take place within the ghetto and its environment, this revolt took on a nihilistic character."[100]

The destruction of the ghetto stood at the center of the Frankist vision. The "impulse" that was to drive the movement outward transformed its own messianic calling into a nihilistic one. "In the restructuring of all values of Jewish tradition propagated by the Frankists," explains Scholem, pointing to the role of external restrictions, "the historical experience of Polish Jewry was coupled with an intense desire for a world that had just failed them."[101] Frankism found supporters among those already let down by the promises of enlightenment, speaking to a Polish Jewry in which the notion of emerging from the ghetto walls still lingered. The Frankists themselves were prime examples of this yearning and consequent rejection. Two worlds were indeed closed to Frankism in the course of its activities: rabbinical Judaism, which vehemently opposes anything perceived as being "law-destroying" and the external vents of Christianity and Islam, which met Frank's conversions with skepticism and repression.[102] Isolation and containment left the nihilistic impulse little choice but to turn inward, explaining the movement of religious nihilism into the main territories of observant tradition, governing the most fundamental aspects of religious life: moral restrictions. "Because the means to political action were closed off to him, Frank focused instead on a moral revolt against the dominant world order."[103] Scholem formulated this tendency more generally in his late essay: "The revolt against the laws, which the nihilist condemns in its very origins and with which he achieves admission to a higher law, finds its closest and most apparent application in a moral law that is worthy of being broken."[104] Since moral law stands at the center of a tradition whose very authority is challenged, the nihilist impulse is directed not simply toward morality itself but rather toward the basis of law and the force that sanctions it.[105] This directed the messianic drive to overturn law altogether through the performance of its reversal; for example, the Sabbatian prayer that transformed the traditional blessing of *mattir assurim*, blessed is He who frees all slaves, to *mattir issurim*, blessed is He who permits the forbidden. According to Scholem, the more repressive rabbinical Judaism reacted to such movement of reversal, the greater the eruption of destructive impulses. The conversion to Islam became the farthest break from rabbinical tradition possible:

> This was seen largely as a masking of the real messianic content that was realized though the antinomian rituals of the sectarian. Unmistakably powerful religious emotions joined together here with anarchistic tendencies that lie hidden deep within human beings. The stricter rabbinical Judaism was with its discipline to ban such impulses, the wilder the outbreaks of radical messianism and its message of the initiation of freedom and redemption, even if this freedom could only be found in secret and underground.[106]

The explosion caused by the encounter between the "law-destroying" impulses of religious nihilism and the "law-generating" impulses in rabbinic Judaism presented in acute form a radical clash of forces that harbored no room for their opposites. Scholem offers a classical dialectical explanation for this phenomenon: "The tremendous energies that went into building religious structures that meant to unite the experience of the world with the transcendent, permitted no room for that which first took place in the crystallization process."[107] The explosion (or implosion, as the case may have been) caused by this confrontation was to yield new constellations of Judaism never seen before. Sabbatianism, through its sheer negativity, was able to help "pave the way for the Haskalah and the reform movement of the nineteenth century, once its original religious impulse was exhausted."[108] A new historical constellation formed, according to Scholem, engendered by a "crisis of faith" that was able to penetrate the most remote corners of Jewish society by the very fact that the emergence of Sabbtianism coincided with a lifting of medieval isolation generally for Jews.[109] Thus the Bakuninist principle that destruction can also be a creative will returns to garnish this rather negative moment in Scholem's conception of anarchism, expressed in messianic terms as "'the transcendence of the Torah as its true fulfillment.'"[110]

The emergence of Sabbatianism, and later Frankism, as an "exceptional explosion of productive energies," were seen by Scholem in expressly dialectical terms.[111] In the case of nihilism, these unyielding destructive forces, working to undo all the binds of Jewish tradition, were to have an historical effect far beyond their intentions:

> The desire for total liberation, which played so tragic a role in the development of Sabbatian nihilism, was by no means a purely self-destructive force; on the contrary, beneath the surface of lawlessness, antinomianism, and catastrophic negation, powerful constructive impulses were at work.[112]

The category of nihilism takes on a whole new meaning in light of Sabbatianism. It, together with anarchism, were to become wholly negative categories—negative, however, with purely unintentional and ultimately creative effects that branched off into the concerns of the enlightenment. "What they themselves brought forth," remarks Scholem on the nihilist contribution to rationalism, "can be seen as a transition to the revolutionary images of the Enlightenment."[113] In this sense Scholem was to link cataclysmic formulations to the "quietistic nihilism" and traditional anarchism of the earliest period by posing the necessity of negation. This connection is most poignantly illustrated in an (until recently) unpublished first introduction to his large work on Sabbatai Zvi. In the following passage we see once again the influence that the early political-theological ideas were to have on Scholem's lifelong research:

> An understanding of the Sabbatian movement, in my opinion, depends on whether the attempt to link the earthly realm, the sphere of history, to the heavenly realm, the sphere of the Kabbalah, is successful and to explain the one in light of the other. For "the worldly is like the heavenly realm." Both truly form a single "realm"—a realm of motion through which human experience unfolds. This cannot be understood merely as "intellectual" or "social" but rather reveals many primary movements.[114]

In this third phase of Scholem's conception of anarchism, we witness a startling new usage of the term, one that, although bearing many of the hallmarks of the first two categories, embarks on an entirely new discussion. Anarchism represents the dialectical necessity of destruction, expressed here in purely religious terms. Scholem stresses the truly religious desire that Sabbatianism embodies. Once expressed in the language of his own early religious-anarchist sentiments, "the flame of true belief burns in its essence only in secret."[115] In a testament to the authentic religious nature of Sabbatian nihilism and their own anarchist pursuit of the "divine world," Scholem concludes his late essay with a perspective harkening back to his own negated messianic pursuits, which were diverted to politics: "The members of this movement were true believers who, in the promise of an anarchist, earthly utopia, found a redemption that rabbinical Judaism failed to provide."[116]

CRITICAL ANARCHISM

In this final transition of the anarchist idea we can now turn to a formulation that found expression late in Scholem's carrier. Just as Judaism was to pay a heavy price for its messianism—in the same way that every historical movement has to pay a price for its activities—the cataclysmic moment was to have a lasting impact on the conception of anarchism. As we have

seen in the previous section, the nihilistic impulse led to the Sabbatian explosion that itself paved the way for an age of enlightenment in Jewish
thought in the eighteenth century. After the onslaught of "law-destroying"
tendencies, the rigid hold that rabbinic authority exercised over Judaism
was no longer as mighty as it once had been, and the *haskalah,* or Jewish
Enlightenment, added a good deal to the decline in influence of "law-
abiding" Judaism as such. Slowly the very heart of Jewish law was brought
into question. If this was not to take place explicitly, then at least unintentionally: for the indisputable basis of lawful Judaism was being undermined, according to Scholem, by the growing disbelief in the divine origins
of Scripture (or in the avoidance of the question altogether). A transcript
of Scholem's comments suggests the startling impact that this phenomenon was thought to be having on Judaism. As he explains:

> The Torah is the sounding of a supernal voice that obliges one in
> an absolute manner. It does not acknowledge the autonomy (au-
> tonomiah) of the individual. To be sure, Jeremiah was promised a
> "Torah of the heart," but only at the end of days. The hasidim, in
> fact, did make an attempt to prepare the "Torah of the heart." A
> hasidic work interprets a passage in Deutoronomy 17 [18f] on the
> king of Israel—"and he shall write for himself in a book a copy of
> the Torah [. . .], and it shall be with him, and he shall read in it all
> the days of his life . . . "—such that the king will read the Torah
> within him, that is, within himself. This autonomous conception of
> the Torah, however, is not compatible with the traditional one.
> Torah has two meanings: the designation of a path, and the trans-
> mission of something. Everything in the world, even a person, can
> be "Torah," but there never is Torah without supernal authority.[117]

A resolute proposition of rabbinic Judaism, as with most forms of Judaism,
is that the Torah is the absolute word of God. This proposition naturally
requires nothing less than total compliance with the Torah, to whose laws
a Jew is unquestionably subjected. This is to say that unless one speaks of
another conception of Torah, there is no autonomy from its laws. There is,
nevertheless, a great difficulty in fulfilling the laws of the Torah. The Written Torah that Moses received is alone not enough to render its laws comprehensible. Scholem continues: "Were we to desire to restrict the Torah
to the Torah, transmitted in writing, we would not be able to read even the

Pentateuch, only the ten commandments. I[t] follows that even the Torah is already Oral Torah."[118] Thus the divine authority of the Torah is always mediated by the understanding oral tradition gives to it, expressed in the Talmud as a "fence around the Torah," defining it, giving it shape and intelligibility. From this he concludes that "the Torah develops and changes, and according to its very nature it cannot be rendered a unified system. The Torah is rather a continuum of questions and answers."[119] Despite the sweeping nature of this statement, there is nothing arbitrary in his notion of the Torah as a "continuum"; the Written Torah is "fixed without the exegesis of the Oral Torah." Scholem concludes his comments with the following three points: "There is no Torah without revelation (maton Torah), and there is no Torah without heteronomy (hetronomiah), and there is no Torah without an authoritative Tradition."[120] This conclusion can be expressed further as: (a) the Torah is revelation in the giving of the Torah to Moses, (b) but revelation in the Torah is accessible through interpretation, (c) and this interpretation has to be authoritative if it is to be capable of explaining the Torah, which is divine. It is this last proposition that has opened the door to what Scholem has termed "religious anarchism."

Unlike other periods in Jewish history, this final proposition on the interpretive authority of divine Scripture has been subjected to intense skepticism and doubt. With the consequential rise in the academic study of Judaism, skepticism concerning divine interpretive authority has been extended to the Torah itself. Scholem articulated this pervasive doubt in an article entitled "Reflections on the Possibility of Jewish Mysticism in Our Time" in uncompromising terms:

> Whoever is unprepared or unable to accept this principle [of the divine origin of the Torah], who lacks the absolute faith of the early believers, having found other beliefs or having been diverted into historical criticism (for many and varied are the forms of doubt in the infallibility of the Torah), is also an anarchist.
>
> Thus, as far as religion is concerned, we are all . . . , to some extent, anarchists today, and this should be plainly stated. Some know it and admit it fully; others . . . twist deviously to avoid facing the essential fact that in our time a continuity of Jewish religious awareness is beyond this principle of the "Law from on High." Such a conclusion inevitably leads to anarchic forms of religion.[121]

Suddenly anarchism is used to describe a condition. It is no longer a set of ideological principles, a critical retreat from history or the internal combustion of "law-destroying" tendencies. It is now a historical moment, brought on, in part, by these three prior anarchic stages. Since we are no longer capable today of identifying where "religious authority" lies, an anarchic moment must be brought into discussion. In an interview Scholem gave shortly after the publication of this essay, he formulated the problem along similar lines: "Someone who has lost his faith in the divine origin of the Bible must today resolve the question to the best of his understanding . . . [Nonetheless,] all of us are anarchists because we do not have an agreed upon authority."[122] In comparison to the orthodox, whose "conviction of the divine character of the Torah" is "beyond historical questioning," contemporary trends in Judaism are burdened by the anarchic condition.[123] Up until our present age the notion of revelation was still bound to the "fundamentalist thesis" of a divine Torah "as the absolute word yield[ing] an absolute system of reference" (jjc:270). Scholem terms this system absolute, but by this he is referring to the faith, or the means to speak of revelation as an aggregate, rather than the worldly knowledge of each particular moment. Indeed, it was this absolute system of reference that enabled an uncensured degree of freedom. Since "revelation was an absolute, its application was impossible without mediation" (jjc:270). Emerging from the divine word, a subjective element was both essential and, at the same time, nearly inexhaustible:

> The infinite meaning of Revelation, which cannot be grasped in the one-time immediacy of its reception, will unfold only in continued relation to time, in the tradition that is a tradition about the word of God and lies at the root of every religious deed. Tradition renders the word of God applicable in time. (jjc:270–1)

The objective basis of individual interpretation gave Oral Torah its "metaphysical legitimation" (jjc:270). In relation to mysticism and the "fundamental thesis," a very similar independence is created in the conviction that a hidden meaning of the divine word has yet to be understood: "This commitment gave firm support to religious individualism without going out of the established framework of the Torah."[124] Today, this fundamental thesis, the groundwork of an absolute system that, nevertheless, created the opportunity for individual mystical traditions to emerge, has been completely undermined by "historical criticism and by the philosophies which supported it,"[125] in other words, enlightenment and rationalist thought. In the context of whether mysticism in our age is possible from the perspective of the individual, Scholem concludes:

> Anyone who tries to bring to the community the fruits of his in-spiration and mystical awareness, but does not consider himself to be in conscience bound to the one great fundamental principle of the "Law from on High," without any reservations, word for word as written—such a person may be considered to be an anarchist.[126]

Thus in his assessment, since most Jews no longer hold this funda-mental thesis to be true, Jews and Judaism are "confronted with the fact of religious anarchism."[127] This confrontation has both an affirmative and negative dimension: Some defy it, but are "anarchists" nonetheless—in-voluntary anarchists, so to speak; others take on this anarchism as part of their condition, in the manner of Scholem himself. Voluntary anarchists recognize the void created by the lack of a system of fundamentals; hence Scholem's claim of not being able to judge whether a given Jewish tradition is "right or wrong."[128] This inability may be seen in an affirmative light, for it is also, in effect, a definite standpoint in relation to the state of knowl-edge, divorced from its foundations. Thus the voluntary anarchist advo-cates an orientation to what is here perceived to be an inherent condition. Scholem grounds this foundationless thesis in the following way: "The en-tire legitimacy of my outlook resides in the fact that I have related to the Judaism of the past, and relate to the Judaism of the future, as a living un-defined phenomenon, whose development possesses a Utopian dimen-sion."[129] Scholem's voluntary renunciation of a foundation for Judaism as such facilitated an ability to examine all forms of Judaism, especially those consciously neglected by the scholars who came before him. His religious anarchism enabled an undogmatic view toward Judaism. Seeing it as a liv-ing force bearing contradictory messages, none of which was too alien to explore, his stance toward this generational loss of divine faith was en-gaged. He was always quite aware of the fact that even his own final cate-gory of religious anarchism could not be considered permanent because of the transitional nature of Judaism. Despite his conclusions on its anarchic state, he always upheld the belief that "Judaism contains utopian aspects that have not yet been revealed,"[130] thus positing a utopianism above and beyond even what he himself could envision. This was expressed as early as 1939 (however much laconically) in a meeting with other like-minded founders of the Hebrew University:

> We are all anarchists. But our anarchism is transitional, for we are the living example that this does not remove us from Judaism. We are not a generation without *mitzvot*, but our *mitzvot* are without authority. . . . We are no less legitimate than our forefathers; they merely had a clearer text. Perhaps we are anarchists, but we oppose anarchy.[131]

To be an anarchist was based on principle—but the state from which it arose was not necessarily agreeable. After the tribulations the concept would undergo, Scholem returns to an anarchism that was to express his own religious politics, and, despite aspects of this politics that he viewed as destructive, his final category of anarchism was one to which he himself could subscribe: "the only social theory that makes sense—religious sense," as he once stated in an interview.[132] Within the complex analysis of anarchism and the drastic changes it was to undergo, Scholem, nevertheless, always left the door open to the possibility of a condition that was, in effect, beyond anarchism as such and ready to embrace a utopian dimension as soon as it revealed itself.

PART II

On the Origins of Language and the True Names of Things

Die Bewegung, in der die Schöpfung zustande kommt, ist also auch als Sprachbewegung deutbar.

The motion which took shape in creation can also be interpreted as linguistic motion.
—Scholem, "The Name of God and the Linguistic Theory of the Kabbalah" (1973)

CHAPTER 3

ON THE ORIGINS OF LANGUAGE

In a collection of commentaries on Genesis first redacted in the third or fourth century, an idea that would have a lasting impact on Jewish speculation concerning the nature of language was proposed: the Torah was created before creation itself.[1] Like a mysterious new discovery fueled by the sayings of Proverbs—"The Lord made me as the beginning of his way," "I was beside him like a little child, I was daily his delight"—something, it was believed, preceded the story of Genesis itself.[2] Various proposals were made in this text, known as *Bereshit Rabbah*, as to what could have possibly been beside God before creation: some argued for the angels, others championed a throne of glory. Then came a rather convincing suggestion: God's creating intentions preceded creation. In the act of creation the Torah stood beside God as a divine notepad in which His thoughts were scribbled out as prototypes on the complicated task before Him. In the tradition of the sages, God formed several models of the earth and universe, furiously creating and destroying prototypes before coming up with the creation of the world.[3] The Torah thus began to function as a divine construction plan or blueprint of how the world should be created, guiding Him through six days of work.[4]

This interpretation set the stage for a host of further speculations concerning the origins of the Torah,[5] the divine hierarchy, the possibilities of knowledge, and foremost the origins and purposes of language. The story of Genesis was no longer to be considered merely a passive description of creation but rather a grammatical explanation of how God gave acoustic expression to his written plans. The Hebrew word for light, *or*, had a hidden dimension, one that was able to create the thing it referred to by being expressed. *Or* was not merely a symbol for light—it was the insignia of the inner expression of light itself. In this way Genesis was to be interpreted as providing clues to an original language that harbored no distinctions between the thing and its name, in which the existence of a thing was inextricably tied to its linguistic expression. Since the fourth century the influence of this idea was to extend on into a wide range of Jewish thought and was later to play host to works like *Sefer Yetzirah* as well as a series of linguistic speculations in the Kabbalah.[6]

In a letter to Scholem dated November 11, 1916, which concerns the focus of his early essay "On Language As Such and the Language of Man," Benjamin seeks to establish a connection between this tradition and his own speculations on language: "I try to address the problem of the essence of language in this work, particularly in an immanent connection to Judaism, as far as I understand it, and the first chapter of Genesis."[7] He reveals to Scholem an inner continuity to his otherwise difficult and rather hermetic essay on language. Judaism was at the center of his speculation, his subject being the principle dimension of the Torah: the story of creation. The texts consulted for the analysis in addition to the Bible and commentary by Samson Raphael Hirsch, as we shall see, were probably the collection of midrashim by August Wünsche, which we know Benjamin later acquired,[8] as well as the work of the Christian Kabbalist Franz Joseph Molitor, which is addressed in the last section of this chapter, "Jewish Linguistic Theory and Christian Kabbalah." For Benjamin the link to the language of creation was not simply a halfhearted attempt to work theoretically with Judaic material but also an attempt to find a basis for his own philosophy—a philosophy in itself as much as it was a philosophy of Judaism. The origin of language is, in this sense, not only the basis of Judaism but also at the heart of Benjamin's thinking on epistemology, law, and aesthetics: "The question regarding the essence of knowledge, law and art," he writes in a letter composed a few years after completing his essay on language, "is linked to the question of the origins of all human expression of the intellect out of the substance of language [*Wesen der Sprache*]."[9]

At the beginning of his essay, he states rather clearly his reasons for pursuing the story of Genesis as an approach to a linguistic philosophy:

> If the essence of language is considered, in the following, on the basis of the first chapters of Genesis, it is not for the purposes of biblical interpretation, nor that the Bible be presented for consideration here as objective revealed truth, but rather to discover what emerges from the biblical text with regard to the nature of language;[10]

Should one take the first part of this statement by itself, it might be possible to assume that Benjamin's use of Genesis was rather accidental to the subject matter at hand.[11] Yet the second part of this paragraph clarifies the degree to which this Genesis-inspired or genesic example is essential:

> and the Bible is *precisely* in this respect indispensable because the explications here are based principally on a notion of language as a last, inexplicable, and mystical reality that can only be considered in its unfolding. The Bible, which is itself considered revelation, must necessarily evolve from the fundamental elements of language.[12]

It is fairly certain that Benjamin could not have hoped his essay would be viewed as a midrashic companion to Genesis. He would have been rather unequipped for that.[13] Instead of wishing to perform a biblical interpretation or engage in pure theological proofs of the objective, "revealed truth" of creation (which few theologians have been tempted to do), Benjamin chose to enter into metaphysical speculations on the nature of language itself, which, if not explicitly postulated in Genesis, is certainly contained in the commentary and tradition that follow. The Bible, he argues, can be read philosophically; it can be read as an exposition of principles based on an idea of language. His argument is such: if the Bible is to be understood as revelation, it must therefore offer the basis for metaphysical speculations concerning the origins and the nature of language.

To begin a linguistic analysis by way of the story of Genesis is not, in itself, a particularly mystical undertaking. By the same token, it cannot be denied that such speculation is indeed embedded in a religious tradition to which mysticism is hardly a stranger. But while it has long been accepted practice to conduct philosophy with examples drawn from Christian theology on their own merits without ever having to question the convictions of the author, this has not been the case with Judaism. The integration of Christianity and philosophy was surely to reach new dimensions in Hegel, where even the most modest barriers fell into disarray. A Jewish philosopher, however, who draws from religious example is either categorized as a Jewish theologian or placed in the context of Christianity. This indeed was to contribute to the fact that the discussion of explicitly Jewish religious notions in pre-Nazi Europe was largely confined to Jews or the scholarship of Judaism. Even today there is scant acknowledgment of the role that Jewish religious speculation has played in the humanities, as the discussion of Judaism in the realm of philosophy is still not a generally open and accepted practice. Benjamin was acutely aware of this and was compelled to situate his work within these confines.

With these preliminary remarks aside, we may now begin a survey of Benjamin's ideas, focusing initially on the distinction of linguistic essence. If we begin by establishing a corollary to the idea presented by *Bereshit Rabbah*, that the Torah existed before creation and that the plan or intention of creation was enacted in the pronunciation of words, we would need to view Benjamin's concept of language as one in which the linguistic substance of a thing or being cannot be divided from its expression. The very first statement in this essay stakes out this claim regarding language as its focus: "Every expression of the spiritual life [*Geistesleben*] of human beings can be understood as a kind of language, and this understanding, in the manner of a true method, everywhere raises new questions."[14] Linguistic expression is understood here as more than the mere exchange of signs with predetermined meanings; it is rather the expression of the very substance of that which is being communicated. In this sense the story of Genesis offers Benjamin an original model of linguistic expression based on the notion of words (more specifically, names, as we shall see later) being the concentrated intentions of God's plan. If language is to be understood as the expression of the spiritual life, or the Geistesleben, of its bearer, as indeed we see here, then God's language expressed would also reflect His being and thinking combined.[15] With the story of Genesis we witness God establishing the primal model of the relationship between word and deed in which the medium of conceptual and linguistic expression is shared by humans to the degree that they are imbued with a linguistic dimension of thinking. If they think in language, every aspect of their intellect can be understood as manifested language and can be expressed in language. This opens up a host of questions when we ask, Is this true?[16]

In this sense Benjamin is clearly not referring to the Geistesleben being expressed in technical language, in terms that are only selectively applicable, but rather as an expression of *geistigen Inhalt* (spiritual or intellectual content), located with its subject matter, in which the content of a given object is not compromised by its expression or its form to content. In short, it concerns the "being of language" [II:140], extending beyond mere human expression to all created things. As Benjamin explains: "There is no event or thing in either animate or inanimate nature that does not in some way partake of language, for it is in the nature of every essential being to communicate the content of its intellect."[17] If language is the expression of geistigen Inhalt, the concentration of geistigen Inhalt must be recognizable in the language of human endeavor, says Benjamin—for example, in poetry and law. Both fields rely on linguistic expression and are measured by the degree to which they accurately match their given content. Thus a poem may only be as true as the expression it finds for its subject, just as a law might be said to be the linguistic expression of rule in which its only determinate is the degree to which it expresses the absolute of rule in momentary form. Similarly, in both examples, language is a substance contained within the expression externalized and completed in the act of speaking. The external expression of language begins with a divine model, guaranteeing its profane existence in a rendered form in human language. The substance of this external expression is present in everything, but resides undivided in the heart of language itself. Benjamin concludes that there is nothing of the living, of the past, nor of the eternal (that is, of the divine or of the profane) that is not in some way part of nature to the degree that it shares an inner core of language and can not help but express this inner core in language, as it exists, i.e., in the expression of its substance of the intellect, its geistige Inhalt, or *geistige Wesen*.

METAPHOR OF THE DIVINE

The first question that arises from this conception of language is the problem of linguistic expression without substance. If language is the expression of the spiritual or intellectual content of a thing, what is a metaphor? Benjamin turns to the *existing* aspect of linguistic expression to distinguish that from what he terms metaphoric expression: "A metaphor, in this usage, is in no way the word 'language.' For it represents a completely substantive knowledge, of which we cannot imagine, in which the substance of the intellect is not communicated in the expression."[18] Since a metaphor is the representation without the existence of a thing, Benjamin suggests that it cannot be understood here within the linguistic framework he establishes.[19] His argument concerns the impossibility to conceive of the inner knowledge of a thing without conveying its existence at the same time. According to Benjamin, language implies just that: the knowledge of its inner existence. A metaphor also presents us with a difficult problem in relation to the genesic model. In Jewish religious speculation there is no obvious place for the concept of metaphor, just as there is no word for "mysticism" as it is understood in Christian theology (and now in scholarship in general). A mystical metaphor, or the spiritual expression of a religious content, be it an idea or an event, is a geistige Inhalt that for many years could not be expressed in the Hebrew language.[20] Thus when Benjamin speaks of a metaphor that is not contained in language, being unable to express its *geistige Wesen* (substance of the intellect) and therefore be fully understood, the problem concerns the expression of an image, that is, how we view the idea that Adam was created in the image of God but is not God himself. How are we to understand the notion of an image if all God's utterances in creation were drawn up in the Torah and executed without flaw or delay? The notion of metaphoric representation, or spiritualization, is something that is therefore resisted by these primary genesic assertions.

Because a metaphor suggests a part of the substance of the intellect that is inexpressible, the smallest degree of consciousness in the representation of the object as a metaphor does not alter the very problem, he asserts. This is to say that whether a thing is animate or inanimate, the question of an inexpressible substance pertaining to the intellect or to the spirit (which here will have to be encompassed under the term *intellect*) applies to both.[21] Thus if a metaphor is the pure representation of a thing without, at the same time, being the thing itself, it is a representation without existence, in other words, a mere abstraction. In the context of an expression, a nonexistent representation would be something that communicates absences rather than substances. In its representation the substance is left behind and merely the form is projected. Thus from the question on the origins and meaning of language a theological metaphor is the "complete absence of language" in any being or thing.[22] It is divorced from its concrete expression and removed from a genesic conception of language. The unrepresented being of a metaphor is hence an abstraction. Benjamin extends this notion of abstraction to the realm of ideas, whereby in comparison to the metaphor, the existence of an idea is generally more certain than its meaning. The question is whether such existence is real or metaphorical. In this regard Benjamin treats us to a very difficult statement: "An existence entirely without relationship to language is an idea, but an idea bearing no fruit even within that realm of ideas whose circumference defines those of God."[23]

Whether the idea of an existence without language belongs to a circle of ideas that God does not permit to be fruitful, or if this circle determines the proximity of certain ideas to God's ideas (those being fruitful ideas), is left rather grammatically ambiguous in this citation.[24] Nevertheless, to speak of God as anything less than the source of ideas would be so far from the idea of God itself that it would bear little meaning. It must therefore be understood as a description of an idea that is rejected by God. But can there be a human idea independent of God? Surely no human idea escapes God, if we understand by the word the originator and safeguard of all ideas. So what is meant by the notion of God having ideas that are capable of being known but are unproductive or unhelpful to the understanding? This is similar to asking whether it is possible to conceive a notion that cannot be expressed in language, itself an absence or a representation of one, and still be conceivable? Certainly modern linguistic philosophy would argue against such an idea. It is most likely that Benjamin too deemed it rather improbable, not so much from a scholastic notion of the goodness of God but rather from an unwillingness to divide thinking from linguistic expression.

Expression therefore is language in its full and complete being. It is the substance of a given object in its existence. Behind this statement lies axiomatic properties on the nature of substance upon which the existence of a thing is premised. Benjamin expressed this in the following way: in order to understand the substance of a thing, one can search for the expression unique to it, as each substance of the intellect is bound to its own expression, from which it can not be severed. If this is so, one is prone to ask which belongs to which, i.e., which expression is constituted to match which substance of the intellect buried within a thing? Given a particular substance, we may ask: What is its expression? Which is the same as saying, How is a given substance expressed? By way of an answer to this question capable of transcending the attempt to establish a theory of direct correlation, Benjamin emphasizes that substance expresses itself in language and not through it. Naturally, the German language is his focus: "The German language, for example, is by no means the expression of everything that we could—presumably—express *through* it, but is the unmediated expression of that which communicates *itself* [*sich*] in it."[25] If we reverse the question from the content of a thing to its expression and begin with a definition of an expression, we are able to condition the discussion from the start were we to say that the expression is not everything that it is possible to express but rather the transference of its *unmediated expression*, itself linguistically communicable.[26] The reflexive pronoun in the citation above, *das Sich*, is emphasized in its German construction to indicate that it is its substance. But it is also a primary indicator that substance is expressed in language. Benjamin argues that the idea of a substance of a thing, existing only in language, is a proposal to which all linguistic theory has thus far fallen prey. He claims that the same contradiction is passed on to the substance and its difference from its expression, leaving a paradox in the existence of the substance to begin with.

In order to better understand the element that remains outside language, Benjamin returns to a central axiom of his discussion: Language communicates its substance of the intellect, the substance that is alone determined for it.[27] This is to say that each thing has both a language and a substance of the intellect, regardless of whether it is living or not. This substance is not transmitted through language but rather within it, as anyone who has had the experience of being a speaker of a foreign language has surly felt.[28] This same principle holds true for the intellectual substance of a particular thing (*geistige Wesen*) that is actively engaged in its linguistic substance (*sprachliche Wesen*). The two are in fact identical to the degree that the substance of a thing is communicable; what is communicable is its linguistic substance. However, the only linguistic difference between the two resides in the fact that while language communicates unconditionally the linguistic substance of a given object, it can only express the communicable portion of its substance of the intellect.

Language expresses itself within the vernacular of expression to the degree that its substance is communicable: "*All language communicates itself,*" such that "*the linguistic being of all things is their language.*"[29] Here Benjamin introduces the rather odd example of a lamp and its language in order to draw attention to the thesis of the indifference of substance to the animate or inanimate state of the object (as far as the principle is concerned). He makes the bold assertion that there is such a thing as a vernacular of the inanimate, such as a lamp, which also expresses its subject of the intellect to the degree that it is communicable. But in the case of all inanimate objects, the substance of the intellect communicable or understandable must be minute, for what would a lamp possibly say if it were to communicate? Since it does not think or write, to what degree can we say that an inanimate object has a geistige Wesen (substance of the intellect)? This would appear to be a rather untenable position.

However, there are possible explanations for his assertion. It might be helpful here to repeat the condition upon which such a statement is made: an inanimate object has a sprachliche Wesen (linguistic substance) to the *degree* that it can be communicated. It is also plausible that the sprachliche Wesen of a thing would be considered a language by way of the fact that its linguistic substance is attributable to its appearance, that its appearance is, in itself, an expression.[30] Benjamin's analysis is not to stop at this rather classical division between appearance and essence but rather seeks to bridge the gap between the two forms of substance. He continues in the following assertion that the linguistic substance of a thing is its language: "that, which is communicable of the substance of the intellect of a given thing."[31] In short, the linguistic substance of a thing is its communicable substance, which is of its intellect and therefore its language.[32] This proposition is not meant as a division of appearance from essence, not that the substance of the intellect of a thing is only that which appears clearly expressed in language, but it is rather language itself, "the language of the substance of the intellect is precisely that part which is communicable."[33] If the substance of the intellect of a thing is communicable language, in which the incommunicable no longer is considered a part of language, then language would not truly be capable of expressing the complete substance of the intellect, i.e., the complete substance of the intellect would not be linguistic. Creation in these terms would be God's expression in the language of the communicable (audible, comprehensible) substance of the intellect from which each thing and being was created.[34]

The Magic of the Inexpressible

If God expressed a language of communicable substance in creation, it would imply that He expressed His audible revelation rather than a translation of His expression rendered audible. Another view is that God did not express His entire substance but only those aspects of His substance directed toward the profane. Would this be a contradiction of Benjamin's thesis?

> The medial, which is the *immediacy* of all communication of the intellect, is the main problem of all linguistic theory, and if one chooses to call this immediacy magic, then the original problem of language is its magic. The notion of the magic of language refers to something else at the same time: its infiniteness.[35]

Magic is here understood to be the original problem of language, identifying the means as the critical problem of linguistic philosophy.[36] The medial is associated with the center of expression, the center from which language would express its substance. What Benjamin proposes here as magic points to a specific aspect of all geistige communication, a dimension expressing differentiation between the divine and profane language: its immediacy. To us it may appear as magic, for its means are not apparent in the association of substance and expression; that is, that substance is deemed existent in its expression, but inexplicably so. Yet when a linguistic model based on creation is applied, the ultimate transparency of the means is associated with a source. Unlike a metaphor, which is the expression of a thing without substance, magic is the expression of substance without a transparency of means.

   In the concept of magic, it seems we are dealing with a reflection of a living, eternal immediacy—an immediacy that could only be conditioned by God. This is the idea that linguistic eternity is measured by nothing other than the immediate expression of the substance inside a given thing.[37] Whether or not the language we know can even remotely express an aspect of this linguistic immediacy is the subject of its "magical" properties. The main focus of these magical properties is the idea of a divine residue thought to have been lodged in language itself as a divinely created and ultimately God-given means. In this sense Benjamin suggests that "all language houses its own incommensurable, uniquely constituted, inner infinity."[38]

   We have arrived at the following conclusions: the substance of the intellect that is communicable is that which is revealed in the process of naming. The difference between humans and objects is an active and a passive substance of the intellect. The active makes itself understood by naming that which it sees, the passive by that which it is or communicates itself to be. The active is a naming language, the passive an implicit language. The linguistic theoretical view that active language is the only form of linguistic expression is mistaken, says Benjamin. But if human language expresses its substance of the intellect in naming, to whom is it being expressed? Human expression occurs not only in one direction, but two, for reception is certainly necessary for that which is being expressed. Thus expression is not void of reception; it is in fact an essential component. Often we know how a thing is meant to be received before it is even expressed.[39] This is to say, we assume we know what it is that we intend to express before we express it, and this knowledge is mediated in part by its reception. According to Benjamin, we find this same principle at work with things and animals.[40] How could humans have named a thing without communicating with it in some form or other? Is there any reason to believe that a *lamp,* a *mountain range,* or a *fox* is able to communicate with us in such a way that we should know that they are called such and not *Lampe, Gebirge,* or *Fuchs,* for example? Is there any way to know if the name we attribute to a thing is truly its proper name and not somehow a case of mistaken identity?

Benjamin gives us another example as to why, if we are to accept that humans are endowed with the ability to express their substance of the intellect in naming, this expression must be done in and not through language. Through mere naming, in the sense of arbitrary words that are passed on through language, humans would not be able to express substance. The bourgeois conception of language is just that, he states, viewing all communicative acts as corresponding to a need or that a particular need has a direct correlate to an expression. In this sense the emphasis is placed on the authority of linguistic creation, without means, object, or addressee, which relies on the genesic process of naming. In the establishment of the name, the substance of the intellect communicates with God:

> The unique significance and incomparably essential meaning that
> the name has in the realm of language is that it is the innermost
> essence of language itself. The name is that *through* which nothing
> more is communicated and *in* which language communicates it-
> self in absolute.[41]

The name is the inner substance of language. Drawn from genesic naming, it is that part of its mean that is not communicable in its origins. God is the creator of language, and in God's language things were shaped from the substance of the intellect, in that they were formed and imbued by substance. The original name, which does not express itself and is not expressible through language. is indeed modeled after the divine name of God, for which no other name of God can be compared. In language God was to express his substance of the intellect (*geistige Wesen*) as He was sure to express Himself acoustically in Genesis. Thus what other substance could He be made out of than geistige Wesen? In language He was to enact creation, construct Adam and everything else in His image. The name therefore must be the quintessential point from which the geistige Wesen of a thing or a person is expressed or expressible. The Tetragrammaton, the unpronounceable name, as the model of the original name, would then be at the core of every name. Since God's infinity must yield a moment in which finite matter can be imitated and thus generated, the name becomes the unchangeable basis from which everything else is capable of being created. Benjamin articulates this in the following way: "The name as the inheritance of human language therefore authenticates the fact that *language as such* is the substance of the intellect of human beings."[42] Humans are their inner geistige Wesen that was given to them by God or transferred to them out of His unpronounceable name. This utterance is ostensibly the reason why only geistige Wesen is completely communicable and why humans stand divided once again from all created forms, i.e., from nature itself: because we speak in names, we speak pure language.

Communicable nature is expressed in language, more specifically, in human language, which itself is expressed in naming. Naming then is the expression of human substance and the communicable substance of nature: "All nature, insofar as it communicates itself, does so in language, and, in this respect, in humanity."[43] We understand that humans are geistige Wesen if we assume that they are the expression of their substance of the intellect. But if geistige Wesen is language, are we to assume that humans themselves are language, and, if they are their own language, are they the medium of nature as well? Since nature has no voice, must it express itself anthropomorphically in human language? The argument implies that since nature expresses itself in language, it expresses itself through human beings. This places humans here, as elsewhere, at the helm of creation and nature.

Adam was the first at the helm. He was to acquire the knowledge of things outside of himself by naming those very things that he encountered in language: "God's creation is completed as things receive their names from human beings, only language speaks through human beings in the name."[44] In Benjamin's rendition of Genesis, God's final approval of the names Adam gave to the animals sanctifies creation and forms a symbiosis between God and humans. In Adam's articulation of imbued, created substance, his language of naming formed a "language of language," if what is meant by this is a medium of expression and not a means, in the sense of prime motion.[45] Humans are alone the speakers of the language of languages, and in this role language encompasses a specifically "metaphysical knowledge" (II:145). A metaphysical question corresponds: is geistiges Wesen truly linguistic? Here we witness a repetition of an earlier discussion when we receive a reply in the affirmative: "Language is then the substance of the intellect of things."[46] This conclusion, however, does not distinguish itself substantially from the initial discussion if the conditional part of the argument—that language is the "communicable" portion of the geistige Wesen (substance of the intellect) of a thing is removed.[47] What we are left with is the proposition that geistiges Wesen is equivalent to sprachliches Wesen (linguistic substance).

Adam is thus the namer, but, at the same time, the *human* speaker of language. The metaphysical question as to the centrality of knowing is bound up with the role of the namer: "The name is however not only the last call, it is also the real call [or address] of language."[48] For the first profane speaker of language, naming is the last appeal or calling out, out of the generality of a thing to its first specific name, while its only true address becomes its proper name. Naming is the "intensive totality of language" in the concentrated totality of a thing within (its completely communicable geistige Wesen) and, at the same time, its "extensive totality," to the degree that it presents a universal substance of being that it names.[49] Thus it follows that *"the individual alone has a complete language in terms of its universality and intensiveness."*[50] This statement is problematic for several reasons. First, because in the present, indicative form it does not reflect the loss of linguistic, human capacity after the first naming. It suggests, rather, the permanence of such capacity. It has already been said that Adam was let in on a divine task; he was creating, so to speak, "in God's image." However, it cannot be suggested that we still retain the ability to will a perfect language. If there is a language in human nature that is perfect, imbued in our creation, which called perfection into life simply out of intention, we can hardly say that we are in possession of it today. A "metaphysics of language" (*Metaphysik der Sprache*) must therefore recognize that our language is not the same as Adam's or the language of creation, though they may be distant relatives.[51]

Rather than being pre-endowed with divine qualities, two dimensions emerge intertwined in linguistic naming independent of intention: the "communicating (naming) and [the] communicable (name) aspects of communication."[52] Communicating as naming and the communicable as name is expressed by the nature of their metaphysical division. They are always radically separate, but join together in naming: "For the metaphysics of language, the equation of linguistic substance with that of the intellect, which knows only gradual differences, yields a graduation of all intellectual being in degrees."[53] Here, in a metaphysical analysis of language through the equation of geistigen Wesen with sprachlichen Wesen, substance of the intellect with linguistic substance, a gradation of *geistigen Sein* (spiritual being) occurs. Through the reduction of the difference between the geistigen Wesen and sprachlichen Wesen of a thing, we are permitted to bear likeness to the divine.[54] This metaphysical differentiation occurs within the substance of the intellect of a thing itself and no longer permits itself to be subsumed under a "higher category."

Theologically informed metaphysics, the course of which began for him before the First World War and came to a crescendo in his 1921 political-theological theses, makes apparent in which direction Benjamin intends to direct his study. The following citation points again to the theological and metaphysical focus of the essay: "[The higher category] leads to the gradation of all intellectual [*geistigen*] as well as linguistic [*sprachlichen*] substance by levels of existence or being, such as was already familiar to the Scholastics with regard to the intellect."[55] This higher category leads to the differentiation of geistigen Wesen from sprachliche Wesen in grades of being. The differentiation of these categories is metaphysically relevant, for it harkens back to a central linguistic tension while, at the same time, demonstrating its inner connection to the philosophy of religion and the notion of revelation. Here we encounter the conflict between the "expressed and expressible with what is inexpressible and unexpressed," what linguistics has since come to refer to in terms of the signifying and the signified.[56] In this confrontation one sees the unpronounceable as the last substance of the intellect that opens up the problem of the equation of the two forms of substance, intellectual/spiritual and linguistic.

Symbolic Revelation

"Exactly this, however, is meant by the concept of revelation, if it considers the inviolability of the word as the only and sufficient condition and characteristic of the divinity of the substance of the intellect that is expressed in it."[57] Should the name be the bearer of substance buried within the object, and the act of naming—the communication of the substance with the name—the process by which the name is able to apprehend substance would therefore be a revelation. And if the imbuing of substance is a divine act, the subject under investigation would concern the architecture of divine revelation and the possibility of its symbolic representation. Revelation is used here in the context of the impenetrability of the word as a precise reference to the divinity (*Göttlichkeit*) of *geistigen Wesen* (intellectual/spiritual substance). If the word presents itself as a symbolic representation of the substance of divinity, perceivable in the profane, revelation would then be the transference of the divine substance of the intellect/spirit in finite form, rendering it knowable: "The highest spiritual region of religion is (in the concept of redemption) at the same time the only one that does not know the inexpressible."[58] The unpronounceable is the very thing withheld from revelation, being nameless and therefore having no expression. At the same time, the inexpressible is the very thing that transmits the finite character of revelation. This enables religion to be the conduit of paradox in which its highest geistige Wesen is formed by humans and the language in them.[59]

Language, seen here in a distinctly esoteric dimension, is then again not fully expressed in things, since the language of things is imperfect and ultimately mute: "Things are deprived the pure, linguistic principle of form: sound."[60] They are unable to concretize their geistige Wesen without the acoustic dimension of communication. They express themselves in an association of materials, an immediate, infinite "magical" collectivity. Human language, however, is purely immaterial in its magical association with things. The work of art, according to Benjamin, is itself formed from the creation of objects out of the language of "the linguistic intellect of things," the language of completed geistigen Wesen.[61] Sound is the symbol of the magical association of things. This is "symbolically" expressed when God blew into the nostrils of Adam, rendering "life, spirit, language," states Benjamin. Here the tripartite explanation of the Hebrew words *nishmat chaim* in this passage on Adam might be better translated as the soul of life, in other words, the divine soul or *Seele*, rather than spirit or *Geist*. Benjamin's rendition touches only upon the borders of the problem of divine spirit being transferred to the world. Missing is something rather obvious here: the first line in Genesis where the divine spirit (*ruakh elohim*) is described as being upon the face of the waters—indeed a rather physical rendering. It is therefore not surprising that Benjamin challenges a physical interpretation of the passage:

> The second version of the story of creation, which tells of the blowing of God's breath, also reports that man was made from earth. In the whole story of creation this is the only reference to the material through which the Creator expresses his will, which is doubtless otherwise expressed as unmediated creation. In this second story of creation the making of man did not take place through the word: God spoke—and there was—but this man, who is not created from the word, is now invested with the *gift* of language and is elevated above nature.[62]

Benjamin, in a letter to Scholem from June 1917, asks him for an explanation of the idea of a "second creation." Benjamin writes that he would need such an explanation for the purposes of a writing project. Generally speaking, however, the source can be said to be self-evident: the second chapter of Genesis begins with a short synopsis of the first seven days of creation, also sometimes referred to as a second version of creation.[63] In chapter 2, verse 7 God brings together the dust of the earth and forms the anatomy of the first human. Whether he resembled a clay sculpture like a golem or merely a loosely formed pile, God took this dust figure and blew into it His spirit of life. The Torah draws a distinction between Adam and all other created beings, comments Samson Raphael Hirsch in his translation of Genesis.[64] Hirsch emphasizes the "individuality" of God's human creation, being modeled after His countenance. In contrast to his worldly, material creation, God sought in the creation of humans "a deeper, higher development that will lead the world He created. . . . [He took] dust from the basis of humanity and blew in his face the breath of life; there man became a living essence."[65] The collection of the dust is underplayed in Hirsch's commentary, where "the earth remained passive in the creation of his body."[66] Only the activity of divine spirit being passed on to His creation marked the creation of Adam. The dust itself was not considered the material of creation, not having been created from itself out of itself, which left living soul, here spirit, as the prime source of creative activity, the "living essence." (*lebendige Wesen*) of creation. Dust is neither the active source nor an integral building block of creation, but merely a passive means. The word, on the other hand, is the only recognized immaterial medium of creation.

It is just this material element that Benjamin sees here as an impediment to the linguistic analysis of creation, the only point in which physical matter is spoken of directly. This is not true, of course; we know for example that Adam's rib or rib cage was used to create Eve. One therefore has to wonder why Benjamin decided that this portion of creation should suddenly be understood as symbolic, whereas, for example, naming should not be.[67] Apparently he views the act of blowing as more physical than speaking. But even the spoken word was an act of God. Is blowing therefore any less anthropomorphic than speaking? Would we say that since the Hebrew word *or* was spoken in the creation of light, it is too physical to be understood as pure light itself and therefore must be symbolically interpreted? God's will is clearly expressed in this passage. Here it is not His words that form Adam but his actions. But if the Torah is to have existed before the creation of the earth, God's intentions would certainly have existed before the act.[68] But why should it be impossible for God merely to pronounce that the dust of the earth should be drawn together to form man, just as He did with the seas and the land. That He gathered the waters does not necessarily mean He took a pump and formed a great pool; he could equally have gathered them by command, linguistically. One thing is certain: it is just not accurate to say that this is the only point where the material of creation is discussed. In the transference of *nishmat chaim* from God to Adam, a transference of a higher task in humans versus all other created things took place. The various aspects of the act of creation facilitated an exemplar from which the importance of the human act takes a new turn in the cast of naming. This may have been reason enough for Benjamin to have emphasized the expressive nature of divine *geistige Wesen* (spiritual substance) rendered linguistic rather than incarnate.

MAGIC AND THE DIVINE WORD

There is no reference to the material of creation in Genesis, according to Benjamin, even if each time it is written "he created," a creation from material was intended.[69] The rhythm of creation is: it was, he created, he named.

The first and last in this list are to stand for the explicitly immaterial, he says: with the power of language, he created. Language is the creating, perfecting, word and name. There is nothing that is more material in the word than the manifestation of the name. They are both conceived in a distinct, genesic relationship to one another: "In God, name is creative because it is word, and the word of God is knowable because it is name."[70] It is, in fact, through manifestation that the divine understanding emerges, for only in the name did God see that creation was good:

> The absolute relation of name to knowledge only exists in God; in God alone is the name the pure medium of knowledge because the name is inwardly identical with the creating word. This means: God made things knowable in their names. Man, however, names them according to knowledge.[71]

God made things knowable, and Adam named them according to his created knowledge. In this way God appears to have considered the relationship between humanity and language and provided for the release of the linguistic element in Adam to serve Him in creation rather then Adam being ordered by language. Thus "God rested when he had left His creativity itself to man. This creativity, relieved of its divine actuality, became knowledge."[72]

In this interpretation God rested not after six days but after He transferred His linguistic force of creation to man. If this is so, the redemptive aspect attributed to His rest would have to be carried over into language itself, giving it a role the Sabbath is poised to represent: a prefigurative, redemptive moment within the profane. The restitution of Adamic names therefore would be an act of redemptive importance not only for the future but above all as a correction. Creation itself is embedded in human language and the collapse of creation in exile from Eden would thus be attainable linguistically, just as it was in the beginning.[73]

God is fully retired in this picture; His creation is completed in the transference of linguistic power and linguistic responsibility. The conversion in this sense does not only pertain to the transformation of power but also to the transformation of linguistic meaning, for now the creative act has been transferred to the human realm. Although not fully traversed, the division between divine and profane has been partially overcome in that the language of creation becomes knowledge. God's differentiation in creation—the heavens from the earth, the sun from the moon, the waters from dry land—is coupled with linguistic power. Language is now not only creation but knowledge.

However, the transference of the divine is driven only to a point and not beyond, as humans are distinguished from God to the degree that He is still the Creator and they the "knowers."[74] God created himself in an image, Benjamin states, so that His knowers could be formed in the image of the Creator. The word is the concentration of creation, God's sprach-lichen Wesen (linguistic substance). Human language is a reflection of the word in the name. Despite the transference of the divine, the name cannot truly replace the manifestation of the word, just as knowledge of creation is not a substitute for the act. In this way Benjamin attempts to remain within the parameters that he was later to express in the 1921 fragment: until a messianic destruction of the division between the holy and the pro-fane, humans are confined to the finite.[75] This observation extends to their language in exile as well: "The infinity of all human language always re-mains limited and analytical in nature in comparison to the absolutely un-limited and creative infinity of the divine word."[76]

Naming is articulated as an act within the relations between God and humanity, representing the "most profound image of this divine word."[77] The notion of proper names, in this way, rests on the "border between finite and infinite language."[78] This border is precisely what Benjamin seeks to un-derstand—a frontier between divine transference in language, elevating hu-mans above all other created forms, and the finite realm where their linguis-tic task is brought to fruition: "Of all beings, man is the only creature who names his kind, just as he is the only creature whom God did not name."[79] Adam is the only part of creation that is permitted to name.[80] In *Bereshit Rabbah* we find Adam naming not only Eve but the animals, himself, and even God.[81] Benjamin associates this act with the tradition of giving a child a name at birth, be it a "Christian" or "Hebrew" name: "By giving names, parents dedicate their children to God."[82] This name, however, does not cor-respond "metaphysically" to any particulars of knowledge, nor should it cor-respond etymologically to any person, past or present. The proper name re-mains the word of God, only here it is pronounced humanly.[83]

Humans are thus likened to God through their name, expressed in their capacity to create.[84] This likeness in the proper name is linked to the creating word of God; His transference is therefore not the only aspect of the *Sprachgemeinschaft* between Adam and God (II:150). Through the word (and here one has to wonder why Benjamin did not apply the first principle of "in" instead of "through" in this sentence) the language of things is coupled with humanity; the human word is the name of things. In this way bourgeois linguistic theory is fundamentally opposed to a "mystical theory of language" in which language is shaped by the convention of establishing the symbol of a thing or the knowledge thereof.[85] But in opposition to a purely mystical linguistic theory, Benjamin voices the argument that the essence of a thing is not in the word, rather the thing is created from God's word and knowable in Adam's. The knowledge of a thing is therefore not spontaneous creation, not creation from out of its eternity and limitlessness but from the name that humanity gives it and in the form in which humanity expresses it:

> In the name the word of God is no longer creating; it has become in part receiving, even if linguistically receiving. This receptivity is directed at the language of things themselves, from which, in turn, the word of God shines forth, silently, in the mute magic of nature.[86]

The following citation raises the problem of Benjamin's stance toward mysticism. Mystical theory may be inclined to avoid the sharp delineations that he requires of his midrash and, in this sense, may not therefore be an appropriate characterization. On the other hand, the linguistic theory he develops here has a distinct relationship to the independent thought that mysticism is able to embody.[87] Moreover, the distinction Benjamin employs, between God's creating word and humanity's naming one, cannot really be said to be alien to mystical thought.[88] Nevertheless, it is interesting to note how Benjamin decides to overcome the problem presented in the interpretation of Genesis: in performing creation, God spoke in words that can be repeated, to the degree that they are presented, but that do not have the same "magical" effect. Thus: *or*, light, does not create light when we utter the word—not even in Hebrew, which suggests that in the transition from divine to human, the creating aspect of language was not transferred in full. Only knowing was given in the language of naming. But this too could not have been complete, for a linguistic theory of absolute knowing would not distinguish itself from mystical linguistic theory in any meaningful way.[89] The creating aspect of language was therefore partly received in the language of things, according to Benjamin, where the unspoken word of God enters nature's silence. And this is what appears to be magic: that God's revelation is embedded in the still language of things and His insignia corresponds to human naming. Magic is the incidental reception of revelation, or the appearance of revelation in the incidental thing, but it is not the mystical oneness within which all distinction is collapsed. The reception of revelation thus becomes the next issue that arises from the question of what aspect of divine transference is conveyed.

What happened to nature when it is moved to a lower form of blessedness? According to Maler Friedrich Müller, Adam saw the nobility (*Adel*) of each animal and was thereby able to give each a name.[90] But, with the expulsion from paradise, nature's silence took on a "deep sadness"[91] caused by its lack of language, with lamentation the only form of linguistic expression lent to it: "Lament, however, is the most undifferentiated and impotent expression of language. It contains scarcely more than the sensuous breath; and even where there is only a rustling of plants, in it, there is always a lament."[92] Lamentation is the lowest form of protest, says Benjamin, the least differentiated statement of intention, which suggests merely the complaints of the senses. But even where the plants rustle, there is lamentation.[93] Because nature is speechless, it mourns. But because it is mourning, it is also speechless: "In all mourning there is the deepest inclination to speechlessness, which is infinitely more than the inability or disinclination to communicate."[94] Mourning is the link to its sadness, not its incapacity to speak. Even when being named in a paradisiacal language, nature was given a secondary position. But being named in an uncountable number of languages, in which the meaning of the name itself has already begun to whither, evokes the deepest state of mourning. As a consequence, the multiplicity of profane languages and the phenomenon of overnaming in each language comes to fill linguistic expression with an abundance of purely arbitrary signs and names. Only in God, says Benjamin, would nature be able to find its proper name again:

> Overnaming, as the deepest linguistic reason for all sadness and (from the point of view of the thing) of all deliberate muteness. Overnaming as the linguistic substance of mourners [*des Traurigen*] points to another curious relation of language: the overdetermination that reigns in the tragic relationship between the languages of human speakers.[95]

Overnaming is the same as calling things by their wrong names. It is said to be the linguistic origins of the mourning of nature and its silence. Overnaming, in becoming the geistige Wesen of nature, becomes overdetermination, which rules the tragic connection between language and humans. In the various spheres of art there are languages for each artistic form based on the language of things and, at the same time, translations of higher forms. However, the nameless, nonacoustic languages of the material world can, he writes, be expressed as the material collectivity of things, rather then a mere, undifferentiated whole. The pursuit of artistic knowledge is therefore bound to the integrated search for the languages of nature, for it encompasses the problem of signs in the composition of language in its written form, expression, and medium (II:156).

RECEPTION AS TRANSLATION

The word was given a divine insignia. It receives the nameless in the name as the translation of languages that pertain to things in human language. For Benjamin, translation is the mode of reception most capable of receiving revelation. The maxim for this: "Every higher language (with the exception of the word of God) can be considered a translation of all the others."[96] Several factors come to the fore with regard to the perception of God's revelation. First, it is clear the word of God is not translatable, for if His name is untranslatable—the heart, so to speak, of the word of God—neither is a word that is peripheral. Second, a higher and a lower language exist, which correspond to a divine and a profane language; third, this higher language can be seen as the translation of all other languages.[97] This last proposition is already expressed in Benjamin's observations on translation: "Translation is the transporting of one language into another through a continuum of transformations. Translation passes through a continua of transformations, not abstractions of identity and similarity."[98] The transition from a divine creating language to a human language was already a translation, the transporting of one language to another in the continuum of transformation and creation. This is Benjamin's answer to the *or* problem (let us call it an *or* problem). If the language of creation is transformative, and God transferred at least a part of the creating word in the *nishmat chaim* of Adam, human language must also be transformative. Translation is thus the capturing of an element of this transformative aspect in language:

The translation of the language of things into that of human language is not only a translation of the mute into the acoustic; it is also the translation of the nameless into names. It is therefore the translation of an imperfect language into a more prefect one and cannot but add something to it, namely, knowledge.[99]

The unyielding, transformative dynamic applies to divine Scripture from this perspective, for even the Torah would appear incomplete if not for God's acoustic expression, rendering scriptural intention into act. The acoustic is not merely the verbal sounding of the written but a translation of the creating word. The sounding of a word is a translation, but it is also a transformative act in the language of things. The translation from the mute to the acoustic not only gives it a sound, it also assigns the meaning of a word. If a word has lost its acoustic form, that is, if it is no longer pronounceable, then it is, in this sense, no longer meaningful. The acoustic attributes the knowledge of a thing in its pronunciation.[100] The naming of things is therefore that which draws them closer to the perfection of the divine realm. Knowledge is a medium in this transition, to be used and to be gained, but the absolute knowledge of things remains solely in the realm of God. In creation God posited the creating name in them and thus created the basis of the knowing of the name. In this sense Adam may be the distributor of the name, but God is its ultimate creator. Naming is the expression of the identity of the creating word and the knowing word as name in God. God does not really abdicate His responsibility in the translation of His language into a human one. To the degree that Adam received the silent, nameless language of things and translated it mimetically into pronounceable names, he merely extended an activity already established by God. This would not have been possible if both the language of God and the language of Adam were not originally located in God Himself, springing from the same creating word in which both things and human language as knowledge shared a common origin, in the "communication of matter in a magical community," their *Sprachgemeinschaft* (community of language).[101]

The connection here between appearance and the act of naming is the inner communicable silence of things and animals in human language:

In the same chapter of the poem, the poet expresses the realization that only the word from which things are created permits man to name them, by communicating itself in the manifold languages of animals, even if mutely, in the image: God gives each beast in turn a sign, whereupon they step before human beings to be named. In an almost sublime way the linguistic community of mute creation with God is thus conveyed in the image of the sign.[102]

Adam named the word from which the thing was created, not the thing itself. The animals came before Adam with a sign that was meted out to them by God, one by one. So, in "sublime fashion," the linguistic association of God with his silent creation is portrayed here in the imagery of the sign. Thus the silent sign Adam discovered in God's creation, permitting him to locate their names, lies buried deep in human knowledge. Profane translation itself could only occur after the fall from grace: "The language of things can pass into *the* language of knowledge and name only through translation—as many translations, so many languages—once humanity fell from the paradisiac state that knew only one language."[103] The development of the plurality of language was set to occur after the fall from paradise when knowledge and names had to be translated into many different languages.[104] The paradisiacal language must have been perfect if knowledge was later to be endlessly differentiated in it, to the point when it had reached the most profane, common level. Only then could creation be expressed in the name.

At the same time, the notion of a language of absolute knowing is contradicted by the tree of knowledge. On the seventh day, Benjamin explains, God had already introduced the meaning of good and evil by the fact that He expressed His approval of creation. The apple was only to transform the meaning of good and evil into knowledge through the act. Even though God had introduced the definition of good, the knowledge of it remained nameless.[105] Thus it is termed an "evil" knowledge, merely external to naming and linguistic knowledge, as the "uncreative imitation of the creative word."[106] Benjamin explains this as the origins of the division between divine and profane language:

The fall from grace marks the birth of the *human word*, in which the name no longer remains intact, stepping out of naming language, the language of knowledge—from what we may call its own immanent magic—in order to become expressly and, indeed, over time, externally magical.[107]

Exile is the point at which Benjamin marks the transition from the creating word to a language that is no longer able to express creation. The magic of this expression, in which linguistic creation was also immanent revelation communicable, was at once lost with the expulsion from paradise. In this the nature of revelatory language was to change along with its magic. If language was once used to express the unfolding of God's divine plan, it was now the mere appearance of the knowledge of how this plan works, a mimicking that is reduced to mere imitation of the creating word. Now that the word must express something outside itself, it typifies "the fall of linguistic spirit."[108] No longer is the spirit of the word capable of being expressed in its name, as all things are to turn faceless with regard to their proper names. The word expresses outwardly as a condition of lost identity.

Misinterpreting the Sign

From the damaged immediacy of language to the departure of meaning associated with the word, the linguistic confusion that followed was a short step. "*Signs* must become confused where things are entangled."[109] Language became enslaved to nonsense, as did things: "Without the latter, all linguistic philosophy remains entirely fragmentary, because the relationship of language to sign (in which that of human language to writing offers only a very particular example) is original and fundamental."[110] We have seen the analysis on language undergo the following steps: language is the expression of the communicable species-being of every created thing and being, termed here the substance of the intellect. This substance, originating from a divine creating word, is transferred to a worldly, naming language through the recognition of divine insignia. This is the theory of transference from divine to profane language, which does not occur materially. The name of the creator, however, remains unknown, itself a nonlinguistic name. Yet where the inexpressible finds some form of expression—and the name of God must somehow have a linguistic connection to every other name—it touches upon the realm of magic. We therefore turn here to the problem of the symbol, which, although it reflects linguistic substance, is mistaken for the substance of another. A reinterpretation of the sign is a necessary task of linguistic philosophy, says Benjamin, even though this basic problem remains largely undetected, suggesting that he may have seen his own work in this light.[111] For a future development of linguistic speculation, an entirely new approach to language was sought:

> Language is in every case not only the communication of the communicable but also, at the same time, a symbol of the noncommunicable. This symbolic side of language is connected to its relation to signs but extends in certain respects, for example, to name and judgment. These have not only a communicating function but most probably also a closely connected symbolic function.[112]

The symbolic side of language begins with the problem that language presents not only the communicable but also often stands in place of it. That is, if the creating name is incommunicable, language must also carry within itself a replication of noncommunicable substance. This makes aspects of language already symbolic before any intention is applied, linking it in a most direct way with the sign, particularly as the sign that is expressed in divine language and understood in a human one. Benjamin here introduces the concept of judgment, which he places on the level of naming. In the next section, as well as in part 3, on justice, this problem will be addressed. Here it is important to recognize the place in which Benjamin seeks to locate the concept of judgment: in its proximity to naming it is one step down from an entirely divine category. Naming and judgment, by standing in relation to the divine, perform a symbolic function of the divine order, where justice is applied in judgment and knowledge in naming:

> The language of an entity is the medium in which the substance of the intellect communicates itself. The uninterrupted flow of this communication runs through the whole of nature from the lowest forms of existence to the individual and from the individual to God. The individual communicates himself to God through name, which he gives to nature and (in proper names) to his own kind, and to nature he gives names according to the communication that he receives from it, for the whole of nature, too, is imbued with a nameless, mute language, the residue of the creating word of God, which is preserved in the individual as the knowing name [*erkennender Name*] and above the individual as pending judgment [*richtendes Urteil*]. The language of nature is comparable to a secret key that each sentry passes to the next in his own

language, but the meaning of the key is the language of the sentry itself. All higher language is a translation of those lower, until in ultimate clarity the word of God unfolds, which is the unity of this linguistic motion [*Sprachbewegung*].[113]

The language of an essence is the medium through which language expresses its substance of the intellect. Its expression occurs in every part of nature, in humans, reaching all the way to God. Humans communicate with God through the naming of nature and themselves. Nature, however, is engaged in the process of naming, for it too was created out of the creating word of God. Nature responds to the search for its name by expressing to humans the intentions God implanted within it as a substance of the intellect. This is the residuum of the divine in every aspect of creation. This residuum for humans remains in the name of knowledge and as judgment. Here a degree of uncertainty settles in. The pursuit of a true language of nature is an attempt to uncover the index by which every substance of the intellect is continuously transferred to another language. The solution to this problem of a true language may lie in the position that one language takes in relation to its transference to another. In this regard, every higher language is a translation of a language coming before it, all the way to the final and complete clarity in the unfolding and revelation of the word of God, which is understood as the unity of all the movement of language. We have located this final unity of language in the unpronounceable name.

JUDGMENT

> The knowledge of things resides in the name, which is that of good and evil. But in the profound sense in which Kierkegaard uses the word chatter, and knows only one purification and uplifting before which also the chatterers, the sinners, are therefore placed: judgment [Gericht].[114]

Knowledge of good and evil is presented as false knowledge, corresponding to sin, which will only be corrected through judgment. Judgment may also be magical, but it represents a markedly different form of magic. Judgment is associated with a word that executed the expulsion from paradise, a judging word that humanity itself expounds from an eternal law. But the judging word that performed the expulsion did so at the same time that it endured the punishment inflicted upon humanity: "In the fall, since the eternal purity of names was violated, the sterner purity of the judging word arose, of judgment [*Urteil*]."[115] In the purity of its act judgment became the purest word upon which the fallen creating language was to rely: justice.[116] This punishment went beyond the expulsion to include a heavy burden, a plague upon the Sprachgemeindschaft (community of language) itself: language became a means, a mere sign (bloße Zeichen) infinitely multiplied, developing what Benjamin termed a "damaged immediacy." Its damaged immediacy reduced expression to the arbitrary production of mere signs, divided among themselves into multitudes of languages. But in this state of profound decay of the agency of naming, the very condition viewed as an infliction of punishment gave rise to the conditions of the restitution of language. Thus within the state of expulsion into which humanity carried the word a new "magic of judgment" was lodged, enabling a full and ultimate redemption of language.[117] This redemptive element, harbored in judgment as justice, was no longer in itself purely divine, now having been located in the world of the profane: in "the restitution of the damaged immediacy of the name from the fall emerges a new immediacy in the magic of judgment that no longer rests blissfully in itself."[118] Justice, which we discover to be a divine state and not a subjective judgment, engenders a magic in the profane, says Benjamin, that enables it to restore itself to the purity of divine judgment. In part 3 we shall see a more elaborate definition of the term.

Language's damaged immediacy gave birth to a multiplicity of languages and served as the impetus for translation, generating its imperative in the profane. The very task of abstraction that translation employed in transporting the transitive substance of the intellect of a thing into another profane language may have lost the linguistic spirit it presented as a consequence of the expulsion. At the same time, it created the need for the abstract: "The origin of abstraction as a faculty of linguistic spirit is also to be sought in the fall."[119] The idea of the abstract within the profane is also, therefore, a qualification of its magic.

Since good and evil were already in existence before the tree of knowledge, the name was able to form the only concrete elements of language before the expulsion, and while both good and evil remained nameless before the partaking of the fruit of the tree, they were inexpressive: "The tree of knowledge did not stand in the garden of God in order to dispense information on good and evil but as a sign of judgment over the questioner. This immense irony marks the mythical origin of law."[120] This notion of the irony of judgment becomes a central point in Benjamin's thinking on justice, forming a background to his essay "The Critique of Violence," as we shall see.[121] Here one find the origins of the notion of good and evil existing before the state of exile, before even the tree of knowledge. The tree stood as a monument to an event that had yet to take place and, in this sense, is paradoxical. Following Kierkegaard's *The Concept of Anxiety*, Benjamin concludes that original sin cannot begin with the eating of the forbidden fruit, for that would mean Adam had already understood the distinction between good and evil.[122] Kierkegaard writes:

> If, in Genesis, God said to Adam: "Only from the tree of knowledge of good and evil, you must not eat," it is self-evident that Adam did not understand these words, for how could he understand the difference between good and evil if the distinction first appears after the indulgence.[123]

The tree with which original sin is meant to originate as worldly decision emerges as a monument to the paradox of justice in Benjamin's reading; it is alive in the profane yet rests upon a notion of divine justice. As with Kierkegaard, Benjamin rejects the idea that the distinction of good and evil emerged in the profane through Adam's indulgence. The event, according to Benjamin, has been mistaken for a sign of worldly transgression when, in fact, it is a sign of judgment. It is the tree of knowledge that deserves our attention, he argues. The tree was planted by God in the garden of Eden as a sign of judgment, having already existed before the alleged transgression. Its message is a judgment—a judgment over the one who questions the idea of knowledge, even before the act. In this sense Benjamin's interest is awakened to the category of judgment, which bears a special relationship to divine justice. As we shall see in part 3, on justice, the idea of judgment is integral to the messianic idea, for, on one hand, it is a profane phenomenon, yet, on the other hand, it bears a link to the divine. Only judgment, in a "magical" association with divine justice, is thus deemed capable of expressing the unpronounceable dimension of language:

> The abstract elements of language . . . are thus rooted in the judging word, of judgment. The immediacy (which, however, is the

linguistic root) of the communicability of abstraction resides in judgment [*im richterlichen Urteil*]. This immediacy in the communication of abstraction came into being as judgment when, in the fall, man abandoned immediacy in the communication of the concrete, the name, and fell into the abyss of the mediacy of all communication, of the word as means, of the empty word, into the abyss of chatter.[124]

The capacity of the abstract, which was once set in the naming word and lost in the expulsion, has been lodged in judgment. A new magic was born in the darkest moment of exile in which all hope was placed on the judging word—a new magic of the word to usher in an ultimate restitution of justice in the dawn of a messianic age. This new magic is therefore also undoubtedly linked to the concept of messianic transformation.

JEWISH LINGUISTIC THEORY AND CHRISTIAN KABBALAH

Franz Joseph Molitor and his book, *Philosophie der Geschichte oder über die Tradition*, (*Philosophy of History; or, On Tradition*, 1827, revised 1857), perhaps the last in a tradition of Christian Kabbalists in the German language, made a great impression on Scholem in his first attempts at unlocking the secret, inner chambers of the Kabbalah. Documenting the importance of Molitor for Jewish history and justifying his own early fascination, Scholem was to remark that Molitor understood considerably more about the Kabbalah than many Jewish theologians of his time.[125] Accordingly, the early journals demonstrate a particular interest in Molitor's linguistic theory based on rabbinic and kabbalistic sources, the historical breath and depth of which, not to speak of Molitor's emphasis on Hebrew as the divine language, led Scholem to call his work "a true ideology of Zionism"[126] despite the obvious partiality of his liberal Catholicism.[127] In a well-publicized letter to Zalman Schocken, Scholem makes clear the central role Molitor played in his decision to study the Kabbalah. Through Molitor "I came to the idea of writing not the history but the metaphysics of the Kabbalah."[128] On November 18, 1916, Scholem made the following entry in his journal: "The letters, *which are the expression of intellectual forces* (Hirsch could have literally written this in his commentary on the Pentateuch!) *have their roots above* (Molitor, vol. 1), meaning in the truth."[129] In the same period that

Benjamin is thought to have written his essay on language (October-November 1916), an intense exchange with Scholem also took place. Scholem makes several references in these two months to heated discussions with Benjamin on Zion, the concept of justice,[130] references to Samson Raphel Hirsch's commentary on Genesis, and Molitor's *Philosophy of History*. In connection to the latter, Scholem was to approach the problem of a philosophy of language in a way that we have already seen as forming the foundation of Benjamin's essay. He writes, "The task [of linguistic philosophy] is the study of language as the revelation of truth; it must determine the truth content of language."[131] He continues a bit farther on in the same passage:

> This problem appears most clearly and unproblematic in the Torah as a divine book: language has to be the language of truth, of all truth, both general and particular, if it is to be the language of God. Every sentence must necessarily be a function of the applied word. . . . It can clearly be said that *truth here is always a continuous function of language.*[132]

One is able to see in the following citation a link to Benjamin in both the terms of a philosophy of language, seeking parallel truths in the claims of revelation and the language of God, as well as contemporaneous reflections of a similar kind. Since Molitor played such an important role in the formation of Scholem's early thoughts on language, which he reports discussing with Benjamin beginning in 1915, a comparative analysis of Molitor in relation to Benjamin is all but necessary.[133] Because he was able to articulate established currents in this tradition in a highly concise form, Molitor could easily have provided a key building block for the theological groundwork of Benjamin's essay. The immediate parallel of themes in the following section makes the connection between the two, in fact, rather suggestive.[134]

The seventh chapter of Molitor's *Philosophy of History* presents us with a concise presentation of his linguistic theory entitled "Über den Ursprung der Sprache und Schrift bei den Ebraern" (On the origins of the language and writing of the Hebrews), which, in many ways, could still be considered a faithful discussion of Jewish linguistics.[135] He begins with the following statement:

> The Jewish tradition . . . maintains that Hebrew was the first original language that Adam spoke in paradise. Even if it can no longer

be taken literally [down to the letter] that the original language spoken by man in his state of bliss before the fall was completely different from all languages today, the Hebrew language must also be the true reproduction of the first, pure, original language (however much embodied in a weaker form) if the Bible is to be seen as the book of divine revelation.[136]

Molitor begins his treatise with a point that affords well with a general linguistic conception of creation in Judaism: if there had once been an original, divine, and creating language, narrated in the book of Genesis, then surely it was Hebrew. The Hebrew language is accordingly at the center of his thesis. Further, if Hebrew today is not itself this genesic language, then it still must be the most splendid profane language known to humanity, uniquely derived from the divine. Should the latter be the case, it would be right to assume that Hebrew is the first, original, profane language, which, because of its unique proximity to divine language, would certainly have maintained divine elements severely reduced in further derivations.[137] In this opening citation Molitor first establishes the basis for Jewish speculation on the divine nature of a Hebrew language whose existence would be no different than the Hebrew we are familiar with; only its meaning and divine character is, as of yet, unknown. Even if not taken "down to the letter" (as Molitor playfully suggests) that an original language existed, once spoken by humans but radically different from the languages that exist today, we are still left with the notion of Scripture as divine revelation. Clearly Hebrew must then be an authentic reproduction (*Abdruck*) of a divine language, regardless of whether it is merely a weaker reflection (*Abglanz*) of its divine origins. He continues in the same passage:

> For just as man in his fallen state still carries within himself the reflection [*reproduction*] of his prior spiritual sublimity, so also must his language contain at least the traces of a magical spirit of creation of a prior original language—that proceeding generations have degenerated, corresponding to the depths to which the human race has sunk.[138]

Human beings were created *betzelem*, in the image of God, out of the expression of divine *nishmat chaim* that God blew into the nostrils of Adam. In this sense, just as we have been endowed with hidden, divine substance, also embedded within the Hebrew language are divine shards of a pure language. Moreover, the tie that binds humanity to its original, profane language also reflects its condition: should an original Hebrew be in a state of decline, it would be in no different a condition then exiled humanity. Only a "magical spirit of creation" afforded to an original creating language of God could redeem this sunken state of human expression. A higher language transfers to a lower one its substance of the spirit/intellect, which would be maintained by the lower in a condensed and sealed fashion.

Summarized and problematized here in a very precise and clear formulation, Molitor would have presented Benjamin with robust inspiration on the nature of Hebrew as the original, divine language in standard midrashic tradition. He would have also incidentally ignited a challenge to Christian interpreters, among them even the revered Hamann.[139] Molitor writes:

> There is no middle position: the testament of creation is either merely a Jewish national myth in which all the names are hebracized as the neologists believe or, if the books of Moses sprang forth from divine revelation, it must also be true that the language in which it was written and the content of the story, which is inseparable from its language, would equally be from a higher origin and the reflection of a true, original language.[140]

If Hebrew is merely another profane language, a mere linguistic thesis of a dead language would do. But if Hebrew is the living word of God's revelation—not the "bourgeois" linguistic theory that views language as a means, as Benjamin argues—then no division is possible between revelation and the language in which it is transmitted. Only then could revelation itself be considered a divine reflection, stemming imminently from on high. The indivisibility of content from form is clearly the intention of Molitor's opening remarks.[141] The meaning that comes from the syntax of Scripture, he goes on to say, is only comprehensible in the context of Hebrew. Particularly in the language of creation and the first act of naming by God—how else would one explain the name Adam if not for the word *adamah*, the earth from which God formed him (1827:330)? In an inserted passage to the 1857 edition Molitor continues in the same vein by claiming that only in Hebrew do biblical passages have "true meaning . . . in which a word is inseparable from the concept of a thing. From this, it can also be ascertained that Genesis was originally thought of solely in the Hebrew language and to be pronounced only by a person who spoke Hebrew."[141] He proceeds to give several etymological explanations for the origins of names in order to further demonstrate that Hebrew is unquestionably "the earthly reflection of the true original language."[143] He concludes with Hieronymus that Hebrew must be the only "pure, holy original language."[144]

The first argument concerns the Hebraic origins of revelation being embedded in language. He introduces next the notion of script (in the sense of Scripture) as written revelation. Naturally, the discussion of the written word in the Torah does not concern profane language, but rather, exclusively, a written form of expression of God's will:

> The entire research into the origins and creation of the original language is actually linked to the first primary question: is the written form merely the work of an artistically inspired reflection, which came about through external needs, or is it based on something internal, necessary, and absolute in humanity?[145]

This proposition is bound to the question whether humans themselves are perfect, created by a perfect God, free to implement His will as He chooses. The answer determines the "naturalist" from the "spiritualist" in the theory of the origins of language, he claims. Though, "if we were to follow the meaning of the Bible faithfully," there can little room for a naturalist theory of "arbitrary signs" in which language is seen as merely a technical aid of meaning.[146] Here Benjamin's critique of language as a means, the necessity of meaningful expression in divine language and the breakdown of divine language into its opposite, "mere signs" compared to the "true signs" of divine judgment, coincides with Molitor's own analysis.[147]

In a genesic conception of language "the individual and his entire being and work [maintain] a far more noble and sublime meaning."[148] Humans are not the product of natural forces, leaving little in the way of "inner spiritual independence and freedom," not a consciousness built from "passive reflex of received external impressions," but, "as the divine writings teach us, the creation in the image of an infinite, absolute intelligence, a living mirror of divinity . . . beyond all natural compulsions."[149] Humans embody a self-generating expression from an internal substance of the intellect. They are their expressive language just as they inhabit the image of His creating holiness.[150] The form this takes in the profane is knowledge: "The intellectual knowledge *of human beings as the image of the divine* is a finite, created representation of the infinite idea of God.[151] Similar to what we have seen in Benjamin, knowledge is that which typifies God's image in humanity, the essence of the *nishmat chaim* imparted to them. Divine implies all knowing and as such its created (and not creating) form is knowledge of the intellect. He continues in the same passage:

> In this respect, the individual with his ideal world of thought is a created image of the divine, which carries within itself the idea of creation from eternity. . . . The word is the transition from the inner ideal to the outer real world—the speaking of an extension, the exteriorization of an inner thought. Here the pure spiritually of thought is limited and an outer image is created from the word.[152]

Knowledge is partly the eternal knowledge of creation, which the imparted word contains as an inner ideality. One is however obliged to recognize a distinct movement away from Benjamin's own concerns in the argument. Where Molitor works to express the pure, inner idea made explicit in its outer reception, in which its multiplicity is expressed through spirit in language, Benjamin steers clear of both an idealist interpretation of Genesis and its Christian implications, that is, in the rendering of spirit to flesh. Benjamin's analysis remains within the realms of the word embodying the transition from an inner ideal in the thoughts of God as a creating language to an outwardly naming one, which is formed by the same act that creating language has at its base i.e., the knowledge of its vocalization.[153]

In this aspect of linguistic theory, based on the concretization of language in speaking, Benjamin lends voice to a perspective beyond Molitor's conclusions. For Molitor "speaking is generally the image of infinite creation, or the bringing into being of the eternal, original image as an existence outside of God." Thus he conceives of speaking as the existence of the divine idea outside the divine realm, since the idea within God is unexpressed (or perhaps inexpressible).[154] But for Benjamin, as we have seen, an existence entirely without relationship to language is an idea, but an idea that bears no fruit even within that realm of ideas whose circumference defines those of God.[155] Benjamin seems to believe that existenceless speaking is an idea that does not bear fruit in the realm of God. God is to think His ideas and express them vocally such that only the idea in acoustic fashion has an external existence. Where Molitor finds a model for the relationship between the spoken and written word in the trinity,[156] Benjamin seeks to view God's ideas as expressive in creation and thus rejects a division between God and His written word, His ideas and their articulation, between, ultimately, idea and thing. Be that as it may, Molitor himself does not remain trapped by this division for very long and, after a short deviation into the moments of the Father and Son, returns to the notion that the spoken word is, in the end, "inseparable from thinking and always in thought, for thinking is nothing other than a inner, spiritually potential word."[157] Benjamin also returns to a similar conclusion. In the implanting of the intellectual/spiritual substance by God into that which He created, Molitor articulates a theory of insignia [*Signatur*] that Adam was later to discover:

> All the constructs of earthly things are also images and expressions
> of spiritual forces and intellectual ideas, and all forms are based on
> spiritual and intellectual [*geistigen und intellektuellen*] principles at
> a higher level; every essence carries within its construction the in-
> signia [*Signatur*] that expresses its inner qualities in an unmedi-
> ated fashion.[158]

All profane creation is reflection and expression of God's spiritual and intellectual ideas, based on rather platonic, divine models. Each created thing carries with it a signature of its craftsmanship, and the written form is considered here again the expression of the inner idea in its outer form.[159] For Molitor, however, this division between implicit and explicit expression is reduced to a minimum of importance, for "all forms in external nature are divine expressions in writing, the entire visible nature is the engraved script of God or the outer revealed word in written form. The acoustic, on the hand, is merely discernible internally in spirit."[160]

For Christian Hebraists of Molitor's caliber, heaven is an open book that humans were once taught to read. Having lost this ability in exile, humanity was to lose its *via mystica* to divine language while retaining merely the arduous task of spelling out the word of God in the profane; for although language was created with Adam, a description of the art of writing is nowhere to be found in the Torah, exclaims Molitor. For this reason, things are able to maintain their insignia despite losing their access to the open transference of divine meaning. Much as we have seen in Benjamin, this transference is what Molitor refers to as *magic*:

> Just as the word in the original language was the pure reproduction of thought and itself had originally magical properties, so too the original script of human beings in every word and act of the figurative expression of the magical word [*magischen Wortes*]. In this way it was magical in its effects.
>
> The original script came into being just as little from arbitrary signs [*willkührlichen Zeichen*] as did the original language from arbitrary sounds.[161]

There is nothing arbitrary in the original language, be it in written or spoken form. Both are reflections of the divine insignia as its magic, its inner substance reflecting God's spirit/intellect. Profane language is then "an imitation of God . . . of the divine speaking and writing [by which] the divine is the single, infinite, all-powerful speaker in the eternally transpiring act of linguistic creation that is always initiating creation from the beginning."[162] Speculation on the nature of human language, being a divinely imparted imitation of God's writing and speaking, leads to the question of the letters themselves being able to contain the hidden concentration of the power of creation. Molitor here comments on the power of those who are able to wield the letters and harness their power: "The letters are the reproductions of divine forces, and God created the heaven and earth through the magic of the letters. One who understand the substitution of the letters would be capable of working wonders."[163] But the power of the letters is not to be had, he now concludes, for the Hebrew language as we know it today cannot be the exact language that God spoke but a second rendition, as if perhaps a broken dialect of a divine language with divine fragments. He terms it "the secondary remains of an old, divine, original language and writings."[164] Modern Hebrew would then be the lefovers from the divine creating language. But better the leftover building blocks of a divine palace then one of the many profane bricks encircling the tower of Babel:

> Just as the actual construction of the Hebrew language points to an inner connection with the original language, the shape of the Hebrew script testifies to a higher origin. The original, true shape of the script could not have been arbitrary signs [*willkührliche Zeichen*]. It had to have been a sculptured expression of sounds and linguistic actions.[165]

It would not have been difficult for Benjamin to construct a theory of translation following the analysis Molitor establishes with regard to the origins of the Hebrew language and the descent into arbitrary signs. As building blocks of divine construction, it cannot be that the letters themselves are arbitrary mediums of communication. They embody, rather, "the traces of their origins."[166] Surely these divine blocks must contain within themselves the power of creating language; it must simply be a matter of application. But their application was not handed down to Adam among the things he received in the divine package, in the transference from creating to naming. Thus, even at the beginning, we might be able to conclude with Benjamin that human language can be seen to be a transference where part of its divine substance was withheld. Such a conclusion is not radically different from the direction of Molitor's argument. Benjamin's own contribution is his emphasis on complete transference, in which Hebrew is no more privileged than any of the other lonely languages that await their restitution to original splendor.

CHAPTER 4

GERSHOM SCHOLEM AND THE NAME OF GOD:
"ON LANGUAGE AS SUCH" RECONSIDERED

Linguistic speculation is metaphysical speculation. With this conclusion from Benjamin's early essay of 1916, Scholem was to draw
a grand survey of Jewish linguistic speculation in his 1970s essay
"Der Name Gottes und die Sprachtheorie der Kabbala," "The
Name of God and the Lingustic Theory of the Kabbalah."[1] Should
this essay achieve what Benjamin earmarked for himself many
years before—to apply his work and spirit to Hebrew literature—
is something that we will never know.[2] But it is certain that, more
than fifty years after Benjamin's influential essay, Scholem returns to many of the themes and categories Benjamin set out in
1916.[3] A fairly close reading of Scholem's late essay reveals an ongoing dialogue with a silent partner whose "instinctive," "deepest
intuition"[4] in regard to Judaism is finally matched up with the
Kabbalah.[5]

   Scholem was fascinated by Benjamin's early philosophy of
language and makes reference to his attempt to translate the work
into Hebrew in *Walter Benjamin: The Story of a Friendship*.[6] Two
versions of this attempt were tucked away in an unremarkable section of the Benjamin Archive in Jerusalem (see figures 4.1, 4.2). Benjamin believed that the Hebrew rendition would allow his words
to come alive as they turned back to the source from which they
had emerged: Genesis and the Hebrew language. He asks Scholem

FIGURES 4.1–4.2 "In the months preceding Benjamin's marriage I occupied myself for some time with the attempt to translate into Hebrew portions of his study of language, which was very close to my heart; this included motifs from our conversations in Seeshaupt. Benjamin insisted that I read the first pages of my translation to him and Dora so that he might hear how his sentences sounded in the *Ursprache* [in the original language], as he put it half-jokingly." Gershom Scholem, *Walter Benjamin: The Story of a Friendship*, p. 38 (New York: Schocken, 1981).
Courtesy of the Scholem Archive, the Jewish National and University Library, Jerusalem.

to read the first page aloud, just to be able to hear his own text in the *Ursprache*, the original language (freund:53). This pursuit, of translating Benjamin's ideas into a language Scholem considered more palpable to their expression, began with these first two Hebrew translations. Yet the act of transferring and applying these ideas went on to become a lifelong goal both in terms of the Hebrew language and his own scholarship. By 1919 Scholem sought to focus on writing a linguistic philosophy of Jewish mysticism, perhaps as a doctoral thesis. On July 28, 1919, he writes in his journals: "I am seriously considering the possibility of [writing] a dissertation in the area of Jewish linguistic theory. If I could only focus for a period of time on the *Zohar* (if only there was such a thing as an index to this book somewhere!), I would perhaps have a fairly simple task and a fine plan."[7] Benjamin, he writes, was also extremely enthusiastic about the idea, and fully encouraged him to dedicate himself to the task (freund:107). However, to formulate such a "linguistic theory of the Kabbalah" during those early years, as he later judges in his autobiography, "was youthful exuberance, if not arrogance."

But as I began to work seriously, it became clear that I knew far too little to deal with the subject matter in a scholarly and responsible manner. It was better to begin systematically and more modestly. The study on the linguistic theory of the Kabbalah, from which I resigned in 1920, I did actually write exactly fifty years later.[8]

The assertion is indeed justified. Scholem gives up the notion of a grand theoretical project at this point and focuses instead on a scholarly edition of the first text in the history of Kabbalah, the *Bahir*, only to return many years later to an overview of his lifelong research into Jewish mysticism with respect to the question of language. What is indeed remarkable is the degree to which that research remains wedded to Benjamin's early ideas. Scholem's opening assertions in this late essay begin with the most primary texts in Judaism, emphasizing the fact that metaphysical speculation of a linguistic nature was not initiated with the most esoteric currents of Jewish thought but with the Torah itself: *rosh devarekhah emet*—the beginning of thy word is truth.[9] In Psalms 119:160 language and truth are viewed in a continuum in which the measure is eternity. The concept of revelation is conceived here (and in rabbinical Judaism in general) as the message of God delivered in a word, this word itself being naturally synonymous with the truth. As such, revelation is immediately linked to a metaphysical conception of truth and, if the study of revelation is the study of truth, a metaphysical conception of revelation is either intentionally or inadvertently linguistic. Revelation in words means, first and foremost, that God spoke His words in the form of acoustic manifestations and, second, that the truth of God itself was conceivable: "According to the meaning originally conceived in Judaism, truth was the word of God that was perceivable acoustically, i.e., linguistically."[10] This is not to suggest that every word of God was receivable; in point of fact, not every word of God is acoustic. Rather, from the perspective of rabbinical Judaism, only those words are receivable that reflect an expressible part of truth.[11]

Acoustic revelation is therefore the medium of divine revelation and is set apart from visual revelation. In contrast to God's acoustic message, there has never been a visual component,[12] nor is speculation concerning visual imagery warranted.[13] We know that imagery thought to represent God is sacrilege and only His voice is to carry the word of His revelation. From this one is assured that in the medium of human language God's message is potentially receivable and understandable, particularly in the idea of prophecy (j3:7).

Revelation, seen from the mainstays of Judaism, can therefore be postulated in the context of metaphysical speculation on the nature of truth in language, in which truth is expressed and received in purely profane expression. That humans are able to receive the word of God is taken as proof alone that the acoustic word can be transformed to embody profane, acoustic expression, thus forming a link between the divine and the profane. But more important, it again raises the question put forward by Molitor whether God's acoustic language was Hebrew as such or whether Hebrew is the transliteration of God's creating language. One way to view Scholem's essay is as a search for an answer to this question within the history of Jewish mysticism, and, while his methodology is historical and philological, it is one of the aims of this chapter to show to what degree his approach to the question is distinctly metaphysical in nature.

Seen from a "metaphysics of language" (II:146), what Scholem articulates as the unifying principals of Jewish mysticism are remarkably similar in word and deed to the categories we find in the early Benjamin:

> Language, the medium in which the spiritual life of humanity is consummated, has an inner dimension, an aspect that does not altogether merge or disappear in the communicative relations between substances [Wesen]. The individual expresses himself, trying to render himself comprehensible to others. In all such attempts, however, something else resonates that is not merely communication, meaning, sign, and expression. The sound upon which all language is built, and the voice that gives form to language, forges from the matter of sound—these are already, prima facie, more than what takes shape in the understanding.[14]

These first few pages of Scholem's essay might appear to be a direct commentary on the 1916 essay. Language is the medium by which humans express that part of their being which is integral to the intellect and spirit and, by doing so, complete their creation.[15] The linguistic aspect of this act is based on the expression of the spiritual or intellectual substance of a thing, in this case understood to be a substance that is brought to the fore by the communicative act—the will to be understood and to understand— an act far more comprehensive than the mere linguistic categories it finds in expression. Linguistic substance pertaining to human beings is drawn to the tonal form as its principle linguistic foundation, which then, in profane vernacular, is expressed as voice in the very same order and structure that it is to be understood in its genesic model.

STRUCTURE OF SYMBOLIC MYSTICISM

Whether language is formed from a prearranged set of symbols and meanings or based on platonic essences is a question that lies at the heart of both Scholem's and Benjamin's studies. Should language be considered more than mere communication, adds Scholem, then the question undoubtedly turns to a "secret" (*Geheim*) dimension of linguistics, which captivates mysticism in every age (j3:8). This hidden dimension can be ascertained by one category alone: "The symbolic character of language."[16] In being able to represent a thing without its existence, the symbol comes to take the place of the notion of metaphor in Benjamin's essay.[17] But since Benjamin was not of the opinion that the substance of the intellect of a thing could be expressed metaphorically without its existence in language, one is confronted with the problem of "magical" expression. And this, in fact, is the very direction that Scholem wishes to take the notion of the symbol in his work: the truth of the inexpressible expressed in the symbol. Its magic would be the presence of substance in every moment where it expresses itself, not merely as a symbol but as solitary revelation of the inexpressible. Is the magic of the symbol therefore its appearanceless existence, or is the symbol a verbal expression of its existence with neither a visual component nor mere communicative meaning? These are Scholem's metaphysical questions, which he clearly links to those of Benjamin:

> Language communicates something beyond the sphere in which
> expression and formation is permissible; the inexpressible [*ein
> Ausdrucksloses*] that only finds expression in symbols, which res-
> onates in every expression and is based on expression . . . shines
> forth through the clefts in the world of expression. . . . (Thus W.
> Benjamin was always clearly a linguistic mystic).[18]

Collective aspects of mystical theory in Scholem's estimation are premised on the view that the symbol stands at the center of the inexpressible, in the very thing to which language cannot give form in the expression. Benjamin's ideas are coalesced under this tier.[19] The paradoxical nature of all symbolism, according to Scholem, expresses that which cannot in any other way be expressed but nevertheless finds its way into expression. This is the task of the mystic who discovers in language an "immanent dimension" within its structure "that does not regulate the communication of the communicable but rather . . . the noncommunicable that is present, expressionless, in the symbol. If indeed the inexpressible had an expression, it would remain nevertheless meaningless, bearing no communicable significance."[20] The immanent dimension of language is inexpressible in the structure of a thing that finds its only expression in the symbolic. Following this view, even if the incommunicable were to be expressed it would not be received as coherent. Mystical linguistic theory is thus foremost concerned with the symbolic language of God, which is itself unquestionably bound to the inner workings of language.

Such theory begins with speculation concerning human language "in order to unveil language as revelation."[21] Language of redemption is language as such, assuming that a part of the divine can be derived from profane language, since the divine gave rise to it. Such a statement generates a host of problems when "the language of the gods or the language of God is interwoven in the spoken language and thus, through this connection, renders itself open to discovery."[22] Such a paradoxical interweaving of God's creating language and that of the profane has introduced a chasm into language that mystics too have been unable to circumvent. This is also reflected in Hamann's recognition of language being both the medium of revelation and of human reason.[23]

On the structure of Jewish linguistic speculation, Scholem presents three theses:

1. The notion that creation and revelation [are] both principally and essentially self-portraits of God. As a consequence and in accordance with the infinite nature of the divinity, certain moments of the divine have occurred, such that everything created in the finite and determined realm can only be communicated in symbols. This is directly associated with the notion of language as the essence of the universe.

2. The central position of the name of God as the metaphysical origin of all language, and the conception of language as the explication

and unfolding of this name, such as it appears principally in the
documents relating to revelation but also in all language as such
[*überhaupt*]. The language of God, which is crystallized in the name
of God and, in the last analysis, in the *one single* name at its center,
is the basis of all spoken language in which His language is reflected
and appears symbolically.

3. The dialectical relation between magic and mysticism in the theory of the name of God is nothing less than the overwhelming
power that is attributed to the pure human word.[24]

In the first thesis Scholem proposes creation and revelation as self-
presentations of God's infinite character that He illustrates momentarily in
finite form. That God manifests Himself at all, under any finite conditions
whatsoever, means that all created things must also be capable of being
formed in symbolic representation of God's substance: as He is His created
object, His symbolic presence in finite matter. This finite symbol bears a
substance similar to the substance of all created things as its linguistic
being. In the second thesis the name of God is proposed as the center of
language and language as the unfolding of the name.[25] Language is conceived as God's linguistic being, concentrated in His divine name, and in
so doing, when the name of God is conveyed, it is merely symbolic. The
third thesis puts forward the notion that magic and mysticism exist in a dynamic within the theory of the name of God and are extended as power in
the pure human word. In one form magic proves itself to be theurgic; in
another, mystical revelation. Nevertheless we see in both cases God's creative power functioning as a divining rod in the profane.

From Scholem's synopsis of Jewish linguistic theory, we can draw
comparisons with Benjamin to see to what degree his early linguistic speculations coincides. To begin with, God concentrating His infinite being
momentarily and linguistically in creation as His essence also forms the
basis of Benjamin's analysis of the transformation of the substance of the
intellect.[26] God is the center of language for both and the center of all linguistic being, which is to say all created being, engaged in the processes of
communicating its inner insignia with the name of God. This communicative act thus constitutes the "basis of every language."[27] Since linguistic things, by their nature, express themselves in relation to God linguistically, they express the experience of an unfolding of revelation, even if
only as a glimpse of an earlier state of sanctity. The name of God remains,

nevertheless, the center of such symbioses, finding its modest symbolic revelation in language. If the symbolic conveys the magic of the inexpressible, then we should be able to see a convergence of opinion. The last supposition of a dialectical tension between magic and mysticism marks a slight departure from the course Benjamin set out, and we shall see to what degree this departure reveals a substantial difference in the textual analysis to follow.

THE CREATING WORD AND UNPRONOUNCEABLE NAME

The Torah does not contain an explicit magical concept for the name of God. Even the Tetragrammaton appearing in a thornbush in Exodus does not, in itself, demand a concept of magic, according to Scholem, for the expression of God's ultimate freedom to do things that are inherently beyond human reason cannot be said to be magical.[28] Yet whether an event is deemed magical or revelatory, it is thought to bear a special message to its receiver, implying a unique relationship between the imparting and the receiving. The same is the case for the name and the thing being named, which Scholem refers to as its magic. The "magic of the name" is based on the conviction "that a close and substantial relation exists between the name and the name's bearer."[29] This corresponds quite naturally to Benjamin's genesic notion of God's creating language being transposed in naming by the fact that Adam recognized the names that God encoded in each being and thing.[30] Like Benjamin, the name is articulated as the concentration of force within the word, embodying a cohesive expression of the essence of the bearer of a name (j3:13). But its magic has found a more definitive focus here than merely the magic of the word. It is explained as an inner substance that extends way beyond the "understanding." In "representing the semantic properties of the word [das Sinnliche des Wortes] in fully speaking," magic resembles a force field of linguistic might.[31] From this perspective one can speak of the "power" of the name and its "practicable magic," a power that originates in the "incredible force" at the root of the name, in which naming itself is the "center of the divine name . . . of the completely untouchable," for the divine name is "an inner-worldly configuration of power active within creation, namely, the omnipotence of God."[32] Here Scholem was to underscore the power dimension of the name, what in many ways lies nascent in Benjamin's linguistic study.[33]

Power is expressed linguistically in creation, generated at its source in the divine name, and handed down to profane language in the mediated form of the act of naming. The power of the name is embedded in its eternity, as expressed in Psalms: "Heaven and earth are perishable, but 'Thy great name lives and endures in eternity.'"[34]

But the theory of names introduces a paradox into religious speculation, Scholem asserts, when "the name, by which God calls himself and to which he is also invocable, withdraws from the audible sphere, becoming *unpronounceable*."[35] Here Benjamin's distinction concerning the divine name reflects the paradoxical. His name is His reference; it is that to which one turns in calling upon God. However, the name, ironically, is unpronounceable; that is, we are to call upon that which we are unable to call upon. Only on rare occasion is the proper name of God even permitted to be spoken, for example, in the case of the *shem ha-meforash* (to follow below), in the Temple through certain blessings of the priests, thereupon drawing back into its unpronounceablity. As Benjamin was to state fifty years before, the name is no longer merely the last *Aufruf* (call) but now the only *Anruf* (address) of language (II:145). This is not simply the process by which Adam called out the hidden insignia of each created thing and animal but the avenue by which the unpronounceably divine was to be referred to in human language. Scholem sees this as a cornerstone of its linguistic power:

> It is precisely this ineffability, by which the name of God can be *addressed* [*angesprochen*] but no longer *expressed* [*ausgesprochen*], that endowed the name with inexhaustible depth from the sensibility of the Jews, evident no less in such a radical exponent of theistic rationalism as Hermann Cohen.[36]

In this process of shrinking back the name of God became that which could be called upon but not pronounced, and it was the depth to which the name was thought to bear, engendered by this transition, that would broadly influence Judaic thought. Scholem draws here on Hermann Cohen, who was to explicate a messianic understanding of the idea of the name of God.[37]

In first- and second-century literature an explanation of the manifold nature of the name is conceived by the term *shem ha-meforash*. Scholem defines *meforash* as released, thoroughly or explicitly explained, literally pronounced or spoken, isolated and hidden—all which capture the nature of this paradoxical notion, a pronounceable but at the same time secret name.[38] In the third century new lists of holy names began to appear, drawn up from Bible verses or from unknown procedures, which were also identified by this term, making their way out of purely mystical speculations and into the mainstay of rabbinic Judaism.[39] A collection of texts from the period makes reference to a creating name of God formed out of twelve, forty-two, and seventy-two letters—even a hundred letters—leaving the only certainty regarding the divine name in the idea that it was the sanctifying force behind creation.[40] In the medieval period of rabbinical Judaism the creating name was often thought to be constructed out of forty-two letters, a belief held by such prominent medieval scholars as Rashi and Hai Gaon.[41] A forty-two-letter divine name did not require that God's name be the unspoken origin of all power, in the sense of being the generating point of creation rather than its fulfillment.[42] This, Scholem explains, is related to the magical element of the divine name:

> If the name of God is seen here as the *agens* of creation, the reason for this is still, apparently, that the magical conception of the power of the names emerges once again. The name is a concentration of divine power, and, in accordance with the different combinations of these concentrated powers, such names can serve different functions. The creating *word* of God, evoking heaven and earth, and substantiated by the account of creation in Genesis as well as the hymns of the Psalmists—"The heavens were made by the word of the Lord" (Ps 33:6)—is for the biblical authors clearly not the name of God itself.[43]

The creative word of God was not His name, but the name was rather the wellspring of His power. The collapse of this difference in later speculations gave rise to the confusion between the word and the name, between the word "that communicates something to a name that itself communicates nothing other than itself."[44] Scholem puts to use here Benjamin's genesic formula: "Every language communicates itself."[45]

The difference between the creating word and the unpronounceable name is explained as the difference between a thing that communicates something and a thing that communicates nothing but itself. One midrash speaks of a precreation in which God and his name were alone. From name, the word was created.[46] This took place in the language of God where "God not only represents and manifests Himself, He communicates with His creation, where the medium of this language comes into existence."[47] The dual nature of God's word as the unspeakable name and the creating word was later able to take on a degree of importance in the Kabbalah. Such a bifurcated linguistic vision of God as word and name was also to place unique emphasis on the letters and, for a Hebrew or Aramaic reader, on the consonants: "The letters of the divine language are what lie at the basis of all creation by way of their combination. These letters, in the Hebrew language, are the letters of an original language and a language of revelation."[48] The letters formed not merely a methodology to uncover further layers of God's revelation but were themselves considered mediums of revelation. Naturally, this was to appeal to mystics, but the methods of linking letters together or blasting them apart constitute a basis of linguistic research, finding expression long before the emergence of the Kabbalah.[49] The power of the word and its proper name were to emerge from a long-standing tradition of genesic thought into a practice that consumed the mystical linguistics of the Kabbalists. The magical, revelatory power of the name fueled their inquiry: "The creative energy that resides in words and names, that quality of immediate and direct effect—in other words, their magic—is based on the fundamental elements in which, for the mystic, the acoustic and written image coincide."[50] The emphasis on the structure of divine language was to break this language down into its perceivable parts in an attempt to discover the hidden, divine combinations of letters and words. How this linkage and atomizing process was to begin to develop in Jewish thought is the focus of the next chapter.

MATTER AND MAGIC IN THE TORAH AND ITS LETTERS

The first question that ensues from a linguistic conception of creation is the power allotted to the word and letter: is the word to be understood in a material form, literally as "building blocks" of creation?[51] It appears Scholem also attempted to respond to the question raised by Benjamin as to a second version of Genesis and the materialist conception of God's creation of Adam:

The divine breath that transforms man into a living being, according to the account in Genesis, and further reveals to man his possibility of speech, is given considerable weight in the so to speak offical Aramaic translation of the Torah, used for religious services in the synagogue. The *Targum Onkelos* renders the sentence in Genesis 2:7, "and man became a living soul," as "man became a spirit endowed with speech." The living essence of man is just that—language. However, for those inclined to speculate, this idea soon gave rise to the question whether this linguistic element was already contained in the breath of God.[52]

While it would be hard to believe that Benjamin made reference to an Aramaic version of Genesis, Scholem was long aware of the similarity. Sometime already in 1917–1918 he notes the importance of the variation in translation with regard to the transference of divine spirit: "This is how the *Targum Onkelos* and Jer. I translates *nefesh chai* fom Genesis 2:7 with *ruach melemalah*, spirit endowed with speech."[53] Rather than the soul that God transfers to Adam, Scholem focuses here on the second part of the sentence, the effect: Adam is turned into *nefesh chai*, a living being, which is rendered as a spirit endowed with speech in *Targum Onkelos*. Scholem, unlike Benjamin, does not focus on the material or symbolic qualities of the act but rather on the linguistic implications of God's transference as the very thing that distinguishes humans from other aspects of creation. Should God have given a part of His spirit to Adam, this would have occured in the form of language as the expression of His spirit; His *ruach* is itself therefore linguistic (j3:21).

In a text, generally thought to have originated somewhere in the third to seventh centuries, known as *Sefer Yetzirah*, ruach appears again in the form of an element of the senses or air.[54] Thus ruach is once again joined together with His breath. However, *Sefer Yetzirah* is particularly concerned with the methodology of creation, where the letters themselves are viewed as fragments of the creating word whose power is locked in combinations. Like a divine padlock, the proper combination was thought to be capable of releasing the means to create. By the combination of the 22 letters as spheres rotating in opposite directions, 231 combinations arise, gates through which all created things are said to pass. The thinking behind these magical combinations was the power of the letters themselves: "The alphabet is the origin of language and, at the same time, the origin of being. 'It

is therefore apparent that all creation and speech are born of one name.'"[55]
What is important for our discussion is not a detailed description of how
these different assemblages of letters were thought to function but the orientation that this type of speculation was to present to the notion of creation. Proceeding from a tradition well established by *Bereshit Rabbah*,
Sefer Yetzirah was to further emphasize and elaborate the dimension of the
power to create within language. As Scholem explains:

> Every facet of reality that exists beyond the divine pneuma thus
> contains linguistic elements, and the clear opinion of the author is
> that all created things have a linguistic substance [*sprachliches
> Wesen*] that takes shape in one of the many combinations of these
> basic letters. Moreover, he allots to the individual letters both pre-
> determined functions as well as objects, such as planets, signs of
> the zodiac in the sky, days of the week, months of the year, and the
> principal organs of the human body.[56]

Sefer Yetzirah makes the assertion that all created things have a linguistic
substance to be found in the combination of letters ascribed to particular
objects. From the smallest particles to the greatest masses, all created
things, according to this work, "are clearly related to each other through
their linguisic substance."[57] The substance of creation breathed the same
"linguistic intellect" as "the divine language in the way it is expressed to
us."[58] If words were believed to contain the power to create, when the right
letters were placed in the proper order to reconstruct a creating language
of names, then the supposition that one could augment the ebb and flow
of revelation through the application of specific, theurgical methods was a
logical outcome. It is possible that *Sefer Yetzirah* may have been read as just
such a manual (j3:26). Another text of a late or post-talmudic period,
Shimushei Torah (the "theurgical application of the Torah"), reports that
when Moses received God's revelation on Mount Sinai he not only received the Torah as it is known today, with its word divisions, but also a series of secret letter combinations, understood to be the names that form
the esoteric totality of the Torah.[59]

By the time this notion reached early medieval Spain, the mystical
character of the Torah was viewed as the all-encompassing name of God.
Nachmanides, the respected figure in the Jewish intellectual world of the
thirteenth century, deemed a genuinely authoritative tradition that the

Torah was formed from the names of God, where "the whole Torah consists of the names of God, such that the words we read there can be divided in a completely different way, that is, in (esoteric) Names."[60] Nachmanides goes on to explain that it may have been possible at one time to read the Torah both traditionally "as history and commandment" and as a list of holy or esoteric names.[61] Moses received the written Torah in particles, as divisible words from divine names, but acoustically he also received teachings on how to read the Torah as a divine list. This imaginative conclusion branches out from the principles established in the previous sources. Here the name clearly existed before creation. Because God applied the name in creation, the name served as a tool. That His name is the nonlinguistic substance of His being, i.e., the only uncreated thing in existence without an acoustic form, not having itself been formed in creation, explains why the Torah, according to Nachmanides, is not able to be used if it has a letter too few or too many. Rather than merely the name of God generating the Torah, the Torah is actually one enormous name of God in its entirety. This was a view shared by many of his contemporaries, particularly that both the Torah and God's throne of glory are either the name of God themselves or the "substance of the glorious name," as it is termed in *Sefer ha-Chayim*.[62] The *Zohar* also speaks of the Torah as "a single, holy, mystical name."[63]

The notion of the Torah as one extended, divine name of God should be understood as more than mystical speculation. Important here is the emphasis on the coherence of the Torah, that in its entirety it forms a distinct unity of purpose to express the "power and omnipotence of God," concentrated in his name.[64] For the Spanish Kabbalist of the thirteenth century Josef Gikatilla, the Torah begins with the Tetragrammaton as the language of God. Drawing on the *Zohar*,[65] it is his view that

the Torah is thus a living garment and textile (a *textus* in the most accurate sense of the word) in which the Tetragrammaton as a basis and leitmotif is woven. This occurs in secret, although occasionally quite openly. In either case, it returns in a plethora metamorphoses and variations.[66]

Gikatilla conceives the Torah to be a (text)ile woven from the names of God, names such as *El, Elohim, Shaddai*, all linked inextricably to the Tetragrammaton as the branches and roots of a tree to its trunk (j3:50). He follows in the footsteps of *Sefer Yetzirah,* where the procedure of linking the letters of the Tetragrammaton to the rest of the alphabet, is explained. In this way it is believed that the core of the Tetragrammaton is revealed.

The principle here is that the Torah can be read both in different ways and differently in various periods of time. The infiniteness of God's name and His language in the Torah means that it is to be reread and reinterpreted continuously. In this world the Torah may appear in a particular form, but its comprehension in the next will be quite varied. "The word of God, which extends to all worlds," Scholem therefore concludes, "is both infinitely pregnant with meaning and yet lacks any fixed significance. Being meaningless, it is purely and simply 'the interpretable' [*das Deutbare*] itself."[67] How is it that God's word is infinitely giving birth to meaning but itself has no meaning? If the word of God is infinite, it would have no meaning distinguishable from anything else and consequently be meaningless to us. The ethical consequences of such a thesis and implications for revelation would be great.[68]

GRAMMARIANS OF THE NAME

Given that the name stands alone at the center and origin of God's creating word, it might be necessary to suspend the principles of semantic meaning to expose the roots of divine language. It is for this reason, says Scholem, that mystics are not to be mistaken for grammarians:

> There exists within human language an image [*Abglanz*], a reflection of divine language that coincides in revelation. Friedrich Schlegel, the great figure in early Romanticism, used to remark that philosophers must be grammarians. One cannot say this of mystics: for the language of God, the "inner world" with which the mystics are concerned, does not have a grammar. It consists of names, which are more than ideas here. The task of recovering the name within the language of humanity is the essential focus of the kabbalistic conception of prayer.[69]

The name is substituted for divine language such that the question of a divine semantic structure is avoided. But, in contrast to Scholem's position, if a mystical linguistic theory is to proceed through speculation, then divine language would require a grammar, as would the divine name, if the basis of divine language were lodged in a "true reflection" (to bring Molitor back into the picture) of itself in the profane.[70] Thus if philosophers are the grammarians of reason, as Schlegel would have us believe, then mystics might very well be the philosophers of divine reason and grammarians of their own language. Substituting the name only turns the focus to the syntax of the letter combinations and does not divert us from the question.

It is within this discussion of a mystical grammar that we encounter in Scholem the writings of Isaac the Blind. His are thought to be some of the oldest kabbalistic speculations pertaining to language, originating in Provence in the twelfth century. Drawing on the Hebrew term *davar,* which can be translated as both thing and object as well as word and speech, the meaning of *geistige Dinge* (spiritual things) for Isaac the Blind would not be distinguishable from *geistige Worte* (spiritual/holy words) (j3:34). His etymological analysis was to extend the notion of language to embrace a slight messianic dimension as well. Since the Hebrew term, *'ot,* or "letter" derives from the word *'ata,* "coming," and *otiot,* the plural of *'ot,* can also mean "das Kommende" (the coming/arriving), Isaac the Blind was to conclude that words and letters are also to be understood as bearing prophetic and messianic messages, as "signs that 'are derived from their origins,' pointing to the hidden origins from which they stem like insignia embedded in all things."[71] In this respect, he entertained no division between the thing and its expression: "In the world of God there is still no such thing as reification, and the *dibb'rim* or *devarim* here are clearly still the words as the creating forces of all things."[72] Drawn from a notion of God's linguistic being, Scholem sees no place in his theory for the concept of alienation—what God projects and what God is are both to be drawn from the same eternal "internalized, mute thinking" that Isaac the Blind was to identify with the infinite core, the *en-sof* ("without end").[73] In his interpretation of *Sefer Yetzirah,* a world of "pure names" is generated out and stands therefore as the principle element of language (j3:35).

The *sefirot* were to play a considerable role in Isaac the Blind's linguistic speculations, where thinking is identified as the first moment, the direction of thinking to creation (in action) as the second. The second moment is termed the "beginning of speech," therefore the origins of the language of God. "It is not yet considered language, but origin and beginning."[74] He was thus to expose the tension between the thought of creation and its execution, what we were to first encounter in *Bereshit Rabbah.* But rather then perishing in logical turmoil, he was instead to embark on a mystical theory of the prestates of language in which the written word forms the center of his speculations on God's revelation as language in language. Scholem terms this a unity of word and thing in spirit: "Everything spoken in the divine world is, at the same time, something written, and every writing is potential speech that is designated to become audible."[75]

This idea may appear to be a slight departure from the first argument on acoustic revelation and, as such, it would also have implications for Benjamin's theory on transference in language. But, in point of fact, Scholem presents these notions of language as being rather consistent, formulating a notion of creation in several linguistic stages: first, revelation was acoustically enacted, even if the written initially preceded it. Written revelation is potentially acoustic but is not always acoustically receivable (as in the Tetragrammaton). Acoustic language can be expressed in writing but written language cannot always be spoken. In the same way, every spoken word has the potential to be written, just as every written word contains the potential to be spoken. Thus in each interaction between word and tone, the division of the spoken and written is only possible with the "potential" God imbued in all linguistic being. But in Benjamin's theory the relation of word to its expression took a "historical" course. He emphasizes the transition of language and locates a realm of transference in language that was lost in the expulsion from paradise. Genesic language is, however, not to be lost forever and is encountered again in the redemptive aspect of judgment. This messianic potential distinguishes the grammarians of language from the mystical grammarians of divine language, placing Benjamin squarely in the company of those for whom the written bears divine messages. For both Benjamin and the Kabbalists the inexpressibility of the written word is, according to Scholem, the true mystery of language:

> While, for the philologist, writing is no more than a secondary and extremely unuseful image [Abbild] of real language, for the Kabbalist it is the true refuge of its mysteries. The phonographic principle of a natural transition from spoken language into writing and, vice versa, from writing into spoken language operates in the Kabbalah with the idea that the divine letters of the alphabet are themselves those lineaments and signs that the modern phonetician would be looking for on his record. The creating word of God is truly and precisely marked along these divine lines. Beyond lan-

guage lies nonlinguistic reflection, which is pure thought contemplating itself—one might say, the mute, inner meaning that is lodged in the nameless.[76]

MICROLINGUISTIC SPECULATION

As the tradition of linguistic speculation began to move from a rabbinic science of creation, focused on filling in the missing pieces of revelation in order to extend divine coherence, the scientific study of creation embarked on a course of abstract analysis in a decidedly microlinguistic direction. Just like the modern attempt to split the atom into its integral parts, the revealing aspects of creation were broken down into their smallest components to see whether it was possible to discover hidden codes that would explain creation's "magic" properties. This transition from the macro- to the microscopic level was also accompanied by a change in focus from acoustic to written expression. In a microscopic view the words that formed God's message were to be split open to reveal their letters. As the building blocks of revelation, the letters themselves were to become the center of speculation. If one recalls the fact that the Torah is already presumed to have existed before its acoustic pronunciation, then surely the letters (not to speak of the words they form in writing) were also the means of creation. But if, however, the Torah, or that which is known as Torah, is not presumed to have existed before creation, there would be no need to think of *or* as the true word for light, but instead as a transliteration of an unknown language into a known one. The written Torah would then merely be a transference of the original story of creation into human language.

Kabbalistic treaties on the letters and the potential for their combination led to a discussion of those letters that constitute the divine name. The anonymous *Sefer ha-Iyyun,* thought to be of the thirteenth century, expresses a combination of light and linguistic mysticism together with a proposition concerning the divine name in which creation, understood as "intelligible lights," is read, at the same time, as intelligible names.[77] A methodological orientation to the science of creation is expounded in this text: the creation of names from letter combinations is based on the Tetragrammaton, "the root of all other names" (j3:37). The latter, however, is taken merely relatively, only appearing "as the symbolic expression of one of the infinite aspects of God's omnipotence."[78] God's is assumed to be the longest and shortest name that exists; one may take a single letter to express it or consider the entire Torah the totality of His name (j3:38).

In another text of the Iyyun circle, *Ma'ayan ha-Chokhmah*, "the fountain of wisdom," the *yud* of the Tetragrammaton is proposed as the first silent letter of the unpronounceable name of God and therefore as the origin of the divine name, the symbolic representation of the "original point of language."[79] The Tetragrammaton itself is the "unity that emerges from the original root of linguistic motion, which is the original ether, the *aura* surrounding God."[80] This leads to the hypothesis that the *alef*, being the first letter of the alphabet, was in fact the first silent letter of God's name, its silence expressing the nonacoustic being of the Tetragrammaton itself. In so doing, the *alef* becomes the "indifference of all speaking," according to Scholem, which, despite its silence and later disappearance from the Tetragrammaton altogether, remains the standpoint from which all creating language is generated.[81]

Scholem applies an expressly dialectical analysis to *Ma'ayan ha-Chokhmah*, focusing on the *Umschlag* (transition/negation), which he suspects to be the author's fascination with the creating movement of the *yud*. The letter *yud* is described as the source of all linguistic motion, both infinitely extending but returning to its center and origins in its "unfolding." Scholem detected something cyclical in this return to origins: "The magical power of speaking is the power of knowing how to imagine being at the root of linguistic motion, capturing in this way all language and expression of substance and capable of penetrating its effects."[82] In the creating motion of the *yud* Scholem reads an attempt to split open the atomic core of the divine name of God, unleashing a "magical" power locked at the root of spoken, linguistic motion. The prime motion released in the *yud* is discovered to be at the core of language and therefore the essence of a thing.

In a slight deviation from the microlinguistic approach, the divine name of God is deemed unrecognizable for all intensive purposes.[83] Another interpretation, perhaps even more radical then the first, is the notion that God's original name is not to be found in the Torah at all, or that hidden behind the Tetragrammaton is the "true original name" which has yet to be revealed (j3:43). Still another formulation found in *Ma'ayan ha-Chokhmah* is that the original name of God is to be found by drawing from the letters *alef, he, vav, yud*, considered the generating letters of the alphabet. *EHVY* is then the name that is thought to be at the core of the divine name from which all other names arose. The same name in *Sefer ha-Iyyun* is proposed as the insignia upon the ring God used to seal creation (j3:41). But like many a hypothesis, it will only be proven when events in time and history reveal themselves as such. So too with the divine name of God, which, according to some traditions, is not truly knowable until the moment of its revelation is at hand:

> It is only in the present eon that the Tetragrammaton—in a Torah whose form has become legible to us—has taken the place of this original name, but in the messianic age, which introduces the end of this eon, the Tetragrammaton will once again be dislodged from its position by the original name.[84]

Born from *sh'mittot*, the theory of eons, also known as the phases of creation through which the world is completed, the Torah is believed to take a form unique to the particular age in which it is read or understood. The Torah itself is actually evolving in the course of time, albeit in enormous periods of slow transformation. At the end of the *Sh'mittot*, everything will return to its origin, no less the name of God itself:

> At the end of this world cycle all things return to their origins in the "great jubilee year," in the third *sefirah binah*, and all the emanations and worlds below disappear. The true name of God, which is also maintained in this condition of the return of all things to the divine womb, is precisely the original name, a revelation of divine being directed solely to itself and nothing outside itself.[85]

From the suggestion that the true name of God does not exist in the present but may exist in the future two positions arise. In the first position God is acutely aware of His name but keeps this name to Himself. The second position, which is presented in the *Zohar*, is that the *deus absconditus* has no name. The Tetragrammaton is called the "essential" or "proper" name of God because it renders the concentrated substance of its endlessness (*en-sof*) immanent in itself, through its emanation. There would therefore be no need for a name beyond it because every name implies a constraint of its unlimitedness.

Thus, in the Iyyun circle's analysis of a "symbolically visible" mystical word of God, Scholem was to detect once again a free-flowing relationship between a thing and its language, here between lights and sounds, which are both considered linguistic substances of the intellect.[86] In this way their linguistic mysticism of the name equipped them with a "metaphorical expression of general theological ideas" in which the "condensation and concentration of God's emissions" in the name was considered part and parcel of a "metaphysical sphere" of speculation in which "the optic and acoustic coincide."[87] In short, it provided them with a theoretical framework for a metaphysics of appearance, drawn from theological principles of a science of creation.

METAPHYSICS OF THE DIVINE NAME

The idea that the theory of the divine name represents the core of the linguistic theory of the Kabbalah was in fact already formulated by Scholem in February 1917 where he wrote that "*the constitution of the mystical conception of language is*: all language is formed by the name of God."[88] He returned to the same idea again in his notebook from Jena, written in the winter of 1917–1918: "The principle of the kabbalistic theory of language is that all language is formed by the name of God."[89] His late essay appears to maintain this earlier view.

Research into the proper name of the divine and its relationship to proper names in the profane was to have a lasting impact on Jewish linguistic speculation, according to Scholem. The discussion of the Kabbalists concerned the relationship of the name to that which Scholem alternately refers to as metaphor or symbol—a reference to the qualities of a thing in the context of a symbolic or equally metaphoric reflection of its existence. Although thoroughly relevant to the science of creation, such speculation was not far from the question of the existence of an imperceivable being in the profane. For Jacob Ha-Kohen of Soria (ca. 1260–1270), this question is anything but incidental. At its very basis lies the meaning of the existence of God. Since language was the avenue to metaphysics, it is therefore understandable why Ha-Kohen sought to prove that the name of God is not mere appearance but essence as well. As such, the twelve, forty-two, or seventy-two letters of the name of God should not be treated as mere visual attributes but recognized as belonging to the essence of the name, Ha-Kohen reminds his readers. Since they are made up of letters that have the capacity to reach the divine, they too must be part of the divine (j3:47). This theory is closely related to a notion of proper names in which the name given to humans is neither accidental nor essential but something "real."[90] The following choice citation of Ha-Kohen, which Scholem renders here into German, suggests the profound impact of Greek philosophy on Kabbalah. At the same time, it points to the clear affinity that Scholem would maintain between Kabbalah and Benjamin:

> The name is thus distinct from essence [*Wesen*] and it is neither substance [*Substanz*] nor attribute, nor anything with a concrete reality. The body, on the other hand, is both substance and attribute, as well as something with a concrete reality. The name is added to essence, but the divine names are essences themselves and powers of the Godhead and their substance is the substance of the "light of life" (one of the highest *sefirot*). Yet if one takes the proper names of humans literally, one finds that they and the essences (that they denote) are such that a name cannot be divided from an essence, nor an essence from a name, for the name is directly linked to essence.[91]

Here we find a very similar conception of the name to that which Benjamin ascribes to Adam's activities in creation. The name presents something "real" of the thing that it names. Adam conveys it to the thing, but it is drawn directly from its essence.[92] Ha-Kohen makes the distinction in the first instance between divine and profane names such that the profane is drawn from essence and the divine is synonymous with it. In the last analysis we see the removal of the first distinction, where the distance between the thing and its profane name is deemed a direct, unmediated connection. From this it is possible to see how Scholem might have had a direct association in mind.[93]

Israel Sarug (a Lurianic Kabbalist active at the beginning of the seventeenth century) advocated a theory of linguistic creation drawn from God's pleasure or joy as the prime motion of all linguistic activity. Envisioned as a *Selbstbegegnung* (encounter) within the *en-sof* itself, Sarug's mystical "pleasure principle" conceives of God's joy within the infinite moment as the transition "'from itself to itself' where the joy of the *en-sof* expresses itself and thereby the secret power of all expression as well."[94] Within this motion an "original texture" (*malbush*) was woven, from which an "original Torah was communicated."[95] This original material presented an initial stage prior to the spoken and the written, a prime root of a "hidden insignia in God," which expressed itself to itself without having an expression, neither in tone nor in image.[96] In the contraction of the *en-sof* within itself (known in Lurianic Kabbalah as the process of *zimzum*), the original Torah was a self-contained entity, generative of creating powers and becoming the "original force of all linguistic motion."[97] This confrontation within itself, without the elements of expression (in the profane), becomes for Sarug the formula of all expression, the locus classicus of all linguistic power. He presents a threefold version of creation where an initial fabric of original motion gave rise to a Torah "as a series of mystical divine names, which are formed by specific combinations of the first elements."[98] This original Torah was revealed with its letters as "angelical forms," appearing in a series of divine names that were inaccessible to the profane reader. Only during a third moment (i.e., a third world) in which the letters of the Torah were shaped into forms with syntactic meaning was the text to appear, originating out of a first incomprehensible list of implicitly divine meaning. In this final form "the names of all things and of all human beings [*menschlichen Wesen*]," meaning "the world of language and the name itself," are contained within the Torah.[99] All of language, and all of its syntactic, speculative, and metaphysical meaning, is to be found in the Torah:

> The original, paradisiacal language of man still had this character of the sacred: language was still immediate and authentically bound to the essence of the things it sought to express. The echo of the divine was still present in this language, for in the breath of divine pneuma the linguistic motion of the Creator was transposed to that of the created.[100]

Just as in Benjamin's initial proposition of an original, creating language that God passed on to Adam in a linguistic and philosophical paradise (with regard to a thing and its meaning), Scholem discovers a "sacral" state of language in Sarug where an "echo" of the divine was lodged in the created through the transference of God's *ruach/nishmat chaim* (II:147–50). To the degree that the sacral is identical with the expressed essence of a thing, Scholem returns to the earlier discussion on the substance of the intellect/spirit (II:140–1). Given that profane language emerged from the descent of divine language, we see Scholem pointing again to the question of the relationship of divine language in the profane or, in Benjamin's words, the translation of a higher language into a lower one (II:151–52). In a broad view of linguistic speculation in the Kabbalah, Scholem presents Sarug's own analysis in light of the widely held opinion in the Kabbalah that Hebrew, as the original language,

> was from the very outset not to be used in the profane. The generation that sought to build the tower of Babel abused this true sacred language in a magical way, in order to imitate to a certain degree the creativity of God with the help of the knowledge of the pure names of things. They sought to obtain, surreptitiously, a "name" that could be used on any given occasion. The linguistic confusion consisted of a far-reaching loss of this language from memory, with the result that those affected had to reinvent and reconceive of the names of each thing. . . . But even the divine language has since become mixed with the profane, just as here and there we still find elements or residues of the divine in the profane languages.[101]

Just as in Molitor's exposition, fragments of a divine language were thought to have been mixed in the profane, with Hebrew retaining a bit more of the pieces of the divine than other profane languages.[102] Here the notion of an original language is distinctly linked to Hebrew such that the misuse of the divine language has consequences, some of which are even incalculable. Benjamin's analysis appears once again in the concept of the misuse of language and the "magical" properties of the name, lodged in the expression of the inexpressible divine insignia (II:153). He too saw the problem of "overnaming" as a consequence of the descent and confusion of language into the profane (II:155–56). That the true name of things could be discovered once again may have been a perspective held by many a linguistic Kabbalist with even a remote messianic yearning, but it was also a dream from which Scholem himself was to abruptly awaken shortly after his arrival in Palestine in 1923.[103]

A MICROLINGUISTIC SCIENCE OF PROPHECY

The Kabbalist Abraham Abulafia, of late thirteenth-century Spain, was to open up to Scholem entirely new realms of linguistic speculation in his methodology of the microlinguistic. He was to take his cue in many respects from Maimonides' metaphysics of Judaism, and its essentially rationalizing and normative teachings that were applied to a linguistically based mystical methodology for a prophecy of the here and now.[104] From both Maimonides and Aristotle, Abulafia borrows the notion of a core of character being eternal and differs only slightly from the theory of the creating word of God, suggesting that even divine acoustics were not to remain isolated in God alone. Divine sounds were linked to the profane, according to Abulafia, through the fact that God wrote creation rather than pronouncing it:

> Creation, revelation, and prophecy for Abulafia are phenomena of the linguistic world: creation as an act of divine writing, in which writing shapes the matter of creation; revelation and prophecy as acts, in which the divine word is infused not just once but repeatedly into human language . . . and endows language, at least potentially, with infinite wealth of immeasurable insight into the interrelation of things.[105]

All major divine events are woven back into a linguistic interpretation, beginning with a genesic starting point that links the word to its expressive medium. But rather than drawing attention to the acoustic sphere, he embarks on a rather unique integration of various forms of linguistic expression. For Abulafia the utterance of the creating word is also an act of divine writing and a divine act of writing is, at once, a momentary act of infinite moments, finding its expression transpired in human language with messianic significance.[106] In terms not unfamiliar to Benjamin, Scholem viewed Abulafia's theory as a conception of "creation as an act of divine writing, in which God embodies things with His language, leaving behind in them His language as an insignia."[107] The written in creation is a reoccurring theme in his work, setting the stage for extensive microlinguistic investigations. For him each letter is itself a symbol of creation, maintaining within itself a powerful atomic core. From the powerful, interforces of letters, Abulafia embarked on a methodology that he termed a "science of prophecy." This consisted primarily of research into word combinations concerning the association between particular words and their aural properties. Through such an undertaking he sought the precursors of linguistic creation, or the prime forces, just as they had been used in creation.

For Abulafia the human ability to bear divine aspects of language (*dibbur 'elohi*) was lodged in the Maimonidean active intellect. As such, it took

Scholem no time to link this concept to Benjamin's geistigen Wesen, for both in Abulafia and in Benjamin the divine substance of the intellect was lodged in every aspect of the created: "Each one of the heavenly spheres of the ptolemaic worldview here corresponded to an inner intelligence that was an intellectual [*geistige*] consequence of the divine will of the Creator."[108] The *intellectus agens* of the *dibbur 'elohi* is a cosmic potential originating out of creation. It is the expression of God's intention in creation, forming every creature and thing with a silent, sanctified intelligence. Perhaps for the first time in Jewish linguistic theory, the active part of the intellect is conceived of linguistically (j3:60). Scholem notes that Abulafia made good use of the medieval attributes of the adjective *devari,* which means both "linguistic," as it is here understood, as well as "rational" or "reasonable." Behind Abulafia's mystical methodology and belief in the experiential practice of prophecy lies a profound conviction in the rationality of his science—in his words, a "'science of the higher, inner logic'"— what Scholem terms a "mystical logic."[109] This was achieved on the basis of a notion of the logical power of language, as Scholem explains: "That which was called the ability of human reason in the language of the philosophers could therefore also be understood as linguistic capacity."[110] As Abulafia himself states on the science of prophecy (in Scholem's translation): "The origin of prophecy resides in the address God spoke through the medium of a perfect language that reached the prophets and encompassed all seventy languages."[111]

Despite the association with the transition of the intellect of naming from God to Adam, a mystical science of self-generating prophecy would not necessarily have appealed to Benjamin. Unlike Abulafia, there is, in fact, every reason to believe that Benjamin's *Sprachmystik* (linguistic mysticism) had little to do with religious practice.[112]

Abulafia viewed God's revelation in written language in no sense metaphorically, as we have seen in Benjamin's application of this term (II:141). The most physical aspects of Scripture were a part of God's being, expressing the unity of His spiritual/intellectual substance—eternally, but also in the moment. A citation from Abulafia: "Thus, for God, hearts are slates and souls are ink, and speech, which comes to them from God and is also knowledge, is like the form of the letters that were inscribed on the tablets of the covenant on both sides."[113] The Tetragrammaton is therefore no less "unreal" in its lack of acoustic expression, its "reality" is no longer determined by the transition from the acoustic to the written. In point of fact, its incommunicability becomes the very measure of its existence: "All created things are endowed with reality inasmuch as they somehow are a part of this 'great name.'"[114] The unspeakable name is thus existence supreme. Abulafia goes on to formulate the "reality" of the created participating in its own creation, implying that the created is always bound to the creating, itself considered an act of scientific prophecy. The link to God is formed by the fact that every act that expresses itself in letters is an "act of knowledge, even when this knowledge remains closed off to us and indecipherable."[115] Knowledge is the cornerstone of linguistic revelation, whether it is acquitted or unattainable.

Scholem's description of Abulafia's *chokhmah ha-tzeruf,* the science of the combinations, has an obvious relationship to Benjamin's theory of the origins of knowledge. The knowledge that was linguistically imparted to Adam by God is not severed from the language he speaks. In fact, the transitive moment in language that finds its expression in translation represents an ongoing act of knowledge (II:151–153). For Abulafia the idea that language is the locus of knowledge implies that even profane languages, such as Greek and Latin, are to serve the divine language, in his words, the "Jewish language."[116] As Scholem explains: "Due to the fact that all languages have come into being through the corruption of the sacred original language, in which the world of names is directly set forth and explained, names are indirectly associated with divine language."[117] Benjamin's analysis of mimicry after the imparting of divine substance as the abuse of the name finds a precursor in Abulafia. Just as in Benjamin's notion of evil knowledge (II:153), Abulafia warns against the misuse of the method, which brings demonic consequences, even conjuring Satan as the spirit of an "unrestituted Nature."[118]

In Scholem's rendition, Abulafia is acutely aware of the "unmediated power" of words (j3:68). Nevertheless, "he adopts an attitude of complete rejection of all practicable magic and theurgy."[119] According to his own formulations, his system, *chokhmah ha-tzeruf,* does not fall under the prohibition concerning magical practices, for his are mystical techniques that encompass a prophetic and equally esoteric form of magic. Despite Abulafia's objections, argues Scholem, "magic does indeed exist for him as the incommunicable, and thus that which radiates out of words."[120] In much the same way that it was defined for us by Benjamin, magic here also is the incommunicable that nevertheless finds a form for its expression (II:142–43). The expression is then deemed magical as the manifestation of revelation in minute, concentrated form. Abulafia's orientation to the question is such that prophetic magic is an integral part of the unfolding of revelation. But since there is an unmediated power contained within the words and a scientific method in their positive combinations, a negative combination is surely possible and naturally merits concern. Thus the former must also be applied in the neutralization of the latter: "As a result of concentrating on the name of God, the center of all creation, a power emerges within himself to 'eliminate the effect of the magician.'"[121] With such a definitive rebuke of magic by one of the standard-bearers of Jewish mysticism (whose method may be characterized as employing magical practices, despite any protest to the contrary), it would be difficult indeed to regard Benjamin's late claims concerning "the elimination of magic" as an authentic attempt to purge any last mystical tendencies from his work.[122]

A MESSIANIC CONCEPTION OF LANGUAGE

In part 2, "On the Origins of Language and the True Names of Things," we have reviewed some of the central ideas of language in Judaism, beginning with the earliest conceptions in the Torah, in *Bereshit Rabbah,* and in rabbinic Judaism in general and extending to the far reaches of mystical speculation in both early and later Kabbalah. Nevertheless, a presentation of Jewish linguistics was never the goal. The aim of this section was to illustrate an integral component of the author's political theology: the concept of language and its place in redemption. We began with an explication of Benjamin's early ideas on language, concentrated particularly in the language of creation. We were able to see many, if not most, of these notions discussed in Molitor's *Philosophy of History.* Then we turned to Scholem and sought to articulate how his early preoccupation with linguistic questions took shape in his mature ideas. To this degree, we have evaluated a short history of linguistic thought in order to show how, despite the development of both Jewish studies and linguistics over the years, we find Scholem formulating many of the same themes and terms that Benjamin first set out in his essay of 1916. We have seen how Scholem returns to the notion that all things and beings express themselves in language and thereby constitute themselves; we have seen how the language of creation was transferred from God to Adam, not metaphorically but linguistically, and we have also seen how, within the fall from the linguistic divinity of Eden into the multiplicity and often redundancy of profane language the judging word of the divine was implanted, offering messianic hope of a manifestation of the divine in the profane. We shall conclude this section on language with Scholem's final remarks, which represent an extremely concise summary of sixty years of linguistic research:

> The name of God is the "essential Name," the origin of all language. Every other name by which God can be called or invoked is connected to a distinct activity, as is shown in the etymology of such biblical names; only this name requires no posterior reference [Rückbesinnung] to an activity. For the Kabbalists this name has no "meaning" in the traditional understanding of the term and no concrete significance. The meaninglessness of the name of God points to its position at the very center of revelation, upon which revelation depends. As the Kabbalists saw it, behind every revelation of meaning in language, and through the Torah, there exists this element beyond significance that endows meaning to everything else, though it has no meaning itself. What speaks to us in creation and revelation, the word of God, is infinitely interpretable and reflects itself in our own language. Its rays [Strahlen] or sounds, which we receive, are not so much communications as calls [Anrufe]. That which has meaning, sense, and form is not this word itself but the tradition behind this word, its mediation and reflection in time. This tradition, which has its own dialectic, transforms itself and eventually becomes a quiet, breathing whisper. There may be times, like our own, in which tradition can no longer be handed down [überliefert] and grows silent. This is the great crisis of language in which we find ourselves, in which the last summit of the mystery that once dwelt within language is no longer comprehensible to us. The fact that language can be spoken is, in the opinion of the Kabbalists, owed to the name, which is present in language. . . . Only poets have an answer to the doubt most mystics have in regard to language, and it is that which links them with the masters of the Kabbalah, even when they reject kabbalistic theological formulation as being too emphatic: a belief in language as an absolute, regardless of the degree to which it is constantly exposed by dialectics. It is a belief in the audible mystery of language.[123]

In a final summary of Scholem's linguistic survey of the Kabbalah we have, in fact, a last return to an early linguistic political theology. At first there was an essential name of God, the genesis of the substance of the intellect to which every other name is related. The etymology of biblical names— Adam from *adamah* (earth), in the words of Molitor—is the active expression of the name of the unmoved mover, itself the most syntactically indefinable proper name in language. But while the divine name attributes meaning to all other names by its insignia, it itself has no meaning. Thus the Kabbalists interpreted the word of God as the infinite in language. In place of a dogma of truth, they carried with them at best a tradition of contextual meaning. Rendering the word of God acoustic was for them however not the expression of context but rather a divine calling—a calling that has become silent in the religious anarchism of our day and age.[124] A crisis in language precipitated a crisis in the notion of a divine origin for Scripture, which can no longer deliver the meaning it once retained.[125] This crisis can be described as one of absolutes—as in the damaged immediacy Benjamin hoped would be repaired by the judging word—but it can also be understood as a crisis in redemption, precipitated by a failing belief in the messianic design of the divine word and a secret dimension to language that awaits its entrance into the realm of the profane.

PART III

A Redemptive Conception of Justice

Der Prophet versteht den Prophetismus nicht; er treibt letzten Endes Politik.

The prophet fails prophecy; in the end he acts politically.
—Scholem on Jonah

CHAPTER 5

PROPHETIC JUSTICE

ON THE ORIGINS OF EVIL

In Benjamin's "Theological-Political Fragment," and in some of the earliest documents on the notion of the messianic, we find elements of messianic fate in the figure of the tragic hero. But as soon as he appears, tragedy is confined to a prison of muteness that sets the hero apart from the sphere of judgment. The silence he is forced to undergo severs expression from a language ripe with genesic insignia, expression from its own genesic code. Isolated from a transformed conception of tragedy and its delineation of time in the word, the notion of character remains unreflected at the intersection between divine intention and the self-constitution of the individual. In this way the ethical imperative of messianic action remains at odds with the idea of tragic decline. Nevertheless, since redemption unfolds in the unintentional will of "free humanity," as Benjamin states, the concept of character is again thrown into question.

What is the relationship between the individual and the tragedy of the world? When transposed to theological terms, the original tragedy is projected onto the individual through the notion of sin. At the same time, as the restitution of original sin has an objective character, so do the terms of justice. Benjamin's analysis of the meaning of justice therefore begins with the responsibility of the individual for original evil. In the chapter on tragic devotion, we have seen him put forward the following arguments: if it is possible to define character as the sum total of the ethical constitution of the individual, then character may serve as a counterpoint to divine intention.[1] The formation of the tension between the character of an individual and divine intention is the history of its first encounter, which Benjamin proposes to be the fall from paradise. Thus the notion of responsibility only takes on meaning following a hypothesis of original sin. Such a view adds a temporal dimension to responsibility, extending beyond the responsibility of a particular individual to the collective responsibility of each individual. But this collective dimension that Benjamin brings to the character of the individual must first be freed from an *Irrtum* (mistake) that has hitherto plagued the discussion: the false assignment of collective responsibility to a collection of individuals rather than the collective responsibility of each individual. This mistaken assignment is the basis of the *Verschuldung* (the attribution of responsibility) of the Jews to holy tragedy.[2] In questioning the nature of responsibility for original sin, Benjamin follows a line of reasoning set out by Kierkegaard in his call for a reevaluation of the ethical notion of character.[3] There are indeed several references in the early letters to a rather extensive project on original sin that was connected to a period in which Benjamin was reading Kierkegaard.[4] Scholem was once apparently in the possession of Benjamin's notebook, entirely dedicated to the subject of original sin,[5] which apparently has not survived. For this reason we must turn back to Kierkegaard to see if it is possible to reconstruct a debate on original sin and ultimately the fragments of a redemptive theory of justice. This begins with the notion of a new ethics.

Kierkegaard proposes in *The Concept of Anxiety*: "The new ethic requires dogma and, with it, original sin. From these two, it defines individual sin."[6] Rather than seeking to hang collective responsibility on eternal events of the past, the fate of the individual is determined by character:

> The concept of sin and responsibility is premised on the individual as individual. It has nothing to do with the world as a whole, or with talk of the past, and is only concerned with the responsibility of individuals. It is by contrast through fate, in everything it

does not entail, that the individual becomes something which the concept of fate transcends. This is what the individual is meant to become through fate.[7]

Sin and responsibility are not formulated in relation to worldly history but directed to the fate of the individual. Here a transformation occurs from blind fate to the willful nature of an individual's character that is determinate, decisive—a character that chooses. First we saw this in Benjamin's tragic hero who chooses fate and goes under. Now we encounter this again with the individual who is freed from the attribution of sin. Through the transformation of fate to a decisive character, Benjamin speculates upon an ethic that would be free from partiality. Proceeding from the ethical and the religious, the dogmatic position on the origin of sin is deeply embedded in the notion of Jewish responsibility and the decline of the Messiah, a full repudiation of which still hangs in the balance.[8] Similar to Benjamin, Kierkegaard explores the origins of sin and evil from the first crisis in the relationship of divine and profane intention. Kierkegaard's speculations on Genesis are also formed from a notion of creation as origin, not with respect to the origin of history but to the idea, more specifically to the problem of good and evil. For this reason the question can certainly not be solved by a dogmatic *Irrtum* (mistake). Rather, the origin of responsibility must begin anew with an idea of sin in which its original character and its character-forming aspects are metaphysically extricated from its genesic beginnings.[9] Genesis is therefore at the center of a new ethical conception of responsibility:

> Unique to our age, the story of original sin in Genesis is mistaken for myth. . . . If the understanding of the mythical is lost, it is rare that anything other than idle chatter [*Geschwätz*] is the result. The story is the only dialectically consistent version; its entire content can be expressed in the sentence: sin entered the world through a sin.[10]

Genesis is read as a single metaphysical statement on the nature of truth, just as it appears in Benjamin. In seeking to move beyond the historically lineal or numerical with regard to the question of creation in favor of a philosophical line of inquiry, we also witness a protest against the mystical or even mythical elements in such an undertaking; with Benjamin, we only need to recall his statement at the outset of the linguistic essay where he puts forward the notion that the truth of Genesis should not be taken a priori as "revealed truth" but, instead, as truth "discovered" in the "nature of language."[11]

The collective, character-forming aspects of responsibility have a relationship to the notion of evil, more specifically to evil intention, which, as sin, brings us to the problem of the origin of sin or original sin. Once idle chatter (*Geschwätz*) is dispensed with, one can explore the principal statement of genesic evil: that sin made its appearance through the first moment of sin.[12] Sin occurs here in the same way that the protagonist of original sin is understood as both individual and collective: since "Adam is the first man, he is both himself and the species," it is therefore possible to view Adam as an individual, a generation, and, up until his creation, all generations—thus an absolute individual and collective in one.[13] This is, in a sense, the means by which Kierkegaard addresses the question of single momentary beginning and eternity in original sin. The difference between Adam and us, however, makes itself apparent in the degree to which his sin is the "iniquity as determining its own consequences" that anticipates and precedes human sin.[14] It is not that Adam created his own first sin—which would take him out of the sphere of the profane altogether—but that, with his act, "a beginning independent of himself" was revealed.[15]

By circuitous route of Adam's mortality, Kierkegaard comes to the conclusion that a beginning occurring before original sin is bound to the question of knowledge: "The story of Genesis," he asserts again, "also presents us with the proper definition of innocence. Innocence is ignorance. It is not the pure being of immediacy but ignorance."[16] Adam's responsibility for introducing sin into the world is paralleled by the question whether it was his intention to contradict divine decree. The supposition of willful knowledge here separates divine immediacy from human innocence. The inability to access immediacy, in the genesic immediacy of language, is the profanity of human activity. As such, it is the dividing point for the first human to be trapped within the profane, to have, in fact, engendered the profane. But at the same time that it provides for its imprisonment it provides a transition from innocence to knowledge.[17]

Despite the boost that Kierkegaard gives to this pursuit of a new ethics of responsibility and, thereby, the first step to a redemptive theory of jus-

tice, he was only partially able to clear the way. It is fairly clear at the outset that Benjamin must diverge paths. Like many other German-Jewish
thinkers at the turn of century, Benjamin was no less accosted than Scholem by the three directions his generation was forced to confront: conversion, assimilation, or Zionism. His rejection of all three meant that he
was also unable to embark from Kierkegaard's universalization of the suffering Messiah, "the only one who took blame for sin out of innocence,"
writes Kierkegaard.[18] Kierkegaard continues in detail on suffering and divine tragedy: "He took the blame for sin not from a fate he was forced to
undergo but as a freely chosen blame for the sin of the whole world and
suffer its punishment."[19] In contrast to each individual forming the contours of all sin, Benjamin proposes an entirely different conception of
character and responsibility. His *Schuldzusammenhang* (relationship of
responsibility) was not a collective guilt linking future generations to
Adam's failure to understand God, for this would only mean that a linguistic fall from divine grace preceded original sin. Rejecting the first particular view that Kierkegaard frees from dogma, Benjamin is not tempted
to embrace a second partiality that sees the origin of good and evil in language (ba:44). On the contrary, he quite explicitly takes up the notion of
evil existing before knowledge.[20] Before the fateful decision, the tree of
knowledge stood in Eden with the distinction of good and evil intact:
"This incredible irony is the distinguishing feature of the mythic origins
of law" (II:154).

Benjamin is not satisfied with the argument that a rejection of the
universal suffering thesis be understood as a Jewish *Angst vor Schuld,*
"fear of responsibility" (ba:106), as Kierkegaard states: "The Jew falls victim to flight, for what would help would be to transcend the relationship
of fear and institute a real relationship."[21] The rejection of a collective responsibility of the individual is deemed a "Jewish" avoidance of collective
responsibility. For Kierkegaard, Judaism appears here merely as a repeated act of citation rather than a particularity that cannot be subsumed
(ba:73). Benjamin too sought a transformation of the notion of responsibility, but not one understood to be Jewish fear, for which the Jew must
reform himself and take on a "true relationship" to the question.[22] In
contrast to the universalization of suffering proposed by Kierkegaard,
Benjamin universalizes the Jew: "Against the dogma of the natural responsibility of human beings, of original responsibility, whose principle
and insolvable state is constituted by the teachings (doctrine) and its

temporary solution, the ritual of hedonism, genius proposes a vision of the natural innocence of humanity."[23]

In a letter to Scholem from the winter of 1917, he appears concerned with drawing a distinction between Christian and Jewish theology, following a close reading of Adolf von Harnack's history of Christian dogma. He asks Scholem for his thoughts on what might constitute the "essential counterpoints to the Christian concept of religion" from the perspective of Judaism.[24] Benjamin's focus is clearly the dogma of original sin. He puts forward a messianic vision of humanity in a condition of natural innocence in place of a fate determined by suffering.[25] Benjamin tries to offset the partiality that Christianity would impose on ethical reason through a reappraisal of the relationship of responsibility to the individual. Collective responsibility was now to be drawn into a process of resanctification such that the individual's role was not determined by the parameters of free choice and suffering, not immersed in dread but a *Schuldzusammenhang*, i.e., a connection to responsibility rather than collective responsibility, embedded in divine intention, which was to span the length of responsibility until a messianic cancellation of *Schuld* (debt/responsibility) would take place.[26] Although the Messiah releases the enslaved from their chains (as the Jewish morning prayer promises), *Schuld* is not viewed here as the dialectical opposite of innocence, for human activity exists before the onset of messianic time. The unexpected suspension of all activity causes Benjamin to dispense with the notion of necessity between fate and fear. Like Rosenzweig's interpretation of neighborly love,[27] choice and divine intention are integrated such that a freedom-fear dynamic in the concept of *mitzvah* (an obligation/an act of goodness) does not enter the picture.[28] Not fear but judgment provides the messianic transition in Benjamin's theory:

> An order whose sole intrinsic concepts are tragedy and responsibility, and within which there is no conceivable road to liberation . . . such an order cannot be religious, no matter how the misunderstood concept of responsibility appears to point to the contrary. Another sphere must therefore be sought in which unhappiness and responsibility alone carry weight, a scale on which bliss and innocence are found to be too light and float upward. This scale is the scale of law.[29]

This *Ordnung* (order), which corresponds to a liberation from irreligious partiality, impairing responsibility and its relationship to happiness, is not merely the internal decision of the individual, however much the figure of the tragic hero puts forward the vision of a self-initiated decline. An external, even divine dimension is brought into the picture with the image of a scale of law. Law introduces messianic judgment into the equation of character, providing an end point from which the latitude of the individual's responsibility can be measured.[30] The messianic moment would then reveal the natural innocence of the individual, allowing a state of blessedness to return to worldly affairs. Law stands for more than merely the imposition of responsibility and administration of debt here. In its active form, as judgment, it provides a link from law to the *Reiche der Gerechtigkeit* (kingdom of justice).[31] It is the *Ordnung* of law that is, at this point, intertwined with the state of iniquity of humanity, albeit intact with distinct identity. Like Kierkegaard, injustice here is also exposed as "demonic," serving as a radical antithesis of the messianic. It is this "order of law that inaugurates the victory over the demons."[32] Law does not establish a kingdom of justice on earth but rather true law, or right, "maintains itself beyond time," initiating the prestages of a messianic era in that, by its virtue, it determines its "relationship to the gods" ("sich über die Zeit hinaus erhaltnis zu den Göttern"; II:174).

As we have seen in the last section on language, Benjamin formulates a linguistic history of the expulsion from paradise, recovering the insertion of paradisiacal truth in the purity of the judging word. In this history another side of the messianic drama was emphasized. In addition to character, judgment itself bore responsibility for the imposition and restitution of the state of bliss.[33] Judgment was the product of the magic of the judging word, which existed before the expulsion from the garden of God. Adam was therefore, in a sense, fooled by the mythical "origins of law," for although he had no knowledge of the sort, the meaning of good and evil existed before his disobeying divine intention.[34] In fact, a distinction that could have been embodied within the fruit of the tree implies a divine judgment on the difference between good and evil preceding profane knowledge. The outcome of this judgment took the form of the decline of immediacy in language. Yet justice was lodged in the judging word, as we are told, a divine insignia that links our law to the "kingdom of justice" (II:174). This notion is predicated on the division of judgment from justice, as we shall see in the next section.

Worldly and Divine Restitution

A newly discovered text by Benjamin casts light on the importance of the concept of justice for the early political theology. Like many of Benjamin's early writings, "Notes to a Study on the Category of Justice" is only found in Scholem's hand.[35] With each text he received from Benjamin, Scholem diligently made a copy for himself, often transcribing it directly into his journal. On October 8 and 9, 1916, he was to do the same with Benjamin's notes on justice.

Following the chronology of the journal, it seems that discussions on justice took place when Scholem and Benjamin met in August 1916 in Munich, specifically in Seeshaupt, where Scholem visited Benjamin and his future wife, Dora Pollak. Their discussions in Seeshaupt spanned a wide spectrum of topics that included the intellectual journals of the day (*Das Ziel, Der Reich*), Benjamin's letter to Buber rejecting his offer to participate in *Der Jude*,[36] Fredrich Schlegel, a Pindar ode (which Benjamin read aloud in the original), Plato's Symposium, Hegel—all recorded in detail in Scholem's journals.[37] But perhaps most important were those on Judaism. In connection with their emerging critique of Buber's *Erlebnis* mysticism, they began to concern themselves with a broad discussion on the questions of Judaism, Zionism, and justice.[38] The impact on Scholem was substantial, as he recorded that evening in his journals:

> During our time together, we spoke at great length on Judaism: on not going to Palestine, "Agro-Zionism," Ahad Haam, "justice," and especially Buber, of whom little remains after the last four days [of criticism]. . . . It is already clear to me how close Benjamin is to Ahad Haam, which will become clearer with respect to a central point: the conception of the role of "justice" in Judaism.[39]

The discussions during those four days in August concerned many of the central issues that moved young German Jewry at the time: whether Zion is a metaphor or a realizable goal,[40] on Martin Buber and the cultural Zionist Ahad Haam as well as the devotion expressed in the idea of *kiddush hashem*.[41] A day after this first remark on Benjamin and Ahad Haam, Scholem again mentions how "incredibly near" Benjamin was to Ahad Haam "from a spiritual core."[42] "'Agriculture *can* be goyish,'" Scholem quotes (as if originating from Benjamin).[43]

In the aftermath of these discussions, Scholem appears somewhat un-settled by the depth of concern that Benjamin demonstrated for Judaism. Rather underestimating this concern beforehand, he seems surprised at the intensity, interpreting Benjamin's words as expressing a shared conviction. Perhaps the following synopsis captures the centrality as well as the radical nature of Benjamin's occupation with Judaism at this time, in Scholem's perception:

> Benjamin's spirit[44] revolves around myth and will continue to do so. He seeks to approach myth from various sides: history, which begins for him with the Romantics; poetry, which commences with Hölderlin; religion, in which his starting point is Judaism, and with law. "If I ever have a philosophy of my own," he told me, "it will somehow be a philosophy of Judaism."[45]

Scholem himself could not believe his friend's devotion to the same questions that were to move him so deeply: "But I'm going to need to talk with him again about everything he said, once in Berlin."[46] In retrospect, one might be inclined to question the passion that Benjamin expressed on that summer evening of 1916, knowing as we do that he was never to truly consummate these passions in a philosophy of Judaism. If this statement was perceived by Scholem as something of an oath to a common goal, it might just point to the basis upon which Scholem was convinced that Benjamin would ultimately turn his attention to Judaism and make good on his promise. Naturally, he was not to question the integrity of such a state-ment. In fact, he would not only overlook the tensions in Benjamin's com-mitment to Judaism but would rather question his own convictions in this regard:

> Everything that we've discussed intensively together, or as a three-some, leaves me with enough to think about for the whole winter— for my whole life, to construct Zionism anew. And I shouldn't fool myself: if I really want to join Benjamin, I've got to revise things tremendously.[47]

Nearly six weeks after this fateful encounter, Scholem made the follow-ing entry in his journal: "Evening with Benjamin, read together Ahad Haam *al sh'nai ha-sayfim* [*Am Scheideweg*]."[48] Afterward, he received Benjamin's notebook with the "Notes to a Study on the Category of Justice."[49] Following is the complete text:

NOTES TO A STUDY ON THE CATEGORY OF JUSTICE

Every good, limited by structures of time and space, has a possessive character trait that is an expression of its ability to pass away. Possession that is trapped by the same finitude, however, is unjust. For this reason, there is no system of possession, regardless of its type, that leads to justice.

This, however, lies in the conditions of a good that cannot be possessed—a good through which all goods become propertyless.

In the concept of society, one seeks to give a good to a proprietor that is able to transcend its possessive character.

For this reason, every socialist or communist theory falls short of its goal, as the right of every individual extends to every good. If individual A has a need z, which can be satisfied by good x, and, for this reason, it is believed just that a good y, which is the same as x, should be given to individual B to placate the same needs— this is incorrect. There is, namely, the entirely abstract right of the subject to every good on principle, a right that is not based on needs but rather on justice and whose last inclination will not possibly concern the right to possession of the individual but a right to goods of the good.

Justice is the striving to turn the world into the highest good.

These thoughts lead to the supposition that justice is not a virtue like other virtues (humility, neighborly love, loyalty, courage), but rather constitutes a new ethical category, one that should probably no longer be called a category of virtue but a category of virtue in relationship to other categories. Justice appears not to be based upon the good will of the subject but forms the state of the world. Justice refers to the ethical category of the existing, virtue the ethical category of the demanded. While virtue can be demanded, justice, in the end, can only be the state of the world or the state of God. In God all virtues take the form of justice—the byword *all* in i.e., all-true, all-knowing, points to this. While virtuous can only be the fulfillment of that which is demanded, righteous is the guarantee of that which exists (through demands that are perhaps no longer determinable but are nevertheless not of the ordinary kind).

Justice is the ethical side of the struggle. Justice is the power of virtue and virtue of power. The responsibility for the world that we share is shielded from the instance of justice.

Our father: do not lead us into temptation, redeem us from evil, a kingdom becomes [two words are illegible], is the request for justice, for the just state of the world. The single, empirical act is related to moral law as an (undefinable) fulfillment of a formal schema. The right to justice, by contrast, is related to the schema of fulfillment. The great impasse of knowledge extending between law and justice is captured by other languages:

ius	themis	mishpat
fas	dike	zedek

The problem of historical time is already presented in the original form of historical counting of time. Years are countable but in contrast to most countable things, cannot be numbered.

NOTIZEN ZU EINER ARBEIT ÜBER DIE KATEGORIE DER GERECHTIGKEIT

Jedem Gute, als in der Zeit- und Raumordnung eingeschränktem, kommt Besitzcharakter als Ausdruck seiner Vergänglichkeit zu. Der Besitz aber, als in der gleichen Endlichkeit befangen, ist immer ungerecht. Daher kann auch keine wie immer geartete Besitzordnung zur Gerechtigkeit führen.

Vielmehr liegt diese in der Bedingung eines Gutes, das nicht Besitz sein kann. Dies ist allein das Gute, durch das die Güter besitzlos werden.

Im Begriff der Gesellschaft versucht man, dem Gut einen Besitzer zu geben, welcher seinen Besitzcharakter aufhebt.

Jede sozialistische oder kommunistische Theorie verfehlt ihr Ziel deshalb, weil der Anspruch des Individuums auf jedes Gut sich erstreckt. Liegt bei einem Individuum A ein Bedürfnis z vor, das durch das Gut x befriedigt werden kann, und glaubt man daher, ein Gut y, welches gleich x ist, einem Individuum B zur Stillung des

gleichen Bedürfnisses gerechterweise geben zu sollen und zu dürfen, so irrt man. Es gibt nämlich den ganz abstrakten Anspruch des
Subjekts prinzipiell auf jedes Gut, ein Anspruch, der keineswegs
auf Bedürfnisse, sondern auf Gerechtigkeit sich zurückführt, und
dessen letzte Richtung möglicherweise nicht auf ein Besitzrecht der
Person, sondern auf ein Guts-Recht des Gutes geht.

Gerechtigkeit ist das Streben, die Welt zum höchsten Gut zu
machen.

Die angedeuteten Gedanken führen zur Vermutung: Gerechtigkeit ist nicht eine Tugend neben anderen Tugenden (Demut,
Nächstenliebe, Treue, Tapferkeit), sondern sie begründet eine
neue ethische Kategorie, die man vielleicht nicht einmal eine Kategorie der Tugend, sondern eine der Tugend gleichgeordnete andere Kategorie wird nennen müssen. Gerechtigkeit scheint sich
nicht auf den guten Willen des Subjekts zu beziehen, sondern
macht einen Zustand der Welt aus, Gerechtigkeit bezeichnet die
ethische Kategorie des Existenten, Tugend die ethische Kategorie
des Geforderten. Tugend kann gefordert werden, Gerechtigkeit
letzten Endes nur sein, als Zustand der Welt oder als Zustand
Gottes. In Gott haben alle Tugenden die Form der Gerechtigkeit,
das Beiwort all in all-gültig, all-wissend u. a. deutet darauf hin.
Tugendhaft kann nur Erfüllung des Geforderten, gerecht nur
Gewährleistung des Existenten (durch Forderungen *vielleicht nicht*
mehr zu bestimmenden, dennoch natürlich nicht eines beliebigen) sein.

Gerechtigkeit ist die ethische Seite des Kampfes, Gerechtigkeit
ist die Macht der Tugend und die Tugend der Macht. Die Verant-
wortung gegen die Welt, die wir haben, bewahrt vor der Instanz
der Gerechtigkeit.

Die Bitte des Vaterunser: Führe uns nicht in Versuchung,
sondern erlöse uns von dem Übel, *ein Reich werde[,] [zwei Wörter*
unleserlich], ist die Bitte um Gerechtigkeit, um den gerechten
Weltzustand. Die empirische einzelne Tat verhält sich zum Sit-
tengesetz irgendwie als (undeduzierbare) Erfüllung des formalen
Schemas. Umgekehrt verhält sich das Recht zur Gerechtigkeit, wie
das Schema zur Erfüllung. Die ungeheure Kluft, die zwischen
Recht und Gerechtigkeit dem Wesen nach klafft, haben andere
Sprachen bezeichnet.

ius	themis	mishpat
fas	dike	zedek

Das Problem der historischen Zeit ist bereits durch die eigentüm-
liche Form der historischen Zeitrechnung gestellt. Die Jahre sind
zählbar, aber zum Unterschied von den meisten Zählbaren, nicht
numerierbar.

Benjamin opens his treatise on justice with a statement that explores
the proximity of the word *good* in an ethical sense to the word *goods* in a
material sense.[50] Every ethical good or good (e), to the degree that it is an
earthly good, a profane good, and not of the divine, contains within itself
its earthly limitation: it exists within a temporal and physical framework.
This is the possessive character of its worldly existence, its *Besitzcharakter*,
a quality embodied within the concept of a profane good. Because it is limited to the finite, it is constituted, as all moral things, to decline. It is therefore a profane good within time and not beyond it. Should however the
quadrants of history come to an end, should this good (e) no longer be re-
strained by temporal and physical limitations, then it can no longer remain
a good (e) in a worldly, civic sense.

This possessive character, which was described as part of every ethical good (e), is part of it by nature of its profane existence. Thus, because
possession is trapped by the very same limitations as the notions of property in the material world (since it would be absurd to speak of possession in the divine world), all things profane are by their nature deemed
unjust. It must also be assumed with this definition that justice is an attribute of the divine, for only then would the divine appear to be the
image of pure justice, and possession essentially profane and unjust.
"Property is theft!" is perhaps the boldest of statements declared by a
French parliamentarian.[51] The injustice of the profane is inherent in the
unjust distribution of possession. For this reason, there can never truly
be a relation of property that is just or that can lead toward justice. This
is the nature of a good (e), which cannot be identified with possession,
beyond its possessive character, which can neither possess nor naturally
be possessed.

Benjamin presents here a notion of "a good [e] through which all
goods [m] become propertyless," a good (e) that is able to unleash property from possession and rescind the ownership of all things. At this stage

in the text we do not have a messianic calling but rather an ethical good that is able to renounce ownership for itself. However, the renunciation of the possessive character of all profane things is, in fact, an ethical good that is capable of returning all things to their rightful "divine" owner. If one is to understand by this an ethical good that is to usher in a "spiritual restitutio in integrum,"[52] we would then actually be dealing with a good that, in its fulfillment, plays a role in the unfolding of a messianic era.

In social and worldly terms one would seek, by this messianic good, a "possessor" capable of lifting off its own possessive character and allowing its own transcendence with regard to the material. But every socialist theory heretofore has been unable to identify this pursuit, says Benjamin, and in this way failed to achieve its goals. This failure is due to a critical misunderstanding: that the claims of the individual to a particular good cannot be defined merely by the needs of a given individual but must be understood in such a way that each individual has a rightful claim to every good. This can be seen in the example of an individual whose needs are satisfied by a good that is unable to satisfy a second individual, even in the case where the needs appear to be the same. If a rightful claim of every individual can be made to every good (m), then the relationship of a good (m) to a good (e) would point to property relations beyond property itself, where the whole nature of possession finds itself suspended indefinitely. As the last example suggests, the equation of individual needs cannot prove to supersede rightful claims that are, in themselves, a priori "abstract" claims of every individual to every good, claims that are not based on needs but on a concept of justice beyond worldly domain, abstract in divine intention.

Justice for which one can strive is here seen not only as the striving for the highest ethical good but also for the highest material good. This is phased simply: "Justice is the striving to turn the world into the highest good." If there is an allusion to a scholastic summum bonum in this phrase, it would be based on the notion of an abstract and divine good in contrast to a worldly and concrete good, for which a conception of the complete, abstract good would serve as a model. It is in this context that Benjamin moves to the question of ethical categories in order to distinguish justice from other virtues such as humility, neighborly love, loyalty, and bravery. More than the quality of character, justice is seen to constitute "a new ethical category," as was seen in the discussion of Kierkegaard on original sin. The "new ethical category" here is comparable to virtue.

This new virtue is not based simply on the "goodwill" of the individual but rather on the condition of the world.

Here Benjamin draws a distinction between justice and virtue. If justice is to refer to the ethical category of that which *is existing*, of worldly affairs, then virtue would stand for the ethical category of those or that which *is demanded*. Justice would here be conceived in the profane, while virtue strives for the abstract good in the category of the existing, as a demand of the living or a challenge to the divine. Whether justice is that which forms the ethical category of the living because of its abstractness or because of, say the contested number of righteous people that prop up the entire world through their *mitzvot* (good deeds/obligations), embedded in the profane, is difficult to determine.[53] Certain here is that justice represents being, either reflecting the "state of the world or the state of God." Virtue—in contrast to the metaphor of matter—can be created and *can be destroyed* and is therefore a matter of demands, of those or that which pushes something forward (*gefordert*), most likely those supporting a certain trajectory, seeking worldly redemption and repentance; certainly all the qualities that make up "the profane order of the profane in the coming of the messianic kingdom," as we saw in the fragment, that is, as virtuous action concerns the profane world.

In the divine realm, in God, all virtue takes the form of justice (whereas if one says "all virtuous actions," one is left with the question whether there is any motion in the divine kingdom). Justice is thus the byword for the *all* in the terms *all-knowing, all-righteous,* says Benjamin.[54] Virtue, by contrast, remains in the realm of demands, of the ethical work of the profane, justified by the defense of the living and the fulfillment of pure, worldly demands. Justice is the ethical dimension of this worldly "struggle." The shared responsibility in relation to the world is preserved in the moment of judgment, the application of the power of justice.

The last section of this text begins with an example of a call to justice, for a righteous state of the world, drawn in explicitly Christian terms: Our father, do not lead us into temptation, redeem us from evil.[55] The single empirical act is related to moral law as an irreducible completion of its formal schema. There could not be moral law without its fulfillment in action. The opposite is the case with law or right to justice. Right is related to justice as a schema to its fulfillment in the sense that justice is the completion of a plan embedded in right. But this, nevertheless, still leaves us with an abyss between right or law on one side and justice on the other. The essence of this difference is expressed in many languages, says Benjamin, giving the following examples without an explanation:

ius	themis	mishpat
fas	dike	tzedek

In this initial comparison we see a lineage of trouble in the distinction between divine and profane.[56] Just as the word *law* is often confused with *justice* in colloquial usage, we see in these words the unmediated integration of divine judgment and profane right, profane law and divine justice. It is highly probable that Benjamin sought to address the correlation of terms in this linguistic schema at some point in the future. However, his notes on justice conclude here without further explanation.

Following the treatise on justice, a final paragraph appears to have been added to the main body of text.[57] Whether it concerns the problem of historical time and its relationship to justice or to the previous linguistic analysis is not clear.[58] Its connection appears to lie in Benjamin's study of messianic time: the problem of historical time, he states, is already present in the standard measurement of time itself. While years are indeed countable, in contrast to most countable things cannot be numbered; in short, while the messianic is temporal, it is not lineal. To this final statement we may add confirmation from Scholem on the nature of the discussion of August 1916:

> We spent a whole afternoon on one difficult remark: although a range of years may be countable, it cannot be numbered. This brought us to counting [in the sense of time], number sequence, and especially . . . direction. Is there direction within counting? "Direction is two objects of different lines" . . . Time is surely passing, but is it directed? For it is a completely metaphysical assumption that time is, as it were, straight.[59]

Scholem was to formulate the question in mathematical terms: if the definition of a direction is based on two masses extending upon the same line, then time would have a direction as a straight line. However, if time proves to have pockets and loopholes, disjointed moments and repeated fragments, then years may lend themselves to be strung together such that they bear coherence but not necessarily numerical order. In fact, we regularly formulate time tables of various sizes and meanings that count time in non-numerical ways.[60]

The restitution of the division of the divine and profane begins to take shape in Benjamin's initial formulation on justice: first in material goods and the highest ethical good, then between individual needs and the collective needs of each individual, and finally the ambiguity of a fallen language in law and justice, where justice is ultimately ascribed to the divine. Scholem's own speculations on the meaning of the latter itself begins with the following notes on the discussion with Benjamin:

> To be read, Baader: *Theory of Sacrifice.* Different meanings of sacrifice and infringement in mythology and Judaism. In the former, the congregation of God is immediacy for which individuals will be killed. In Judaism, since only the individual is killed, *the "turn" begins.* In mythological hedonism law is the highest form, in Judaism it is justice. What is most important is that, in Hebrew, *mishpat* and *tz'dakah*, come from totally different roots. Mishpat does not reveal itself (Isaiah 58), only tz'dakah does. Law and justice are two completely different things. *The essence of Judaism is justice.* A divine category. Christianity wanted to remake the space that is Judaism through three coordinates: belief, love, hope; if Judaism can be penetrated as a point penetrates space, it is always relegated to a lower dimension. In Judaism one does not believe, one is simply righteous. In this sense the Jewish "act" is to be taken as completing space.[61]

While a close reading of Baader's *Theorie des Opfers* seems to offer less than Scholem hoped for in terms of the concept of sacrifice (far less than Kierkegaard, for example), the discussion here of Judaism, of the distinction in the concept of the individual in the face of divine justice, apparently led the discussion. Whereas in hedonism worldly right is understood as the highest good, justice is the highest state in this conception of Judaism. The division of mishpat from tzedek (or tz'dakah) comprises the cornerstone of Scholem's views on justice, as the next section will show. Here mishpat is associated with law, tz'dakah with prophetic justice, originating from on high. Divine tz'dakah reflects the essence of Judaism, worldly tz'dakah the act that is contrasted to the Christian call to faith. And the link between the act and the messianic era is suggested in the fulfillment of the spatial realm in the act of tz'dakah in the profane.[62]

Theses on the Concept of Justice

In addition to the notes we have on the discussions on justice from 1916, an unbound, hand-written text from the Scholem archives in Jerusalem may help shed light on the concept of justice in these early debates.[63] The unpublished document, entitled "Thesen über den Begriff der Gerechtigkeit" (Theses on the Concept of Justice), is divided into two parts, with the first appearing to be a direct commentary on Benjamin's notes on the category of justice, following rather systematically the formulations and propositions in Benjamin's text. There are two dates, in Scholem's hand, written at the top of the page: 1919 and 1925. The first part appears to have been written either in conjunction with the transcription of Benjamin's text in October 1916, or, indeed, as late as 1919; the second part was probably written later, most likely after Scholem's own text on Jonah (1919), Benjamin's "Critique of Violence" (1921), and possibly as late as 1925.[64] A portion may have been read to Walter and Dora Benjamin by Scholem in Switzerland.[65] The following is a translation of the "Theses" and the first publication of the German original:

> *Theses on the Concept of Justice*
>   A
>   1) It is impossible to arrive at a concept of justice from the realm of the *theory of goods*. Regardless of its form, justice in the distribution of goods cannot be realized, even as an idea. *Every good* in the perceivable world has a possessive character trait as an "index of its temporality," as an expression of its ability to pass away. The possessive character trait of all goods is *objective*, meaning that there is an *absolute* right of *each* individual to *every* good. This truly fundamental right makes every definition of justice illusory within a socialist or communist distribution system which hopes to eliminate the possessive character of goods either through the fictitious anonymity of its possessor (that is, society!) or by avoiding the immanent catastrophe of this right through a foundationless theory of the "justified needs" of the individual.

2) The concept of relative justified needs must be stricken from ethics as chimerical. Theoretically no measure of justification can be proposed which would not be incidental (one which would be arbitrary linked to a particular level of consciousness: say, for example, the harmonious education of humanity). It had to be said that the catastrophic nature of the right to possession, defined, as above, by the essence of time, is rendered no less extreme by *practical* economic theory.

3) Justice is not a virtue, (where V [virtue] defines the ethical category of the *demanded*) but rather (provisionally) the C [category] of the ethically *existing*. For this reason, all virtue takes on the form of justice in God (the little word "all" in the theory of attributes points to this).

Truth is not a mover—it is deeply unrevolutionary. Revolutionary are those positions whose demands are absurd (objectively) and obvious (subjectively). But truth is limited by its ironic appearance (which is the only moving force).

4) Justice as a demand is the virtue of violence—the most revolutionary and catastrophic of all demands. Virtue has, in particular, an *individual* subject; the humble have a clear, uncomplicated relationship to humility. The subject of *violence*—which is a more complex phenomenon as virtue—is however as an individual *only* symbolic; the true, non-symbolic proprietor of violence is anonymous: society. The demand, which is *necessarily* directed to the proprietor of violence, thus expects a virtue in justice, which, from the viewpoint of ethics, has no subject. Symbolic forms are not attributable to virtues. In this way, the demand, which is a sublime irony, only prevails in a fundamental catastrophe of violence through which revolutionary politics are determined. It is not determined in a non ironic connection to religion.

5) In this sense, justice can be defined, albeit unsatisfactory, as the attempt to make the world into the highest good.

B) The concept of justice finds its true context in the philosophy of religion. This concept should be the easiest to find in the context of the theory of law and its borders with religion.

1) Judgment is possible. For every act of human judgment, there is a corresponding execution of judgment which *transcends*

it. (Banal!) Between judgment and execution, a fundamental impasse exists (myth of the legal system!)

Divine Judgment is also its own execution.

2) Every human action elicits a divine judgment about itself with absolute certainty.

3) Justice is the idea of the historical annihilation of divine judgment; just are those actions which neutralize divine judgment over itself. The idea of divine judgment over the world means: the Last Judgment. Every sphere, in which the appearance of divine judgment is indefinitely postponed, is justice—the indifference to the Last Judgment.

4) Messianic is the kingdom that is not followed by a Last Judgment. For this reason, the prophets demand justice: so that the L. J. [Last Judgment] is finally eliminated. The messianic is established *directly* upon righteous actions.

Messianic time as eternal present and justice as becoming, as substantial, are related. If justice was not *present*, the messianic kingdom would not only not be present, but impossible. Justice (like all other central concepts in Judaism) is not a conceptual limit, not a "regulating notion."

5) "From what the sages call the world to come, it cannot be understood that the world to come is not yet here, that it will come only after the decline of this world. This is not the meaning, but that the world to come is continuously becoming" (Maimonides). And the mystics, where they have not fallen prey to the political revolutionary-ism of the apocalyptics (the politicians of Judaism), define the messianic kingdom with infinite precision as the "world, which is continuously arriving"—the eternal present.

6) Prophecy is the vision of the eternal now. It becomes comical when it meets up with an empirical now. (Jonah)

7) Human actions form a whole. A space can be saved with great effort for ethically relevant actions. Saved from what? From violence, which can be termed 'myth.' Almost all realms of human action are subject to mythical categories, from which fate alone attributes meaning. *Justice is the elimination of fate from action.* The righteous act has neither fate nor meaning. The nonsymbolism of an action—the destruction of appearance which alone attributes meaning—turns the act into a justified one.

8) *Postponement* and *transformation* are both constituents of the righteous act, death and the birth of the righteous. The act of transformation, e.g., the rebirth of the ineffectual act, is true evil, the unjust act, which is identifiable by its singularity. The injustice of our lives is manifested in the abundance of singular and fate-bound actions in living.

9) To allow the messianic world to break through, the perspective of redemption needs only a *virtual* shift. "The messianic world will look exactly like this one, just a little different." This virtual shift from the center of our lives is the most difficult. The apocalyptic depiction of the messianic kingdom has the value and truth of revolutionary propaganda—it tries to invoke the final conflict of violence in which myth declines. The character of the Messiah represents the redemptive and therefore catastrophic power of life without fate. His personality, in an individual sense, is political irony that is effective solely in a world in which the voice of god, the bearer of justice and the unmetaphorical object of the just life is perceptible only in silence.

10) Justice bridges the abyss which stretches between judgment and execution. In God, whose essence—to the degree that we may inquire into it—is turned toward the world and manifested in divine judgment, is this abyss closed.

THESEN ÜBER DEN BEGRIFF DER GERECHTIGKEIT

A

1) Es ist unmöglich zu einem Begriff der Gerechtigkeit zu gelangen aus dem Bezirk der *Güterlehre* heraus. Gerechtigkeit als Verteilung von Gütern, in welcher Art immer, läßt sich auch als Idee nicht realisieren. *Jedem* Gut der sichtbaren Welt kommt als "Index seiner Zeitlichkeit", als Ausdruck seiner Vergänglichkeit, Besitzcharakter zu. Dieser Besitzcharakter der Güter ist *objektiv*, das heißt: Es besteht ein *absoluter* Anspruch *jedes* In[d]ividuums auf *jedes* Gut. Dieser, höchst fundamentale, Anspruch ist es, der jede Definition der Gerechtigkeit innerhalb eines sozialistischen oder kommunistischen Systems der Güterverteilung illusorisch macht, das hofft den Besitzcharakter der Güter entweder durch eine fingierte Anonymität ihres Inhabers (nämlich der *Gesellschaft*!) aufheben zu können, oder durch eine bodenlose Theorie

der "berechtigen Bedürfnisse" des Individuums seiner immanenten Katastrophalität zu entgehen.[66]

2) Der Begriff von, relativen, berechtigten Bedürfnissen ist als chimärisch aus der Ethik zu streichen. Theoretisch läßt sich kein Maßstab dieser Berechtigung angeben, der nicht zufällig wäre (d.h. zum Beispiel an gewisse Bewusstsseinstadien völlig *willkürlich* gebunden wäre, wie etwa der der harmonischen Ausbildung der Humanität). Behauptet werden muß, daß die katastrophale Natur des Besitzanspruches, der, wie gesagt, im Wesen der Zeit begründet ist, durch keine *praktische* ökonomische Theorie gemildert wird.

3) Gerechtigkeit ist keine Tugend (wobei T[ugend] die ethische Kategorie des *Geforderten* bezeichnet), sondern etwa (vorläufig) die K[ategorie] des ethisch Existenten. Daher alle Tugenden in Gott die Form der Gerechtigkeit annehmen, (das Wörtchen "all-" in der Attributenlehre deutet darauf hin).

Die Wahrheit bewegt nichts, sie ist tief unrevolutionär. Revolutionär sind diejenigen Haltungen, deren Forderungen absurd (objektiv) und einleuchtend (subjektiv) sind, aber die Wahrheit durch deren ironische Darstellung (die allein *bewegend* wirkt) limitiert.

4) Gerechtigkeit als Forderung ist die Tugend der Gewalt. Sie ist die revolutionärste und katastrophalste aller Forderungen. Tugend nämlich hat einen *individuellen* Träger, der Demütige steht in einem eindeutigen, unkomplizierten, Verhältnis zur Demut. Der Träger der *Gewalt* dagegen—die ein viel tieferes Phänomen als die Tugend ist—ist als Individuum *nur* symbolisch, da der eigentliche, unsymbolische Inhaber der Gewalt anonym ist: die Gesellschaft. Die Forderung, die *notwendig* an den Inhaber der Gewalt gerichtet wird, verlangt also in der Gerechtigkeit eine Tugend, die im Sinne der Ethik keinen Träger hat. Symbolischen Figuren kommen Tugenden nicht zu. So läßt sich diese Forderung, die eine erhabene Ironie ist, nur in einer fundamentalen Katastrophe der Gewalt durchsetzen. In ihr, nicht in dem unironischen Zusammenhang der Religion, bestimmt sich revolutionäre Politik.

5) In diesem Sinn läßt sich, *durchaus* unbefriedigend, von der Ethik aus, Gerechtigkeit als das Verhalten definieren, das die Welt zum höchsten Gut macht.

B) Der Begriff der Gerechtigkeit gewinnt seinen wahren Zusammenhang in der Religionsphilosophie. Es dürfte am leichtesten sein, Zugang zu diesem Begriffszusammenhang aus der Rechtslehre und ihrer Grenze zur Religion hin zu suchen.

1) Es ist möglich zu urteilen. Dem Urteil des menschlichen Gerichts entspricht, ihm *transzendent,* eine Exekutive dieses Urteils. (Banal!) Zwischen Urteil und Exekutive besteht ein fundamentaler Abgrund. (Mythologie der Rechtsordnung!)

Das *Gottesurteil* ist dasjenige Urteil, das seine eigene Vollstreckung ist.

2) *Jede* Handlung des Menschen excitiert[67] mit absoluter Sicherheit ein Gottesurteil über sie.

3) Gerechtigkeit ist die Idee der historischen Annihilation des Gottesurteils, und gerecht ist diejenige Tat, die das Gottesurteil über sie neutralisiert, indem sie es aufschiebt. Die Idee des Gottesurteils über die Welt heißt: Jüngstes Gericht. Jene Sphäre, in der der Eintritt des jüngsten Gerichtes unendlich aufgeschoben wird, ist die der Gerechtigkeit, der Indifferenz des jüngsten Gerichts.

4) Messianisch ist das Reich, auf das kein jüngstes Gericht folgt. Darum fordern die Propheten Gerechtigkeit: um das j[üngste] G[ericht] unendlich zu eliminieren. In den gerechten Handlungen wird das Messianische *unmittelbar* aufgerichtet.

Die messianische Zeit als ewige Gegenwart und die Gerechtigkeit als Daseiendes, Substantielles, entsprechen sich. Wäre Gerechtigkeit nicht *da,* wäre auch das messianische Reich nicht nur ebenfalls nicht da, sondern unmöglich. Gerechtigkeit (wie alle anderen Zentralideen des Judentums) ist kein Grenzbegriff, keine "regulative Idee".

5) "Was die Weisen die kommende Welt nennen, das hat seinen Grund nicht etwa darin, daß diese kommende Welt nicht jetzt schon vorhanden wäre, daß erst nach dem Vergehen dieser Welt jene käme. So verhält sich die Sache nicht, sondern jene Welt ist beständig daseiend". (Maimonides) Und die Mystiker, wo sie nicht dem politischen Revolutionarismus der Apokalyptiker (der Politiker des Judentums) verfallen sind, definieren das messianische Reich mit unendlicher Genauigkeit als "die Welt, die ständig kommt"—die ewige Gegenwart.

6) Prophetie ist Weissagung über die ewige Gegenwart. Sie wird zum Witz, wo sie die empirische betrifft (Jona).

7) Die Handlungen des Menschen bilden ein Ganzes. Unter fürchterlichen Krämpfen ist ein Gebiet, das der ethisch relevanten Handlungen, abgerungen worden. Wem? Der Gewalt, die man 'Mythos' zu nennen pflegt. Fast alle Bezirke des menschlichen Handelns unterstehen noch immer den mythischen Kategorien, allen voran dem Schicksal, das Bedeutung verleiht. *Gerechtigkeit ist die Elimination des Schicksals aus den Handlungen.* Die gerechte Tat ist schicksalslos und bedeutet nichts. Das unsymbolische an einer Handlung, die Vernichtung des *Scheins*, welcher Bedeutung allein verleiht, macht sie zur gerechten.

8) *Aufschub* und *Verwandlung* sind die beiden Konstituenten der gerechten Tat, der Tod und die Geburt des Gerechten. Die der Verwandelung, d. i. der Wiedergeburt unfähige Tat ist die eigentlich böse, *ungerechte* Tat, die an ihrer Singularität erkennbar ist. Die Ungerechtigkeit unseres Lebens manifestiert sich in der Fülle singulärer und schicksalhafter Handlungen in ihm.

9) Die messianische Welt hervorbrechen zu lassen, die Perspektive der Erlösung erfordert nur eine virtuelle Verschiebung. "Die messianische Welt wird genau so aussehen wie diese, nur ein ganz klein wenig anders". Diese *virtuelle* Verschiebung des Zentrums unseres Lebens ist die schwerste. Die apokalyptische Ausmalung des messianischen Reichs hat den Wert und die Wahrheit revolutionärer Propaganda—sie sucht den letzten Konflikt der Gewalt hervorzurufen, in der der Mythos untergeht. In der Person des Messias ist die katastrophale, weil erlösende, Macht des schicksaallosen [sic] Lebens dargestellt, seine *Persönlichkeit* im individuellen Sinn ist politische Ironie, welche *allein* in einem Weltzeitalter *wirkt*, in dem die Stimme Gottes, des Trägers der Gerechtigkeit und unmetaphorischen Gegenstandes des gerechten Lebens, nur aus dem Schweigen heraus vernehmbar ist.

10) Die Gerechtigkeit füllt den Abgrund aus, der zwischen Urteil und Vollstreckung klafft; In Gott, dessen Wesen, soweit es *erfragbar* d.h. hier: der Welt zugekehrt ist, im Gottesurteil sich manifestiert, ist dieser Abgrund geschlossen.

In Scholem's first thesis we find him attempting to pinpoint the school of thought from which Benjamin's discussion originates. However, a short review of the concept of justice seems to suggest once again to what degree Benjamin drew only marginally from other sources. The *Güterlehre* (theory of good) beginning with the ancient Greeks appears to provide only the most basic groundwork for a notion of justice: *The Republic* offers the most general definitions in the *techne* of justice and injustice leading to a discourse on the state; Aristotle's *Nicomachean Ethics* may set the stage to the degree that he establishes the question whether justice is the practice of perfect virtue and its determination through the categories of distributive and remedial (or corrective) justice.[68] However, Scholem's attempt to locate Benjamin's text in the tradition of the *Güterlehre*[69] may more likely reflect the enthusiasm of the younger discussion partner rather than any immanent or pivotal connection.[70]

Next Scholem moves to the difference between the concept of justice and the distribution of goods. He remarks that it is impossible to arrive at justice through the theory of what is good (*Güterlehre*). A concept of justice cannot be reduced to the fair distribution of goods—the distributive cannot approach the abstract "idea" of justice itself. Thus every material good in the profane world can be read as having embedded within it a temporal index that functions just as an insignia would, yet here expressing the finite quality of worldly goods. It seems that whereas Benjamin attempts to bend the meaning of the words "good" and "goods," Scholem's commentary can be understood as a more linear discussion of the material dimension of goods. For Scholem, the "possessive character" of every material good is "objective" to the degree that its objective nature justifies the rightful claims of every individual to every material good. He identifies the objective nature of the possessive character of things as that which insures the right of each individual to every thing. Possession is that which signifies their objectivity despite the fact that it becomes actual only in its individuality, i.e., the collective possession of each individual. And the emphasis on the singular aspect of this objective claim is key, for it is deemed the dominant problem in the notion of justice in socialist or communist systems. While their notions of justice concentrate on the attempt to universalize the distributive idea, justice wanders into the oblivion of possession.[71] While the task of transcending the possessive character of goods is either hoisted onto "society" as such or upon the individual based on a figurative needs structure, neither plan is ultimately able to address the possessive character of material goods, nor the abstract idea of justice, he states. A formulation of the distributive notion continues in the second thesis, where the concept of "relative" justified needs is refused as an ethical category: while the right of ownership is measured by its relation to time, the possessive character cannot be transcended through a "practical economic theory." This is due to the fact that the possessive character of things are objective-individual and not relative, needs-based universal. The nullification of its possessive character can therefore only be sought outside the framework of the profane.

"Walter Benjamin defines justice as the will to make the world the highest good," comments Scholem in his journal notebook, drawing on Samson Raphael Hirsch's commentary on Genesis, "there is an old Jewish saying: *tzadikim yashkinu shekhinah ba-aretz,*" the righteous allow the Shekhinah to reside upon the earth.[72] When we read in the theses that justice is not a virtue but a call or demand of the ethically existing, Scholem clearly echoes Benjamin's distinction and terminology. But Scholem introduces a variation on this call or demand, one that can be described in the variations on the word for justice in Hebrew, from *tzedek* to *tzadik* and *tz'-dakah*. If tzedek is first to represent justice, with the meaning of a state of righteousness linked to divine intention, the second, *tzadik* would be the practice of right, i.e., he or she who practices worldly justice or the righteous practice of tz'dakah. From divine tzedek to tz'dakah, the practice of the righteous (righteousness/charity), is a lineage of divine to profane. While tzedek is found in absolute form in God, tz'dakah is the practice of worldly agency, conceived in the image of the divine. Virtue finds its absolute model as divine justice in a theory of attributes.

Although Scholem has yet to articulate this lineage here, he does take up the debate with Benjamin on mishpat and tzedek in his journals, as we have seen above (tag I:392). He enters into a discussion of the absolute divine in contrast to worldly agency in the form of revolution. Justice is coupled with truth to the degree that it is not a practiced virtue. Truth, like justice, does nothing; at best, it just is. Truth is "deeply unrevolutionary," he writes. What is revolutionary is something that causes, or aims to cause, a radical, worldly transformation; in a critical moment its perspective is formally "absurd" but, at the same time, "illuminating." It is truth that portrays the ironic in the limiting movement of all revolutionary forces, whereas the absolute is that which indeed makes revolution possible:

"Truth is limited by its ironic appearance (which it the only moving force)."

Scholem turns here to the means of revolution: *Gewalt* (authority/violence).[73] Scholem treats the latter in the context of Benjamin's formulation of the virtue of power and the power of virtue. By this he understands the means of justice as a demand—i.e., tz'dakah as a worldly goal is the virtue of Gewalt. Justice is therefore "the most revolutionary and catastrophic" of all demands. The catastrophic emerges from the fact that the will to divine justice in the profane seeks an immanent revolutionary transformation of the world through the messianic act. On one hand, the redemption of the world is its virtue; on the other, its revolutionary, cataclysmic vision demands Gewalt. Virtue itself is carried by individuals in the self-assured image of the *tzadikim* (righteous). It is they who stand in an uncomplicated relationship to humility and are implicitly the symbol of virtue. Their relationship to those who demand authority/violence, however, is purely "symbolic," in the same way that authority/violence is to the demands of the individual. While the application of revolutionary Gewalt must have a claim to virtue at its disposal, so long as it is attributed to the individual its claim can never be absolute. The only true possessor of authority/violence, concludes Scholem, is the collective.

Thus there are two paired categories that remain abstract to the individual and his or her actions: authority/violence, which is retained in the collective, as well as truth/justice, which is represented symbolically in the profane. From this tension the demands and actions of the individual for justice are, in effect, calls for virtues that are attributes of an ethical authority and, therefore, in a word, an ethics. This new ethics calls for a justice that can only be established through authority/violence. In the final thesis of the first part of this text, it is no longer sufficient to define justice from the perspective of ethical behavior, from virtuous action in which the world is transformed to the summum bonum, the highest good in and of itself. The good is dependent on truth, which, like justice, requires a divine and a symbolic form.

The second part of the "Theses" moves slightly beyond the themes outlined in Benjamin's notes and Scholem's commentary to them here. The implications of a theory of justice is brought into the realm of the philosophy of religion through the categories in the first part. But whereas, in the first part, the idea of the abstract-divine is a given, the second part explores the implications of such an assumption, comprising a further ten theses. It is quite probable this second part was written several years after the first, even possibly late in life.[74] For this reason, we shall break off from the text here in order to introduce ideas that appear to have exerted an influence upon it and rejoin with a short synopsis in the final section.

THE JUSTICE OF PROPHECY

Another newly published text in Scholem's archival papers is a short essay entitled "Über Jona und den Begriff der Gerechtigkeit," (On Jonah and the Concept of Justice). Written more than two years after the transcription of Benjamin's "Notes to a Study on the Category of Justice," it appears that Scholem continued to formulate a notion of justice that drew and expanded upon Benjamin's initial, materialistic reflections on the relationship between good and goods. It is, however, unclear whether Benjamin was familiar with this text when Scholem composed it in Switzerland. Several years later, in December 1924, Benjamin certainly received a copy from Ernst Simon, although it is possible that he may have already been in possession of the text.[75] In "On Jonah and the Concept of Justice" Scholem turns to the idea of a prophetic notion of justice, informed by Jonah, Isaiah, and Job, as well as the juridical precepts of the Psalms. As in the first part of his "Theses on the Concept of Justice," Scholem concludes this text with twelve theses on prophetic justice that appear to form the foundation of the second part of the "Theses," written no earlier than January 1921, and perhaps many years later.[76] Several of the statements in the second part of the "Theses" appear to be transcriptions with slight changes of the theses that conclude the discourse on Jonah.[77] Moreover, the Hebrew categories that form a central part of the discussion—tzedek and mishpat—not only correspond to Benjamin's speculation toward the end of his text but were to appear again in Scholem's late essay "Die Lehre vom 'Gerechten' in der jüdischen Mystik" ("The Teachings of the 'Just" in Jewish Mysticism"), thus pointing again to Scholem's lifelong commitment to the early political theology.[78]

In the discourse on Jonah justice is understood as the central concern of the prophets. But, in contrast to the others, the paradoxical event is deemed "key to the understanding of the prophetic idea" itself.[79] Both the major and minor voices of the prophets are either articulating the word of God, imploring for repentance, or prophesying the meaning of time. Ful-

filling these tasks with both pedagogical and didactic meaning, Jonah attempts to circumvent the "immortality of the divine word" as the plot
seeks to transcend the finite expression of divine prophecy.[80] The prophets
offer the ultimate form of Jewish instruction in that their prophetic teachings reveal a glimpse of the true nature of "the order of the righteous," says
Scholem. The didactic character of the text is itself deemed a prophetic category.[81] But the pedagogical ensues not from the word of the prophet, as is
the case with the other narratives, but from "the greater problem inaugurated by divine postponement."[82] For this reason Jonah's prophecy plays a
crucial, liturgical role in Judaism, Scholem explains, as a result of the revelation of divine postponement that transpires.[83]

The turning point in the concept of justice occurs at the outset, at the
moment when the city of Nineveh heeds the words of the prophet and re-
pents.[84] Rather than rebelling, we find the congregation repenting before
the prophecy explaining that God's wrath will fall upon the city dwellers if
they fail to heed His messenger. But as the congregation complies, the reaction of God follows a most unusual course. In the words of Psalms 94:15,
God will not forsake his people, for he "turns law to justice" (*ki al tzedek
yashuv mishpat*).[85] Both the transformation of Nineveh and of God's judgment gives rise to metaphysical speculations on the nature of judgment
and divine providence. The greatest inquiries are conducted by the
prophets themselves, says Scholem, and in this way Jonah bears a special
linguistic affinity to Job. Both are overwhelmed by the linguistic meaning
and implications of divine justice, which become the central question in
the idea of justice.[86]

> Both books are themselves questions and both offer no answers:
> the question itself is the solution. Jonah concludes with a question
> that, in contrast to the law of nature, is brought to life through his-
> tory. Job, in its entirety, is a question, a cosmogonical question
> that becomes permanent in every single "where were you . . . "
> (chapter 38).[87]

"Where were you when I laid the foundations of the earth?" God asks
Job after his relentless suffering, setting the stage for God to throw everything into question. Even his existence hangs in the balance. Job's pre-
sumption regarding his own guilt and innocence emerges from God's cate-
chism through a state of permanent questioning in relation to the divine

plan. At the same time, he unintentionally contemplates his suffering as a divine attribute. But, in the end, when God finally appears to determine fate, He does so not by way of rectifying divine conception but worldly misconception. Error is found to reside not in the divine but in the nature of the question. God does not deliver comprehensible answers to cosmological questions, Scholem states: he rectifies the question. The "Jewish question," he writes, cannot mediate answers, for Judaism knows no answers at its very core: "This means its answer is essentially again a question."[88] And in this way the irony of the fate of both Job and Jonah come to the fore. Job asks a question and receives only questions in reply, questions far more disconcerting than even his own, while Jonah suffers prophetic irony and is therefore unable to achieve the task before him. "Another forty days" and the great city "Nineveh shall be overthrown," says Jonah (3:4). But just as the modern revolutionary loses the pure certainty of dialectical necessity, "the prophet fails prophecy. In the end, he acts politically."[89]

The irony of the prophets is the politics to which they are compelled, in forging answers to an answerless state. Their irony lies in the shards of the divine in the profane. "Politics," comments Scholem in his journals, "is the prophecy (*Weissagung*) of the imaginary about time that is neither past, present, nor future. This is the incredible irony of prophetic politics, whose politics are divine irony. Theocracy completely negates the idea of politics."[90] Only theocracy, the city of God, what Nineveh lacks by reason of its hedonism, is the solution to divine irony. The Torah embodies equivocation as well, he says, for it neither asks questions nor returns answers. Scholem places emphasis here on the word *t'shuvah*, which he translates both as answer, with accent on *reply*, and an act of righteousness.[91] In the same way, Jonah receives his sign from God but tries to circumvent it and ends up prophesying a future that does not actually come about. His prophecy is meant as a warning, but Jonah understands it as history. He carries the message of judgment as law (*Recht*). God, however, transforms judgment to justice, as the Psalms instructs:

> Jonah stands for law, and from this standpoint he is in the right, whereas God stands for justice; God denies law [mystical law] in history.[92] In the return law is overcome and judgment is not executed . . . for this alone implies justice in the deepest sense: a judgment can be made, but its execution must remain completely separate. The clear relationship between the judicial judgment and its

execution, its true legal order, is transcended in the postponement of execution.[93]

Jonah delivers his message as if by prophetic judgment of the future. The dispatcher of the message, however, is not limited to the message. In this sense Scholem concludes that God denies a definitive notion of historical law. In the relationship between tzedek and mishpat all normative meanings are set aside. As in an executive notion of law, the linguistic relations between ends and means are suspended. Justice itself, the postponement of punishment after judgment, becomes a lifting of sin rather than its attribution. Divine violence is understood similarly here to Benjamin's description of God's administration of justice in the "Critique of Violence."[94] *Aufschub* (postponement) becomes the means by which God manifests divine justice in the profane.

At this stage Scholem begins with a string of twelve theses that are meant to capture not only the idea of justice in Jonah "but also, to the greatest extent, Judaism in its entirety."[95] Justice is defined here as the annihilation of God's judgment in time and place as history. Just as that which is capable of neutralizing divine judgment, indifferent to divine wrath, providing a sphere in itself in which the Last Judgment is permanently *aufgeschoben* (postponed). The meaning of this eternal postponement is clear: it is the making way for the entrance of the messianic kingdom. There is a footnote to this passage that concerns the concept of "death as motion"[96] in monotheism, explained by way of divine Aufschub. In the Aufschub that God oversees between judgment and its implementation, he is, in effect, ruling over life and death. The notion of the transmigration and rejuvenation of the souls as bloodless, which in Benjamin's interpretation constitutes the basis of God's destruction in Numbers 16:31,[97] emerges in Jonah 3 as reprieve: "Filled life in this order is judgment [*Gericht*]; the idea of a Last Judgment is the establishment in absolute of a temporal order for which death is its pure life."[98] The difference between law or judgment (*Recht*) and divine justice (*Gerechtigkeit*) is manifested in the temporal cleft between life and death. Whereas a just life in worldly affairs is the application of what is right (or even what is law), the abolition of life itself is the Last Judgment in this world, on the way to a just one. Ironically, death is the worldly outcome of both the just and the unjust, the pure and the impure. In the same way, an eternal life in this world is hardly a gratifying reward for the righteous. Only an eternal life, which is lodged in the integrity of the soul, is able in this world to distinguish between the two and present the meaning of the idea of death as motion in the next. Once beyond the idea of a temporal limitation caused by death, the Last Judgment loses its meaning, being set to define the temporal order of the world of injustice. Where a just life is reached, the Last Judgment is necessarily eliminated, he concludes.

"Death as motion" in the pursuit of justice is thus incumbent upon a notion of righteous character because it is "death as motion . . . into the other world."[99] As Scholem comments elsewhere in his journals: "The death of the righteous is the last, absolute postponement, in which distance is transcended and the faithful move on to God. The death of the righteous is a mediating principle of his life, and of life itself."[100] Death must form the center of the "religious topography" of all monotheisms, says Scholem, and thereby begins with an idea of prophecy whose essential characteristic is expressed by distance.[101] This accounts for the nature of the *righteous/Gerechte/tzadik*—the righteous personifying the nearness of divine postponement. Distance is perhaps better expressed as proximity, as the Psalms explain: "The nearness of God is my good."[102] Since the character of the tzadik is encapsulated in his proximity to the divine, the distance between judgment and its execution, or simply length, is therefore "the *being* of justice."[103] The highest characteristic of righteousness, both in the divine and the profane, is therefore postponement: the existence of justice is manifested in its divine Aufschub.

Divine judgment is therefore its own execution. Scholem denotes the proximity of *Vollstreckung* (execution) to *Urteil* (judgment) to show that just as there is no linguistic partition between thought and act, a division between judgment and execution in God is also inconceivable. God actively intervenes in fate in the postponement of Jonah's prophecy. Justice, as a manifest postponement, is dependent upon the implementation of postponement in the actualization of judgment. Divine judgment establishes the relationship first through the fact that it is its own execution. Postponement of punishment in Jonah's prophecy must then signify an ultimate link to fate as divine intention. But, in its need to annihilate the distinction altogether, proximity does as much to establish a link to the divine as destroy it. This is envisaged as an execution that neutralizes the Last Judgment: divine judgment, which has no temporal index itself, "anticipates" that which its Aufschub denies, i.e., the Last Judgment, which concludes profane existence. And while divine judgment is an eternal now, it is constantly anticipating judgment. This occurs, for example, in prophecy. But in the act of anticipating the end, prophecy "neutralizes and annihilates" the idea of continuous divine judgment.[104] Justice is, in this sense, alone, manifested as an "indifference to the Last Judgment" in the sign of postponement.

Divine resolution of the profane in the form of tz'dakah, according to Scholem, is the just act that both establishes and denies justice: it is "justice as act," which, through its action, is "postponement that has become action."[105] An example of this may be found in the divine inequality of tz'-dakah, for although both rich and poor are to be judged equally, "this judgment is not to be executed [because] the poor are answerable to God."[106] While there may be an impartiality of judgment, justice reflects the partiality of postponement. The redemption of the poor is not the cause of love, not a "culture of the heart," as Benjamin suggests, but divine partiality.[107] While love of the poor means the "annihilation of judgment, justice is the [love] of execution," a love supreme.[108] Where judgment is eternally suspended by the postponement of the execution of judgment, an execution emerges that is administered only by love, perhaps better said, neighborly love. Scholem bases his notion of tz'dakah on Hirsch: "The good deed, for example charity, as the act to which the poor lay claim, not in the name of law but in the name of God (S. R. Hirsch), is the postponement of execution through another execution."[109] In the substitution of divine Gewalt for the right of law, another form of execution emerges as postponement, which is engendered by a form of execution symbolized in tz'dakah.

Scholem here turns to the meaning of the righteous act in Proverbs 10:2, which promises that "righteousness delivers from death" (utz'dakah tatzil mimavet). Scholem renders righteousness here acting in postponement: "acting in postponement rescues from death."[110] The division of life and death emerge as death and Talmudic postponement in Benjamin's discussion of the "Judaic" concept of the death penalty and the state in the Critique of Violence.[111] In a separate commentary on Jonah found in one of Scholem's notebooks from August 1918–1919, which is most likely the basis for the later manuscript, he elaborates on the role of the death penalty and its meaning for the distinction between divine and profane justice:

> The Torah knows the death penalty. It becomes one of the great triumphs of justice in Talmudic law: the possibility of the death penalty exists, i.e., to sentence a person to death, but the execution does not. This principle idea is realized in the burden of proof with

all things that are connected to the death penalty. This leads deep into the essence of Talmudic Judaism. A court that executed a single death penalty in seventy years was called the court of murder [Mishnah Makkot 1,10]. Justice permits judgment but not the execution of the death penalty, and, for this reason, judgment, in *practice*, is made impossible retroactively through complications. But the idea is always: judgment is possible, execution by human beings is not. Divine judgment can be defined as the judgment that is its own execution. Divine judgment is *therefore* always somehow an event in the sense of an occurrence: an absolute event that unfolds on the phenomenological level of absolute experience. Thus a worldly verdict is transcended by its execution, though connected to the verdict through *law*. In specific cases such a verdict should not be executed. However, the idea of justice fills the abyss between judgment and execution. With divine judgment, judgment is the execution. Divine judgment is the medium of history.[112]

Precisely as Benjamin outlines, we find Scholem in the early years articulating the difference between the Torah and Talmud regarding the death penalty. While the Torah refers to the ultimate punishment, Scholem states, the Talmud only "knows" its Aufschub, manifested as postponement. The idea of righteousness remains constant, on one hand, its actualization in the world unattainable, on the other. In a similar formulation to the paragraph cited above, Scholem restates the same terms in a more concise version in his seventh thesis: "Judgment is possible, execution is not. A worldly verdict is transcended by its execution. Justice fills the abyss between them."[113] The gap between judgment and execution is encompassed by the possibility of transcendence in divine justice, that which would transform profane judgment to justice. Justice alone, however, can make this possibility real.

Having articulated a notion of eternal postponement with the cancellation of prophecy, Scholem attempts to move to a theory of action. Seeing in postponement symbolic punishment, the just act is defined as the "symbolic act."[114] This very formulation is even attributed to Benjamin in a journal entry that follows the paragraph on the death penalty: the symbolic act is righteous, for "it is the execution of every divine judgment (Benjamin)," suggesting a realm of symbolic action that might transcend the worldly prescript of judgment and reach the sphere of justice.[115] If "acting in postponement," i.e., the active postponement of tz'dakah, connotes the cancellation of the implementation of judgment, it also insinuates the elimination of the meaning of judgment, purging meaning from action itself. And if "the meaningful act is a mythical act that is subject to fate," as stated by Scholem, we are therefore able to understand the statement that "justice eliminates fate."[116] This phrase is then reformulated in the "Theses on the Concept of Justice" such that justice is understood as "the elimination of fate from action" altogether.[117] Fate here is not unlike Benjamin's tragic conception in which the active individual achieves his or her fate in free will, in a decline in the act of "pure means."[118] To eliminate the realm of fate is associated with the elimination of the mythical entirely—the point at which the messianic enters the profane: "Isaiah 65:19–24 does not only mean the elimination of fate from messianic time but also presents the method of this elimination in the idea of postponement."[119] In his notes elsewhere, he writes that this cancelation of fate lies at the core of the relationship between messianism and justice: "for in truth, there are no sinners, and this ironically relates to the messianic center of justice, as 'all of you people are just' in messianic time."[120] A theory of action of postponement is messianic action, which makes its appearance here in a most intricate metaphysics: it promises a means of postponement that does not tally before the onset of a messianic age but, at the same time, appears to offer little by way of the profane. It corresponds to the "eternal now" of the historical idea of the Torah, Scholem states.

Just as the canonical forms tradition in Judaism, it also constitutes justice. But although we are readily able to articulate "tradition," the canonical has us at a loss. Scholem sees this stemming from the paradox of a "practicality" of the written Torah that "cannot be applied."[121] The Torah is the "idea of tradition" that, like judgment, "pertains to divine law, which is not yet justice, transforming itself in the infinite postponement of tradition. In tradition, revelation and messianic time are inseparably linked."[122] The process of transformation is that from the divine law to justice, *ki al tzedek yashuv mishpat.*[123] Revelation does not take place in time, for time in line with a messianic epoch has no constitution, no spatial dimension. Prophetic time, as with prophecy itself, is therefore an *ewige Gegenwart* (eternal now)—an idea that Jonah did not harbor and that unleashed the ironic dimension in his story: "It is clear he mistakes the eternal now for momentary presence. He is to prophesize the eternal now in Nineveh, but he himself considers this prophecy as one above the others."[124] The ironic or, perhaps better expressed, paradoxical, reflects an eternal time that admits change.

Only in this atmosphere could the rather miraculous postponement of execution take place. There must therefore be an eternity, if not a bad infinity, in a justice that requires redemption just as much as a redemption that requires justice. Justice therefore can serve neither as "a determining concept" nor as a "mechanistically infinite, regulating idea that is approachable."[125] It is not mechanistically infinite but an eternal state, both infinite and finite. It cannot serve as a border to the profane, just as redemption or revelation cannot merely serve as a limit to the world or worldly knowledge. It is worldly by the fact that it is the hidden dimension of the divine in the profane, for justice is "the order of the world (*tikkuno shel olam*) and the messianic kingdom is the world of order (*olam hatikkun*)."[126] The eruption of an order of justice, redemption, and revelation in this world is to be broached by an arriving messianic dimension initiated by the acts of the righteous:

> In the same way that a coming world exists, there exists a coming justice. This coming is its unfolding. Tz'dakah does not become, it reveals, it unfolds (Isaiah 56:1).[127] Its coming is only the penetration of a radiating means in darkness. For this reason, the tzadik, the just (in Chasidism) is only a *mitgaleh* [the one who reveals]. No one can become a tzadik, a person can only be one. Yet the "hidden righteous" is a category through which prophecy developed the idea of tradition. Tradition is the living heritage of prophecy in the center of the Jewish people. The communalist [*Mitmensch*] is the hidden righteous. He recounts the nameless things.[128]

A theory of postponed action is here expressed in the figure of the tzadik who is able to embody "ethically determined actions" that unintentionally transform law to justice.[129] Justice is not enacted by the righteous but unfolds in his or her character. That is the nature of the "coming" of justice in the form of ethical action. As self-revelation, it sunders the darkness of profane ignorance in its unintentional act of redemption. It cannot be willed or desired. It can only be there, hidden, intentionless, transpiring in the spirit of prophecy, the center of the congregation, in history. The *Mitmensch*, the collectivist dimension of the ethical character of the righteous, is a redemptive figure that is able to unify all the aspects of redemption in response to the suffering of a fellow human being, but doing so, all the while, as a hidden agent.

CHAPTER 6

JUSTICE, VIOLENCE, AND REDEMPTION

JUDAISM AND REVOLUTION

No other period was more crucial for Scholem's political thought in the early years than the point at which he joined Benjamin in the highly resigned atmosphere that characterized their discussions in Switzerland.[1] This moment of transition in Scholem's thinking, which culminated in the reevaluation of his earliest political activities, led to a phase that I have already termed a form of anarchist nihilism.[2] Raging war and disappointment in the Zionist and youth movements had brought their contact with the outside world to a near halt.[3] Yet something was to suddenly disrupt these intimate discussions in their sanctuary of practical resignation: the Russian revolution. As we have read in a letter to Werner Kraft from Bern: "I have never in my life seen a more humanist and politically sincere text than the documents of the maximalist [Bolshevik] revolution."[4] In his journals from November 13, 1917, Scholem adds "the *first* official text of world history that every decent person can sign."[5] He augments his comments to Kraft by signaling that although Bolshevism reflects elements of a theocratic revolution with anarchism as a "precursor" (*Vorstufe*), he still is reminded of the "principle difference" between his vision and that of the Bolsheviks. Later he reflects on the relationship between the three—anarchism, Bolshevism, and theocracy—in his journal, probably written as a draft of a letter to his friend, Albert Baer:

> The more it becomes clear to me that theocracy is the only organized communal and state structure for humanity, the clearer the criteria emerges for both the idea as well as the value of revolutions. I am considered very sympathetic to Bolshevism. Yet despite the extraordinary absurdity of this opinion, there is something to it: to the degree that I see in Bolshevism—meaning the idea that views the unconditional dictatorship of poverty as the only means of establishing the messianic kingdom—a resolute revolutionary intensity with regard to a history of the here and now. I completely reject this here and now, but should I ever accept it, Bolshevism would appear be the unavoidable result. Since theocracy has yet to be achieved, I choose the anarchist over the Bolshevik method (which are wrongly mistaken for one another). Anarchism (not socialism) is the only conceivable ideal precursor, if one may call it that, of the state of God. This does not mean that anarchy should be sought as a condition, but that the theocratic position in opposition to every noneternal now is anarchism.[6]

These emphatic observations were not the only ones Scholem would make on the events taking place in Russia. Among the newly published papers in the Scholem archive is a text written in 1918 entitled "On the Bolshevik Revolution." In it Scholem articulates his views on revolution in relation to his earlier anarchist Zionism and emerging nihilistic politics. As in the "Theses on the Concept of Justice," here as well he raises the question of authority and justice in the context of a messianic perspective, independent of but fully intertwined with Benjamin's own. Anarchism, if implicit, is nevertheless one of the key themes of the paper. Like other anarchists of his period, Scholem first embraces aspects of the Bolshevik revolution but then launches into a critique of the movement and upheaval, which, in his own messianic terms, falls far short of the kingdom of God on earth—the very quality that appears to set it apart from other movements. The following is the complete text and translation:

THE BOLSHEVIK REVOLUTION

Bolshevism has a central idea which lends magic to its movement: the messianic kingdom can only unfold in the dictatorship of poverty. (The error is perhaps that it cannot unfold *in* itself—which is Tolstoyism. This serious confusion brought so many followers of Tolstoy to the movement.) This connotes that only the judgment of the impoverished has revolutionary power. The poor may not be just but they can never be unjust. Poverty, even where it is dictatorial, is not *Gewalt*. Moscow's theory of the firing squad appears as ethical outcome: the unjust kingdom stands trail. Bolshevism is the attempt to stand divine judgment on its head. It kills in the name of a mission.

Revolution exists where the messianic kingdom is to be established without the teachings. For this reason, there *can* be *no* revolution for the Jews. The Jewish revolution has to be reconnected to the teachings. A revolution that is clearly based on the messianic kingdom, like the Bolshevik or French revolution, must be principally distinguished from the frail pseudo-revolutions that are centered on "progress," like Germany in 1848. The messianic kingdom, the eternal now of history, cannot be reached gradually. Liberalism is a conforming imitation of Messianism that functions by a rule of operation. In key moments, it is extended indefinitely and thus loses its conformity. Asymptotes are the guidelines of liberalism. The circle turns from hyperbole to the imaginary.

Revolutions fail. But this is not, nor can it ever be, an argument against them. Revolutions convey time and again the silent teachings of the unambiguity of history.

Intrinsically the Bolshevik revolution, like every legitimate revolution, has a double point in which *Gewalt* emerges through the inner collision of structures (that have to appear due to the exclusion of the Torah).

The great historical paradox put forward is that *exactly* where poverty *reigns*, it remains poverty nonetheless—as if the *faithfulness* of the poor to poverty would be the only and highest guarantee of the Bolshevik idea. Is this possible or sensible? Such a system would be revolutionary consistency—an absolute, self-sustaining system. And precisely because, unlike liberalism, revolutions lack a form of consistency understood in this sense, they fail.

Anatole France, in his book, *La révolte des anges,* set a limit for the idea of the teachings with ironic necessity. His true, deep, and perhaps unutterable question, is: how can one overcome the prescriptive circular reasoning of revolution? He does not answer the question. But true mysticism can, which considers circular reasoning a legitimate fundamental idea.

Even though the Bolshevik revolution will be caught up in bloodshed (and precisely the fact that it will not drown in its own blood is the miraculous thing about it), it will nevertheless serve as the only high-point of the history of the world war and, however saddening it may be, the messianic reaction against it. Zionism has nothing in common with the world war, to which it does not respond but turns away. Whoever affirms the history of today has to be a Bolshevist, seeing in it the futuristic and purest form of the present in blood and misdeed.

One might be able to designate revolutionary actions as those distinguishable from both the ordinary and historical in that they are conducted in good faith while standing in the face of history. The person who *knows* that he is acting historically, is revolutionary. Yet Bolshevism does more than this: it acts not only conscious of standing in the face of history, it seeks *at the same time* to act *futurist* in a specific sense. But with action, this is not simultaneously possible. Bolshevism tries—perhaps with grandeur but surely for naught—to suspend judgment over itself through the permanence of its singular point of *Gewalt* which appears to itself as the future that it anticipates. *For this reason,* it is unjust and the root of its reprehensibility, independent of its position on spirituality and labor.

DIE BOLSCHEWISTISCHE REVOLUTION

Der Bolschewismus hat eine zentrale Idee, die seiner Bewegung revolutionäre Magie verleiht. Dies ist: das messianische Reich kann nur durch die Diktatur der Armut entfaltet werden. (Der Irrtum ist vielleicht, daß es nicht *in* ihr entfaltet werden kann—was Tolstojanismus ist, und eben diese folgenschwere Verwechselung hat so viele Tolstojaner zur Mitarbeit dort gebracht.) Dies besagt: das Urteil des Armen hat allein revolutionäre Macht. Der Arme ist vielleicht nicht gerecht, aber er kann niemals ungerecht sein. Die Armut, auch wo sie diktatorisch ist, ist nicht Gewalt. Die Moskauer Schießtheorie erscheint als ethische Konsequenz: der Reiche, der der Ungerechte ist, steht vor dem Gerichte. Der Bolschewismus ist der Versuch eines auf den Kopf gestellten Gottesurteils. Er tötet im Namen einer Aufgabe.

Revolution ist dort, wo das messianische Reich ohne die Lehre aufgerichtet werden soll. Im letzten Grunde *kann* es für den Juden *keine* Revolution geben. Die jüdische Revolution ist allein der Wiederanschluß an die Lehre. Eine Revolution, die jedenfalls auf das messianische Reich gerichtet ist wie die bolschewistische oder die französische, ist prinzipiell zu trennen von den schwächlichen Pseudorevolutionen wie der deutschen 48er, die vom „Fortschritt" zentriert ist. Das messianische Reich, die ewige Gegenwart der Geschichte, kann nicht allmählich erreicht werden. Liberalismus ist eine konforme Abbildung des Messianischen unter einem Funktionsgesetz, das in den entscheidenden Punkten es ins Unendliche gedehnt hat, also die Konformität verloren gegangen ist. Asymptoten sind die Leitlinien des Liberalismus. Der Kreis wird zur Hyperbel ins Imaginäre hinein.

Die Revolutionen scheitern. Aber dies ist und kann niemals ein *Argument* gegen sie sein. Die Revolutionen überliefern immer wieder den Generationen die stumme Lehre von der Eindeutigkeit der Geschichte.

Die bolschewistische wie *wesensmäßig* jede legitime Revolution hat Doppelpunkte, an denen durch inneren Zusammenprall von Ordnungen (der durch die Ausschaltung der Thora notwendig eintreten muß) die Gewalt entsteht.

Es ist die ungeheure historische Paradoxie, daß gefordert wird, daß die Armut auch und *grade* da, wo sie *herrscht*, doch und dennoch die Armut bleibt. Die *Treue* des Armen zu der Armut wäre die einzige und hohe Bürgschaft der bolschewistischen Idee. Ob sie möglich und sinnvoll ist? Diese Ordnung wäre die revolutionäre Konstanz, sie wäre das sich absolut Erhaltende, und eben weil den Revolutionen eine in diesem Sinne, der nicht der liberale ist, verstandene Konstanz mangelt, scheitern sie.

Anatole France hat in seinem großen Buch *La révolte des anges* mit ironischer Notwendigkeit die Idee der Lehre limitiert. Seine eigentlichste und tiefste, vielleicht unausgesprochene Frage dort ist: wie kann der gesetzmäßige Zirkelschluß der Revolution durchbrochen werden? Er antwortet nicht. Aber die wahre Mystik, in der der Zirkelschluß eine legitime fundamentale Idee ist, kann antworten.

Die bolschewistische Revolution wird in Blut erstickt werden (und eben daß sie in ihrem eigenen Blute nicht erstickt, scheint das Wunderbare an ihr zu sein), aber sie wird dennoch als der eigentliche Höhepunkt der Geschichte des Weltkrieges und die ihm entsprechende (und angemessene, so traurig das Wort auch sein mag) messianische Reaktion gegen ihn wirken. Der Zionismus hat mit dem Weltkrieg nichts gemein, auf den er nicht reagiert, da er sich abkehrt. Wer die heutige Geschichte aber bejaht, muß dem Bolschewismus anhängen, muß in ihm die zukünftigste und in Blut und Untat reinste Gestalt der Gegenwart erblicken.

Vielleicht kann man als revolutionär die Taten bezeichnen, die sich von den gewöhnlichen einerseits und den historischen andererseits dadurch scheiden, daß sie mit dem legitimen Bewußtsein getan werden, im Angesicht der Geschichte zu stehen. Derjenige, der *weiß*, daß er historisch handelt, ist ein Revolutionär. Dies ist der weiteste Begriff von Revolution. Der Bolschewismus aber tut mehr: er handelt nicht nur im Bewußtsein, angesichts der Geschichte zu stehen, sondern will *zugleich* in einem präzisen Sinne *zukünftig* handeln. Das aber ist beim Handelnden nicht zusammen möglich. Der Bolschewismus versucht, vielleicht großartig, sicher aber umsonst, das Gericht über sich selbst auszuschalten: durch Permanenz der singulären Gewaltpunkte, das ihm als ein Zukünftiges erscheinen muß, das er antizipiert. *Hierdurch* wird er ungerecht, und hier ist die Wurzel seiner Verwerflichkeit, von seiner Stellung zum Geistigen und der Arbeit ganz abgesehen.[7]

The voracious tone of this text recalls a political congress. But if Scholem had such a gathering in mind it would have been a society constituted by two: himself and Benjamin. It seems that the key to Scholem's fascination with the events in Russia, and with the idea of revolution in general, is well summarized in the first two lines: "Bolshevism has a central idea that lends magic to its movement: the messianic kingdom can only unfold in the dictatorship of poverty."[8] Scholem attributes a prophetic element to Bolshevism, an idea, he writes, that fills its ranks with a magical force. This magical idea is that only the dictatorship of the impoverished will open the floodgates of redemption. If we are to understand magic here in terms of the linguistic magic embedded in the transition from a creating word to profane expression, in which the redemptive aspects of the creating word is understood to be magical, being lodged in the profane, then the ability of a class that has been promised its restitution in the world to come is no unlikely candidate for the initiation of the coming world in the here and now.[9] And should the gap between these two worlds encompass the tension between the divine and profane, then the merger of these two realms necessitates the existence of a fragment of the divine a priori in the profane as its "magic."

The impoverished class that has been promised its restitution could well be capable of initiating redemption through the revolutionary authority of its judgment. But Scholem immediately draws a distinction between that very class redeeming itself within itself and the restitution in which it participates under revolutionary conditions: "The great historical paradox put forward is that exactly where poverty reigns it remains poverty nonetheless." Paradox ensues when the very condition poised to be transformed is actually institutionalized, in which impoverishment and disenfranchisement form the basis of a class that seeks the preservation of its authority in the administration of justice. In this respect he expresses marvel at the authenticity of the Russian revolutionary attempt to establish the kingdom of God on earth—an attempt that, save for France, far outweighs the German "pseudo revolution" of 1848, as he calls it, with its unyielding notion of progress.[10] In contrast to the attempt to transform redemption by a progressive notion of reform, "the messianic kingdom, the eternal now of history, cannot be reached gradually [allmählich]." But while redemption of the impoverished is the vital aspect of the Bolshevik revolution—the recognition of which brought many a religious anarchist to the movement under the teachings of Tolstoy, says Scholem—redemption does not take place within a revolutionary agent but before society as a whole. If those who are weak are to be made strong, that is not to be achieved by the rotation of the master but by the complete rupture of slavery altogether. A messianic revolution must expressly destroy the basis of worldly power itself as, for example, in the prophecy of Isaiah: "His burden shall be taken away from off thy shoulder, and his yoke from thy neck, and the yoke shall be destroyed."[11] Thus, according to Scholem, the cardinal dilemma of the Bolshevik revolution is the collapse of justice into impoverishment, since, in this world, the impoverished are the bearers of absolute injustice. Although impoverishment is unjust, he writes, it does not necessarily form the basis of justified authority/violence: "The impoverished may not be just but can never exist as unjust," say Scholem. "Poverty, even where it is dictatorial, is not Gewalt." In lining up the bourgeois class before judgment, Bolshevism neutralizes the task of the divine by reversing the Last Judgment. Recalling Marx's famous claim regarding the flawed premises of the Hegelian system, Scholem writes: "Bolshevism is the attempt to stand divine judgment on its head." Unlike divine violence, however, its task is executed through the barrel of a gun.

In the application of revolutionary violence to achieve messianic ends, great importance is placed on the meaning of redemption. Not only must the agent of revolution extend beyond the universalization of an internal redemption, says Scholem, redemption itself must be bound to a *Lehre*, a teaching or tradition. In its neutralization of the divine, revolution is itself an attempt to establish a radical kingdom of God without God. It therefore does not appear as a "redemptive" act, nor does it correspond to an anarchistic conception of the return to Zion that was to capture Scholem's imagination. For him the "Jewish revolution has to be reconnected to the teachings," meaning the teachings of the Torah. A revolution for the Jews as Jews without that connection would be impossible, he writes.

Scholem here proposes an interpretation of messianic events that reflects the apocalypse of the prophets: that the kingdom of God is not to be achieved through evolutionary measures but by a sudden breach in the flow of worldly events. Thus the Bolshevik revolutionary act is an attempt at an "eternal now of history" ascribed to redemption. It is precisely the place in which redemption is initiated without teachings or tradition. Its messianism stands in contrast to the liberalism of the revolutions of 1848, which may have neutralized divine judgment, he writes, but spawned in its place a bad eternity from the task of redemption. Liberalism itself reflects a "conforming imitation of the messianic" that loses its link to messianism by severing justice from redemption and placing it in the realm of reform. In this respect liberalism is just as much a political failure in Scholem's view as it is a theological one.

Yet revolutions also fail. If there is something that frees them from the bad eternity of liberalism, this would be the transposition of the legacy of redemption: "Revolutions repeatedly convey the silent teachings of the unambiguity of history." In this respect the Bolshevik revolution, as in "every legitimate revolution," is capable of generating its own Gewalt—its authority/violence—as a convolute of order in the neutralization of the divine. In this process the impoverished class becomes the norm rather than teachings, tradition, the Torah. In contrast to liberalism, which loses its intimate connection to messianic transformation in the unending continuity of reform, paradox is the only constant in revolution. In this way liberalism never truly establishes a just and noncontradictory means to redemption, he states, for it is prone to circuitous reasoning. In that paradox inevitably turns to compulsion and failure, revolution is also unable to provide an answer. "True mysticism," however, "which considers circular reasoning a legitimate, fundamental idea," is able to answer the question. How this might occur, however, is left open to interpretation.

The final part of Scholem's treatise is divided into two paragraphs on the historical role of the revolutionary force of Bolshevism, its relationship to history, and a more subtle and authentic messianic response. The Bolshevik revolution may end in bloodshed, Scholem asserts in 1918, but a bloodshed that is not its own. Thus the revolution may be the final act of the First World War evoking a messianic response:

> Even though the Bolshevik revolution will be caught up in bloodshed (and precisely the fact that it will not drown in its own blood is the miraculous thing about it), it will nevertheless serve as the only high point in the history of the world war and, however saddening it may be, the messianic reaction against it.

A bloody end to a purposeless war could hardly be deemed "miraculous" (*wunderbar*) by any account, and Scholem surely does not mean to imply by this a belief in the necessity of Bolshevik violence. Rather, in an interpretation of the Bolshevik revolution as a messianic reaction, he appears to suggest just the opposite. His vision of an anarchic Zionism will have nothing to do with the war or the salvaging of its ruins. In this sense a Bolshevik messianic reaction is directed at the war that, although conjuring up images of salvation, can nonetheless never be truly messianic. One senses here an attempt to define a political and practical messianism in response to an apocalypticism derived from the impossibility of worldly barbarism as a means to redemption. "Whoever affirms the history of today," argues Scholem, "has to be a Bolshevist, seeing in it the futurist and purest form of the present through blood and misdeed." Unlike messianism in this respect, the

Bolshevik revolution comes to represent the history of the future. Out of the bloodshed of an utterly meaningless war, it is able to project itself as a futuristic form of the present. It may not reach an "eternal now" of redemption, nor suffer the bad eternity of liberalism, but it is a force heralding the profane future in the historical moment.

Scholem's comments seem to attribute to Bolshevism a historical force it has always been prone to assert about itself. But here he essentially asks if it is possible to divide the historical from the quotidian. If so, revolution would mean to act "with a legitimate consciousness . . . in the face of history." But this implies the capacity to know history in order to transform it through revolution. Bolshevism, however, does more than this. It does not merely act in a consciously historical way but is "*futurist* in a specific sense." It is futuristic but, at the same time, unable to judge its own actions or have its own acts tried by a court of the future. This means that, while promising a justice of the future, Bolshevism can only deliver a justice of a here and now. The permanence of its *Gewaltpunkte* (point of violence/authority), which makes it necessary to appear as the historical future to come through the attempt "to suspend the judgment over itself through the permanence of its sole *Gewaltpunkte*," is the very force that makes it "unjust" and "the root of its reprehensibility."

In Scholem's distinction between justice and judgment, a divine verdict is synonymous with justice itself; no space is conceived between word and act, unlike worldly judgment where the two are most clearly remote from one another. In his fourth thesis on Jonah, drawing on the saying of Proverbs 16:33 that places all faith in divine ruling, Scholem writes, "Divine judgment is both judgment and its own execution" (tag II:527). In the case of Bolshevism this crucial distinction was lost, making it perhaps the nearest attempt at the divine kingdom on earth, and its most monstrous antithesis, precisely because it seeks to eliminate the distinction between justice and judgment, according to Scholem's critique. In transcending the question posed by the tension between the divine and profane in messianism, Bolshevism initiates its downfall in injustice. Its futuristic judgment, with all its claims to historical necessity, is the only basis for its monopolized Gewaltpunkte and not the legitimacy of a messianic eternal now. It remains trapped within the profane world, in the conditions that it sought to overthrow within itself. The dictatorship of its historical futurism—Scholem predicts in conclusion to his treatise, itself written less than a year after the Russian Revolution—is constituted to end in demise.

Violence and the Politics of Pure Means

Given the title of Benjamin's essay from 1921, the "Critique of Violence," it would appear to be the most expressly political of the early writings. But despite the fact that it concerns the question of justified violence in the pursuit of revolutionary goals, there is surprising little by way of politics here. His analysis of general strikes, ethical action, the principles of anarchism—even the notion of violence itself—is not written to rally for one party or another, nor is it concerned with distributive justice as is "Notes to a Study on the Category of Justice," where the interests of each person is recognized in the interests of humanity.[12] It appears more directed at a politics of "pure means" and a "culture of the heart," geared once again toward the activities of the individual.[13] More than a political analysis of violence, all these aspects together seem best to be described as a metaphysical discourse on justice.[14] And, like many pieces that comprise the early writings, there is a very distinct movement in this work to articulate an authentic theology of the role of violence in messianic redemption.

The essay revolves around the juxtaposition of various juridical, political, and theological categories. These include the mediation of ends and means, natural and positive law, law-forming and law-maintaining violence, divine and profane, laws and rights, and, finally, violence/nonviolence. Violence is articulated by the word *Gewalt,* a term that cannot be rendered easily in any language.[15] Gewalt represents both the role of authority and the application of violence. Here the linguistic ambiguity that finds expression both in constitutional law as well as in common parlance harbors a political uncertainty concerning the nature of justice. Benjamin asks the question, How is it possible to determine and implement what is just, which is to say, how is it possible to implement justice justly? In this sense, determining the idea of violence has to be one of the primary aims of any attempt to clarify the meaning of justice itself, seen in terms of language. This would initially require a discussion of the ambiguity of the term *Gewalt.*

Benjamin proposes an initial series of suppositions that attempt to define Gewalt in relation to the notion of law. His first proposition is that Gewalt can only be defined meaningfully in the context of an ethical realm constituted by law. The term *law* is predicated by the question of what is right, expressed by the word *Recht.*[16] While law is first to be determined in the context of the relationship of means to ends, justice is taken out of this framework altogether. Benjamin assigns justice purely to sphere of ends; it is a state, not a means, and therefore cannot be understood from the perspective of that which is applicable. To this degree, law distinguishes itself from justice in that its existence is its applicability. Without the possibility to view law as a means, the ends of a particular act could never be completely subscribed to justice. If justice, however, is to be viewed as a state in which only ends are known, then justified means would have little to do with its condition, for neither means nor ends have a role in an order made solely of ends or, in the same way, an order that has no concept of means or ends as, for example, in a divine order. Justice is therefore reserved for a later moment in favor first of a discussion of means.

If law is therefore a means, what is Gewalt? If it is also a means, can it be applied justifiably toward certain ends? By asking this, Gewalt is identified by its application and not by principle. Yet if we define it as a means to a justified end, Gewalt itself would have to be an ethical category. It is therefore necessary to divide means from ends such that application and justification are not presented as one and the same, which is reflected in the difference between a philosophy of right (*Rechtsphilosophie*) and natural law (*Naturrecht*).[17]

From the perspective of natural law, the relation between a violent (*gewaltsamer*) means to justified ends is a matter of application, as in the science of propulsion.[18] There is no ethical conception of means in natural law.[19] Gewalt is here conceived as "a product of nature, as it were a raw material, the use of which is in no way problematic, unless force is misused for unjust ends."[20] The application of natural law to a philosophy of right is easily transformed into a philosophy of state, i.e., positive law. One only has to think of a Hegelian *Rechtsphilosophie* in order to view Gewalt as the submission of the individual to the state, to conceive of the subject exercising the capacity for violence for the purposes of the state.[21] While natural law attempts to justify means via the justice of ends, positive law seeks to "guarantee" the justice of ends through the justification of means. In the form of Darwinian biology (which Benjamin refers to as Darwinian popular philosophy), violence is not only deemed natural in the pursuit of ends but justified as well.[22] Both positive and natural law share the same dogma: "Just ends can be attained by justified means, justified means used for just ends."[23] The inherent dichotomy between ends and means cannot be resolved as long as just goals are met with justified means and justified means are applied to just goals. A critique of violence must in this sense transcend a search for a justified application of violence and reflect on violence itself (II:181). But while natural law theory appears hermetically guarded against a critique in its conception of naturalized Gewalt, positive law distinguishes between various types of Gewalt and attempts to establish an autonomous norm for Gewalt independent of its application. In this sense it offers a possible starting point for a critique. Positive law is law executed by the state. Where the power of the state is concerned, the relevant categories of a critique are located in the difference between sanctioned and non-sanctioned violence, which means, in fact, "historically recognized" violence. The discussion turns to two examples of sanctioned and nonsanctioned Gewalt: the police and the general strike.

The institution of the police is an example of an unnatural, sanctioned Gewalt embedded within the institution of state. It is a form of Gewalt in legal means with the authority to determine the boundaries of the means themselves. At the same time, it conceives of itself as powerless in the face of the state: "Unlike law, which acknowledges in the 'decision' (determined by place and time) a metaphysical category that gives it a claim to critical evaluation, the institution of the police cannot be considered anything essential."[24] Benjamin conceives of police Gewalt as a means of managing an already decree-organized existence with outright brutality, and, compared to the metaphysical determination of right within a temporal and spatial dimension, it is a vacuous expression of Gewalt.[25] Here one is confronted with the ambiguity of omnipotence and impotence at the heart of the monopoly of state violence. In applying the law of the state, police apply *law-maintaining* Gewalt in order to put law into action, maintaining law as enforceable. But, while maintaining law, law itself is being applied within a temporal and spatial arena and is therefore forming itself at the moment of its application. The application of law is therefore also achieved through *law-forming* Gewalt.[26] Gewalt is either law forming or law maintaining. When it claims neither, it is no longer Gewalt, for it is no longer applicable. The distinction between law-forming and law-maintaining Gewalt appears to fall apart in the institution of the police. If law-forming Gewalt is required to establish authority, then it is based on the limitations of law-maintaining (and state-maintaining) Gewalt. But it is actually free from the restraints of both spheres: it is law forming through the regulation of exemption and law maintaining by the fact that it has complete access to ends. The ends of police violence and that of law however cannot be seen as identical.

Benjamin argues that the law or right of the police is in fact determined at the very instant where the state is unable to protect the rule of law:

> The "law" of the police essentially marks the point at which the state, whether from impotence or because of the immanent connections within any legal system, can no longer guarantee through the legal system the empirical ends it seeks to attain at any price.[27]

The state is unable to ensure its ends, to be achieved through the rule of law, because of its powerlessness in light of the "immanent" structure of every law, says Benjamin. The threat of violence lies behind its structure, as is the case with divine justice. And this violence, when applied, is not purely determined by right but is rather established by its own force. Thus, in the application of law, the law-forming aspect of violence is always at work, determining the meaning of the rule of law at any given moment, and particularly the moment of its application.

In terms of sanctioned violence, Benjamin here asserts the most principal element of political theology: that power is the main force behind law-maintaining Gewalt: "Law making is power making and to that extent an immediate manifestation of violence."[28] In this form Gewalt is self-perpetuating. The law-maintaining act is the establishment and preservation of power itself. In the name of Sorel Benjamin cordons off these observations from the cultural or historical sphere; they are, he says, metaphysical in nature. In contrast to a state of justice, this world knows no equality save the equalities of the powerful: "From the point of view of violence, which alone can guarantee law, there is no equality but, at the most, equally . . . violent forces."[29] Only the ability to apply violence is the measure of worldly equality. This is the law of states, in which all rights reside in the possession of the powerful.[30]

The Strike As Revolutionary Means

A strike is another example of Gewalt that plays a distinctly oppositional role to the power of the state. In contrast to the other examples, it does not necessarily rely on action. Unlike rights that exist only when they are actualized, a strike is by definition the cessation of action. Moreover, the paradox of the Gewalt of a strike is that, in its nonaction, it is often held to be quintessential nonviolence.[31] It is this conception of the strike as nonviolent nonaction that facilitated sanctioning of the right to strike by the state. In cases where the state does not recognize the right to strike, however, the strike is deemed Gewalt; we may also say moreover that it thereby has a right to Gewalt. As a nonsanctioned right, what form of Gewalt can the strike apply? If a strike employs Gewalt and a right in an active form, it is either an active disruption of the legal order or a passive disruption in the form of blackmail. The strike can therefore be seen as a fulfillment of a right, although its Gewalt may contravene the legal order that guarantees that right in the first place: "Understood in this way—from the perspective of labor, which is opposed to that of the state—the right to strike constitutes the right to use force in attaining certain ends."[32] The right to strike means in this case the right to apply Gewalt in the fulfillment of certain ends in which the interests of the working class are conceived as fully contrary to that of the state. According to Benjamin, the working class is the only "legal subject" (*Rechtssubjekt*) outside the state that has a right to Gewalt, thereby legitimizing the concept of the *revolutionary general strike*.[33]

In a revolutionary general strike the working class is called into action as the state contests the right to strike as an abuse of right altogether. This reveals a contradiction in the legal basis of the state, which guarantees a right that, if the state is to maintain the sole right to the monopoly of rights, it must fully oppose, while the right itself is achieved at the expense of legal order: "For, however paradoxical this may appear at first sight, even conduct involving the exercise of a right can nevertheless, under certain circumstances, be described as violent."[34] Gewalt makes its appearance therefore as a right. In Gewalt a right is expressed as such; it may exist without Gewalt but only assumes form with it.

Gewalt appears, in this example, as a mere means and, therefore, as thieving violence.[35] The right of the subject to sanction Gewalt is relegated to "natural" means and falls easily into conflict with the question of what is natural. If the violence of theft is normative, "original[,] and reflects an original image," and thus a "natural means," Gewalt takes on a law-forming character (*Rechtsetzender*).[36] Law-forming Gewalt would then be definable as thieving violence. This is the tendency of modern law, which accepts the "violence directed at [the] natural ends of the individual" as the subject bearing rights—only in the application of violence sanctioned as "natural."[37] The state responds to law-forming crime in the same way that it does to the right of theft and the right to strike: great crimes threaten to be law-forming acts.

Sorel distinguishes between two forms of the general strike: the political and the proletarian.[38] But only the revolutionary general strike is able to use the proletarian strike in the "task of destroying state power."[39] One form of strike rallies for an altercation in labor conditions, the other for a pure nonviolent means. Far beyond its appearance and reference to Sorel, here the concept of the revolutionary general strike is anything but syndicalist. With regard to the question of the working class, Benjamin's interest is clearly limited to the ability to define it as a "legal subject" (*Rechtssubjekt*) for the purposes of analysis of unsanctioned Gewalt. His conception has, in fact, little to do with the question of labor or the capitalist means of production. It does not seek new labor relations but rather a complete transformation of labor itself. This form of strike does not merely create the conditions for a political cataclysm; it aims to induce a complete historical rupture. Whereas the strike that transforms working conditions actually upholds a ruptured state of existence, the revolutionary general strike messianically abolishes it. A messianic conception of labor is therefore a "wholly transformed work, no longer enforced by the state . . . an upheaval that this kind of strike not so much causes as consummates. For this reason, the first of these undertakings is lawmaking but the second is anarchistic."[40] The revolutionary general strike rejects all forms of plans, programs, or even utopian projects of a revolutionary society. With its anarchist critique of the state, it is directed beyond parliamentary revolutionaries and professional intellectuals alike. In Benjamin's estimation Sorel's vision moves beyond the politics of the profane; his revolutionary general strike is taken as messianic politics. Others might well read Sorel's anti-intellectualism and his vision of proletarian revolution rather differently, questioning the notion of the divine embedded in his model of the world to come.[41] Yet Benjamin interprets Sorel's vision as one of moral integrity and, despite its cataclysmic consequences, argues that it is not to be understood as advocating violence for its own sake. Violence, both in an everyday sense and in that which erupts in a transitory moment, is not caused by the means used to end a state of violence. For this reason the Gewalt of revolution as well as the Gewalt of redemption cannot be evaluated through their existence as events, effects, or even less as ends, but rather only through an inner determination, "from the law of its means."[42]

Punishment and Fate

We have seen how a revolutionary notion of the strike bears greater resemblance to the idea of messianic redemption than the transformation of
the ownership of the means of production. In much the same way, we saw
how Benjamin's interpretation of the idea of fate reveals a distinctly theological approach. In the sphere of Gewalt the idea of fate returns again in
the form of the temporal and spatial meaning of death and immortality in
the realm of punishment.[43] Fate represents the structure of a particular life
span and, at the same time, the interests of humanity within each individual. In the case of punishment, fate is determined by external factors.
Nowhere is this more the case than with the death penalty which is the ultimate realm of legalized Gewalt. He writes:

> For if violence [Gewalt], crowned by fate, is the origin of law, then
> it may be readily supposed that in cases where the highest violence
> occurs in the legal system—that concerning life and death—the
> origin of the legal system is representative in that which exists and
> that manifests itself in awe.[44]

The determination of life and death is the deliverance of crowned sovereignty to the state. First, state Gewalt is based on the neutralization of divine
Gewalt, for it is ultimately divine authority that sanctions life and administers death as much as it guarantees immortality: from a theological-
metaphysical analysis of life and death the power to authorize one over the
other is a divine task. The origins of that sovereignty precisely defines the
way in which the transgression of law will be addressed. In the neutralization of divine authority the purpose of the death penalty is not "to punish
the infringement of law but to establish new law."[45] Benjamin's idea apears
to be informed by a discussion with Scholem on the idea of the death
penalty in rabbinic Judaism.[46]

The purpose of the verdict concerning life and death is not so much to
inflict punishment but to define the very basis of its law, a new law that
neutralizes an old law. The elimination of the concept of death is, at the
same time, the exclusion of divine principles in worldly affairs. "Lawmaking," says Benjamin, "is power making" (II:198), and this principle is most
evident in the power to rule over death—a power rightly delegated to the
old law, the law of the Torah, the law of God. This neutralization is, however, chimerical, he argues. The neutralization of the divine by the state

leads Benjamin to speculate on the manifestation of the divine in the profane: "Justice is the principle of all godly formation of ends, power the principle of all mythical formation of laws."[47] Although law is based on justice, which is divine, it is always limited to the profane sphere, making the decision of legal death a leap to a mythical divine power. Fate makes reference to divine origin, but comes to reflect the mythical generation of worldly right. We will return to the mythical aspect shortly.

Pacifism, Anarchism, and Violence

The focus of Benjamin's comments on the idea of pacifism in the context of the politics of the First World War are twofold in nature. He criticizes absolute nonviolence based on a fundamental rejection of the ends and means of war while, at the same time, recognizing the passionate critique of Gewalt to which the pacifist movement gave voice—a critique that extended into the heart of positive law. Central to that argument was the rejection of compulsory military service: "Militarism is the compulsory, universal use of violence as a means to the ends of the state."[48] Benjamin expresses himself in complete accordance with the pacifists here, not only abstractly but in the actual fact that both he and Scholem successfully avoided the trenches of the First World War.[49] Militarism, as articulated by the pacifists, rests in the hands of the state to apply Gewalt as it sees fit in reaching its ends by any means. As the only party who opposed the war from the perspective on violence and who took this compulsory aspect to task, the pacifists were able to arrive at a critique of the application of Gewalt itself, says Benjamin. Gewalt, in their analysis, has another function: not only the fictive application of "natural means" but the application of natural means as a "means of legal ends" (*Rechtszweck*; II:186). The submission of the citizen to law, particularly in compulsory military service, is an example of such "legal ends."

Yet where Gewalt is law forming, in the submission of a population to law, compulsory military service is law maintaining. Rather than the source of all Gewalt as the "pacifists and activists" believe, it is merely an example of its law-maintaining form, i.e., a law of violence (II:187). This notion also forms the second aspect of Benjamin's critique. Whereas the pacifists proclaim a "childish anarchism . . . that refuses to acknowledge any constraint of the individual and declares 'what pleases is permitted,' " they fail to account for a dimension of action that would be "moral and historical."[50] In

the rejection of compulsion altogether, they overlook an objective structure of justice that immanently negates a theory of private needs in favor
of a more compelling view of freedom. In that respect Benjamin returns to
the notion that the interests of humanity are to be recognized in the interests of each individual, just as he does in the notes on the category of justice.[51] Rather than a freedom without restraints, Benjamin proposes a categorical imperative with a theological dimension: "Act in such a way that
you employ humanity—your own humanity as well as that of the next person—always as ends, never merely as a means."[52] Even this, he says, is a
limited version of positive rights in practice. In addition, a sphere beyond
the worldly actions of the individual must be preserved. As we have seen
several times before, fate is a category in which divine intention and
worldly actions confront one another in Benjamin's thinking. The positive
rights of mutuality between individuals has an interest in preserving "the
representation and preservation of a fateful order," not a "formless 'freedom'" manifested in the first form of anarchism but a "higher order of
freedom" of a distinctly religious nature.[53] Ethical action must also point
to a higher notion of freedom beyond the mere atomization of single ethical acts existing for all time. This extends a critique to the anarchists' call
for a "formless freedom" that remains unable to articulate even the contours of such a demand, allowing the collective aspect of fate, otherwise expressed here in the form of the tragic hero, to wander into the realm of the
private satisfaction of needs.

While Benjamin uses the term *anarchism* to launch a critique of pacifism, he apparently maintained a twofold conception of the term.[54] Compare this positive statement on the anarchists that follows shortly thereafter:

> Significantly, the decay of parliaments has perhaps turned away
> as many minds from the ideal of a nonviolent resolution to polit-
> ical conflicts as were attracted to it by the war. The pacifists stand
> in contrast to the Bolsheviks and syndicalists. They have articu-
> lated a devastating and, on the whole, apt critique of present-day
> parliaments.[55]

A similar sentiment may be found in Benjamin's notes on "Das Recht
zur Gewaltanwendung" (The Right to Use Violence), written in response
to an article of the same title published in the *Blätter für religiösen Sozialismus* (Journal for Religious Socialism; September 1920).[56] The author of the

article, H. Vorwerk, begins with the statement that only the state has the right to the use of violence. In reply, Benjamin considers three positions on authority: 1. the state is the highest legal institution, 2. power is the source of authority from its own or another source, i.e., the notion of a self-contained, perfect form of power (*Machtvollkommenheit*), 3. authority is established through "worldly theocracy." To these possibilities he matches the following conclusions: the use of violence is or should be A) denied for both state and individual, B) sanctioned for both state and individual, C) justified for the state, or D) justified for the individual. Vorwerk puts forward his argument specifically against what he terms ethical anarchism. Benjamin, however, takes up the term as the most appropriate description of his own political views:

> The material impossibility of this view appears to have disturbed the author so greatly that he fails to establish its logical possibility as a distinct position, referring to it instead as an inconsequential, one-sided application of ethical anarchism. This view has to be represented in the case where, on the one hand (in opposition to A), he sees no principle contradiction between violence and morality and, on the other hand (in contrast to C), he sees a principle contradiction between morality and the state (or law). The exposition of this position is one of the tasks of my moral philosophy where the term *anarchism* can surely be used. It calls for a theory that does not reject a moral right to violence in itself, but rather in every human institution, community, or individuality that accords itelf a monopoly on violence or reserves the right to violence on principle, in general, or from some other perspective, rather than revere violence as the providence of divine power—as perfect power in a single moment.[57]

Benjamin defends the idea of an ethical anarchism that takes as its goal a neutralization of the paradox of the moral application of violence. He theoretically develops a political notion concerning the abolition of Gewalt through moral, humanistic institutions, societies, and individuals themselves. The right to such a human state is ensured and guaranteed by nothing less then divine power, as no profane institution is able to match divine Gewalt.

The article on the right to violence led Benjamin to speculate on an ethical anarchism based on morally acting individuals and social institutions, yet whose authority would, however, ultimately rest on divine Gewalt. The focus of his concern is the elimination of Gewalt from the worldly realm altogether. He asks, Is it possible to solve human problems through pure, nonviolent means? Indeed, like many of the anarchists, it appears that Benjamin sought a measure of utopian behavior in the social realm of individuals. His proposition is rather unambiguous here: "Nonviolent agreement is possible wherever a culture of the heart has given humanity the use of pure means of agreement. Legal and illegal means of every kind, which are all forms of violence, may be confronted with nonviolent ones as a pure means."[58] A model for conflict resolution is to be sought not within the political sphere but within society. In this respect the *Nächstenliebe* edict of the Psalms to love thy neighbor is perhaps the force that is best able to construct a "culture of the heart" (Kultur des Herzens).[59] Benjamin's call to a "culture of the heart" may appear rather vague. However, if we take Ahad Haam's essay "Die Lehre des Herzens" ("The Teachings of the Heart") from *Am Scheidewege*, which Benjamin and Scholem read together, we find something on the order of a Judaic categorical imperative in the words of Hillel: "That which you hate yourself, do not afflict on your neighbor—with this is the entire teachings."[60] This mutuality was, for Ahad Haam, the cornerstone of a rejuvenation of Judaism beyond mere soil, penetrating into the "heart" of social relations. Benjamin's "culture of the heart" sought to extend this maxim of cultural Zionism, with its clear disdain for the dominance of practical goals of the colonialist mentality, to a general maxim. In this he sought to apply the demands of the cultural Zionists to all culture. In addition to this text from Ahad Haam, we have already identified such a culture with the worldly activity of "messianic intensity" (Fragment) of mutual recognition and cooperation. Benjamin names the other virtues here that form the basis of a culture of the heart: "courtesy, sympathy, love of peace, trust."[61] From his analysis of the state we are able to envisage a political realm dominated by the powerful, seeking to establish rules and rights to serve their own interest. He appears to place all hope, therefore, in a messianic transformation of society and the individual. That these qualities or virtues take shape in society defines the "law" of their objective character, so he argues. Such pure means are therefore immediate means.[62]

Social relations through the medium of pure means is the framework of a cultural-categorical imperative; it is also a cultural arena of material goods existing in an ethical matrix, similar to his notes on justice: "In the material connection of human conflicts to goods, the realm of pure means is opened."[63] The relationship between good and goods is articulated as a politics of technique, of civilized agreement, that functions under the principle of the exclusion of Gewalt. Here Benjamin introduces a problem in the communicative sphere: how would one attempt to exclude Gewalt from civil society when active, verbal fraudulence is unremittingly tolerated by the state, existing shoulder to shoulder with truth. Since there has never been such a thing as due process in language, the origins of fraudulence, i.e., the lie, has never been dealt with in connection to judgment. However, "there is a sphere of human agreement that is nonviolent to the extent that it is wholly inaccessible to violence: the true sphere of 'understanding' [is] language."[64] Where the lie is expressed, it remains uncontested, having largely been removed from juridical consideration in a worldly sense and deemed unattainable in its language. It is the very opposite of an understanding; it is, in fact, a purposeful misunderstanding. By the time that law intervenes in language to address the lie, it is too late. It has already become professional deceit. Nevertheless, because the legal order assumes its ability to destroy lawlessness as it appears and because fraudulence is not considered a part of the realm of Gewalt, law is unable to address the origins of deceit, says Benjamin.[65] Just as in the case of the strike, fear is the instrument that lies behind the lawful action of the state, remaining all the while powerless to the true, linguistic origins of fraudulence.

Benjamin therefore rejects the notion that positive law is able to resolve the very thing it promises to ensure. Nor is there a political solution to the problem of Gewalt. The only answer can be found in the divine as it makes its entrance into the social realm. The social realm is radically transformed by a messianic general strike, on the one hand, and a daily politics of pure means on the other. This vision of a worldly form of justice is found in the "natural" rapport of individuals—a series of utopian relationships in a broader social context. For Benjamin, this politics of pure means would be based on the "peaceful intercourse between private persons" that is capable of solving conflicts in much the same way as diplomacy, where "private, personal" conflict resolution is transcribed into worldly, political dimensions based on individual virtues such as honesty.[66] Where a politics of pure means is envisioned in an individual form, it is not to be reduced merely to the private realm. On the contrary, the pure means of all individuals are to be claimed by every individual.

Violence and Myth

Even within a culture born from a politics of pure means the difficulty conceiving of a society completely removed from the problem of violence is contingent on an appropriate concept of rights and laws. There is no worldly realm that is, in and of itself, free of Gewalt:

> Since, however, every conceivable solution to human tasks—not to speak of redemption from the tracks of world-historical existence hitherto—remains impossible if violence is totally excluded in principle, the question necessarily arises as to kinds of violence other than all those envisaged by legal theory.[67]

To be sure, a principled culture of pure means would not be able to isolate every aspect of the profane that contains a realm of Gewalt, since Gewalt is manifested in almost every sphere of existence. However, when existence itself is freed by a "redemption from the tracks of world-historical existence hitherto," Gewalt would no longer be tied to ends, determined neither by justified nor unjustified means, but drawn in an entirely new direction, says Benjamin. This direction would be capable of applying violence as "fateful Gewalt."[68] A magical connection? Certainly this "insolubility of all legal problems" in the material world is only solvable in a divine one, as the only force capable of judging rights and laws in Benjamin's system appears to be God alone.[69] The idea of pure violence of a supreme judge enables Benjamin to provide a further imperative in this regard: "For it is never reason that decides on the justification of means and the justice of ends, but fateful violence on the former and God on the latter."[70] Benjamin's model for a determinate, historically rupturing Gewalt is formed from God's ultimate authority/violence, which is "valid in all cases."[71]

Just as in a culture of pure means, the transformation of worldly Gewalt is expressed as unmediated, everyday experience of the individual. Anger and fright, for example, are not so much the means of planned ends but interpreted here as "manifestations." Manifestation is assigned to the purest form of Gewalt by the image of the divine, where divine justice is capable of thoroughly piercing worldly experience and permeating all aspects of human intention and justification. Ends must appear, in short, as manifestations rather than any concrete effort on the part of God within the profane. Benjamin concludes, therefore, that the only objectively realizable manifestation of Gewalt in the profane is mythical. Seen from the perspective of the profane, the only objective of divine manifestation appears in the form of mythical violence: "Mythical violence in its original form is a mere manifestation of the gods. Not a means to their ends, scarcely a manifestation of their will, but first of all a manifestation of their existence."[72] We have already seen in Benjamin's work how references to mythical gods have rendered themselves equally valid for a monotheisic God and, as such, have led to the suspicion that the Greeks may have lent an acceptable face to "oriental" speculation.[73] Like divine intervention in the life of the righteous— for example, the idea of justice manifested in Job's fate—mythical violence is bound to the fate of the tragic hero:

> How little such divine violence meant to the ancients [in relation to] the law-preserving violence of punishment is shown by the heroic legends in which the hero—for example, Prometheus— challenges fate with dignified courage, fights it with varying fortunes [*Glück*], and is not left by the legend without hope of one day bringing a new law to humanity.[74]

The hero introduces a new law and breaks the weak, law-maintaining violence of the gods. The unmediated, divine Gewalt that Benjamin presents here in mythical form appears to us as divine manifestation in which heavenly, thieving violence falls back on a law-maintaining world. But as worldly manifestation of myth is ultimately juxtaposed to a true and ultimately divine manifestation, a contradiction in myth is exposed. In this process myth must rescind on the claim to delineate fate, for even though an intimate and necessary relationship between myth and God exists, both are ultimately opposed to one another:

> Far from inaugurating a purer sphere, the mythical manifestation of immediate violence shows itself to be fundamentally identical with all legal violence, and turns suspicion concerning the latter into the certainty of the decay of its historical function, the destruction of which thus becomes obligatory. The very task of de-

struction poses again, in the last instance, the question of a pure immediate violence that might be able to call a halt to mythical violence, just as, in all spheres God confronts myth, mythical violence is confronted by the divine.[75]

The mythical manifestation of Gewalt is unmediated, legal violence. But if mythical Gewalt is law-maintaining, divine Gewalt is the destruction of law, for whereas mythical law establishes borders, the divine recognizes no borders; if the mythical attributes blame, the divine revokes blame. Consequently, mythical violence legitimizes the sanctioning of state violence (*Rechtsgewalt*) as it does responsibility and sin.[76] In this sense the law of violence, state of violence, and right of violence are all tied to the origins of sin and the attempt to attribute sin to humanity. A jettison of the mythical manifestation of Gewalt requires a return to the question of the origins of sin, states Benjamin again here.

In contrast to feudal barons for whom power forms the only definitive stakes of worldly barriers, Gewalt knew no boundaries in an original state, neither the meaning of Gewalt in the sense of power, nor the meaning of the transgression of law. Transgression before expulsion was not prohibited but prohibitive—the lack of knowledge made not only prohibition but punishment nonexistent. Therefore the origin of the first sin was a consequence of such a transgression rather than a punishment. The fall from paradise thus introduced an element of choice, as Benjamin understands it, and it is this choice that made the entrance of humanity into the domain of law a matter of necessity: "Its entrance is, in the sense of law, not chance but fate."[77] Just as the fate of the tragic hero is embedded in the will to decline, so too is fate embedded in will in the decline from Eden. This decline opened up the reality of the profane. In a true, natural human condition, humanity was neither capable of being guilty of sin nor of suffering the slavery of law: "The dominion of existence under law ends with mere life."[78] Only in a return to a natural state will law cease to dominate everything living: "Mythical Gewalt is the blood Gewalt against mere life for its own sake; divine Gewalt is pure Gewalt over all life for the sake of the living."[79]

The Gewalt of God is of a different caliber then that of myth. While God's conflagration of things and people is unmitigated and exhaustive, it is not punishment but purification. Resistance to the will of God may define sin but divine Gewalt comes as rectification through destruction. An example of this is the fact that God's destruction is bloodless, says Benjamin.[80] This reveals "a deep connection between the lack of bloodshed and the expiatory character of this violence."[81] God destroys without spilling blood—itself considered here the "symbol of mere life" (Symbol des bloßen Lebens)—because His violence is propelled out of the sphere of violence altogether. He can therefore destroy profane forms and rectify sin at the same time. Just as the sinners no longer remain, neither does sin. Blood and sin are both aspects of the profane world, expressed here as "mere life."[82] Divine Gewalt is thus manifested in the profane world and not solely as tradition: "This divine Gewalt makes itself evident not only through religious tradition but also appears in present-day life in at least one sanctified manifestation."[83] Within the profane world, within history, a repaired manifestation emerges but, at the same moment, ends history altogether. Divine Gewalt is not merely a manifestation for its own sake but enters worldly affairs to cleanse humanity and destroy evil, not "that God Himself works miracles in unmediated appearances but through the moment of bloodless overwhelming, execution without sin."[84] God is Himself whole in His actions. He does not send a manifestation of Himself as a miracle such that one would ask why a correction in His divine plan was needed. God's manifestation comes rather as the sanctifying, redeeming, completion of worldly affairs: "finally through the absence of all legal formation as relief and liberation from the suffering of administrative law."[85]

Although divine Gewalt is destructive in relation to things, rights, and life, it is not in terms of "souls of the living" (II:200). In this regard, action preceding sin initiates the final stage of the discussion and concludes this chapter of the critique of violence. Benjamin asserts here, perhaps in contrast to Kierkegaard,[86] that if action did not take place judgment itself would be impossible. The reality of an act like murder, however, conceived of as an event God would be unable to predict or prevent, would make the idea of God improbable. The commandment prohibiting murder must therefore be seen not as a means of judgment but rather as an ethical norm that reflects the "divinity of life."[87] Benjamin leads a small discussion here on the justification for murder and the relationship to its prohibition in the Torah. He argues that while the commandment cannot be read as a measure of judgment, of whether a particular murder is just or unjust, it serves as a measure of action. It is not law that condemns murder but the structure of a society's action to confront the ethical isolation of the individual.

Scholem, who distinguishes between the Torah and the oral tradition with regard to the death penalty, may have been the source for Benjamin's speculation in his treatment of Talmudic jurisprudence in thesis 7 of his essay on Jonah.[88] In Benjamin's program ethics becomes the means for a "divinity of life" as the search for an ethical theorem in the process of sanctification en route toward the divine. For a world to appear to match the "not-yet-attained condition of the just human being,"[89] the real existing world, with its limitation and material suffering, would have to decline: "Just as much as man is holy (or the life in him that is identical in worldly existence, death and afterlife), there is little sacred in his condition, in his corporal, vulnerable life in the collective."[90]

There is something divine embedded in mere living, something of an original, natural state. What is divine in humanity is profane beyond mortality, something that is bound to worldly affairs but, in one instant, able to transcend the limitations of the body as well as the collective. Hence the individual's divine potential is the ability to overcome death in choosing fate. In this respect it appears Benjamin did not consider the divine aspects of the living as formed experience but rather as original embodiment. Concerning an "origin of the dogma of the divinity of life," he writes, "what is here pronounced sacred was according to ancient mythical thought the marked bearer of the attribution of guilt: mere life."[91] Here it seems rather apparent that the beginning of a search for the origins of the divine within the profane would start with the notion of a natural humanity as "mere life" that preceded the concept of sin. He focuses his attention on the attribution of guilt or responsibility to mere life in the form of the fall from paradise and the attempt to liberate it from eternal responsibility. Just as in the initial discussion of the origins of evil in this section, Benjamin states that if there was no true concept of sin before sin, equally there can never be a proper attribution of guilt to the former residents of Eden. God's judgment cannot be understood as punishment but only as cleansing. In cleansing rather than revenge God preserves the natural and divine aspects of humanity from the damage that would occur in the relocation from Eden. The revelation of pure humanity, its release from eternal sin, is therefore a messianic task:

> On the breaking of this cycle that is maintained by mythical forms of law, on the suspension of law, with all the forces on which it depends, and thus finally on the abolition of state power, a new historical epoch is founded.[92]

Divine Postponement, Judgment, and the Question of Violence

With the "Critique of Violence" Benjamin introduced into the discussion a range of new formulations in the difficult relationship of worldly injustice to divine providence. Beginning with a philosophy of right, we saw him apply the discussion on justice to a debate on the justification of ends and means. He takes up the problem of the administration of worldly rights through the institutions and counterinstitutions of power; violence being the measure of these competing claims to rights and means. Events of the day such as the general strike and antiwar pacifism form the background to the notion of the fate of the individual and the meaning of justice in the divine realm. Ultimate Gewalt appears as the true manifestation of God in the world that redeems the profane, as the critique concludes with an attempt to articulate a politics of pure means that afford terms for constructing a new ethics.

Several aspects of this critique is evident in the second part of Scholem's "Theses on the Concept of Justice." Here Scholem breaks away slightly from Benjamin's "Notes to a Study of the Category of Justice" and points to a larger commentary on his early works as a whole, particularly his studies of violence and authority that begin with the early essay on language and culminate in the "Critique of Violence." Referring back to the "Critique of Violence," Scholem announces at the outset of the second part that the contextual basis for the concept of justice is to be sought within the framework of the philosophy of right, not with regard to the tension between law-forming and law-maintaining violence but the distinction between a philosophy of politics and authority and one of religion. This distinction is all the more relevant because the philosophy of right, says Scholem, so closely borders the sphere of religion in this respect. The question of justice is first and foremost a pillar of the philosophy of religion, he argues.

Scholem begins his analysis with the possibility of judgment. As it appears in the conclusion to Benjamin's early speculations on language (II:153–53), judgment is examined in terms of its existence in the profane. In defining justified judgment as resting on postponement, the question whether judgment is possible refers back to its worldly execution. Scholem reiterates the notion that judgment is dependent on the juridical application of Gewalt. The effectiveness of judgment is therefore linked to the jurisdiction the authority of judgment is able to establish, namely, its power of execution. But between judgment and execution a contradiction is to emerge that only God can solve, the one force simultaneously capable of both divine judgment and its execution: "Between judgment and execution a fundamental impasse exists," says Scholem. The contradiction of worldly judgment, which attempts to transcend the problem of postponement, is what he here defines as the "mythology of the legal system." This leads Scholem to the thesis that every human action exists in God's awareness and by His judgment, and, just as every human judgment must be sanctioned by divine judgment, the judging attribute of God rests solely on His judgment with regard to the profane, which is manifest in His Last Judgment. In this final form there is a tallying of all human action in a divine administration.[93]

Similar to Benjamin in his discussion of fate and justice, Scholem also postulates God permitting human activity through His judgment: "Every human action elicits a divine judgment about itself with absolute certainty," says Scholem, introducing a new problem in the notion of justice: justice on earth, i.e., the execution of profane judgment as justice implies the full negation of divine judgment. If that which is just is capable of *annihilating* the notion that every human action necessitates a divine judgment, it institutes a postponement in its place. The idea of justice in Jonah's prophecy is manifested in the annihilation of God's judgment against the great city, thus turning His own prophet and prophecy on its head. But if worldly justice is the elimination of divine judgment, the question turns naturally to the existence of God, which Scholem claims never to have doubted.[94] While Scholem does appear to lay the groundwork for the exclusion of the divine, he appears not to be referring to the complete neutralization of God from the sphere of justice but rather the "historical annihilation of divine judgment" in its manifestation. It is here that Scholem formulates the eternal suspension of His judging to constitute the messianic, for that which is capable of postponing the Last Judgment introduces divine justice into worldly affairs and thereby neutralizes the tension between the divine and the profane. Scholem formulates this in his fourth thesis: "Messianic is the kingdom that is not followed by a Last Judgment." The prophets are deemed messianic precursors in their call for justice because they sought the elimination of the Last Judgment. Jonah may in fact be the best example of this, first in his attempt to avoid prophecy, then in the reversal of his delivered prophecy. Just actions imply therefore the "immediate" establishment of the messianic.

This means the transformation of time from the historical to the eternal now and justice from the abstract to the concrete.

Justice is therefore not merely a conceptual "border," as one might be lead to see it in Benjamin's formulations, but a living, breathing, realizable cornerstone of Judaism. Maimonides, whom Scholem draws upon in his fifth thesis on the continuous coming of the future world, if lacking a penchant for the revolutionary, apocalyptic politics of immanent redemption, still articulates an "eternal now" of the messianic kingdom. If not one letter of the Torah will be altered upon the arrival of the Messiah, as Maimonides stipulates in his epistle to the Jews of Yemen, then essentially he prescribes a kingdom that is always coming, or always becoming. Prophecy is therefore a vision of the eternal now, "the word that is always coming." "This is why the prophets demand justice: in order to finally eliminate the Last Judgment. In the just act the messianic is established immediately."

Postponement is the "all" of the divine attributes of justice. Scholem now turns to agency in modeling this attribute, postulating the role of human activity in the establishment of a just realm. The mitigating factor in achieving justice is not abstract power but Gewalt, he states, drawing on the "Critique of Violence." In the latter we are able to identify both the terms *authority* and the *force* that establishes authority, i.e., violence, either as a threat or as an actuality. Here Scholem takes up the mythical dimension of violence that Benjamin formulates as the symbolic manifestation of the divine.[95] Revealing its contradiction, we have seen how a "mythical origin of law" in Benjamin's essay on language gives way to a divine conception of Gewalt in the "Critique of Violence."[96] Here Scholem adopts Benjamin's categories concerning myth, drafting human activity in the image of the profane locked in battle with worldly, mythical violence: "Almost all realms of human action are (still) subject to mythical categories from which fate alone attributes meaning." Scholem places emphasis here on Benjamin's ideas on fate and character, attempting to carve out a sphere of human behavior leading beyond the realm of myth, which is, in a sense, the imitation of divine Gewalt. At the same time, he seeks to move beyond the fate of profane destination based on a will to decline, which itself is merely a symbolic version of the "eternal now." In his theory of postponement *"Justice is the elimination of fate from action."* Justice is therefore not only an eternal annihilation of divine activity in the realm of judgment, it is also the complete elimination of the myth of the tragic hero while moving into a kingdom beyond fate. The righteous act, Scholem explains, "has no

fate."[97] Thus postponement and transformation, like the act of righteousness, both point beyond the world of injustice.

The final, two concluding theses are perhaps Scholem's most prescriptive. In seeking some form of mediation between a radical transcendence
of the profane through active postponement, that is, through the *transformation*,[98] *elimination*, and *annihilation* endemic to an apocalyptic revolution, and a Maimonidian conviction that the messianic world will appear
exactly the same as this one—"just a little different"[99]—Scholem arrives at
a thesis of messianic action. He writes, "To allow the messianic world to
break through requires only *virtual* postponement of the perspective on redemption." A vision that enables the eruption of the messianic world requires "virtual" postponement and substitution. But this moderate, virtual
moment is radically contrasted to an apocalyptic, cataclysmic one, which
he defines in thesis 5 as the real politics of Judaism. We can detect here two
strands of messianic tension: on the one hand, a messianism of the act, initiated by violence, and, on the other, the quietistic acquisition of a vision
of redemption. It is the former, in Scholem's estimation, that draws closer
to the program of transcendence in Benjamin's "Critique of Violence":
"The apocalyptic vision of the messianic kingdom has the value and truth
of revolutionary propaganda—it seeks to provoke the final conflict of
Gewalt where myth declines." Taking the form of revolutionary propaganda, the apocalyptic scenario is able to bring to a head a final battle of
Gewalt in which mythical forms finally disappear. The ironic figure of the
Messiah enters here, a nonfigured but also nonfigurative characterization
of the cataclysmic. His character represents the power of a life without fate,
the same *schicksalslos* (fatelessness) that Benjamin describes in the words of
Hölderlin in his "Fate and Character" (II:174). It is the personality of the
Messiah that forms the ironic dimension of messianism—an individual
who represents the impersonal. It is however the only figure of the messianic that Scholem claims to be able to break through this "demonic
fate."[100] Only through the introduction of the ironic Messiah into the
"world epoch," itself characterized by Scholem as the "catastrophic," can
the redemptive power "of a life without fate be presented" in a historical
epoch beyond history.[101]

In the second part of the "Theses on the Concept of Justice" Scholem
aims to incorporate the postponement of the divine in the profane, seeking the category of justice to bridge the abyss between judgment and its
execution. He works to articulate the messianic act as both action and the

reception of divine providence in a unity of thought and action, which we first observed in his linguistic analysis of the name of God. Such a messianic thought-action would be capable of pointing to a "history" beyond a theory of attributes and the problem of the physical aspects of God, a state of open revelation where *die Stimme Gottes,* "the voice of God," would ring freely in the sound of justice, the unmoving, eternal being of a just life. The good life would be audible in the silent voice of God, emitting the "unmetaphorical object of the just life."[102]

The Righteous, the Pious, the Scholar

A penchant for the science of redemption is perhaps one of the most enduring aspects of the early political theology that served Scholem in his lifelong research into Judaism. The incipient constitution of a practical messianism in the early intellectual exchange with Benjamin constituted, in many ways, the greatest impetus for this pursuit. Although it is not possible here to analyze every instance of this ongoing dialogue in connection with Scholem's later work, I would like to conclude with a glimpse into Scholem's later conception of justice in order to explore how these ideas continue to form the basis for speculation in his late work. Scholem's essay, "Die Lehre vom 'Gerechten' in der jüdischen Mystik," "The Teachings of the 'Just' in Jewish Mysticism," was first published in 1958 in the *Eranos Jahrbuch* and was again presented as the third chapter in *Von der mystischen Gestalt der Gottheit* under the title "Zaddik; der Gerechte" (in English: *On the Mystical Shape of the Godhead,* "Zaddik: The Righteous One").[103] Following the early speculations, here the notion of justice is expressed in the form of an ideal character. Yet these are not merely late observations. Already in his notebooks from 1918–1919, following upon his study of Jonah, he formulated a threefold concept of the just figure: "The Torah speaks of the divinely righteous, the prophecy of the hidden righteous, while tradition establishes the concept of the just, which encompasses both. Revelation and messianic time are inseparably linked to the oral teachings."[104] But whereas, in the earlier text on Jonah, embodiment takes form only in the category of the righteous, Scholem resumes the same line of investigation in his late work by distinguishing between three ideal types in Jewish society: the righteous, the pious, and the scholar—tzadik, chasid, and *talmid chakham.*[105]

First, following the line of analysis within the discussion of prophetic justice, the notion of tzedek is drawn from a divine exemplar. The relationship between "justice and its bearers" and "divine justice"[106] is one that is informed by the association of subject and attribute.[107] It is expressed in a linguistic association of the name of God between *tzedek* and *tzadik* (justice and the righteous). In this way, the Torah is able to refer to God as the righteous of the world or the righteous one who lives eternally (*tzadiko shel 'olam, tzadik chai 'olamim*; ges:87/mys:91). The standard of justice is measured by divine wisdom, the knowledge of good and evil, the ability to judge and refrain from execution (Jonah)—in short, to do that which is beyond the capacity of mortals. This ideal status forms the basis for further speculation on the manifestation of justice, more specifically, in ideal prototypes of just behavior or worldly personifications of justice. The tzadik, the chasid, and the talmid chakham are redemptive figures contrasted to this notion of tzedek. All three form ideal character types in a "religious society,"[108] and although it is somewhat difficult to form a definitive picture of the three among various traditions, Scholem is able to articulate a few primary features.[109]

Whereas the scholar (talmid chakham) sees it as his most important task to be the bearer of the tradition of the divine word and its interpretation, the tzadik and chasid are less concerned with exegesis than with the absolute fulfillment of tradition. The cardinal feature of their identity is not intellectual prowess but rather a "moral and religious power" in the fulfillment of obligation.[110] In searching for a distinction between tzadik and chasid, the righteous and the pious, Scholem marks the chasid as being somewhat higher than the tzadik. He does so based on the distinction between that which is required of the devoted and that which is beyond the realm of demands, reminding one of the distinction introduced by Benjamin in his "Notes to a Study on the Concept of Justice." The tzadik is motivated by the fulfillment of moral obligations. Should he succeed in this task, he is prepared to take his rightful place as a tzadik. In this sense it is a rank of self-achievement open to all who are devoted and not a question of leadership or political charisma (ges:85). The chasid, on the other hand, is motivated by a real and compelling zeal that transverses the ordinary boundaries of religious obligations. If one is able to point to the tzadik as a state of accomplishment, it is a merit deserved in a somewhat ordinary sense. The chasid, however, is a truly extraordinary figure. In Benjamin's notes on justice we encountered a distinction between two figures, circulating around the unusual phrasing of a *Geforderte* (that or the one being demanded). He stipulates that virtue is the ethical category of that which is demanded. While virtue is the true achievement of the worldly demands of the *Geforderte*, the righteous (*gerecht*) preserves existence. We are reminded here of a phrase from Proverbs 10:2, "Righteousness delivers from death," which was an important component of Scholem's early repertoire of biblical citations. Here the righteous could be identified with the preservation of the world, a nondescript or "hidden" righteous figure who rather accidentally preserves the worldly. These are individuals who stand nearest to God and His divine justice.[111] In Benjamin's early formulations, "while virtuous can only be the fulfillment of that which is demanded, righteous is the guarantee of that which exists (through demands that are *perhaps* no longer determinable, but are nevertheless not of the ordinary kind)."[112] Drawing from these statements, we find Scholem's analysis mirrored in the categories of the pious chasid as the *Ungeforderte* (undemanded):

> The pious does not perform that which is required or demanded but that which is not demanded, and, even when carrying out a legal demand, he acts with such radical exuberance and subtlety that an entire world is revealed to him in the fulfillment of a commandment. An entire lifetime may be needed just to carry out one commandment properly.[113]

All three figures, the scholar, the righteous, and the pious, exercise discrete roles in Jewish society. While the scholar fulfills his role through study, the righteous carries out the completion of moral duties. However, in this "religious society," the chasid exhibits a revolutionary quality marked by extremity. His pursuit is not the mere fulfillment of obligation but an attempt to comply with the very root of moral law. Thus the term *radical* discriminates most appropriately between the other two figures. Consequently, a political dimension is invoked within religious society—"an anarchist element," says Scholem—that is characterized by the charismatic leadership of the chasid:

> He is a radical Jew who goes into extremes in an attempting to realize his destiny. This extremism—as inseparable from the nature of the pious man as it is alien to that of the righteous—may assume the most diverse forms. . . . He demands nothing of others

and everything of himself, and it is just this radicalness that sets him apart from the sober figure of the just, who gives to each what is due. In this lingering extremism, which never reaches a point of equilibrium, an anarchist element resides.[114]

It is certain from these reflections on the character of the chasid that Scholem is drawing on various aspects of his own political theory. Anarchism here, by the nature of its intensity, has a cataclysmic tone, reminding one of the Sabbatian model from which such a notion emerged. Scholem's formula of an apocalyptic or cataclysmic anarchism comes to the fore once again as critical inquiry. The charismatic aspect of the chasid appears to draw on the analysis of the Frankists—even the character description brings to mind Scholem's often psychological sketches of these leading figures. To be sure, the character type of this pious anarchist offers a quasi-messianic ideal to those seeking revolutionary leadership. With particular regard to a desired neutralization of the more cataclysmic aspects of the messianic wish, the radically ideal piousness of an equally radical conservatism (in terms of rites and obligations) would avail themselves of the political and religious turmoil that remained in the wake of the Sabbatians.[115] But, in addition, the pious anarchist was to represent a more primary aspect of the cause. A deepseated dismissal of worldly affairs marked the chasid with "something absurd and often offensive to bourgeois mentality."[116] Scholem comments that hardly a paradoxical act exists from which the pious would shy away if it meant the fulfillment of the true meaning of moral obligations.[117]

Scholem's analysis of divine postponement in the case of Jonah's prophecy led to a string of conjectures on the meaning of justice. *Aufschub* (postponement) became the most apparent sign of the manifestation of justice, typified by the notion of divine judgment suspending its execution. The nature of this suspension is not momentary, as with Nineveh, the redeemed city, but rather the divine connotation of all time and place. Scholem resumes this earlier course of thought, where the idea of justice in Jewish mysticism is depicted as "the elimination of the element of judgment":

The righteous is no longer the righteous judge; God as judge also presents an entirely different aspect of divinity in the Kabbalah than that of God as the righteous. *Law and justice or God as the bearer of justice are two different sides of God.* The uniqueness of this concept is most evident when the Kabbalists discuss not the earthly righteous but the just as an aspect of divinity, as a symbol of a status in God.[118]

The tzadik, like his forebear Job, is the righteous servant of God. The measure of his just character is not qualified by his actions as a judge but by the abandonment of the execution of judgment. But unlike the course of prophetic justice pursuant to the early speculations, Scholem states that the judging character of God is given a different configuration in the Kabbalah. Be that as it may, the linguistic focus remains constant. The distance from *Recht* (law) to *Gerechtigkeit* (justice) that forms the cornerstone of both Benjamin's main texts presented in this chapter is taken up again categorically: "*din* and *mishpat* (law and judgment) are different from *tzadik* and *tzedek* (righteous and righteousness)," remarks Scholem tersely in a footnote to the above citation.[119] The emphasis here lies in the idea of justice as a facet of the divine rather than the culmination of moral activity. Judgment and law form one side of this embankment, justice and the righteous the other. The distance rather than the "nearness" of the Psalms expresses their rapport.[120] But despite the proximity of *tzadik* to *tzedek*, there still remains an abyss through which the righteous may not pass.

The categorical distinction between the righteous and the pious is transformed again in the Kabbalah, says Scholem. In reference to the thirteenth-century Kabbalist Joseph Gikatilla and his book *Sha'are Tzedek* (the Gates of Justice), Scholem writes, "The main focus of the perspective of the just is the master of the living, if he is to be understood as a mystical symbol."[121] Quoting from this text, Scholem draws upon an aspect of redemption that Benjamin attempts to formulate as the restituto in integrem:

> "Know that for this reason the righteous are called righteous [*tzadikim*]: because they set all the inner things in their place within, and all outer things in their place without, and nothing leaves the boundary set for it. And that is why they are known as the righteous." [Scholem:] We find here the first major definition of the new understanding of the ideal figure of the tzadik, as it was later formulated in kabbalistic ethics: the righteous is the one who sets everything in the world in its proper place. But the simplicity of this definition should not deceive us as to the messianic significance and utopian explosiveness that resides within it, for a world in which everything is in its proper place would be,

considered from the point of view of Judaism, a redeemed world.
The dialectic of the righteous merges with the dialectic of the
messianic.[122]

The focus of a messianic restituto in integrem is a type of distributive justice that is able to return every disturbed thing and being to its rightful
place. The distinction between material goods and the ethical good is no
longer significant here, since both are objects that have lost their original
purpose. This presents a paradigmatic example of the ethical behavior of
the worldly righteous, first and foremost, in this world.[123] Nevertheless, the
messianic implications of such activity are made explicit in a "dialectic"
that begins with the restoration of the worldly and discovers within it a
rushing, messianic current leading beyond itself.[124] In referring to a dialectic, this lengthy citation is followed by one of Scholem's most cherished
phrases: "The repose of the organic within its movement."[125] That sentence, from Hegel's *Phenomenology of Spirit,* was first to come to Scholem's
attention in a discussion with Benjamin on a Saturday in the summer of
1916.[126] To find it reappearing here, nearly a half century later, points again
to the importance of that Saturday afternoon discussion.

The concept of justice as completion appears again in this essay after a
rather lengthy reference to Franz Joseph Molitor (mys:110). Scholem places
emphasis here on the messianic aspect of justice, in which the just, in Benjamin's terms, are endowed with the task of the "guarantee of the living."[127]
This leads into a discussion of the term *shalom:*

> The essence of the righteous, according to the symbolism of the
> living [*Lebendigen*] and sustaining life, consists in the establish-
> ment of harmony and peace—conceived in the Hebrew word
> *shalom* where the two merge. Strictly speaking, *shalom* represents
> a state of completeness or integrity, and it is only in these terms
> that it also refers to peace.[128]

In Hebrew script both *shalom* and *scholem* are visually undifferentiated, the
former being the Hebrew pronunciation and the latter Yiddish. This reinterpretation here of a linguistic analysis of the term harks back to earlier
considerations on the idea of perfection and its redemptive dimension. In
one of his early journal entries Scholem is prone to read into his own name
a messianic calling: "I will not alter the name that came across my lips as

the natural consequence of my activities, uninvited and yet welcome: . . . harbinger of redemption." "Who among us young Jews[129] has not had the same dream and seen himself as Jesus and the Messiah of the oppressed? . . . I've considered this dream so real as to be possible."[130] Scholem concludes these speculations on his own innate, redemptive qualities with a return to the name: "The way of the naive is the way to redemption. And the dreamer—whose name has him marked as the awaited: Scholem, the perfect—equipped himself for his work and began to act furiously to forge his weapons of knowledge."[131] It is perhaps slightly ironic that, in the first analysis, the term *shalom* is interpreted as the peaceful, messianic reconciliation of all that is misplaced and, in the second, the call to arms of a young man who ponders his own messiahship.[132] One sees here a definite interweaving of the concept of justice as a peaceful event, as a messianic battle, and as the redemption of society. All three faces of justice are public. They are conducted on an open, historical plane in relationship to humanity. Scholem's own early tendencies in this regard, as I tried to convey in the chapter on his early theological politics, cannot be categorized as wild flights of fancy. Despite the abandonment of his own messianic calling, he remains, in fact, true to the contours of such a calling in his theoretical analysis: the terms and conditions of a true, divine conception of justice secures a messianic moment for humanity in time.

The radical nature of this calling is always at the forefront of Scholem's consciousness. In the tradition of the Baal Shem, says Scholem, the "'children of the world to come'" are among the children in the open markets of this world.[133] Asked their role in this world, the children reply: "'We are jesters. If someone is feeling sad, we try to cheer him up, and if we see people fighting, we try to make peace between them.'"[134] These "clowns"— *Spaßmacher,* as Scholem calls them—are the true righteous in the eyes of the Baal Shem: "They do not sit at home thinking about their own salvation, but work in the dirty bustling marketplace, as he himself loved to do. The strength of their communion with God is proved in their ability to permeate coarse matter and raise it to the level of spirituality."[135] In contrast to Scholem's own messianic desires, these clowns appear not only to reflect the perfect form of the righteous in the eyes of the Baal Shem but in Scholem's own anarchist conception of justice as well.[136] The private, intensive communion with God is transformed into a religiosity of the "collectivists" (*Mitmenschen*), drawn from a profound concern with the redemption of the profane world. The purity of this first "nearness" is naturally compromised by the distance to the profane. In the proximity of this world to the next lies a paradox that the chasid inherited from the anarchism of the Sabbatians:

> The righteous enters the social sphere originally in order to spiritualize it and to restore active life to its contemplative roots; in doing so, however, the righteous is himself transformed. The true friend of God becomes the true friend of humanity, as the accent shifts imperceptibly.[137]

The transformation of the redemptive task to the ethical task of the revolutionary "collectivist" (*Mitmensch*) who seeks worldly redemption in the aspirations of the divine, injects a degree of ambiguity into the paradoxical messianism of this transformation. To be sure, the tzadik here is a public figure, a political activist working toward the "justification" of the public sphere. Publicity is his messianic dominion and his "isolation" (an *Einsamkeit* we also encountered in Benjamin's fragment) is the mark of his radical "collectivity" (*Mitmenschlichkeit*).[138] The righteous are no longer measured by the divine but rallied by the just character of wandering preachers. In this way justice undergoes a "dialectical" transformation that extends beyond textual justice into a transhistorical realm determined by the public sphere:

> The chasidic authors well understood that the relationship of the just to his fellow human beings has its own dialectic. . . . By attempting to lift up his fellow human beings, he himself is raised; the more he fulfills his function as the center of the community, the more his own stature grows.[139]

The charisma of the righteous figure, the chasidic tzadik, becomes the determinate of his own redemptive powers. He is engaged in a process of rising and falling from a realm of blessedness to that of quotidian commonality and material suffering. The paradox of his transgressive nature is embodied in his connection to society. But despite a clear relationship to a heretical Sabbatian legacy, the paradox of this chasidic tzadik is able to acquire for itself a "constructive meaning." "It is no longer a matter of treachery, apostasy, or demonic preoccupation with evil; instead, it involves the performance of a task essential to the survival of society."[140]

A righteous figure who is capable of intervening in the profane with his or her "nearness" to the divine, able to rectify both material displacement as well as the origin of sin, who can unleash the power of language as well as bridge the chasm between intention and action—this figure embodies the meaning of Benjamin's and Scholem's early political theology as they conceived of it together in the first decades of the twentieth century. These ideas were to expand and permeate the corpus of Scholem's work, the study of Judaism, and have a lasting effect on philosophy and cultural history at the end of the twentieth century. In short, these ideas constitute a political theology of redemption.

ABBREVIATIONS

II	Benjamin, *Gesammelte Schriften*, vol. II:1
GB	Benjamin, *Gesammelte Briefe,* vols. I–II
briefe	Benjamin, *Briefe*, vols. I–II
ref	Benjamin, *Reflections*
tag	Scholem, *Tagebücher*, vols. I–II
B	Scholem, *Briefe*, vols. I–III
von berlin	Scholem, *Von Berlin nach Jerusalem*, expanded version
freund	Scholem, *Walter Benjamin. Die Geschichte einer Freundschaft*
ges	Scholem, *Von der mystischen Gestallt der Gottheit*
mys	Scholem, *On the Mystical Shape of the Godhead*
j	Scholem, *Judaica*, vols. I–VI
jjc	Scholem, *On Jews and Judaism in Crisis*
zur kab	Scholem, *Zur Kabbala und ihrer Symbolik*
SdE	Franz Rosenzweig, *Stern der Erlösung*
GdU	Ernst Bloch, *Geist der Utopie,* first edition
ba	Søren Kierkegaard, *Der Begriff Angst*
1827	Franz Joseph Molitor, *Philosophie der Geschichte,* vol. 1, first edition
1857	Franz Joseph Molitor, *Philosophie der Geschichte,* vol. 1, second edition

NOTES

Introduction

1. Wyneken's key texts from this period are *Schule und Jugendkultur*, *Die neue Jugend: ihr Kampf um Freiheit und Wahrheit*, and *Der Kampf für die Jugend*. It is doubtful whether Wyneken had a lasting impact on Benjamin. On Wyneken, his turn to anti-Semitism, and Benjamin's break with the movement see Brodersen, *Spinne im eigenen Netz*, pp. 52–56.

2. See Scholem, *Von Berlin nach Jerusalem*, pp. 49 (hereafter von berlin:49); and *Walter Benjamin. Die Geschichte einer Freundschaft*, pp. 10–11 (hereafter freund:10–11).

3. Scholem records this meeting quite memorably in his journal: "Ich komme ins Bibliotheks-Katalogzimmer, steht da mein Herr Benjamin und kuckt auf und kann seine Augen überhaupt nicht mehr von mir trennen. Ich sehe meine Sachen nach, jener geht hinaus; schön, denke ich, weg bist du. Aber siehe da, die Tür öffnet sich wieder, zurück kommt Herr Benjamin, auf mich zu, macht eine formvollendete Verbeugung und fragt mich, ob ich jener Herr sei, der auf dem Hiller-Abend gesprochen hätte?" Scholem, *Tagebücher* 1:131 (hereafter tag 1:131).

4. Benjamin, Scholem, *Briefwechsel*. Other sources include Scholem's late recollections in his autobiography (von berlin), his book on the partnership (freund), and the collection of essays entitled *Walter Benjamin und sein Engel*.

5. With the publication of Scholem's journals and letters we now have a very reliable record of their early discussions. See tag 1 and 2.

6. Werner Scholem remained committed to both Germany and socialism to the very end. He was murdered in Buchenwald in 1940. Benjamin's brother, Georg, in many ways a mirror of Scholem's brother, was murdered in Mauthausen in August 1942.

7. See von berlin:59–61, 66–67 and, in depth, in the journals.

8. tag 1:71.

9. I have included several works of this type in the bibliography. Two examples are Witte, *Walter Benjamin*; and Brodersen, *Spinne im eigenen Netz*.

10. I have chosen this approach for two reasons: first, with regard to Benjamin, the secondary literature is rife with personal and often rather arbitrary associations. I have tried here to consider Benjamin's work as a part of the corpus of German thought, open to inquiry and investigation, rather than as a private reserve for insiders with references that have taken on purely cult significance. Second, Scholem's early texts remain unknown and in need of explanation. I have concentrated on exposing this critical dimension in Scholem's thought for those who seek an understanding of the origins of his most innovative approach to Jewish history and culture.

11. "Das Problem des jüdischen Geistes ist einer der größten und beharrendsten Gegenstände meines Denkens." Benjamin, *Gesammelte Briefe* 1:283 (hereafter GB 1:283).

12. tag 1:391. Scholem reproduces this journal entry in freund:45.

13. "Metaphysik ist die Theorie im legitimen Konjunktiv. Dies ist die beste Definition, die ich bisher gefunden habe. Sie sagt alles." tag 2:267.

14. As of late, there has been some discussion of a "secularizing" effect with regard to Scholem. See, for example, Werblowsky, "Tradition in 'säkularer' Kultur," pp. 70–80; and Wohlfarth, "'Haarscharf an der Grenze zwischen Religion und Nihilismus,'" pp. 176–257, in Schäfer and Smith, *Gershom Scholem*. With Benjamin, see also the discussion in Witte, "'Wie Welt," pp. 26–37.

15. Schmitt, *Politische Theologie*. On Benjamin's later connection to Schmitt, see Fadini, "Esperienze della modernità," pp. 43–58; and Figal, "Vom Sinn der Geschichte." Having been published only at the end of this early period, Schmitt does not enter this discussion.

16. On Schmitt's claim, see his letter to Armin Mohler from April 14, 1952, in Taubes, *Ad Carl Schmitt*, p. 36. Meier, in his *Carl Schmitt, Leo Strauss*, pp. 84–85, believes that Schmitt took the term from the anarchist Michail Bakunin's *La Théologie Politique de Mazzini et l'Internationale* (St. Imier, 1871) in Bakunin, *Oeuvres complètes de Bakounine*. However, if Schmitt had indeed sought to plagiarize from Bakunin, it would have been easier to read the shorter but complete Italian and French manuscripts rather than the fragmented manuscript Meier cites. These can be found on pp. 93–106, 282–298 of the same volume.

17. See the discussion of theocracy in chapter 1, section 1.

18. A good example of this can be found in the debates of the Russian revolutionaries in the nineteenth century. Their question was whether a socialist society could be established without first undergoing a capitalist phase. See Venturi, *Roots of Revolution*.

19. By the end of the war Scholem has difficulty even imagining Benjamin as a political thinker. tag 2:146.

20. freund:100–101.

1. The Messianic Idea in Walter Benjamin's Early Writings

1. Benjamin, "Gedanken über Gerhart Hautpmanns Festspiel" in *Gesammelte Schriften*, Band II.1, pp. 60 (hereafter II:60).

2. Titled by Adorno in a 1955 publication of Walter Benjamin's writings.

3. Note on the translation: several points in this text make a natural rendering rather impossible, or, when feasible as a translation, only with substantial clarification. Surely the first translator was aware of these problems (*Reflections;* New York: Schocken, 1976) but remained unable to address the ambiguity of several phrases. For instance, the conjugational phrase *Darum,* which appears four times in the first paragraph, seems unable to be rendered easily in English, keeping the programmatic, rhythmic, and cumulative effect of the original without introducing a monotonous tone. In the second paragraph I have tried to preserve the superlative within the genitive phrase *seines leisesten Nahens* that was lost in the Schocken version. Finally, the term *Glück* with its corresponding *Unglück* presents a problem to any translator. While the former may be rendered as "happiness," it would be grounds for misunderstanding to render the latter "misfortune," for while the term *misfortune* does convey the "unhappiness" of an event, it unwillingly also introduces the notion of fortune. Thus I have chosen the term *tragedy,* which seems to best express the meaning of *Unglück* in the context of Benjamin's early work, a point to which I devote considerable attention in this chapter. See for example the use of the word in II:173.

4. Benjamin's interest in messianism is evident throughout his early writings. At a certain stage in his doctoral thesis it became important to reformulate the meaning of Schlegel's affirmative stance toward progress in order to maintain a coherent view of him as messianically inspired. There is a linguistic component as well; he quotes Schlegel, "Der Buchstab' ist der echte Zauberstab," and Novalis, "Mehrere Namen sind einer Idee vorteilhaft," in this respect. See I:92–93. Bullock, in his book *Romanticism and Marxism,* believes that the thesis adds very little to the understanding of matters that it claims to consider, suffering under the weight of a priori messianic notions. Relevant to this discussion is Benjamin's letter to E. Schoen in GB II:23.

5. For two contrary opinions, see Jennings, *Dialectical Images,* p. 59; and Nieraad, "Walter Benjamins Glück," who places the fragment largely in the context of the later writings. See also Picker, "Darstellung als Entsprechung."

6. On Martin Buber and the war, see von berlin:65, 76 and Benjamin's letter to Buber from July 17, 1916, in GB I:325.

7. One could cite a dozen sources for the claim that, for example, the "Theses on the Philosophy of History" from 1940 was written, in part, in response to the Hitler-Stalin pact.

8. There is also some evidence concerning the type of paper used in the manuscript which would correspond to the earlier period, but these findings can not be considered conclusive. See Anmerkungen in II:946–949.

9. "Ich halte es für unbezweifelbar, daß diese Seiten 1920–1921 im Zusammenhang mit der »Kritik der Gewalt« geschrieben wurden und noch keine Beziehung zu marxistischen Auffassungen unterhielten. Sie stellen einen metaphysischen Anarchismus dar, der den Ideen des Autors vor 1924 entsprach. Adorno datiert sie aus dem Jahr 1937. [. . .] Meine Antwort darauf ist, daß es sich um einen Witz handelt, um zu wissen, ob Adorno einen mystisch-anarchistischen Text für einen kürzlich geschriebenen marxistischen Versuch nehmen würde. Benjamin pflegte übrigens solche Experimente anzustellen." This is taken from a letter by Scholem to the French editor of Benjamin's work, dated November 11, 1970. Walter Benjamin, *Mythe et Violence*, p. 149 (Paris: Denoël, 1971). Originally in Wohlfarth, "Immer radikal, niemals konsequent," p. 30. It is unfortunately not included in the published collection of Scholem's letters. See also Scholem's comments in freund:117, where he writes: "Alles an diesen zwei Seiten [of the fragment] entspricht genau seinen Gedankengängen und seiner spezifischen Terminologie um 1920/1921."

10. See Scholem's account of this statement in tag I:391. He reproduces this journal entry in freund:45.

11. To chart the course between the *Spirit of Utopia* and several years of independent theological and political thought appears to have been the task, later cartographed and guided by the *Star of Redemption*. The relationship between Benjamin and Bloch, unlike Benjamin's single encounter with Rosenzweig in December 1922, was extensive and complex. It lies beyond the realm of the discussion here to attempt to explicate the myriad overlapping affinities, influences, perhaps even rivalries between these two thinkers, which has already received scholarly attention. The importance of Bloch's book for Benjamin, however, as indicated in the reference in the text itself, points to a key influence that no interpretation of the fragment can ignore. See the first references in GB II:44, 58, 61, 67 from November 1919. With regard to Rosenzweig, the influence is somewhat more determinable. Apparently, Benjamin was familiar with Rosenzweig's book before July 9, 1921 (GB II:63), receiving his copy from Scholem by post that month (GB II:170). He writes again to Scholem on November 8, 1921, after just completing a first reading, although he makes little comment immediately, claiming to want to reserve judgment for a second round (GB II: 208–209). The emphasis on evaluating the work and its structure raises the possibility that the fragment was partly a first attempt at a close analysis of Rosenzweig in the context of his own theological speculations, which date from an earlier period. On this point see the opinion of Michael Löwy, who also recognizes Rosenzweig's influence in the fragment. Löwy, *Redemption and Utopia*, pp. 101–102.

12. "Denn es ist so, wie der Baalschem sagt, daß erst dann der Messias kommen kann, wenn sich alle Gäste an den Tisch gesetzt haben; dieser aber ist zunächst der Tisch der Arbeit und dann erst der Tisch des Herrn—die Organisation der Erde besitzt im Geheimnis des Reichs ihre unmittelbar einwirkende, unmittelbar deduzierende Metaphysik. " Bloch, *Geist der Utopie;* see also Bloch, *Gesammelte Schriften,* vol. 16. Hereafter page numbers from *Geist der Utopie* follow each citation as GdU:411. I later discovered the same passage marked in Scholem's edition from 1918, Scholem Library Jerusalem, no. 16253.

13. Eliezer Schweid, for example, defines the messianic idea as following four distinct and perhaps cumulative phases: 1. the onset of evil, 2. the necessity of suffering leading to an end, 3. prophetic visions of redemption, and 4. the restitution of a Davidic kingdom as redemption. See Schweid, "Jewish Messianism," p. 61.

14. For expository purposes, a few representative (but in no way exhaustive) postbiblical examples are given here. On *Sefer Zerubabbel* (ca. seventh century), in *Encyclopaedia Judaica* 16:1002ff; and Levi, "Sefer Zerubabbel."

15. On the "Treatise on the Left Emanation" see Dan, *The Early Kabbalah,* pp. 36, 151–183. In the *Zohar* we find both a Messiah in rags and Ha-Kohen's critical influence, in which the Messiah as warrior intervenes to stop human history, to the degree that human history is imbued with suffering and evil, and releases a metahistory from its imprisonment in falsehood.

16. See Scholem, *Major Trends in Jewish Mysticism,* pp. 244–286. In Nathan of Gaza we see a strategic merger of the two ideas: humanity prepares prehistory, it can work to redeem the shards of divine light that have been broken off into sparks, yet only the Messiah can perform the final capturing of the last sparks, which, when redeemed from their fallen state, bring on a redemption prepared for in every other way by human agency. On Sabbatai Zvi, see Scholem, *Major Trends in Jewish Mysticism,* pp. 287–324; "Redemption Through Sin" in *The Messianic Idea in Judaism;* and *Sabbatai Sevi.* Perhaps the most interesting and creative development of Scholem's work on Zvi are to be found in the late and, as of yet, untranslated novels of the Japanese author Kenzaburo Oe, particularly *Chûgaeri* (Somersault; Tokyo: Kodansha, 1999).

17. "Im Gedanken des messianischen Reiches ist das größte Bild der Geschichte gefunden worden, auf dem sich ihre unendlich tiefe Beziehung zu Religion und Ethik aufbaut. Walter sagte einmal: Das messianische Reich ist immer da. Diese Einsicht ist von der *größen* Wahrheit—aber erst auf einer Sphäre, die meines Wissens nach niemand nach den Propheten erreicht hat." tag II:70. Scholem copies the same sentence in his notebook from the period ("Kleine Anmerkungen über Judentum 1917/18—Minor Notes on Judaism")—an exact duplicate, although this time leaving out the reference to Benjamin and adding the sentence "Offenbarung und messianisches Reich als die ewigen Pole der Gegenwart sind die Fundamente der jüdischen Geschichtsauffassung, deren Einheit die Lehre ist." "Revelation and messianic kingdom as the eternal poles of the present are the foundations of the Jewish concept of history, whose unity is the teachings." tag II:203.

18. This argument on messianism is put forward by Scholem in *Über einige Grundbegriffe des Judentums*, pp. 123–125, in English, *The Messianic Idea in Judaism.*

19. Benjamin's interest in the early Christians, expressed elsewhere in the early writings, does not lend support to the idea of viewing his messianism in a post-Judaic context. It is far more probable that Benjamin sought to read the early Christians in their Judaic element. This becomes readily apparent if one compares Benjamin's to Bloch's approach to Christianity in the *Spirit of Utopia*. See note 83, this chapter.

20. The Judaic dimension of Benjamin's thought is still bitterly contested in Germany today. The sometimes almost racial tone of the debate is a further indication that the effects of the Shoah on intellectual life are hardly a thing of the past. See, for example, Menninghaus, *Walter Benjamins Theorie der Sprachmagie*. An analysis of Benjamin through the "Kabbala" (read Judaism), he argues, promotes "die Dunkelheit von Benjamins Texten, statt sie zu erhellen, vollends ins Ungreifbare und Unsinnige abgleitet" (190–191). Scholem's own response to these lines in the margin of his copy reads rather unsurprisingly characteristic: "Nein. Leere Behauptung!" Scholem Library, National and University Library Jerusalem.

21. This is the nature of messianic creation, which returns to its origins in the process of redemption, completes the remains, and constitutes itself at the same time, as it would be in an undivided divine realm.

22. As Benjamin states elsewhere in an early fragment: "Geschichte hat ein Ende aber kein Ziel." *Gesammelte Schriften,* VI:94.

23. Franz Rosenzweig, in his *Stern der Erlösung* formulates a similar conception of divine completion: "So wird [Gott] bis zum Ende. Alles was geschieht, ist an ihm Werden.[. . .] So ist jenes Werden Gottes für ihn kein Sichverändern, kein Wachsen, kein Zunehmen, sondern er ist von Anfang an und ist in jedem Augenblick und ist immer im Kommen. [. . .] 'Gott is ewig' bedeutet also: für ihn ist die Ewigkeit seine Voll-endung." Rosenzweig, *Stern der Erlösung,* §264 (hereafter SdE§264; citations refer to the paragraph rather than the page number). Everything that takes place in Him is "be-coming," says Rosenzweig; no growth as such, but simply impending arrival, his existence as "coming." His eternity has no beginning and no end, which as categories can no longer maintain themselves as essentially different.

24. tag II:261. "Der neue Himmel ist der Himmel ohne Nacht. Die neue Schöpfung ist die Zeit, die, wie Walter sagt, am Ende der Zeiten sich erhebt."

25. In his dissertation on the idea and the critique of art, Benjamin formulates the role of criticism as the "Vollendung des Werkes" itself. *Gesammelte Schriften,* I:108. Completion here is understood as an action of creation. But since a critique is a human endeavor, this notion of completion, if meant to uphold the category we have before us here, can only be seen as anticipatory and not final.

26. SdE§236.

27. Within the heart of this complex imagery, one may be tempted to see a reformulated Lurianic structure, which undoubtedly had meaningful impact on both Rosenzweig and Bloch as well as Benjamin. With regard to Rosenzweig, see particularly SdE§236.

28. Rosenzweig terms this a "gehaltvoller beseelter Zusammenhang" that is capable of arriving at "ein im ästhetischen Sinn, Fertiges, Abschließendes zustande." SdE§238.

29. GdU:437. "So hat also die Welt wie einen Anfang so ein Ende in der Zeit weil sie nur als Prozeß begreifbar ist, weil allein Geschichte die auftreffende, wesentliche Methode der Welterkenntnis bildet."

30. Evil, which stands at the end of a messianic conception of history, waits at the end of Bloch's historical process as well. He also refers here approvingly to Maimonides' critique of Aristotle's second proof of the eternity of the world and formulates a notion of time that is not merely the history of progress but rather knowledge of the world as history. However, Maimonides' real views on the matter may not be so clear. See, for example, Silver, *Maimonidean Criticism*.

31. On this point, see the discussion in part 3 on justice.

32. Regarding political theology, Jacob Taubes's article on the fragment makes the unfortunate claim that only Jewish theocracy is political, whereas (early) Christian theocracy is able to take on purely religious dimensions. He appears to resurrect the old ghost of Christianity as a "spiritual" religion versus a Jewish "religion of the book" in order to construct a haphazard critique of Scholem's notion of the Jewish messianic idea taking place in history. Out of this myriad of competing themes, he comes to the wayward conclusion that Benjamin was a modern version of Marcion, although the reader is hard-pressed for a reason. Taubes, "Walter Benjamin—ein moderner Marcionit?" See especially pp.139–140.

33. See Wohlfarth, "Immer radikal, niemals konsequent," p. 118.

34. Bloch's writes that a distinct but nevertheless concentrated effort among German Jewry toward Judaism "hat derart viel gelernt, sowohl von den Antisemiten, die jeder stolze Jude an Schmerz und Haß tausendfach überbietet, wie auch von den Strebungen eines staatlich festgelegten Zionismus; dessen Schaden freilich ist, daß er die gesamte Kraft des Auserwähltseins leugnet und derart mit dem Begriff des Nationalstaats, wie er im neunzehnten Jahrhundert ephemer genug kursierte, aus Judäa eine Art von asiatischem Balkanstaat machen möchte." GdU:320.

35. II:837–838. Letter of October 10, 1912 to Ludwig Strauß. The exchange is now printed in GB I:61–88. See also the discussion in Brodersen, *Spinne im eigenen Netz*, pp. 52–56.

36. GB I:71. "Ich empfinde das Judentum als mein Kernhaftes."

37. GB I:72. "Sie propagieren Palästina und saufen deutsch."

38. GB I: 83, 85. "Ein jüdisch-geistiges Unternehmen."

39. We can only speculate as to Benjamin's true intentions concerning the move to Palestine in the 1930s. Had he gone, he would not have been the first to emigrate to Palestine while still entirely wedded to Europe linguistically, culturally, and, above all, politically.

40. See the interview with Gershom Scholem in Ehud Ben Ezer, ed., "Zionism: Dialectic of Continuity and Rebellion," pp. 265–267. In this respect the vigorous exchange between Benjamin and Scholem in the later years must be examined not

only from the perspective of Scholem's criticisms of Benjamin's attempt to merge his earlier political ideas with elements of Marxism as a rejection of Jewish theology but also as a loosening of his commitment to anarchism.

41. See the articles by Bernhard Lang, "Theokratie" and Hubert Cancik, "Theokratie und Priesterherrschaft," in Taubes, *Religionstheorie und Politische Theologie*, pp. 11–15, 65–76.

42. See R. A. Horsley, "Popular Messianic Movements Around the Time of Jesus," in Saperstein, *Essential Papers on Messianic Movements*, p. 87; Jacob Taubes, "Theokratie," in Taubes, *Religionstheorie und Politische Theologie*; "Staatsrecht," *Jüdisches Lexikon*, vol. IV:2 (1930), pp. 618–623.

43. In Scholem's description of the period in Bern, he defines his discussions on politics with Benjamin as concerning a "theocratic anarchism:" "Wir sprachen auch viel über Politik und Sozialismus, über den wir, wie über den Stand des Menschen bei seiner eventuellen Realisierung, große Bedenken hatten. Noch immer lief es bei uns auf theokratischen Anarchismus als die sinnvollste Antwort auf die Politik hinaus." freund:108. We may understand theocracy as a necessary dimension of Messianism and anarchism as the most "sensible" political position. See also Scholem, *On Jews and Judaism in Crisis*, p. 33 (henceforth jjc), where he makes a similar statement. Benjamin's rejection of "political" or historical theocracy would favor here an abstract role for this "theocratic anarchism."

44. II:125. "Das Reich Gottes und das Reich der Welt"; "Die Himmlischen sind zu Zeichen des unendlichen Lebens geworden, das aber gegen ihn begrenzt ist." Benjamin, *Selected Writings*, 1:35 (modified).

45. In Scholem's own comments on the role of dialectics in his early conception of political theology, we find the curious statement that he was not to learn as much "from Hegel or the Marxists, but from my own experiences and from pondering the labyrinths of Zionism as I was trying to implement it." jjc:36. Whether the use of dialectical theory in the historiography of the Kabbalah is justified, is worthy of further exploration.

46. Rather, Rosenzweig continues, "Das Reich Gottes setzt sich durch in der Welt, indem es die Welt durchsetzt. Von der Welt aus ist ohnehin, wie zum Zeichen dieser Unvergleichbarkeit, nur ein Teil des kommenden Gottesreichs überhaupt wahrnehmbar, nämlich nur der Mittelteil, der »Dual« der Nächstenliebe." SdE§232.

47. It is my inclination here to view the parallel of concepts and categories as an indication of Benjamin's affinity with Rosenzweig, in regard to ideas he himself had worked out nearly seven years prior to the publication of the *Star of Redemption*, particularly in his essay on Hölderlin. Bloch's own consideration of this problem may have also contributed to Benjamin's understanding. Nevertheless, it is therefore important to note here the use of language, categorical similarity, and the formal juxtaposition of the categories in the fragment, which may reveal an indebtedness to Rosenzweig.

48. Profane activity contains within it a magnetic tension for Rosenzweig, to which *die Nächstenliebe* is drawn. See especially SdE§144.

49. This is indeed the element of secularization that Benjamin also sought to introduce, in a markedly different way.

50. GdU:276. "Überweltliche Sphäre, eine utopische Wirklichkeit oder eine noch nicht erreichte, wohl aber geltende Realität der Idee," an "übersinnliche," "überempirische Welt" which exists for the "utopische-absolute Subjekt," in contrast to a "sinnliche," "untere empirische Welt." Here the two realms are mediated through their tension: "So wird schon die Geschichte in zwei Räume geteilt; in einen unteren, irdischen und einen oberen, unsichtbaren, zwischen denen sich dieser Rotationswechsel der zwei Gruppen und Zeiten vollzieht, sofern in dem oberen Raum als dem Raum der Abgeschiedenen, als dem Zwischenreich zwischen Hier und Dort, die Geschichte oder Typologie des nächsten Zeitraums jeweils ihre wesentliche kausale Prägung erhält." GdU:430.

51. As with the rest of this elusive fragment, the author does not allude to what aspect of image making he deems problematic. Nevertheless, it is possible that our author did have in mind the problem of the concept of image in connection with the corporeality of God.

52. II:75. "Abbild eines höchsten, metaphysischen, Standes." Benjamin, "The Life of Students," *Selected Writings*, 1:37 (modified).

53. If this image is a divine image in representation, its dissonance is the expression of "damaged immediacy," as Benjamin articulates the present condition of language in his essay from 1916. Its immediacy, however, poses a problem, for God is naturally far greater than the things he created. Thus human language falls shy of being able to express the nature of God, and merely lends itself to its conception. This is to say that through this dynamic, the divine kingdom only finds its true form when it is faced by its linguistic limit in historical agency. This agency takes form at the same time that it is fundamentally and inherently formless.

54. II:117. "jede Bilddissonanz, der in äußerstem Nachdruck eine lautliche anklingt, hat die Funktion, die innewohnende geistige Zeitordnung der Freude sinnbar, lautbar zu machen, in der Kette eines unendlich erstreckten Geschehens, das den unendlichen Möglichkeiten des Reimes entspricht. So rief die Dissonanz im Bilde des Wahren und [. . .] die Beschreitbarkeit als einende Beziehung der Ordnungen hervor, wie die »Gelegenheit« die geistig-zeitliche Identität (die Wahrheit) der Lage bedeutete. Diese Dissonanzen heben im dichterischen Gefüge die aller räumlichen Beziehung einwohnende zeitliche Identität und damit die absolut bestimmende Natur des geistigen Daseins innerhalb der identischen Erstreckung hervor." Benjamin, "Two Poems by Friedrich Hölderlin," *Selected Writings*, 1:29 (modified).

55. See Scholem, tag I:390, 401, freund:45, as well as Benjamin, *Gesammelte Schriften*, VI:90, 682, and the discussion in section three.

56. "B'tzelem" (Gen. 1:26), "rosh d'var'cha emet" (Ps. 119:160).

57. We can see this tradition dating back to the inconceivable measurements of God in the text *Shiur Komah* and its abhorrence by most rationalist readers. See Scholem, *Die jüdische Mystik*, 68–70, 38 n. 82, and *Von der mystischen Gestalt der*

Gottheit, chapter 1; Dan, *Ancient Jewish Mysticism*, pp. 48–58; M.S. Cohen, *The Shiur Qomah*.

58. SdE§455,459, GdU:347.

59. Maimonides begins his tractate with an exegetical exposition of the terms image (*tzelem*), likeness (*demuth*), and form (*to'ar*). See the first chapter of *The Guide of the Perplexed*. Benjamin makes reference to Maimonides in his article for the *Encyclopedia Judaica*, "Juden in der deutschen Kultur." II:807. The article, however, cannot be considered authoritative due to the irrevocable altering of the text. See II:1521.

60. See the discussions in chapter 3 on language and on justice and violence in chapter 6.

61. SdE§456. "Wir sprechen in Bildern. Aber die Bilder sind nicht willkürlich. Es gibt notwendige und zufällige Bilder. Die Unverkehrbarkeit der Wahrheit läßt sich nur in dem Bilde eines Lebendigen aussprechen. Denn im Lebendigen allein ist schon von Natur und vor aller Setzung und Satzung ein Oben und Unten ausgezeichnet." He continues in the same passage: "weil es in der Wahrheit Oben und Unten gibt, deshalb dürfen nicht bloß, sondern müssen wir sie das Antlitz Gottes heißen." SdE:422. In Maimonides' terms, this means to have a natural and not merely a general form.

62. Like Maimonides, Rosenzweig follows that "nicht Gott, aber Gottes Wahrheit ward mir zum Spiegel." For each element of holiness we are permitted to view forms "in der Welt selber ein Stück Überwelt, ein Leben jenseits des Lebens." SdE§459.

63. SdE§459. "die Schau auf der Höhe der erlösten Überwelt." SdE:422 (modified).

64. Bloch refers to a "menschliche glücksuchende Wille" in reference to Marx's notion of a humanity that is not "completely rotten" and whose moral will is able to be determined by a "Wille als revolutionäres Klasseninteresse bereits durch die einfache Tatsache der Gemeinschaft des Wollens." Bloch, *Gesammelte Schriften*, p. 300. This will is explained in the first edition of *Spirit of Utopia* as the will to be free from the alienation of production. "Der Mann, der immer nur Teile zu bearbeiten hat und niemals das Glück der ganzen und Fertigproduktion genießen kann." GdU:20.

65. Benjamin's critical views toward the pleasure-seeking aspect of modern society appear several times in the early writings. In "Dialog über die Religiosität der Gegenwart," we find reference to the idea of a unity in bourgeois pleasure and progress: "Was hat aller Fortschritt, alle Weltlichkeit mit Religion zu tun, wenn sie uns nicht eine freudige Ruhe geben? [. . .] Wir sind gehetzt von Lebensfreude. Es ist unsere verdammte Pflicht und Schuldigkeit, sie zu fühlen. Kunst, Verkehr, Luxus, alles ist verpflichtend." II:18. I will be returning to this point in the section on tragedy in this chapter.

66. II:134,154. I deal with these ideas more thoroughly in the context of Benjamin's concept of language. See chapter 3 on "Über Sprache überhaupt und über die Sprache des Menschen."

67. Benjamin had a long-standing interest in evil, Satan, and demonic forces, an interest that perhaps should not be taken as a form of occultism but rather, as I argue here, a necessary component of messianism. On the devil, see II:101 and Scholem's reflections on Benjamin's intrigue with the demonic in *Walter Benjamin und sein Engel*, pp. 46–49, as well as Agamben's essay, "Walter Benjamin und das Dämonische."

68. On the difference between divine and profane intension, see the related theme of *Selbstzweck* and *göttlicher Selbstzweck* in the "Dialog über die Religiosität der Gegenwart." II:17.

69. Benjamin's "Glücksuchen der Freien Menschheit" here can be compared to Rosenzweig's formulation of free will with regard to "redemption-intentions." Rosenzweig's free will is determinate in relation to God's complete freedom. The noncoercive free act of love that is applied to the neighbor is the pursuit of happiness in the anarchic sense. This pursuit is an event that takes place in the world but, at the same time, evokes the coming of the next, for in Rosenzweig's structure redemption is not beyond human participation. In this sense he bears a Lurianic legacy. See Moshe Idel's article "Franz Rosenzweig and the Kabbalah" in Mendes-Flohr, *The Philosophy of Franz Rosenzweig,* on some kabbalistic features. A broader explication of the Lurianic elements embedded in the corpus of the *Star of Redemption* is still, however, needed.

70. In Rosenzweig worldliness is "de-thingified" or "enchanted" (*entdinglicht*) as everything entering the *Jewish* world contains a twofold meaning: "einmal auf »diese« und dann auf die »kommende« Welt.[. . .] In »dieser« Welt dient es zum gemeinen Gebrauch, kaum anders als ob es ungesegnet geblieben wäre, aber gleichzeitig ist es jetzt einer der Steine geworden, aus denen sich die »kommende« Welt erbaut. [. . .] Diese Spaltung durchdringt das ganze Leben, als Gegensatz von Heilig und Gemein, Sabbat und Werktag, »Thora und Weg der Erde«, Leben im Geist und Geschäft. [. . .] Und wie der Segen alles Gemeine erfaßt und nichts mehr gemein bleiben läßt, sondern alles heiligt, so werden es auch" das ewige Leben in der künftigen Welt. SdE§328.

71. SdE§328. "Vergängnis zur Ewigkeit." We find this juxtaposition in Benjamin in the sense of the holy and worldly standing in direct relationship to each other through human activity. For holiness to exist in Rosenzweig's system, the division here is necessary, being resolved only in the moment of redemption. Just as the blessed ultimately absorbs into itself everything external, leaving nothing simply profane but instead forming holiness, "so too will it be in the eternal life of the coming world."

72. Dan, *Gershom Scholem*, pp. 292. A more readily known example is the suffering of the devoted Job.

73. Isaiah 53.

74. See SdE§145–146, 191–198.

75. II:78. "Strebungen des inneren Menschen."

76. See, for example, Löwy, *Redemption and Utopia*, pp. 14–26; Rabinbach, "Between Enlightenment and Apocalypse."

77. It is important here to note that, although his ideas are directed toward the individual, Benjamin's politics cannot be reduced to a brand of individualism. See the critical remarks on individualism in II:25.

78. This concept was received quite differently by Benjamin, Bloch, and Rosenzweig. As a model for the rebirth of tragedy, Rosenzweig rejects it out of hand; for Benjamin the divinity of the poet/artist is problematic; for Bloch it is accepted and incorporated in the secularizing task of the *Spirit of Utopia*.

79. This appears to have been the consensus of both Rosenzweig and Bloch.

80. See Mosès, "Walter Benjamin and Franz Rosenzweig."

81. In the *Trauerspiel* book Benjamin brings together his own earlier reflections of fate and character with Rosenzweig's concept of the decline of the tragic hero to introduce the notion of Trauerspiel as religious tragedy. Only through the drama of the martyr is the Trauerspiel as "heilige Tragödie" believable. "Im sterbenden Sokrates," he writes, "ist das Märtyrerdrama als Parodie der Tragödie entsprungen." I:292. Indeed, this is not the first discussion of the figure of Socrates in Benjamin. Here Socrates represents the immortality of the character of the hero. He freely chooses fate, rather than allowing the despotism of the events leading to his death to succeed in his involuntary capitulation to fate, and in this way no longer remains a victim of arbitrary forces. This paradox points to the end of tragedy as such. See also "Sokrates" (II:129), written around June 1916.

82. SdE§70. "In der Tragödie wird leicht der Anschein erweckt, als müßte der Untergang des Einzelnen irgend ein gestörtes Gleichgewicht der Dinge wiederherstellen. Aber dieser Anschein beruht nur auf dem Widerspruch zwischen dem tragischen Charakter und der dramatischen Fabel; das Drama als Kunstwerk braucht beide Hälften dieses Widerspruchs, um zu bestehen; aber das eigentlich Tragische wird dadurch verwischt. Der Held als solcher muß nur untergehen, weil der Untergang ihm die höchste Verheldung, nämlich die geschlossenste Verselbstung seines Selbst ermöglicht. Er verlangt nach der Einsamkeit des Untergangs, weil es keine größere Einsamkeit gibt als diese. Deshalb stirbt der Held eigentlich auch nicht. Der Tod sperrt ihm gewissermaßen nur die Temporalien der Individualität. Der zum heldischen Selbst geronnene Charakter ist unsterblich." SdE:78–79 (modified).

83. As in Rosenzweig, we also find recourse to "heilige Tragödie" in Bloch. But unlike Benjamin, Bloch's notion emphasizes the idea of Jesus, son of Joseph as Messiah in what amounts to a mystical and sometimes rather ahistorical materialist theology in the use of Kabbalah and Talmud: "Zudem haben viele anerkannte jüdische Lehrer die Erwähnung und weissagende Beschreibung des Gottesknechts Jesus im Deuterojesaja auf den Messias bezogen, in guter Übereinstimmung mit der Haggada, die sehr wohl einen leidenden Messias kennt, wenn auch unter der Einschränkung, daß man den leidenden, den Sohn Josefs, durchgängig von dem herrschendem Messias als dem Sohn Davids unterschied." GdU:325. Had he applied himself to the blood-soaked question of the suffering Messiah more thoroughly, he might have seen that he was not the first to apply Jesus to the idea of the two Messiahs. Indeed, in his well-known *Vikuah,* which reports the transcripts of

the forced disputation of Barcelona (1263), Nachmanides rebukes the necessity of Jesus having been either of the two Messiahs. See Maccoby, *Judaism on Trial*, p. 42f.

84. "Über Sprache überhaupt und über die Sprache des Menschen," November 1916.

85. II:133. "Die tiefere Erfassung des Tragischen hat vielleicht nicht nur und nicht sowohl von der Kunst als von der Geschichte auszugehen." Benjamin, "*Trauerspiel* and Tragedy," *Selected Writings* 1:54 (modified).

86. II:133. "Die Zeit der Geschichte geht an bestimmten und hervorragenden Punkten ihres Verlaufs in die tragische Zeit über: und zwar in den Aktionen der großen Individuen. Zwischen Größe im Sinn der Geschichte und Tragik besteht ein wesensnotwendiger Zusammenhang—der sich freilich nicht in Identität auflösen läßt." Benjamin, "Trauerspiel and Tragedy," 1:54 (modified).

87. II:134. "Unendlich in jeder Richtung und unerfüllt in jedem Augenblick"; "Die Zeit ist für das empirische Geschehen nur eine Form, aber was wichtiger ist, eine als Form unerfüllte. Das Geschehnis erfüllt die formale Natur der Zeit in der es liegt nicht. Denn es ist ja nicht so zu denken, daß Zeit nichts anders sei als das Maß, mit dem die Dauer einer mechanischen Veränderung gemessen wird. Diese Zeit ist freilich eine relativ leere Form, deren Ausfüllung zu denken keinen Sinn bietet."

88. II:134. "Bestimmte Kraft der historischen Zeit."

89. The concept of time is addressed in the chapter on worldly and divine restitution in part 3.

90. tag II:302. "Der Zeitbegriff des Judentums ist: ewige Gegenwart."

91. II:134."Im Sinne der Geschichte vollkommen sei"; "Diese Idee der erfüllten Zeit heißt in der Bibel als deren beherrschende historische Idee: die messianische Zeit." Benjamin, "*Trauerspiel* and Tragedy," 1:54 (modified).

92. II:134. "Die tragische Zeit von der messianischen."

93. II:134. "Keiner zu leben vermag."

94. II:135. "Stirbt an Unsterblichkeit"; "Ursprung der tragischen Helden"; "der tragischen Schuld"; "eigentliche Ausdruck der Schuld." Benjamin, "*Trauerspiel* and Tragedy," vol. 1:54 (modified).

95. II:135. "Individuation als der Urschuld."

96. II:135. "Völlige Passivität"; "Denn nicht selten sind es die völligen Ruhepausen, gleichsam der Schlaf des Helden, in dem sich das Verhängnis seiner Zeit erfüllt, und gleichermaßen tritt die Bedeutung der erfüllten Zeit im tragischen Schicksal in den großen Momenten der Passivität hervor: im tragischen Entschluß, im retardierenden Moment, in der Katastrophe." Benjamin, "*Trauerspiel* and Tragedy," 1:55–56 (modified).

97. In *Spirit of Utopia* we see a very similar concept of the tragic hero forming himself out of his own choice in the face of a predetermined destiny. Drawing on Lukács, Bloch writes: "Alles ist ja schon vorher auf das Ende gerichtet gewesen, nicht als Unglück oder Strafe. [. . .] Sondern das tragische Sterben ist das Vorrecht der Größe [. . .] So kann der tragische Tod nach dieser Betrachtung nicht anders definiert werden als der durchaus von hier geschehende, zurückkehrende, immanente, durchaus unmystische Zwang zur Form, zum Horos, zur Gestalt und dem

endgültigen Terminus des Ichs." GdU:68. In tragic death what appears as tragedy or punishment becomes the triumphal march of victory. The death of the tragic hero, for Bloch, "ist nicht weniger, nicht anders real als die Heiligenlegende, wenn auch durch charakteristische utopische Gegenstands- und Sphärengrade von dieser verschieden, und so wird die letzthinige Beziehung des tragischen Problems auf den Tod Christi als dem Inhalt der paulinischen »Gnadendramatik« in der religiösen Sphäre unausweichlich. Denn der Held geht nicht unter, weil er wesenhaft geworden ist, sondern weil er wesenhaft geworden ist, geht er unter; erst dieses macht das ernsthafte zu sich selber Gekommensein zum Heroismus, zur Kategorie des gewaltigen Schicksals und der Tragödie, die den Menschen erhebt, den sie zermalmt, indem sie ihn zermalmt." GdU:77. In his death the tragic hero again reaches his own essence as finished; Bloch stresses that his essentiality causes his passing. For our purposes it is the relationship between form and decline that finds affinity with Benjamin's notion of the individual. Here the figure of the hero secures his character in his *Untergang*, as does the individual who is able to destroy the tragedy that pulverizes him. This is what Bloch calls the "eine—vom Charakter stammende—Absichtlichtkeit im Schicksal der Einzelnen." GdU:351. In the face of tragedy, that portion of the individual which has the possibility of becoming fixed is completed and springs heroically into tragedy out of free will. This final leap, not into faith but into fate, is the propulsion of the hero out of the realm of drama, out of the malignancy of time, and through the gates of redemption: "wenn uns Luft und Boden entzogen werden und alle Räume des physischen Vorbei [. . .] dann stehen wir nackt vor Gott, halb, lau, unklar und doch »vollendet«, im Sinn der tragischen Situation vollendet, wenngleich aus ganz anderen Wünschen, Zusammenhängen und Zeitmaßen zerschlagen als aus denen unseres Werks und seiner dem Satan mühevoll abgerungenen Zeit." GdU:439.

98. II:123. "Mut ist Hingabe an die Gefahr, welche die Welt bedroht; Mut ist das Lebensgefühl des Menschen, der sich der Gefahr preisgibt, dadurch sie in seinem Tode zur Gefahr der Welt erweitert und überwindet zugleich. Die Größe der Gefahr entspringt im Mutigen—erst indem sie ihn trifft, in seiner ganzen Hingabe an sie, trifft sie die Welt. In seinem Tode aber ist sie überwunden, hat die Welt erreicht, der sie nicht mehr droht;" Benjamin, "Two Poems by Friedrich Hölderlin," 1:33–34 (modified).

99. Since it is proceeded by a reference to Kol Nidre, the prayer service associated with Yom Kippur, it was possibly written after September 1918.

100. tag II:345. "Die Idee des historischen Todes aller Wesen in der messianischen Zeit vernichtet das Schicksal. Die Schicksalslosigkeit dieser Ordnung spricht auf deutlichste aus Jesaja 65, 19–24. Die Verwandlung der Landschaft in den Schauplatz (historischen Ort) heißt im Judentum Erlösung. [. . .] Und *darum* versteht man im letzten Grunde die Idee des messianischen Todes als Erlösung."

101. II:137. "Zeitcharakter"; "ist in der dramatischen Form erschöpft und gestaltet." Benjamin, "*Trauerspiel* and Tragedy," 1:57 (modified).

102. II:136. "Es gilt das Gesetz eines höhern Lebens im dem beschränkten Raum des Erdendaseins, und alle spielen, bis der Tod das Spiel beendet, um in

einer andern Welt die größere Wiederholung des gleichen Spiels fortzutreiben."
Benjamin, "*Trauerspiel* and Tragedy," 1:57 (modified).

103. II:136. "Bild eines höheren Lebens, sondern nichts als das eine von zwei
Spiegelbildern, und seine Fortsetzung ist nicht minder schemenhaft als es selbst. Die
Toten werden Gespenster." Benjamin, "*Trauerspiel* and Tragedy," 1:57 (modified).

104. II:137. "Die Idee seiner Auflösung"; "innerhalb des dramatischen
Bezirks." Benjamin, "*Trauerspiel* and Tragedy," 1:57 (modified).

105. II:139. "Das Spiel muß aber die Erlösung finden, und für das Trauerspiel
ist das erlösende Mysterium die Musik; die Wiedergeburt der Gefühle in einer
übersinnlichen Natur." Benjamin, "Language in *Trauerspiel* and Tragedy," 1:61
(modified).

106. His interest in this relationship begins in 1916, but it is not until the
Trauerspiel work of 1923–1926 that these notions are fully explicated, there finding
expression in direct connection to the *Star of Redemption*. See II:418. Stéphane
Mosès first mentions this connection but gives a different interpretation. See his
"Walter Benjamin and Franz Rosenzweig" and *Der Engel der Geschichte*.

107. II:172. "Die Möglichkeit einer Vorhersagung des Schicksals rationell be-
greiflich zu machen." Benjamin, "Fate and Character," *Selected Writings*, 1:202–203
(modified).

108. II:172. "Die Hoheit oberer Sphären und Begriffe."

109. II:173. "Dieser Irrtum ist mit Beziehung auf den Begriff des Schicksals
durch dessen Verbindung mit dem Begriff der Schuld veranlaßt. So wird, um den
typischen Fall zu nennen, das schicksalhafte Unglück als die Antwort Gottes oder
der Götter auf religiöse Verschuldung angesehen."

110. On the following page Benjamin states that this understanding of responsibility cannot be seen as being religious at all. The reference here is undoubtedly
to Christian dogma on the origins of evil and the Jews. See the discussion in chapter 5, on the origins of evil.

111. II:174. "In der griechischen klassischen Ausgestaltung des Schicksals-
gedankens wird das Glück, das einem Menschen zuteil wird, ganz und gar nicht als
die Bestätigung seines unschuldigen Lebenswandels aufgefaßt, sondern als die Versuchung zu schwerster Verschuldung, zur Hybris." Benjamin, "Fate and Character," 1:202–203 (modified).

112. The reference here to the gods could easily refer to a single God, leading
one to the assumption that the statement seeks to either hide or legitimize Jewish mystical ideas, brought to the project through the Greeks. Whether this is to
be understood as legitimation or concealment depends on the standpoint of the
reader. This is also applicable to the reference to the early Christians and the
Genesis conception of word and deed. See II:74 and the section on immortality
in this chapter.

113. II:174. "Den Glücklichen aus der Verkettung der Schicksale und aus dem
Netz des eignen." Benjamin, "Fate and Character," 1:23 (modified).

114. II:174. "Das Glück und Seligkeit führen also ebenso aus der Sphäre des
Schicksals heraus wie die Unschuld."

115. II:96. "Es stellt mit hoffnungslosem Ernst die Frage, in welcher Zeit der Mensch lebt. Daß er in keiner Zeit lebt haben die Denkenden immer gewußt. Die Unsterblichkeit der Gedanken und Taten verbannt ihn in Zeitlosigkeit, in deren Mitte lauert der unbegreifliche Tod. Zeitlebens umspannt ihn Leere der Zeit und dennoch Unsterblichkeit nicht." Benjamin, "The Metaphysics of Youth," *Selected Writings*,1:37 (modified).

116. We see this terminology in Rosenzweig: "Denn wenn wir sonst nichts von Ewigkeit wissen, dies ist sicher: daß sie das Un-vergängliche ist. Dieser Bestimmung durch ein unendliches Nun muß also das zur Ewigkeit geschaffene Heute zuvörderst entsprechen." SdE§304. In Rosenzweig's concept of redemption, time becomes an infinite now. It is no longer a *Leerlauf* of progress but the filled time of the moment, where all past events have been resolved and its historical end becomes the future as now-time.

117. Rosenzweig makes several categorical distinctions in this regard, centered on what he ultimately considers the groundwork of all philosophy, which for him is none other than death. He writes: "Vergänglichkeit, die Gott und Göttern fremde, der Welt das bestürzende Erlebnis ihrer eigenen, sich allzeit erneuernden Kraft, ist dem Menschen die immerwährende Atmosphäre, die ihn umgibt, die er mit jedem Zug seines Atems einsaugt und ausstößt. Der Mensch ist vergänglich, Vergänglichsein ist sein Wesen, wie es das Wesen Gottes ist, unsterblich und unbedingt, das Wesen der Welt, allgemein und notwendig zu sein." SdE§55.

118. Rosenzweig turns to the Platonic doctrine of the soul and posits the first contradiction to the principle of immortality, which is set in direct correlation to the character of the tragic hero. In the psychology of the ancients the psyche is that part of the notion of immortality that is truly "Nichtsterbenkönnen," says Rosenzweig. SdE§71. It is something that, although part of nature, is eternal. In this way, it is found divided in ancient philosophy from its corporeality—the soul contains the self. Rosenzweig judges this to be problematic precisely because the soul, although entwined in nature, is always capable of transmigration; not death, not messianic end, but eternal travel. Yet this is an immortality of a single dimension, whereas redemptive immortality requires "eine Unsterblichkeit ohne Wandel und Wanderung," beyond an "Unbeschränktheit seines vergänglichen Wesens" of the self. SdE§71. This, in turn, posits a false dichotomy between body and soul, he goes on to say, which proves unable to resolve the transformation of the profane into the holy. A reformulation of the paired relationship in which the two are fully mediated—not merely as soul wandering but the end of wandering altogether—could then provide a conception of the unity of character of the tragic hero and the principle of the eternity of the soul: "Würde das Selbst zur Seele in diesem Sinn, dann wäre ihm auch Unsterblichkeit in einem neuen Sinn gewiß, und der gespenstische Gedanke der Seelenwanderung verlöre seine Kraft." SdE§71.

119. II:20. "Die Religion garantiert uns ein Ewiges"; "Der Gegenstand der Religion ist Unendlichkeit." II:97.

120. GdU:442. "Das seelische Leben schwingt zwar über den Leib hinaus, es gibt ein seelisches Keimplasma und die transphysiologische Unsterblichkeit wird

vom Verlust des Leibes nicht betroffen. Aber daß das seelische Leben auch über die Vernichtung der Welt hinausschwinge, dazu muß es im tiefsten Sinn »fertig« geworden sein und seine Taue mit Glück um die Pfosten der jenseitigen Landung-stelle geworfen haben, soll nicht auch das seelische Keimplasma in den Abgrund des ewigen Todes gerissen, und das Ziel, auf das es bei der Organisierung des Er-denlebens vor allem ankommt, das ewige Leben, die auch transkosmologische Un-sterblichkeit, die alleinige Realität des Seelenreichs, die Restitutio in integrum aus dem Labyrinth der Welt—durch Satans Erbarmen verfehlt werden."

121. One cannot help but notice that the concept of soul here, both in Bloch and in Rosenzweig, bears some similarity to the Maimondian rational core of the individual, which achieves its transphysiological, transcosmological form not from moral activity in the world, which we know is the greater materialist understand-ing of restitutio in integrum in Bloch, but through acquisition of abstract knowl-edge. However much Bloch actually departs from Maimonides' rather central, an-timessianic tenents, the immortal core that is constituted as independent of worldly affairs, i.e., transcendent of them, and the necessity to avoid evil in the pur-suit of immortality, clearly parallels Benjamin.

122. GdU:430. "Das absolute Zentrum der Realität": "die Geburt und Einset-zung aller Dinge und Wesen in ihr Eigentum."

123. Here the emphasis on redemption is individual in contrast to a messianic conception that would be collective in constitution. See GdU:42.

124. Regarding the inheritance of the term, see also the comments of Löwy, *Re-demption and Utopia*, p. 102.

125. Wohlfahrt presents a different view of secularization in his essay "'Haarscharf an der Grenze zwischen Religion und Nihilismus.'"

126. II:98. "Aber diesem, der Geburt der unsterblichen Zeit, geschieht Zeit nicht mehr. Das Zeitlose widerfährt ihm, in ihm sind alle Dinge versammelt, ihm bei. Allmächtig lebt es im Abstand, im Abstand (dem Schweigen des Tage-buches) widerfährt dem Ich seine eigene, die reine Zeit. Im Abstand ist es in sich selbst gesammelt, kein Ding drängt sich in sein unsterbliches Beieinander. Hier schöpft es Kraft, den Dingen zu widerfahren, sie in sich zu reißen, sein Schick-sal zu verkennen." Benjamin, "Metaphysics of Youth," *Selected Writings*, 1:12 (modified).

127. The praise of God, explains Rosenzweig, lends further validity to the quest for immortality as a necessary part of the transformation to the messianic age. "Die Wir" which he borrows from "Aber wir, wir loben Gott von nun an bis in Ewigkeit" (Ps. 115:18), "ist ewig; vor diesem Triumphgeschrei der Ewigkeit stürzt der Tod ins Nichts. Das Leben wird unsterblich im ewigen Lobgesang der Erlö-sung." SdE§253. In this formulation there is no completion of God's plan without entering into the divine, where human eternity, which was "gepflanzt in den Boden der Schöpfung" (SdE§265), eventually makes its appearance in the final day of re-demption. Death no longer holds substance; the concept of evil itself has lost its meaning. For as with the immortality of God and the divine realm, so must hu-manity be constituted in redemption.

128. II:73. "Kein Ding, keinen Menschen. [. . .] "darf die Jugend verwerfen, denn in jedem (in der Litfaßsäule und im Verbrecher) kann das Symbol oder der Heilige erstehen" "Die religiöse Stellung der neuen Jugend."

129. II:74. "Viele Züge mag man diese Jugend mit den ersten Christen teilen, denen auch die Welt so überfließend schien von Heiligem, das in jedem erstehen konnte, daß es ihnen das Wort und die Tat benahm."

130. Benjamin's appreciation of the early Christian doctrine of worldly activity and the social calling of Christian anarchists like Leo Tolstoy found expression in his early writings. In "Das Leben der Studenten," Benjamin mentions the challenge made by the early Christians to the division of civitas and dei, civil and religious, profane and holy: "Die frühen Christen gaben die mögliche Lösung für die civitas dei: Sie verwarfen die Einzelheit in Beiden." II:84. This is the direct opposite of Nietzsche, who criticizes the Christians for failing in "die Kunst des diesseitigen Trostes." Friedrich Nietzsche, *Der Geburt der Trägodie* (Köln: Könemann, 1994), 1:17.

131. The tragic hero for Bloch is undoubtedly the enlightener Prometheus, but a Prometheus whose drama unfolds under the direction of Isaac Luria. In this sense, Bloch's expressionistic statements such as "denn wir tragen den Funken des Endes durch den Gang" (GdU:382) and "der Funke ihres Endes" (die Idee). GdU:387 must be understood within the context of an attempt to secularize the activist and collectivist structure of Lurianic Kabbalah. This can most clearly be seen in his reworking of the drama of redemption, a scenario marked by God's failure with thoroughly Lurianic consequences: "Erst wenn wir ganz gottlos geworden sind, werden wir wieder eine Tragödie haben. [. . .] Gott muß die Bühne verlassen (denn, so fügen wir hinzu, er ist nicht, er gilt, es soll nicht als Gott sein), doch Zuschauer muß er noch bleiben: das ist wie die noch einzig mögliche neue Frömmigkeit, so auch die historische, die utopische Möglichkeit tragischer Zeitalter." GdU:69.

132. "Inkognito des Einzelnen kann nur vor sich selber, ja letzthin nur am Ende der Tage vor Gott enthüllt werden, wie sich Gott selbst enthüllt." GdU:347. The individual transcends his isolation in the final revelation of God. The anonymity of the individual is matched by God's exile. Unity is not with God proper but with humanity: "Worauf ja auch die Auferstehung aller Toten im einfachen Unsterblichkeitsdogma hinweist, am letzten Ereignis der Geschichte subjektiv existent zu sein. *Alles könnte vergehen, aber das Haus der Menschheit muß vollzählig erhalten bleiben und erleuchtet stehen,* damit dereinst, wenn draußen der Untergang rast, Gott darin wohnen und uns helfen kann—und solches führt aus der Seelenwanderung heraus auf den Sinn der echten sozialen, historischen und kulturellen Ideologie." GdU:429 (my emphasis).

133. II:22. "Dialog über die Religiosität der Gegenwart"; "ein inniges Streben nach Vereinigung mit Gott." In this sense, his earlier mixing of redeemer and redeemed (II:100–101) and attributing divine qualities to the poet (II:110–114) gave way, I believe, to a more nuanced understanding of immortality, particularly in the concept of tragedy.

134. In "Zwei Gedichte von Friedrich Hölderlin," Benjamin in fact quotes a fragment of Heraclitus to this effect: "Im Wachen sehen wir zwar den Tod, im Schlafe aber den Schlaf." II:120.

135. The term *Rhythmus* seems to describe the understanding of a dynamic motion, of essentially objects in passing, without seeking to overly determine them by linking them to time as such. We find repeated usage of the term in the early writings. See, for example, pp. 18, 87, 100, 103–104, 111, 113 in vol. II of *Gesammelte Schriften*.

136. tag II:344. "Vielleicht ist das letzte Zentrum der messianischen Idee die Aufhebung der Natur in der reinen Historie, denn die messianische Zeit ist als die zu definieren, in der *alles* Geschehen historisch ist. Die Ereignisse des Naturreiches werden in ihr zu historischen [. . .] und die Landschaft wird im messianischen Reiche zum reinen Schauplatz [historischen Ort]. (Der Begriff 'Schauplatz' für den Ort des historischen Geschehens stammt von Benjamin.)"

137. II:75. "Den immanenten Zustand der Vollkommenheit rein zum absoluten zu gestalten, ihn sichtbar und herrschend in der Gegenwart zu machen, ist die geschichtliche Aufgabe." Benjamin, "The Life of Students," 1:37 (modified).

138. "Rettung des Toten als der Restitution des entstellten Lebens." Adorno, "Charakteristik Walter Benjamins," p. 171.

139. Benjamin, *Gesammelte Schriften*, VI:106. "Die Darlegung dieses Standpunkts gehört zu den Aufgaben meiner Moralphilosophie, in deren Zusammenhang der Terminus Anarchismus sehr wohl für eine Theorie gebraucht werden darf, welche das sittliche Recht nicht der Gewalt als solcher, sondern allein jeder menschlichen Institution, Gemeinschaft oder Individualität abspricht, welche sich ein Monopol auf sie zuspricht oder das Recht auf sie auch nur prinzipiell und allgemein in irgend einer Perspektive sich selbst einräumt, anstatt sie als eine Gabe der göttlichen Macht, als *Machtvollkommenheit* im einzelnen Falle zu verehren." Written circa April 1920. Benjamin, "The Right to Use Force," *Selected Writings*, 1:233 (modified).

140. On the importance of the anarchists in the Spanish Civil War, see, for example, Bookchin, *The Spanish Anarchists*.

2. Gershom Scholem's Theological Politics

1. tag I:158. "Ich glaube in dieser Stunde nicht mehr, wie ich es einmal geglaubt habe, daß ich der Messias bin."

2. tag II:270. "Es gibt nur zwei große Möglichkeiten der Politik: die anarchistische und die theokratische."

3. Some of the relevant material, however, has not yet reached the shelves and is either being prepared for publication or is still lingering in the Scholem archive in the National and University Library in Jerusalem. In this regard, I would like to thank Michael Löwy for his unpublished essay "Esoterica—Metaphisica: les papiers inédits du jeune Gershom Scholem."

4. On the formation of Jewish messianism, see Scholem, *Über einige Grundbegriffe des Judentums*, pp. 123–125 (Eng. *The Messianic Idea in Judaism*).

5. freund:14. "Ich las damals viel über Sozialismus, historischen Materialismus und vor allem über Anarchismus, dem meine Sympathien am meisten galten. Nettlaus Biographie von Bakunin und die Schriften Kropotkins und Elisé Reclus' hatten auf mich tiefen Eindruck gemacht, wozu 1915 die Lektüre der Schriften Gustav Landauers trat, vor allem dessen Aufruf zum Sozialismus." Scholem, *Walter Benjamin: The Story of a Friendship*, p. 6.

6. B I:5. "Die Organisation ist wie ein trüber See, in den der schöne reißende Strom der Idee mündet und der ihn nicht mehr hinausläßt. Organisation ist ein Synomina (!) von Tod. Nicht nur bei den Sozialdemokraten—auch bei den sonstigen isten und ismen gilt dies, nur bei den Sozialisten in furchtbarer Art. Sie wollen so schönes, und die Menschen befreien ist ihr Ziel—und sie zwangen sie in Organisationen! Ironie!"

7. B I:14. "Sag mal, was sollen denn nun die Sozialisten machen, wenn sie sich nicht organisieren? [. . .] Wie kann die Partei den politischen Kampf führen [. . .] oder soll sie vielleicht keinen führen, damit die Arbeiter Mann für Mann Zentrum oder Liberal wählen?"

8. B I:13 "Die Flamme des Sozialismus, die Flamme eines heiligen Volkswillens darf nicht der Nahrung beraubt werden, indem man ihr ein Gefäß überstülpt, nämlich die Organisation."

9. See Scholem's comments on the utopian socialists, whom he compares with the likes of Schopenhauer, Marx, and Hegel, in tag I:79.

10. "Jede Organisation einer sogenannten provisorischen und revolutionären politischen Macht, um diese Zerstörung herbeizuführen, könnte nur ein neuer Betrug sein und für das Proletariat ebenso gefährlich wäre, als alle heute bestehenden Regierungen." Von der zweiten Resolution des internationalen Kongreß. Saint-Imier. September 1872. In Nettlau, *Geschichte der Anarchie*, vol. 2. See also Nettlau, *Michael Bakunin*.

11. "Die notwendigerweise revolutionäre Politik des Proletariats soll die Zerstörung der Staaten zum unmittelbaren und einzigen Gegenstand haben. [. . .] Wir geben nicht zu, nicht einmal als revolutionäre Übergangsformen, weder nationale Konventionen, noch konstituierende Versammlungen, noch provisorische Regierungen, noch sogenannte revolutionäre Diktaturen, weil wir überzeugt sind, daß die Revolution nur in den Massen aufrichtig, ehrlich und wirklich ist, und daß, wenn sie in den Händen einiger regierender Personen konzentriert ist, sie unvermeidlich und unverzüglich zur Reaktion wird." Nettlau, *Geschichte der Anarchie*, 2:200.

12. B I:6. "Ich möchte gern wissen, ob ihr Marxisten die Moral für etwas wirkliches, d.h. uns eingeborenes, oder für etwas erfundenes haltet. Es ist das sowohl für das Verständnis eurer Stellung zur Anarchie als auch der Gründe, der tieferen Gründe der sozialistischen Ideen notwendig."

13. Kropotkin's work, which was written primarily as a response to the Social Darwinism (particularly T. H. Huxley) in vogue at the turn of the century in Lon-

don, promotes a theory of natural selection that is based not so much on the competition of species and the survival of the fittest but on a "law of mutual aid" in which an alliance of species in a cooperative manner—whether in the collective hunting methods of pelicans or "compound families" of elephants—enables their "struggle for life" to be carried on through organic nature. See Peter Kropokin, *Mutual Aid: A Factor of Evolution* (London: 1972), pp. 43–71, and Paul Avrich's fine introduction to this edition.

14. "Einer von der ethischen Seite des Anarchismus, und er glaubt an die Moral." B I:6.

15. These include *Die Revolution* (tag I:44, 48), *Ein Weg deutscher Geist* as well as the essays "Strindbergs 'Neue Jugend'" (tag I:396), "Stelle Dich, Sozialist!" (tag I:142), "Martin Buber" (tag I:126), "Sind das Ketzergedanken?" (tag I:83/tag II:85), and "Doktrinarismus" (tag I:83), with the last two essays appearing in *Vom Judentum* (1913). It is also quite likely that in conjunction with his interest in Fritz Mauthner's *Beitrag zu einer Kritik der Sprache*, Scholem read Landauer's *Skepsis und Mystik*—a philosophical review of Mauthner. tag I:271. Scholem reports discussing both the essay on Martin Buber and "Stelle Dich, Sozialist!" which appeared in the first issue of the journal *Der Aufbruch,* with Benjamin. tag I:142. He also records Benjamin's critical stance toward Mauthner's linguistic philosophy. tag I:136.

16. Landauer's lectures took place on December 12, 1915, January 29 and March 11, 1916. See tag I:197, 250, 284.

17. tag I:250. "Stehe dem Zionismus sehr nahe."

18. tag I:81. "Unser Grundzug: das ist die Revolution! Revolution überall! Wir wollen keine Reformationen oder Umbildung, wir wollen Revolution oder Erneuerung. Wir wollen die Revolution in unsere Verfassung aufnehmen. Äußere und innere Revolution. [. . .] Revolution gegen die Familie, gegen das Elternhaus. [. . .] Wir wollen Revolution aber vor allen Dingen im Judentum. Wir wollen den Zionismus revolutionieren und den Anarchismus predigen, das ist die Herrschaftslosigkeit."

19. Scholem reports reading this work together with Benjamin and having extensive discussions with him on Ahad Haam in tag I: 391, 400. Scholem makes several references in his journals to a perceived affinity between Benjamin and Ahad Haam. See Ahad Haam, *Am Scheidewege.* On Ahad Haam's influence on Benjamin, see chapter 6 on a "politics of pure means."

20. Benjamin to Ludwig Strauß. II:835–844.

21. B I:91. "Ja alle Judenfragen [. . .] zu lösen [. . .] das wäre: Heilig zu leben."

22. B I:116–117. "Wir sind Zionisten, und das heißt: wir wollen mehr als das reine Nationaljudentum, das uns noch leer und schematisch erscheint [. . .] Wir wollen, wie Ahad Haam, ein Judentum mit jüdischen Inhalten."

23. tag I:81–82. "Den lehnen wir ab. Denn wir predigen den Anarchismus. Das ist: wir wollen keinen Staat, sondern eine freie Gesellschaft.[. . .]Wir wollen nicht nach Palästina, um einen Staat zu gründen—o du kleinliches Philistertum—und in neue Fesseln aus den alten zu geraten, wir wollen nach Palästina aus Freiheitsdurst und Zukunftssehnsucht, denn dem Orient gehört die Zukunft."

24. tag I:83. "Die erhabenste anarchistische Lehre." An analysis of the concept of the Orient, drawing on Edward Said's *Orientalism* (New York: Pantheon Books, 1978), would not be inappropriate here.

25. tag I:414. "Uns ist der Zionismus das Judentum."

26. tag I:353. "Von Zion geht die Thora aus und das Wort Gottes von Jerusalem."

27. B I:48. "Die Thora [. . .] nach dem Prophetenworte—geht von Zion aus, und das verstehe ich auch innerlich: daß der innere Ausgangspunkt der Thora für uns Zion sein muß—*Zion ist ein Religiöses Symbol*—daß Zion ein innerlichstes Zentrum der Thora ist, äußerlich und innerlich, und daß wer ein Zionist ist, nach Thora streben muß, nicht nach Erlebnissen, sondern nach Leben, und daß der Zionist das Wort Gottes nur von Jerusalem vernehmen kann."

28. tag II:152. "Ich finde in der Religion in unsagbar tiefem Sinne den Zionismus beschlossen und allein legitimiert, und mein 'Volkstum' ist ein religiöser Begriff: goy kadosh." "Goy kadosh" is a reference to Exodus 19:6, where God instructs Moses to preach that the Israelites are a kingdom of priests and a holy nation. Scholem's friend, Aharon Heller, preaches the same to Scholem, as we shall see in the next section, "A Programmatic Torah."

29. von berlin:74. "Zion war für mich ein Symbol, das unseren Ursprung und unser utopisches Ziel in einem eher religiösen als geographischen Sinne verband." Scholem, *From Berlin to Jerusalem*, p. 69.

30. See Agudas Jisroel, *Berichte und Materialen*.

31. tag II:302. "Zion ist keine Metapher."

32. B I:34. "Nicht bei Gott, wie Sie, [Fischer] sondern bei den Menschen stehen muß. Ich scheide zwischen mir und Ihnen deshalb, weil Ihnen die civitas dei nicht nur wichtiger ist als die civitas humana, sondern allein wichtig. Für uns[. . .]gibt es aber keinen anderen Weg zur civitas dei als durch civitas humana, das ist über Zion."

33. tag I:388. "Am ersten Abend sprachen wir auch darüber, ob Zion eine Metapher sei, was ich bejahte—denn nur Gott ist keine—und Benjamin verneinte. Wir kamen durch die Propheten darauf, denn Benjamin behauptete, man dürfe die Propheten nicht metaphorisch benützen, wenn man die göttliche Autorität der Bibel anerkennt." –

34. See, for example, tag II:225–227.

35. GB I:82–83. "So wie er existiert und allein existeren kann: mit dem Nationalismus als letztem Wert."

36. In this way the fundamental distinction between Scholem and Benjamin in these matters has little to do with what one often is led to believe under the terms of Zionism or anti-Zionism but rather with a differentiated conception of Judaism and, although often misunderstood, of anarchism.

37. tag II:37. "Is Walter Benjamin wirklich ein Zionist? Ist nicht da doch noch eine ungeheure Kluft zwischen uns? Ist nicht auch er *für* das *zentrale Leben* und nicht für *Zion*? Hat er wirklich in sich schon die große Synthese vollzogen, die die

eigentlich zionistische ist: die Anlegung des Maßstabes der Lehre? Er ist der rein theoretische Mensch."

38. II:136. Benjamin, "Trauerspiel and Tragedy," 1:57. See the discussion in the section on "Tragic Devotion."

39. B I:89. "Unser Ziel ist Verwirklichung des Zionismus = Verwirklichung der Tora"; "Und Ihr sollt mir ein priester Reich sein und ein heiliges Volk."

40. B I:89. "Was ist Thora? Ich verstehe folgendes darunter: I) das Prinzip, nach dem die Ordnungen der Dinge gestaltet sind. Nach der Ansicht des Judentums nun ist dies Prinzip als Sprache Gottes auch, und sogar in besonderer Weise, in den Überlieferungen der Menschen erkennbar.[. . .]daher II) Thora bedeutet das Integral, den Inbegriff der religiösen Überlieferungen der Judenheit von den Tagen der Urzeit bis zu den Tagen des Messias, ein Integral, das dem Judentum in eigentümlicher Weise mit dem Gesetz der Dinge und ebenso mit dem in einem *Buche*, der "Thora" als Wort Gottes angesprochenen geistigen Wesen der Welt zwar nicht identisch ist, aber koinzidiert."

41. This is the subject of the part 2, on language.

42. B I:90. "Für mich ist Zion das Zentrum.[. . .]Ob Gott das Zentrum der Dinge ist, weiß ich nicht. Ich glaube es aber nicht. Von Zentrum aus kann Gott erst erkannt werden."

43. jjc:26.

44. B I:361. "Lieber Ewig im Golus und meine Sünden allein tragen als in [Eretz Yisroel] ein heidnisches Leben führen."

45. "Besserung der Herzen"; See Achad Haam, "Die Lehre des Herzens," in *Am Scheidewege*, 1:96–110.

46. B I:80. "Das sexuelle Verhältnis"; "Wir alle müssen einsehen, daß ein Stück Asketentum (in allen Dingen) dazu gehört, aufzubauen, was wir aufbauen wollen. Ich muß ja hier beim Militär auf die furchtbarste Art erfahren, was sexuelle Unreinheit aus den Menschen macht. Wenn wir die Volksgesundheit in dem Sinne erstreben wie etwa die Deutschen, mit denen zusammen ich hier eingezogen bin, ein gesundes Volk sind, so sind wir verloren, denn jeder Zugang zum Heiligkeit ist hier durch die Zote versperrt.[. . .]Wollen wir aber heilig sein[. . .]so müssen wir uns in der Einsamkeit verbinden. Jede Gemeinschaft, die jetzt nicht aus wirklicher Einsamkeit hervorwächst, ist ein Schwindel, denn sie hat das Golus noch nicht überwunden, trägt vielmehr sein Hauptgift im Herzen." See also B I:89.

47. Scholem was eventually diagnosed as suffering from an "incurable schizophrenia" and released from military duty in July/August of 1917. von berlin:108.

48. "Ein Nihilismus quietistischer Natur." See "Der Nihilismus als religiöses Phänomen" in *Judaica* 4 (Frankfurt: Suhrkamp, 1984), p. 131.

49. B I:66. "Wir sind uns alle einig darüber, daß wir vorläufig auf die sogenannte 'Außenarbeit' im Sinne großer Veranstaltungen[. . .]verzichten, und intern die Sache machen."

50. This reference to a politics in postponement or reserve appears in several places in Scholem's writings. See the discussion in chapters 5 and 6.

51. See B I:81–2. A defense of the *Geheimbund* also appears in "Abschied" roughly a year later: "Die Jugend, die eines Bundes würdig ist, ist noch nicht da, und wenn sie da ist, wie können Sie glauben, daß sie sich anders organisieren wird als in einem Geheimbunde, der die einzige Möglichkeit einsamer Gemeinschaft darstellt, die in der Verborgenheit verwirklicht wird." B I:465. Scholem is aware of the criticism levied again himself and Jung Juda, but rejects it out of hand. See, for example, tag II:41

52. In a letter to a friend on May 28, 1918, just prior to the Bernfeld letter, Scholem refers to the importance that "Abschied" was to have: "Ich werde nun draußen in Muri den offenen Brief an Bernfeld schreiben (den wir beide, mein Freund Benjamin und ich, unterzeichnen werden), und wenn er so wird, wie wir es uns denken, so wirst du staunen. Es wird die nackte Wahrheit darin stehen, die über die metaphysische Haltung der jungen Zionisten gesagt werden muß. Da ich jetzt Gott sei Dank keinen mehr vor Augen habe, kann ich aus der Distanz das Bild desto deutlicher sehen." B I:156. Little has changed in Scholem's nihilism by November 1, 1918, in a letter to Ludwig Strauß: "Ich lebe nach wie vor völlig zurückgezogen und komme mit hiesigen 'Zionisten' gar nicht zusammen." B I:182.

53. GB I:396. "Wir werden uns in der Tat mit Ihrem Austritt aus der zionistischen Organisation beide der Einheit unsres Denkens versichern."

54. Scholem remarks in his journals: "Der offene Brief an Bernfeld soll von uns beiden unterzeichnet werden." tag II:223.

55. B I:462. "Gemeinschaft verlangt Einsamkeit: nicht die Möglichkeit, zusammen das Gleiche zu wollen, sondern allein die gemeinsamer Einsamkeit begründet die Gemeinschaft. Zion, die Quelle unseres Volkstums, ist die gemeinsame [...] Einsamkeit aller Juden.[...]Solange dies Zentrum nicht mit strahlender Heiligkeit restituiert ist, muß die Ordnung unserer Seele, zu der sich zu bekennen die Ehrlichkeit gebietet eine anarchische sein. Im Galuth kann es keine vor Gott gültige jüdische Gemeinschaft geben. Und wenn Gemeinschaft zwischen Menschen in der Tat das Höchste ist, was gefordert werden kann, welchen Sinn hätte der Zionismus, wenn er im Galuth verwirklicht werden könnte." Scholem, "Farewell," jjc:55 (modified).

56. Other commentators have also remarked on the particularly fundamentalist tone of Scholem's text. Gert Mattenklott sees it as a "Kritik am Gemeinschaftskult der Jugendbewegung" but equally a call to establish "intellektuelle Eliten" with "ordensähnlicher Disziplin von Einzelgängern." See Mattenklott, "Mythologie Messianismus Macht," p. 193.

57. Several years earlier, Benjamin outlined his own theory of community and solitude: "Ich glaube, daß nur in der Gemeinschaft, und zwar in der innigsten Gemeinschaft der Gläubigen ein Mensch wirklich einsam sein kann: in der Einsamkeit, in der sein Ich gegen die Idee sich erhebt, um zu sich zu kommen.[...]Die tiefste Einsamkeit ist die des idealen Menschen in der Beziehung zur Idee, die sein Menschliches vernichtet. Und diese Einsamkeit, die tiefere, haben wir erst von einer vollkommen Gemeinschaft zu erwarten." GB I:160–161.

58. B I:463. "Wie die Jugend nicht einsam sein kann, so kann sie auch nicht schweigen. Das Schweigen, in dem sich Wort und Tat vereinigen, ist ihr fremd [. . .] Menschen aber, die nicht schweigen können, können im letzten Grunde auch nicht miteinander reden [. . .] in [dem Geschwätz] vermischen sich in unterschiedsloser Weise alle Dinge und verkehren sich: Zion zum Zukunftsstaat, das Judentum zum Geist. [. . .] Der Jugend die Sprache wiederzugeben ist die Aufgabe." Scholem, "Farewell," jjc:56–57 (modified).

59. B I:465–466. "Ihrem Auftreten und ihren Ansprüchen, sondern in der Zurückgezogenheit, in der sie ihre Aufgabe erfaßt, und in der Größe des Verzichtes, in dem ihre Fülle Gestalt annimmt." jjc:60 (modified).

60. B I:464. "Zion wäre keine symbolische Metapher mehr." Scholem, "Farewell," jjc:57 (modified). This assertion, that "Zion kommt hier nur metaphorisch vor," appears twice in "Abschied," lending emphasis to the concept and particularly to the difference with Benjamin. See also freund:94.

61. tag II:418–420. "Mein Zusammensein mit Walter ist keine anarchistische Gemeinschaft, die ganz stetig ist, sondern ist noch von historischen Gesetzen beherrscht: nur in Revolutionen sei unsere Beziehung realisierbar. . . . Im letzten Grunde ist es wohl eben ein verschiedener Begriff vom Verzicht, der die Widersprüche unseres Verhältnisses enthält und periodisch erneuert. Mein Begriff von Verzicht ist so, daß es *nichts* Irrelevantes in bezug auf ihn gibt, für Walter und Dora aber gibt es Dinge, auf die sie glauben ein Recht zu haben nicht verzichten zu müssen. [. . .] *Ich habe mich geirrt*, als ich schrieb . . . daß ich zu Walter ein völlig positives Verhältnis habe. Und diesen Irrtum muß ich wiederrufen, und auch wenn es die jetzigen Krämpfe kostet. Drei Jahre hat diese versuchte und irrealisierte Gemeinschaft mich belehrt, erzogen, gefördert und gehemmt."

62. tag II:418. "Rückkehr nach Deutschland."

63. "Ich sagte wohl viel, aber eigentlich doch nur symbolisch, denn ich konnte nicht direkt vom Zionismus sprechen. Jedenfalls hatten sie eine Idee, worum es geht." tag II:418.

64. Peter Kropotkin, Emma Goldman, and Alexander Berkman, to name just three who returned to Russia embracing the revolution. All, including Scholem, were terribly disillusioned. Kropotkin, however, was saved from the worst aspects, having died a few years before Lenin's own death.

65. B I:125. "In meinem Leben habe ich noch keine so menschlich ergreifenden und wahren politischen Schriftstücke gesehen wie die Dokumente der maximalistischen [Bolschwistischen] Revolution."

66. B I:184. "Die Differenz meiner Haltung zum Krieg und zur Revolution ist sehr klar: Zwar in beiden Fällen beteilige ich mich nicht. Aber dort wandte ich mich ab und hier sehe ich zu. Ich nehme diese Revolution, die zweifellos historische Legitimität besitzt, in mein Gesichtsfeld auf—nicht mehr, aber auch nicht weniger. Solange die Stellung des Geistes in der neuen Ordnung der Dinge noch nicht durchaus verletzt ist, ist es meine Pflicht eine 'wohlwollende Neutralität' nicht zu verlassen. Da aber natürlich die Revolution, an der mich zu *beteiligen* die größte Aufgabe wäre: die theokratische Revolution gewiß nicht mit dieser identisch ist (auch

wenn sie irgendwo natürlich etwas Messianisches hat) kann ich nicht mehr tun."
The term *well-meaning neutrality, wohlwollende Neutralität* emerges again in opposition to his brother Werner. tag II:427.

67. tag II:406. "Die prinzipielle Differenz zwischen Sozialismus und Anarchismus (der Vorstufe der Theokratie) ist jetzt klar."

68. Scholem's later views on these matters are complex and deserve much
more attention than I am capable of providing here. His growing dissatisfaction
with the Zionist movement in Palestine, from the emergence of Hebrew as a truly
secular language to the Arab-Israeli conflict (particularly his activities with the
group Brit Shalom) mark distinct turns in his development. In contrast to his earlier messianic Zionism, he develops a distinctly antimessianic approach when arriving in Palestine, ascribing such views to the followers of Jabotinsky and the
Right. On his post-European views, see Scholem, "Ist die Verständigung mit den
Arabern gescheitert?" "Zur Frage des Parlaments," "On Our Language," *Od Davar*
(Hebr.), pp. 68–71 and 85–90 on Brit Shalom, especially 88–89 for a critique of messianic Zionism and "Ahad Haam v'anachnu," 72.

69. Since this period extends beyond the scope of the thesis (which is focused
on the German years), I have decided to sketch only briefly the development that
was to take place in Scholem's thinking after his arrival in Palestine in order to contextualize political ideas discussed in this chapter.

70. Evidence, however, of a growing interest in the subject dates back from
the earliest journal entries from 1914 (tag I:31–32), on through to the essay on
Sabbatianism in *Der Jude 9, Sonderheft* 5 (1928), and again in his article for the
Encyclopaedia Judaica (1932) on Kabbalah. There has been some confusion concerning the date of "Redemption Through Sin," identified as either having appeared in 1936 or 1937. From a letter to Hans-Joachim Schoeps dated March 1,
1937, in which Scholem mentions enclosing a copy the article, it would seem to
have been written in 1936.

71. Some have interpreted this essay (as well as Scholem's interest in Sabbatianism) as a critique of political Zionism, leaving aside its scholarly importance in
reviving one of the most earth-shattering and radically suppressed events in the
annals of Jewish history. On the history of the debate, see Biale, *Gershom Scholem*,
pp. 172–173, 187–194. Perhaps the only thing to add to Biale is Scholem's own description of Frank as a "Territorialist" in "the language of modern Zionism." See
"Der Nihilismus als religiöses Phänomen," *Judaica* 4 (Frankfurt: Suhrkamp, 1987),
p. 181 (henceforth jIV).

72. "Allgemeinen Umbruchs und Kataklysmus." See "Die Metamorphose des
häretischen Messianismus der Sabbatianer in religiösen Nihilismus im 18. Jahrhundert," *Judaica* 3 (Frankfurt: Suhrkamp, 1984), p. 212 (henceforth jIII).

73. Grundsätzliche Bestreiter jeglicher Authorität, der keinerlei Prinzipien auf
Glauben hin annimmt, ganz gleich welche Achtung solches Prinzip umgeben
möge." See also jV:122–124.

74. jIV139. "Unheimlichste aller Gäste." This occurred without succumbing to
the instrumentalism of positivism.

75. jIV:130. "Die Anarchisten nahmen den Begriff aktiv in ihre Propaganda auf und wurden so für das Bewußtsein weiter Kreise die klassischen Vertreter des Nihilismus, bevor noch Nietzsche, ganz jenseits der politischen Sphäre und im Durchdenken der Implikationen des Zusammenbruchs der Überlieferung der autoritären Wertsysteme, den Nihilismus als jenen steinernen Gast erkannte, der an der Tür unserer Feste wartet."

76. jIV:131. "Die Zerstörung aller Institutionen, um herauszufinden, was etwa als guter Fonds in ihnen solcher Zerstörung widersteht."

77. jIV:131. "Der konsequente Kampf für die Freiheit des Individuums gegen tyrannische und heuchlerische Institutionen und zugunsten des freien Zusammenschlusses einander helfend beistehender Gemeinschaften."

78. jIV:130. "Der Verfall der alten autoritären, noch auf Offenbarung gegründeten Wertordnungen der Religionen wurde dann, im Verfolg jener religionskritischen und philosophischen Strömungen als Nihilismus, als die Folge des Zusammenbruchs der religiösen Welt ausgerufen."

79. jIV:131. "Nicht Institutionen oder gar die Realität schlechthin im aktiven Aufstand, sondern in der Kontemplation und von einem metaphysischen archimedischen Punkt her negiert oder auch zerstört werden."

80. Scholem, "Redemption Through Sin," p. 84.

81. Ibid., p. 116.

82. Ibid., p. 88.

83. Ibid., pp. 127, 131. Scholem writes elsewhere: "Frank war ein Nihilist, und sein Nihilismus besaß ein seltenes Maß von Authentizität. . . . Er stellt nicht etwa einen Mystiker, einen Visionär oder einen Staatsmann als Messias vor, sondern einen Kraftmenschen, wenn man so sagen dürfte, einen Athleten-Messias." jIV:171.

84. jIV:178. "Ständig wiederholt Frank das doppelte Grundmotiv seiner Lehre: *Abschaffung* aller Werte, positiven Gesetze und Religionen im Namen der Befreiung des *Lebens*. Der Weg dazu führt durch den Abgrund der Zerstörung. Dieser Begriff des Lebens stellt für Frank ein Schlüsselwort dar, in dem sein anarchisches Pathos sich ausdrückt. Leben ist für ihn nicht die harmonische Ordnung der Natur und ihr sanftes Gesetz; er ist kein Anhänger der Rückkehr zur Natur im Sinne Rousseaus. . . . Leben ist Freiheit von Bindung und Gesetz. Das anarchische Leben ist Gegenstand und Inhalt seiner Utopie, in der ein primitives Streben nach einem gesetzlosen Begriff von Freiheit und von der Promiskuität aller Dinge sich ankündigt. Dies anarchische Leben rauscht von dem 'großen Bruder' und erhält bei Frank alle positiven Töne und Obertöne, die dieser Begriff sonst in der religiösen Überlieferung, wenn auch in ganz anderem Sinne hat. Hundert Jahre vor Bakunin hat Frank die erlösende Macht der Zerstörung ins Zentrum seiner Utopie gestellt."

85. Even this emphasis on "life" precedes Scholem's research on Frank. He applies a similar construction to the debate between Brenner and Bialik regarding Halakhah and Aggadah. See tag II:606.

86. Compare the opening lines of Wilde, "The Soul of Man Under Socialism," pp. 121–185, especially pp.184 and 134.

87. jIII:207. Frank: "Wo ich gehe, wird alles zerstört. Ich muß zerstören und annihilieren—was ich aber bauen werde, wird ewig stehen."

88. jIII:207. "Vorläufig ist die Zeit für solches Bauen aber noch nicht gekommen. Vielmehr ergreift das Ringen um die Zerstörung, ein ursprünglicher und echter Anarchismus, alle Schichten unserer Existenz."

89. jIII:207. "die Vision der nihilistischen Erlösung"; "die Aufhebung aller Gesetze und Normen."

90. jIV:177. "Diese Welt wird von 'unwürdigen Gesetzen' regiert. Daher besteht die eigentliche Aufgabe darin, der Herrschaft dieser Gesetze—*aller* Gesetze dieser Welt—ein Ende zu bereiten, die ja Gesetze des Todes sind und die Würde des Menschen verletzen."

91. jIII:208–209. "Nichts der Religion"; "das Nichttheologische." One sees in this formulation a parallel to the "Nichts der Offenbarung" he uses to characterize the 'kabbalistische Sprachwelt' of Kafka's struggle with the disappearance of God. Would this imply that a nothingness of religion born from the condition of the nothingness of revelation is "das Nichttheologische" or theological nihilism?

92. Rather than signaling the end of the movement, the great messianic act of Sabbatai Zvi in his conversion to Islam, as Scholem points out, was actually in many ways its beginning. See Scholem's *Sabbatai Sevi.*

93. "Redemption Through Sin," p. 84.

94. Ibid., p. 89.

95. Ibid., p. 109.

96. See jjc:32, where Scholem refers again to his fear of the terror unleashed by absolute freedom based on optimistic, transhistorical assumptions concerning human nature.

97. Scholem, "Redemption Through Sin," p. 109. Scholem was to support these conclusions many years later in his essay on nihilism published in honor of Adorno: "Wenn wir unsere Aufmerksamkeit auf das Judentum richten, so ist von vornherein das Auftreten antinomistischer und bis ins Nihilistische gehender Tendenzen besonders unerwartet. Stellt doch das historische Judentum, wie es sich in dem festen Gefüge des Gesetzes der Tora und der Halacha kristallisiert hat, eine Religionsverfassung von ungewöhnlicher Disziplin und Festigkeit dar, die in jedem Stück auflösenden und die festen Ordnungen abbauenden Bestrebungen sich entgegenstellt." jIV:61

98. On mysticism and authority, see Scholem's "Religiöse Autorität und Mystik" in *Zur Kabbala und ihrer Symbolik.*

99. Cf. jIII:198.

100. jIII:211–212. "Solange kein positiver Weg sichtbar war, durch den eine messianische Revolte gegen das Ghetto und seine Umwelt von innen her vollzogen werden konnte, nahm diese Revolte einen nihilistischen Charakter an."

101. jIV:182. "In der Umwertung aller Werte der jüdischen Überlieferung, die der Nihilismus der Frankisten propagierte, verkoppelte sich die historische Erfahrung des polnischen Juden mit einer intensiven Sehnsucht gerade nach der Welt, die ihm versagt war."

102. Frank spent over thirteen years as prisoner of the Catholic Church in Czestochowa. Scholem, *Kabbalah*, p. 301.

103. jIV:80. "Da Frank der Weg der politischen Aktion versagt ist, betont er vorläufig den moralischen Aufstand gegen die herrschenden Wertordnungen."

104. jIV:138. "Der Aufstand gegen die Gesetze, die der Nihilist gerade ihres Ursprungs wegen verwirft und mit dem er zugleich den Eintritt unter ein höheres Gesetz vollzieht, fand seine nächstliegende und sichtbarste Anwendung auf das Moralgesetz, das zu brechen Verdienst wurde."

105. This is quite evident in the theology of Baruchja Russo, a leader of the Döhme sect at the beginning of the eighteenth century, whose teachings sought to overturn all the laws that would pertain to a Torah of creation, particularly those that would be deemed "civilization forming" or necessary. These would include, following Moses 3:19, "die Sexuellen Tabus und Inzestverbote. In der neuen Ära seien diese Verbote nicht nur aufgehoben, sondern würden vielmehr zu Geboten, die dem neuen Weltzustand entsprächen.[. . .] Die Propaganda der Abrogation der Schöpfung-Tora und ihrer Ersetzung durch eine mystisch-libertinische, die dem neuen Stand entspräche, wurde begreiflicherweise von den Hütern der Überlieferung als totaler Umsturz gewertet und dementsprechend bekämpft. In der Tat war der Weg von hier zu einem konsequenten Nihilismus auf religiöser Grundlage nicht weit." jIV:170.

106. jIV:166. "Dies wurde aber eher als eine Maskierung des eigentlichen messianischen Inhalts angesehen, der in antinomistischen Ritualen der Sektierer verwirklicht wurde. Hier verbanden sich unverkennbar machtvolle religiöse Emotionen mit anarchischen Neigungen, wie sie tief im Menschlichen verborgen liegen. Je stärker die Disziplin war, mit der das rabbinische Judentum solche Impulse gebändigt hatte, desto wilder war ihr Ausbruch im Verfolg des radikalen Messianismus und seiner Botschaft eines Anbruchs der Freiheit und Erlösung, selbst wenn diese Freiheit sich nur im Untergrund und geheimen bestätigen konnte."

107. jIV:134. "Die ungeheuren Energien, die in den Aufbau religiöser Strukturen gingen, in denen die Erfahrung der Welt mit der der Transzendenz sich verbinden sollte, ließen keinen Raum für den Abbau dessen, was erst im Prozeß der Kristallisation sich befand."

108. Scholem, "Redemption Through Sin," p. 88.

109. Ibid., p. 84.

110. "'Aufhebung der Tora als deren wahrer Erfüllung'"; "Ursprünge, Widersprüche und Auswirkungen des Sabbatianismus" (Einleitung zu Sabbatai Zwi aus dem Nachlaß). jV:130.

111. jIII:198. "ungewöhnliche Explosion neuer produktiver Kräfte."

112. "Redemption Through Sin," p. 84.

113. jIV:187. "Was sie aber selber vorbringen, stellt einen Übergang der revolutionären Bilderwelt in die der Aufklärung dar."

114. jV:130. "Ein Verständnis der sabbatianischen Bewegung hängt meiner Ansicht nach davon ab, ob der Versuch gelingt, das irdische Reich—das Gebiet der Geschichte—mit dem himmlischen Reich—dem Gebiet der Kabbala—zu verbinden

und das eine im Licht des anderen zu deuten. Denn 'das irdische ist wie das himm-lische Reich'. Beide bilden ja in Wahrheit ein einziges 'Reich'—das Reich der Bewe-gung, in der die menschliche Erfahrung sich entfaltet, die sich weder allein 'geistig' noch allein 'gesellschaftlich' verstehen läßt, sondern viele Gesichter hat und in jedem ihrer Gesichter dieselbe Grundbewegung offenbart."

115. jIV:166 "die Flamme des wahren Glaubens brennt ihrem Wesen nach nur im verborgenen." See B I:13 and the debate with Werner Scholem in the section on "Tradition and Anarchism" in this chapter.

116. jIII:217. "die Anhänger dieser Bewegung waren echte Gläubige, die in den Verheißungen einer anarchistischen irdischen Utopie eine Erlösung fanden, die ihnen das rabbinische Judentum versagte." Scholem also repeats this same sentence in the last lines of his "Der Nihilismus als religiöses Phänomen." Here he leaves out the word "irdischen" in the phrase "einer anarchistischen Utopie." See jIV:188.

117. Translated from the Hebrew by Mendes-Flohr in *Divided Passions*, pp. 344–345.

118. Ibid., p. 345.

119. Ibid.

120. Ibid.

121. Scholem, "Reflections on the Possibility of Jewish Mysticism," p. 50.

122. Scholem, "Zionism: Dialectic of Continuity and Rebellion," p. 279.

123. Scholem, "Reflections on Jewish Theology" (1974) in jjc:263

124. Scholem, "Reflections on the Possibility of Jewish Mysticism," p. 49.

125. Ibid.

126. "Reflections on the Possibility of Jewish Mysticism," p. 50.

127. Ibid.

128. See "Zionism: Dialectic of Continuity and Rebellion," pp. 278, 282. This represents what David Biale refers to as Scholem's concept of anarchism, which only reflects part of Scholem's use of the term. See his book, *Gershom Scholem: Kabbalah and Counter-History*, and the discussion on pp. 7–9, 65, 90, 102–103, 112, 115, and 186.

129. "Zionism: Dialectic of Continuity and Rebellion," p. 291.

130. Ibid., p. 276.

131. Mendes-Flohr, *Divided Passions*, p. 346.

132. See jjc:33.

3. On the Origins of Language

1. *Bereshit Rabbah* contains a host of interpretations on how the Torah existed before the world. Something, however, was with Him in His work. *Bereshit Rabbah* I:1–2/Proverbs 8:30–31. Six things are suggested to have either come before cre-ation, or were at least considered candidates for creation. Three seem to take pri-ority over the others with the intention of God's creation being seen as the most probable of the three. I:5.

2. Proverbs 8:22, 8:30–31.

3. *Bereshit Rabbah* I:1–2.

4. *Bereshit Rabbah* I:1. In agreement with the basic terms of Jewish linguistic speculation, Benjamin lends his voice to the idea that creation was a linguistic event but appears undecided and ultimately unimpressed with the notion of Hebrew being the language of revelation. His argument: even if Hebrew was God's language the profane form is merely a representation. The fact that he does not take up Hebrew as the original language, however, should not be misinterpreted as a statement on Hebrew as a "national" language, as we shall see in Molitor. The chances that he was aware of *Bereshit Rabbah*, despite the availability in the königliche Bibliothek in Berlin of a translation (Wünsche, *Der Midrasch)* from this perspective is slight (aside for the reference to a second Genesis story). On the other hand, Molitor, whom Benjamin did read, was familiar with this text and convinced of the linguistic revelation only occurring in Hebrew. The consequences of such a theory without Hebrew might have led to ambiguity, which Benjamin admits to Scholem in a letter from March 30, 1918, in briefe I:181–183.

5. *Bereshit Rabbah* VIII:2 has it that the Torah was created two thousand years before the world.

6. The growth and development of this idea is truly a study of its own. See for example, Neusner, *Genesis Rabbah*; Neusner, *Genesis and Judaism*; Wünsche, *Kleine Midraschim zur jüdischen Ethik.*

7. GB I:343. "Im übrigen aber versuche ich in dieser Arbeit mich mit dem Wesen der Sprache auseinander zu setzen und zwar—soweit ich es verstehe: in immanenter Beziehung auf das Judentum und mit Beziehung auf die ersten Kapitel Genesis."

8. Wünsche, *Die kleine Midrashim zur jüdischen Ethik*, which Benjamin discusses in a letter to Scholem. GB II:92. It is therefore also highly probable that Benjamin was familiar with Wünsche's rendition of *Bereshit Rabbah.*

9. GB I:437. "Für mich hängen die Fragen nach dem Wesen der Erkenntnis, Recht, Kunst zusammen mit der Frage nach dem Ursprung aller menschlichen Geistesäußerung aus dem Wesen der Sprache."

10. ref 322. "Wenn im folgenden das Wesen der Sprache auf Grund der ersten Genesiskapitel betrachtet wird, so soll damit weder Bibelinterpretation als Zweck verfolgt noch auch die Bibel an dieser Stelle objektiv als offenbarte Wahrheit dem Nachdenken zugrunde gelegt werden, sondern das, was aus dem Bibeltext in Ansehung der Natur der Sprache selbst sich ergibt, soll aufgefunden werden." II:147.

11. See Menninghaus, *Walter Benjamins Theorie der Sprachmagie*, p. 22. Menninghaus, however, is criticized by Speth, *Wahrheit und Ästhetik*, p. 257, yet whose own reliance on a "jüdisch-christlichen Geschichtserfahrung" (p. 263), is purely chimerical at best. He is also criticized along similar lines by Bröcker, *Die Grundlosigkeit der Wahrheit*, p. 105–106. Benjamin's study indeed needs to be divorced from the mystery shrouding this discussion. I refer to the opinion that (a) to compare Benjamin with Jewish thought is tantamount to "unkritischen Mystizismus" (as if critical mysticism is a meaningful idea), or that linguistic speculation

informed by Judaism is necessarily Kabbalistic. See Menninghaus, *Walter Benjamins Theorie der Sprachmagie*, pp. 189–191.

12. ref 322. "und die Bibel ist *zunächst* in dieser Absicht nur darum unersetzlich, weil diese Ausführungen im Prinzipiellen ihr darin folgen, daß in ihnen die Sprache als eine letzte, nur in ihrer Entfaltung zu betrachtende, unerklärliche und mystische Wirklichkeit vorausgesetzt wird. Die Bibel, indem sie sich selbst als Offenbarung betrachtet, muß notwendig die sprachlichen Grundtatsachen entwickeln." II:147.

13. He was also under no illusions concerning this matter. See Benjamin's own views of his knowledge of Judaism in letters to Scholem (briefe I:182) and Scholem's estimation of this period (freund:92–93).

14. ref 314. "Jede Äußerung menschlichen Geisteslebens kann als eine Art der Sprache aufgefaßt werden, und diese Auffassung erschließt nach Art einer wahrhaften Methode überall neue Fragestellungen." II:140.

15. This interpretation of Genesis immediately draws attention to an unwanted opposition between God's intention and his act. It is difficult to determine conclusively if this problem lies inherent in Benjamin's early essay. It is certain, however, that he brings the question of intention to the forefront of his work, particularly in the later *Trauerspiel* book.

16. The focus here is not to restrict the observations on the nature of language in pursuit of reason but of truth. For this reason there is no shying away from the paradoxical in Benjamin analysis, should this serve the interests of truth. That the truth may very well be unreasonable is not a position the author may indeed have sought to deny, which is all the more noteworthy in light of the scholarship that sometimes mistakes the truthful for the reasonable, an assumption modern religious scholarship has shown to be problematic.

17. ref 314. "Es gibt kein Geschehen oder Ding weder in der belebten noch in der unbelebten Natur, das nicht in gewisser Weise an der Sprache teilhätte, denn es ist jedem wesentlich, seinen geistigen Inhalt mitzuteilen." II:140–141.

18. ref 314. "Eine Metapher aber ist das Wort "Sprache" in solchem Gebrauche durchaus nicht. Denn es ist eine volle inhaltliche Erkenntnis, daß wir uns nichts vorstellen können, das sein geistiges Wesen nicht im Ausdruck mitteilt." II:141. The term *inhaltliche* is translated here as "substantive" and *Wesen* as "substance."

19. Benjamin's concept of the metaphor, particularly in relation to a separate notion of the symbolic, undergoes a tremendous development in his work as a whole, beginning with his earliest texts, such as the essay on language, taking on more complicated form in the dissertation on the Romantics, and again receiving attention in the *Trauerspiel* book as well as in many places in the later writings. The difference between metaphor and symbol was also to concern Scholem, even at an early stage. This makes a definition of the term *metaphor* for our purposes here extremely difficult. After reviewing the later texts, I have come to the conclusion that the understanding of the term here is somewhat different than in, for example, the *Trauerspiel* and have therefore sought to begin with a *peshat* (simple) interpretation. A full analysis of the concept of metaphor, however, is surely due in future study.

20. For "mysticism" modern Hebrew has merely borrowed the Latin term. See Dan, "The Language of the Mystics in Medieval Germany," p. 6–7.

21. Since rendering the term *Geist* in the English language leaves little choice but to select from one of the two directions contained in the German, I have favored here the term *intellect*.

22. II:141. "Völlige Abwesenheit der Sprache."

23. ref 315. "Ein Dasein, welches ganz ohne Beziehung zur Sprache wäre, ist eine Idee; aber diese Idee läßt sich auch im Bezirk der Ideen, deren Umkreis diejenige Gottes bezeichnet, nicht fruchtbar machen." II:141.

24. For a very different philosophical interpretation of high caliber, see Fenvis, "The Genesis of Judgement," pp. 81–82.

25. ref 315. "Die deutsche Sprache z.B. ist keineswegs der Ausdruck für alles, was wir *durch* sie—vermeintlich— ausdrücken können, sondern sie ist der unmittelbare Ausdruck dessen, was *sich* in ihr mitteilt." II:141.

26. The "unmediated expression" of its *geistige Inhalt/Wesen* or what I would prefer to term its substance of the intellect.

27. "Was teilt die Sprache mit? Sie teilt das ihr entsprechende geistige Wesen mit." II:142.

28. That a foreign speaker of a particular language has no choice but to communicate what he or she is capable of in that language is all the more apparent in the exchange between a first language which is radically different from a second. It may appear that a foreign speaker is communicating an idea generated in a first language and expressing it merely through the second, but this reveals itself to be nothing more than an impoverished translation of the former when more complex forms of expression are undertaken by the foreign speaker, yielding more fully formed ideas in the second language.

29. ref 316. "*Jede Sprache teilt sich selbst mit*," such that "*Das sprachliche Wesen der Dinge ist ihre Sprache.*" II:142.

30. One commentator attempts to explain this problem in the following way: "Die Sprachen umschließen nicht nur die menschliche, worthafte Sprache und das Gebiet aller anderen menschlichen Geistesäußerungen, sondern auch die Natur, die unbelebte, materielle Welt sowie das Geschehen in ihr, so daß der Bereich der Natur wie die Kultur als Ausdruck menschlicher Tätigkeiten gleichermaßen als Sprachen zu beschreiben sind. Auf der äußeren Sinnebene gilt somit alles als Sprache, was sich mitteilt, ausdrückt, darstellt—ungeachtet der Unterschiede in der Weise, *wie* sich etwas mitteilt." Kather, "*Über Sprache überhaupt*, p. 37.

31. ref 316. "Das, was an einem geistigen Wesen mitteilbar ist." II:142.

32. One might be tempted to formulate this in German such that *das sprachliche Wesen ist dem geistigen Wesen mitteilbar.*

33. ref 316. "Die Sprache eines geistigen Wesens ist unmittelbar dasjenige, was an ihm mitteilbar ist." II:142.

34. We can turn to no other explanation of this paradoxical statement than to the creational model. A reasonable explanation must give way therefore to a theological one, if every language is understood as communicating itself in itself.

35. ref 317. "Das Mediale, das ist die *Unmittel*barkeit aller geistigen Mitteilung, ist das Grundproblem der Sprachtheorie, und wenn man diese Unmittelbarkeit magisch nennen will, so ist das Urproblem der Sprache ihre Magie. Zugleich deutet das Wort von der Magie der Sprache auf ein anderes: auf ihre Unendlichkeit." II:142–143.

36. See also Benjamin's letter to Martin Buber, refusing his offer to write for the journal *Der Jude*. GB I:325–327.

37. Only its linguistic substance determines this border, which is the same as saying its (primary) substance and not its "verbal content." This is true for things as well as for people but in distinctly different ways, for humans communicate in words and express their primary substance in naming: "Der Mensch teilt also sein eignes geistiges Wesen (sofern als mitteilbar ist) mit, indem er alle anderen Dinge benennt." II:143.

38. ref 317. "Darum wohnt jeder Sprache ihre inkommensurable einziggeartete Unendlichkeit inne." II:143.

39. Think, for example, of mediums and situations where the communication of a particular substance is essential: an important letter, conversation, presentation. For a further development of Benjamin's thought in the direction of media with a distinctly analytical component, see the work of Konitzer, *Sprachkrise und Verbildlichung*.

40. II:143. Clearly the type of questions Benjamin proposes leads us back to theological speculation on Genesis.

41. ref 318. "Der Name hat im Bereich der Sprache einzig diesen Sinn und diese unvergleichlich hohe Bedeutung: daß er das innerste Wesen der Sprache selbst ist. Der Name ist dasjenige, *durch* das sich nichts mehr, und *in* dem die Sprache selbst und absolut sich mitteilt." II:144.

42. ref 318. "Der Name als Erbteil der Menschensprache verbürgt also, daß *die Sprache schlechthin* das geistige Wesen des Menschen ist." II:144.

43. ref 318. "Alle Natur, sofern sie sich mitteilt, teilt sich in der Sprache mit, also letzten Endes im Menschen." II:144.

44. ref 319. "Gottes Schöpfung vollendet sich, indem die Dinge ihren Namen vom Menschen erhalten, aus dem im Namen die Sprache allein spricht." II:144.

45. II:144. Stéphane Mosès detects three languages in Benjamin's analysis: an original/divine, an Adamic, and a fallen language. It is a question to what degree Mosès understands a final, redemptive, restitution of language to be a true return to origins. See his "Benjamin's Metaphors of Origin," p. 140–142.

46. ref 320. "Sprache ist dann das geistige Wesen der Dinge." II:145.

47. "Es wird das geistige Wesen also von vornherein als mitteilbar gesetzt, oder vielmehr gerade *in* die Mitteilbarkeit gesetzt, und die Thesis: das sprachliche Wesen der Dinge ist mit ihrem geistigen, sofern letzteres mitteilbar ist, identisch, wird in ihrem 'sofern' zu einer Tautologie. *Einen Inhalt der Sprache gibt es nicht; als Mitteilung teilt die Sprache ein geistiges Wesen, d.i. eine Mitteilbarkeit schlechthin mit.*" II:145–46.

48. ref 319. "Der Name ist aber nicht allein der letzte Ausruf, er ist auch der eigentliche Anruf der Sprache." II:145.

49. II:145. "Intensive Totalität der Sprache"; "extensive Totalität."

50. ref 319. *Der Mensch allein hat die nach Universalität und Intensität vollkommene Sprache.*" II:145.

51. II:146. We are compelled to note the inconsistency in the division of the divine and the profane here, a point he was to stress toward the end of his early writings in the thesis of 1921. A similar weakness appears once again in the essay on Hölderlin, where the divine qualities of the poet seems to supersede the partition of humans and God. But since we also know from later passages in this essay on language that Benjamin did not intend to confound this division (see, for example, II:150), one might be lead to assume that if humanity posses a complete and universal language, it carried it unknowingly through the profane.

52. ref 320. "Des Mitteilenden (Benennenden) und des Mitteilbaren (Namen) in der Mitteilung." II:146.

53. ref 320. "Für die Metaphysik der Sprache ergibt die Gleichsetzung des geistigen mit dem sprachlichen Wesen, welches nur graduelle Unterschiede kennt, eine Abstufung allen geistigen Seins in Gradstufen." II:146.

54. See note 55. The reference is to II:146.

55. ref 320. "Sie [the higher category] führt daher auf die Abstufung aller geistigen wie sprachlichen Wesen nach Existenzgraden oder nach Seinsgraden, wie sie bezüglich der geistigen schon die Scholastik gewohnt war." II:146.

56. ref 320. "Ausgesprochenen und Ausprechlichen mit dem Unaussprechlichen und Unausgesprochenen." II:146.

57. ref 321. "Genau das meint aber der Begriff der Offenbarung, wenn er die Unabtastbarkeit des Wortes für die einzige und hinreichende Bedingung und Kennzeichnung der Göttlichkeit des geistigen Wesens, das sich in ihm ausspricht, nimmt." II:146.

58. ref 321. "Das höchste Geistesgebiet der Religion ist (im Begriff der Offenbarung) zugleich das einzige, welches das Unaussprechliche nicht kennt." II:147.

59. Benjamin introduces here a quotation from Hamann, which interrupts the flow of ideas from the paragraph before it. (The beginning of the next paragraph picks up where the last ended). The same quotation is found in Scholem's essay and seems to have yielded a common basis if we take into account Scholem's view that Benjamin's "Metaphysik der Sprache" was to be the linguistic continuation of Hamann and Humboldt (letter from Scholem to Benjamin, March 1931, reproduced in full in freund:284). While a legacy of the latter was refuted by Menninghaus in his study (*Walter Benjamins Theorie der Sprachmagie*, pp.11–12), the former is taken up as the wellsprings of Benjamin's thought. Several commentators have noted that both authors appeared to draw from Unger's *Hamanns Sprachtheorie,* where the citation "Bei mir ist weder von Physik noch von Theologie die Rede, sondern Sprache, die Mutter der Vernunft und Offenbarung, ihr A und O," Hamann to Jacobi, 28 Dec. 1785, is found on the title page. Benjamin's linguistic

theory, however, differentiates itself from that of Hamann, and ultimately Molitor, as we shall see, in that he does not attribute an incarnation of Christ to a theory of the letters or to the magic of worldly revelation. Hamann's attempt to establish parallels between the letters and an "Offenbarung Gottes im Fleisch" as it is conceived in the "fleischgewordene Logos" of John's evangelium—in short, an entire theory of incarnation based on the word of God and the body of Christ—is entirely absent in Benjamin. Unger, *Hamanns Sprachtheorie*, pp. 66–67. In addition, there is reason to believe Benjamin rejected an emphasis on the physical in creation in his rather oblique references to the formation of Adam. II:147. The notion that Judaism is the "Universalgeschichte" of Christianity (letter to Herder January 1, 1780, in Unger, *Hamanns Sprachtheorie*, p. 113), that "Die Erlösung der ganzen sichtbaren Natur von ihren Windeln und Fesseln beruht auf der Offenbarung des Christentums" (Hamann, *Schriften*, VI:20–21; Unger, *Hamanns Sprachtheorie*, p.121), and that God revealed "in niedriger Gestalt, in seinem 'Worte,' im Logos, d.h. in der irdischen Erscheinung Christi und in der Schrift, dem Zeugnusee des Heiligen Geistes" (Unger, *Hamanns Sprachtheorie*, p. 137) all run counter to Benjamin's expressed goals in this essay. A further analysis of one of the mainstays of Christian theology, however, is at least implicitly addressed in Benjamin's notion of translation. See the discussion in the chapter entitled "Reception As Translation."

60. ref 321. "Den Dingen ist das reine sprachliche Formprinzip—der Laut—versagt." II:147.

61. ref 321. "Dinglichem Sprachgeist." II:147.

62. ref 322. "Die zweite Fassung der Schöpfungsgeschichte, die vom Einblasen des Odems erzählt, berichtet zugleich, der Mensch sei aus Erde gemacht worden. Dies ist in der ganzen Schöpfungsgeschichte die einzige Stelle, an der von einem Material des Schöpfers die Rede ist, in welchem dieser seinen Willen, der sonst doch wohl unmittelbar schaffend gedacht ist, ausdrückt. Es ist in dieser zweiten Schöpfungsgechichte die Erschaffung des Menschen nicht durch das Wort geschehen: Gott sprach—und es geschah—, sondern diesem nicht aus dem Worte geschaffenen Menschen wird nun die *Gabe* der Sprache beigelegt, und er wird über die Natur erhoben." II:147–148.

63. See GB I:364. We find a reference to the Aramaic translation (Targum Onkelos) in Scholem's notebooks from 1918–1919, presenting the possibility of a second story of creation. This text becomes relevant in Scholem's late essay on language precisely because this passage in the Aramaic translation has a unique linguistic meaning, as we shall see. It is indeed even possible that Scholem knew about the *Targum Onkelos* rendition of nishmat chaim earlier, as many of the texts in this particular notebook of Scholem's are copies of earlier texts. See tag II:284 as well as the section on matter and magic in this chapter. *Bereshit Rabbah* also always remains a possibility with regard to a second creation story, either independently or together with Franz Joseph Molitor's interpretation.

64. Benjamin apparently consulted Hirsch at this time. See the letter to Scholem from November 11, 1916 (briefe I:129), and later in freund:50. It is therefore also

far more likely that Benjamin consulted the Hirsch translation rather then the Lutherian as the editors of Benjamin's *Gesammelte Werke* suggest. See II:935.

65. "Eine fernere, höhere Entwickelung der von ihm geschaffenen Erdwelt einleiten will [. . .] er nahm Staub von dem Menschen-Boden, und hauchte in sein Antlitz Odem des Lebens, da ward der Mensch zu einem lebendigen Wesen." Hirsch, *Der Pentateuch*, p. 47.

66. Ibid. "bei der Schöpfung seines Leibes, war die Erde passiv."

67. It is indeed possible that Benjamin sought to distinguish himself from Hamann (and Christian mysticism in general) in terms of the incarnation of the body of God in language. Menninghaus presents this "Mit Hammans eigenen Wortern: 'Der Geist Gottes in seinem Worte offenbart sich wie das Selbständige—in Knechtgestalt, ist Fleisch'" but remains unable to articulate this crucial difference, which touches the very heart of German Jewry. See Menninghaus, *Walter Benjamins Theorie der Sprachmagie*, p. 209 and the attentive discussion in Menke, *Sprachfiguren*, pp. 60–66.

68. *Bereshit Rabbah* III:7 presents a very active God playing even perhaps a physical part in creation, not just as a speaker but someone busy creating and destroying worlds.

69. Benjamin also makes reference to the passage in Genesis 1:27 where the word *created* appears three times in conjunction with God's act.

70. ref 323. "In Gott ist der Name schöpferisch, weil er Wort ist, und Gottes Wort ist erkennend, weil es Name ist." II:148.

71. ref 323. "Das absolute Verhältnis des Namens zur Erkenntnis besteht allein in Gott, nur dort ist der Name, weil er im innersten mit dem schaffenden Wort identisch ist, das reine Medium der Erkenntnis. Das heißt: Gott machte die Dinge in ihren Namen erkennbar. Der Mensch aber benennt sie maßen der Erkenntis." II:148.

72. ref 323. "Gott ruhte, als er im Menschen sein Schöpferisches sich selbst überließ. Dieses Schöpferische, seiner göttlichen Aktualität entledigt, wurde Erkenntnis." II:149.

73. One sees this idea of the Sabbath, for example, in the *Star of Redemption*, where Rosenzweig situates it within the necessary stages of redemption. The dire necessity of a perfect Sabbath to redeem the world in a Lurianic sense can be linked to the original cessation of labor. A return to creation is, for Rosenzweig as well as Benjamin, a cornerstone of the messianic idea. See SdE§337, 339, 346.

74. One would have to disagree with Irving Wohlfarth when he writes, "Die adamitische Namensgebung ist die Übersetzung einer stummen in eine wörtliche Sprache. Sie nimmt am großen Kreislauf des göttlichen Logos teil." The emphasis in Benjamin appears to be on a transference of linguistic power, on Adam discovering the divine insignia for each thing God created, not the invention of an acoustic language that God must surely have known, if Adam was participating in His divine plan, nor the incarceration of a Hamannian Logos in the body of the word. See Wohlfarth, "Die Willkür der Zeichen," p. 134.

75. See chapter 1, section 2 on the idea of division of the holy and profane.

76. ref 323. "Die Unendlichkeit aller menschlichen Sprache bleibt immer eingeschränkten und analytischen Wesens im Vergleich mit der absoluten uneingeschränkten und schaffenden Unendlichkeit des Gotteswortes." II:149.

77. II:149. "tiefste Abbild dieses göttlichen Wortes." In the fragment, an *Abbild* is the form in which a mystical conception of history is perceivable.

78. ref 324. "Grenze der endlichen gegen die unendliche Sprache." II:149.

79. ref 324. "Von allen Wesen ist der Mensch das einzige, das seinesgleichen selbst benennt, wie es denn das einzige ist, das Gott nicht benannt hat." II:149.

80. Genesis 2:20.

81. *Bereshit Rabbah* XVII:4.

82. ref 324. "Mit der Gebung des Namen weihen die Eltern ihre Kinder Gott." II:149–150.

83. It is a common practice in Jewish tradition to name a newborn in honor of a close family member recently deceased. Scholem was the first to draw out Benjamin's interest in this tradition in his analysis of Benjamin's mystical text "Angesilaus Santander." See Scholem, *Walter Benjamin und sein Engel*, p. 41f.

84. In connection with the first chapter, where Benjamin presents messianism in light of the tragic hero, he here also comments that Greek tragedy had it that the name was linked to fate (II:150). This conception of the name was to have serious messianic implications for Scholem.

85. II:150. "Mystische Sprachtheorie."

86. ref 325. "Im Namen ist das Wort Gottes nicht schaffend geblieben, es ist an einem Teil empfangend, wenn auch sprachempfangend, geworden. Auf die Sprache der Dinge selbst, aus denen wiederum lautlos und in der stummen Magie der Natur das Wort Gottes hervorstrahlt, ist diese Empfängnis gerichtet." II:150.

87. Scholem explains mystical activity as both authority forming and authority destroying in his essay on authority and mysticism. See *Zur Kabbala und ihrer Symbolik*, pp. 21, 27–28, 48 (hereafter zur kab:21, 27–28, 48)/*On the Kabbalah and Its Symbolism*, pp. 12, 16–17, 31.

88. Despite a long history of linguistic mysticism, it remains for many a scathing critique. One can only suppose that a similar drive lead Rosenzweig to attack mysticism so forcefully in the *Star of Redemption*. (His goal, as he interpreted it, was *in philosophos!*). The question of his or indeed Benjamin's relationship to mysticism, however, cannot be settled by the mere disclaimers of either author.

89. On "mystical" disclaimers of magic, see, for example, the discussion of Abulafia in this chapter.

90. Müller, *Adams erstes Erwachen*, p. 49. "(Erscheinung Gottes). Gott kündigt Adam seinem Beruf an. Adam Giebt vor Gott den Thieren Namen." See II:936.

91. II:155. "Tiefe Traurigkeit."

92. ref 329. "Die Klage ist aber der undifferenzierteste, ohnmächtige Ausdruck der Sprache, sie enthält fast nur den sinnlichen Hauch; und wo auch nur Pflanzen rauschen, klingt immer eine Klage mit." II:155.

93. In formulating a conception of lamentation in relation to mourning, Benjamin may very well be anticipating a discussion with Scholem on the subject. We

know that Benjamin received a text of Scholem's entitled "Über Klage und Klagelied" (Scholem arc 40 1599/277, National and University Library, Jerusalem, now in tag II:128–133), which he discusses in a letter to Scholem from March 30, 1918, nearly a year and a half after completing this essay on language. In it he compares his "Die Bedeutung der Sprache in Trauerspiel und Tragödie" (II:137) of November 1916, written nearly contemporaneously with the essay on language, to Scholem's essay on Lamentations. Central to Benjamin's reading is the difference between the German and Hebrew languages: "Jetzt sehe ich nun in Ihrer Arbeit daß die Fragestellung die mich damals [the period of these two earlier text] bewegte auf Grund der hebräischen Klage gestellt werden muß." briefe I:182. Benjamin alludes to a distinction he sought to make in "Die Bedeutung der Sprache in Trauerspiel und Tragödie" between mourning and tragedy that is not reflected in Scholem's thesis but that, in both his own thought and in Scholem's, is "nicht genügend ausgearbeitet um diese Frage lösen zu können." He also questions Scholem's approach to the German language as the receiving vernacular of his translations (Lamentations and the Song of Songs): "Ob sich die Klagelieder jenseits einer solchen Beziehung auf das Deutsche auch noch in die Sprache übersetzen lassen vermag ich natürlich nicht zu entscheiden und Ihre Arbeit scheint es zu verneinen." briefe I:183. This difference in the notion of Hebrew as a translatable language must have indeed been a point of contention based on the interpretation of the meaning of the word of God. Although Scholem does articulate a unique status for the "original" language, the very fact that he is engaged in its transference to another language implies a certain degree of faith in the integrity of such an undertaking, rather then the "Unfähigkeit oder Unlust zur Mitteilung" Benjamin ascribes to Lamentations itself. II:155. See also freund:67 on the debate as well as tag II: 129–133, in which Scholem elaborates on the relationship between symbol and lamentation.

94. ref 329. "Es ist in aller Trauer der tiefste Hang zur Sprachlosigkeit, und das ist unendlich viel mehr als Unfähigkeit oder Unlust zur Mitteilung." II:155.

95. ref 330. "Überbenennung als tiefster sprachlicher Grund aller Traurigkeit und (vom Ding aus betrachtet) allen Verstummens. Die Überbenennung als sprachliches Wesen des Traurigen deutet auf ein anderes merkwürdiges Verhältnis der Sprache: auf die Überbestimmtheit, die im tragischen Verhältnis zwischen den Sprachen der sprechenden Menschen waltet." II:155–156.

96. ref 325. "Daß jede höhere Sprache (mit Ausname des Wortes Gottes) als Übersetzung aller anderen betrachtet werden kann." II:151.

97. It is interesting to compare once again Benjamin's own history of the reception of language to Hamann's rather expressionistic views on translation. "Reden ist Übersetzen—aus einer Engelsprache in eine Menschensprache, das heißt, Gedanken in Worte—Sachen in Namen—Bilder in Zeichen; die poetische oder kyriologische—historisch oder symbolisch oder hieroglyphisch— und philosophisch oder charakteristisch sein können" (letter to G. E. Linder, Königsberg, August 3, 1759, in Unger, *Hamanns Sprachtheorie*, p.146). In contrast to Hamann, Benjamin views the higher, divine language in constant transformation

of the lower form rather then the word of God being constantly transformed in worldly translations. While the former is Benjamin's own formulation based on an understanding of creation, the latter is endemic to Christianity. It seems apparent to this author that Benjamin did have in mind this central aspect of the idea of revelation in Christian theology (that he also encounters, to some degree, in Molitor), and distinguishes it from his own views accordingly.

98. ref 325. "Die Übersetzung ist die Überführung der einen Sprache in die andere durch ein Kontinuum von Verwandlungen. Kontinua der Verwandlung, nicht abstrakte Gleichheits- und Ähnlichkeitsbezirke durchmißt die Übersetzung." II:151.

99. ref 325. "Die Übersetzung der Sprache der Dinge in die des Menschen ist nicht nur Übersetzung des Stummen in das Lauthafte, sie ist die Übersetzung des Namenlosen in den Namen. Das ist also die Übersetzung einer unvollkommenen Sprache in eine vollkommenere, sie kann nicht anders als etwas dazu tun, nämlich die Erkenntnis." II:151.

100. In the transition of the "Stummen in das Lauthafte" one must keep in mind the structure of the Hebrew language in its written form, which, in very often being formed without vocalization signs, can arrive at a word whose pronunciation is unknown. This gives rise to an unpronounceable divine name such as YHVH or a list of divine names that best resemble strings of largely unintelligible consonants in cacophonous patterns. In the transformation of the silent into the audibly recognizable, the process by which the Hebrew language is spoken, discovered, and rediscovered could serve as a model for the idea of a constant translation. Joseph Dan interprets the unpronounceable name as representing a semiotic conception of language. See Dan, "The Name of God, the Name of the Rose."

101. ref 326. "Mitteilung der Materie in magischer Gemeinschaft," II:151.

102. ref 326. "In demselben Kapitel der Dichtung spricht aus dem Dichter [Müller] die Erkenntnis, daß nur das Wort, aus dem die Dinge geschaffen sind, ihre Benennung dem Menschen erlaubt, indem es sich in den mannigfachen Sprachen der Tiere, wenn auch stumm, mitteilt in dem Bild: Gott gibt den Tieren der Reihe nach ein Zeichen, auf das hin sie vor den Menschen zur Benennung treten. Auf eine fast sublime Weise ist so die Sprachgemeinschaft der stummen Schöpfung mit Gott im Bilde des Zeichens gegeben." II:152.

103. ref 326. "Die Sprache der Dinge kann in *die* Sprache der Erkenntnis und des Namens nur in der Übersetzung eingehen—soviel Übersetzungen, soviel Sprachen, sobald nämlich der Menschen einmal aus dem paradiesischen Zustand, der nur eine Sprache kannte, gefallen ist." II:152.

104. The proximity of historical events to the transformation of language, once a common notion of the middle ages, is brought to the fore here in Benjamin's analysis. Giorgio Agamben's study on the relationship between history and language is relevant here. He links the two realms through power, i.e., the power of language is historical: "La condizione storica dell'uomo è inseparabile dalla sua condizione di essere parlante ed è iscritta nella modalità stessa del suo accesso al linguaggio." See his "Lingua e storia," p. 70. Agamben's consideration of the only

universal language in our time, Esperanto, is indeed a coherent outgrowth of Benjamin's thought.

105. Benjamin describes this namelessness, interesting enough, as the only evil known in paradise. In the analysis of evil, it appears the discussion is drawn, in part, from Kierkegaard. We shall return to Kierkegaard and a discussion of *The Concept of Anxiety* in chapter 5 on the origins of evil and the concept of justice.

106. ref 327. "Unschöpferische Nachahmung des schaffenden Wortes." II:153.

107. ref 327. "Der Sündenfall ist die Geburtsstunde des *menschlichen Wortes*, in dem der Name nicht mehr unverletzt lebte, das aus der Namensprache, der erkennenden, man sagen darf: der immanenten eigenen Magie heraustrat, um ausdrücklich, von außen gleichsam, magisch zu werden." II:153.

108. ref 327. "Der Sündenfall des Sprachgeistes." II:153.

109. ref 329. "*Zeichen* müssen sich verwirren, wo sich die Dinge verwickeln." II:154.

110. ref 331. "Ohne diese bleibt überhaupt jede Sprachphilosophie gänzlich fragmentarisch, weil die Beziehung zwischen Sprache und Zeichen (wofür die zwischen Menschensprache und Schrift nur ein ganz besonderes Beispiel bildet) ursprünglich und fundamental ist." II:156.

111. See his letter to Scholem from March 30, 1918, in breife I:182.

112. ref 331. "Sprache ist in jedem Falle nicht allein Mitteilung des Mitteilbaren, sondern zugleich Symbol des Nicht-Mitteilbaren. Diese symbolische Seite der Sprache hängt mit ihrer Beziehung zum Zeichen zusammen, aber erstreckt sich zum Beispiel in gewisser Beziehung auch über Name und Urteil. Diese haben nicht allein eine mitteilende, sondern höchstwahrscheinlich auch eine mit ihr eng verbundene symbolische Funktion." II:156. Benjamin ultimately develops the notion of knowledge as the center point of divine transference into a call for a linguistic order of knowledge in his program on the coming philosophy, "Über das Programm der kommenden Philosophie" (II:157). The expulsion from paradise tarnished an original knowledge far broader then the "mathematical-mechanical" view that dominates epistemology. A correction would be rightly defined as a metaphysic of language, he writes. II:168. See the comments of Kather, "*Über Sprache überhaupt*," pp 73–77.

113. ref 372. "Die Sprache eines Wesens ist das Medium, in dem sich sein geistiges Wesen mitteilt. Der ununterbrochene Strom dieser Mitteilung fließt durch die ganze Natur vom niedersten Existierenden bis zum Menschen und vom Menschen zu Gott. Der Mensch teilt sich Gott durch den Namen mit, den er der Natur und seinesgleichen (im Eigennamen) gibt, und der Natur gibt er den Namen nach der Mitteilung, die er von ihr empfängt, denn auch die ganze Natur ist von einer namenlosen stummen Sprache durchzogen, dem Residuum des schaffenden Gotteswortes, welches im Menschen als erkennender Name und über dem Menschen als richtendes Urteil schwebend sich erhalten hat. Die Sprache der Natur ist einer geheimen Losung zu vergleichen, die jeder Posten dem nächsten in seiner eigenen Sprache weitergibt, der Inhalt der Losung aber ist die Sprache des Postens selbst. Alle höhere Sprache ist Übersetzung der niederen, bis in der letzten

Klarheit sich das Wort Gottes entfaltet, das die Einheit dieser Sprachbewegung ist." II:157.

114. ref 327. "Die Erkenntnis der Dinge beruht im Namen, die des Guten und Bösen ist aber in dem tiefen Sinne, in dem Kierkegaard dieses Wort faßt, "Geschwätz" und kennt nur eine Reinigung und Erhöhung, unter die denn auch der geschwätzige Mensch, der Sündige, gestellt wurde: das Gericht." II:153.

115. ref 328. "Im Sündenfall, da die ewige Reinheit des Namens angetastet wurde, erhob sich die strengere Reinheit des richtenden Wortes, des Urteils." II:153.

116. Gillian Rose detects a measure of uncertainty in the emergence of the notion of judgment from the pains of expulsion when she writes, "Judgment is ambiguous: both a new immediacy and the mediation of abstraction." By associating the mythical origins of law to this ambiguity, she appears to view it as a paradox. On the other hand, a messianic lodging of the pure word in the midst of the decline of language might be the linguistic equivalent of Rabbi Akiva laughing at the destruction of the Temple, knowing full well that the birth of the Messiah has come. See Rose, *Judaism and Modernity*, p. 185.

117. II:153. "Magie des Urteils."

118. ref 327. "Daß nun aus dem Sündenfall als die Restitution der in ihm verletzten Unmittelbarkeit des Namens eine neue, die Magie des Urteils, sich erhebt, die nicht mehr selig in sich selbst ruht." II:153.

119. ref 328. "Daß auch der Ursprung der Abstraktion als eines Vermögens des Sprachgeistes im Sündenfall zu suchen sei." II:154.

120. ref 328. "Der Baum der Erkenntnis stand nicht wegen der Aufschlüsse über Gut und Böse, die er zu geben vermocht hätte, im Garten Gottes, sondern als Wahrzeichen des Gerichts über den Fragenden. Diese ungeheure Ironie ist das Kennzeichen des mythischen Ursprungs des Rechtes." II:154.

121. See the discussion on "Violence and the Politics of Pure Means" in part 3.

122. We know from Benjamin's letters that he had been reading Kierkegaard's *The Concept of Axiety* and considering the problem of original sin two years before his comments on the mythical origins of law. See GB I: 51, 168.

123. Kierkegaard, *Gessammelte Werk: Der Begriff Angst*, p. 42 (henceforth ba:42). "Wenn es somit in der Genesis heißt, daß Gott zu Adam sprach: 'Allein von dem Baum der Erkenntnis des Guten und Bösen sollst du nicht essen', so versteht es sich ja von selbst, daß Adam dies Wort eigentlich nicht verstanden hat; denn wie sollte er wohl den Unterschied von Gut und Böse verstehen, da diese Unterscheidung doch erst mit dem Genuß sich einselllte." Scholem comments on the point in his journals: "Das Wissen, das nicht prinzipiell durch die Lehre in mir hervorgerufen werden kann, ist Geschwätz. In diesem Sinne ist es auch zu verstehen, wenn Benjamin das Wissen Adams um Gut und Böse Geschwätz nennt." tag II:385.

124. "Die abstrakten Sprachelemente aber [. . .] wurzeln im richtenden Worte, im Urteil. Die Unmittelbarkeit (das ist aber die sprachliche Wurzel) der Mitteilbarkeit der Abstraktion ist im richterlichen Urteil gelegen. Diese Unmittelbarkeit in der Mitteilung der Abstraktion stellte sich richtend ein, als im Sündenfall der Mensch die Unmittelbarkeit in der Mitteilung des Konkreten, den Namen,

verließ und in den Abgrund der Mittelbarkeit aller Mitteilung, des Wortes als Mittel, des eitlen Wortes verfiel, in den Abgrund des Geschwätzes." II:154.

125. Scholem mentioned this in his autobiography as well as in an article on Molitor for *Encyclopaedia Judaica*. David Biale comments, "It is possible . . . that Scholem's early positive attitude toward the Kabbalah was more a result of his reading of Molitor than of any Jewish historian." See his *Gershom Scholem*, p. 32.

126. tag I:405. "Eine wahrhafte Ideologie des Zionismus." Zionism here is only understandable in the context of Scholem's early religious notions of Zionism, capable of viewing Molitor's historical and religious writings as a contribution to a cultural-political, ultimately religious Zionism that is described in chapter 2. It would not be understandable in terms of his later conception of Zionism.

127. Despite its "grundlos [. . .] christologische Wendung," remarks Scholem on the meaning of Molitor for his and Benjamin's early discussions, "ist das Buch noch immer beachtenswert." freund:53.

128. B I:471. "So kam ich mit der Absicht, nicht die Historie, sondern die Metaphysik der Kabbala zu schreiben." We know, however, that it was not Molitor alone who introduced the interest in metaphysics, even if this interest is also reflected in Molitor's *Philosophy of History*. It is indeed Benjamin.

129. tag I:422. "Die Buchstaben, *welche der Ausdruck geistiger Kräfte sind* (könnte wörtlich Hirsch im Pentateuchkommentar geschrieben haben!), *haben ihre Wurzeln oben* (Molitor I), d.h. in der Wahrheit."

130. Including a newly discovered text from Benjamin on the subject entitled "Notizen zu einer Arbeit über die Kategorie der Gerechtigkeit" (entry of 8/9 Oct. 1916). tag I:401. In chapter 5 we will explore the importance of this text for Scholem.

131. tag I:420. "Ihre Aufgabe [der Sprachphilosophie] ist die Untersuchung der Sprache als Offenbarung der Wahrheit, sie hat den Wahrheitsgehalt der Sprache zu bestimmen." Scholem goes on to claim that, upon this statement, Wilhelm von Humboldt should be considered a linguistic philosopher. Humboldt connection to Scholem's own religious speculations on language, however, is far from apparent here. Benjamin's views on Humboldt, who indeed overlooked the "magische Seite der Sprache," were quite negative. See Benjamin, "Reflektionen zu Humboldt," *Gesammelte Schriften*, VI:26–27, VI:648–652, suspected to having been written around 1925–1928.

132. tag I:421. "In der Thora als einem göttlichen Buche erscheint dies Problem am ehesten und unproblematischsten: als Sprache Gottes muß sie notwendig Sprache der Wahrheit sein, *jeder* Wahrheit, und die in jedem Satze ausgedrückte allgemeine und besondere Wahrheit muß notwendigerweise eine Funktion der angewandten Worte sein. [. . .] Man kann durchaus mit Recht sagen, *daß* hier *die Wahrheit eine stetige Funktion der Sprache sei*" (November 18, 1916).

133. Scholem was to note, for example, in his copy of Menninghaus, *Walter Benjamins Theorie der Sprachmagie*, p. 191, that, in his opinion, it was Molitor and not Franz von Baader who was to have a critical influence on Benjamin. On Scholem's discussions of Baader's *Vorlesung über eine künftige Theorie des Opfers* with Benjamin, see chapter 5.

134. In 1981 Scholem wrote a short and highly critical review of Fuld, *Walter Benjamin*, focusing on Fuld's argument that Benjamin's "Theses on the Philosophy of History" (1940) was based on Franz von Baader's "Elementarbegriffe über die Zeit" (1831). Scholem thoroughly rejects Fuld's thesis. However, a secondary comment by Scholem on Molitor confirms again the content of letters from Benjamin to Scholem from 1917 (briefe I:134–139/GB I: 357, 361, GB II:19) on the occasion of receiving Molitor's work. It would not be overly speculative to suggest that Benjamin was already somewhat familiar with Molitor before ordering the four volumes, care of Scholem. A copy of the book was available in the library in Berlin during the period that he wrote his essay. See Scholem, "Benjamin and Baader" in *Walter Benjamin und sein Engel*, pp. 201–203.

135. Albeit in catholic guise, which I shall address in this chapter.

136. "Die jüdische Tradition [. . .] behauptet, das Ebräische sey die erste Ursprache gewesen, die Adam im Paradiese gesprochen. Obgleich nun solches nicht nach dem buchstäblichen Sinne genommen werden darf, indem die Ursprache, welche der Mensch in seiner Geistigkeit vor dem Falle geredet, von ganz anderer Art als alle jetzt bestehende Sprachen gewesen, so muß doch, wenn die Bibel das Buch der göttlichen Offenbarung seyn soll, die ebräische Sprache ein zwar geschwächter verkörperter, aber doch treuer Abdruck jener ersten, reinen Ursprache seyn." Molitor, *Philosophie der Geschichte*, pp. 329–330, henceforth 1827:329–330, or, if the citation refers to the second edition, 1857:520.

137. Certainly another possibility not formulated by Molitor is that both a divine, creating language and a semidivine naming language existed, out of which profane language derived; Adam's naming language being a lesser but still divinely imbued form. Hence a genesic and an adamic language. Hebrew, which would then have been a language transferred to the Torah, would belong to a third category. The possible speculations in this regard are seemingly endless. Important here are only the general parameters of the discussion that are capable of determining the species of linguistic considerations, i.e., if a given analysis can be considered a part of genesic speculations.

138. 1827:330. "Denn gleichwie der Mensch auch noch in seinem gefallenen Zustand den Abglanz [*Abdruck*] seiner ehemaligen geistigen Hoheit an sich trägt, so muß auch seine Sprache wenigstens die Spuren jenes magischen Schöpfungsgeistes der frühern Ursprache noch behalten haben; die in seinen Nachkommen sich immer mehr degenerirte, je tiefer das Menschengeschlecht nach und nach sank." In parentheses, I have included the word *Abdruck* which he substitutes for *Abglanz* in his "zweite, neu bearbeitete und vermehrte Auflage" of 1857. It is interesting to note how the term *Abglanz* finds expression in Benjamin's aesthetic speculation, beginning with the prohibition of the image and its *Abdruck*.

139. Like Molitor, Hamann uses a *midrashic* interpretation to explain Christian principles and does not distinguish himself here from the body of Christian Kabbalists beginning with Johannes Reuchlin. What is particularly remarkable in Molitor, however, is the length to which he goes to remain philologically (and otherwise) faithful to *midrashic* tradition in the first volume of the *Philosophy of His-*

tory from 1827. This integrity is all the more apparent in contrast to the second edition of 1857, in which, under the influence, in part, of Franz von Baader, he was to alter many of the passages of this chapter to emphasize Christian aims in the study of Kabbalah, particularly where he chooses to employ a trinitarian structure that ends up merely hovering over the citations below.

140. 1827:330. "Es bleibt also hier kein Mittelweg übrig: entweder ist die Schöpungsurkunde eine bloße jüdische National-Mythe, in welcher alle Namen ebräisirt sind, wie die Neologen behaupten; oder wenn die Bücher Moscheh aus göttlicher Offenbarung geflossen, so muß zugleich auch die Sprache, in der sie verfaßt ist, und die von dem Inhalte der Erzählung völlig untrennbar ist, von höherer Abkunft, und der Abglanz der wahren Ursprache seyn."

141. Molitor was in fact ahead of more contemporary critics of Benjamin's genesic speculations. If the notion of Hebrew as a divine language could not be reduced to "eine bloß jüdische Nation-Mythe" in 1827, one has to wonder why we are left with only two choices in interpreting Benjamin's early conception of language today, either private and mystical, perhaps part national myth, or rationalist, universalist, and ultimately Christian, meaning naturally also messianic, partial, and mystical.

142. 1857:526. "Wirkliche Bedeutung [. . .] indem hier das Wort und der Begriff der Sache untrennbar sind, woraus also unleugbar folgt, daß die Genesis ursprünglich nur in der ebräischen Sprache gedacht und zunächst für ebräisch redende Personen ausgesprochen sein kann." This is taken from the 1857 edition to illustrate a point that is expressed generally in the first edition. Although the second edition contains most everything in that of the first, the latter places undue emphasis on the independence of God and Christianity (particularly its victory through reason), suggesting the possibility that the later inserts were meant as a response to a contrary position or critique. Scholem suggests the influence of Baader in the second edition in his article on Molitor in the *Encyclopaedia Judaica*.

143. 1827:331. "Der irdische Abglanz der wahren Ursprache." "Irdische Abglanz" should be noted as being the preferred wording of Benjamin on several occasions.

144. 1827:332. "Reine heilige Ursprache."

145. 1827:336. "Die ganze Untersuchung über den Ursprung und die Beschaffenheit der Urschrift hängt eigentlich von der ersten Vorfrage ab: ist die Schrift blos das Werk einer künstlichen, durch das äußere Bedürfnis geweckten Reflexion, oder liegt ihr etwas Inneres, Nothwendiges, Absolutes im Menschen zum Grunde?"

146. 1827:337. "Wenn wir mit glaubigem Gemüthe dem Sinne der Bibel folgen"; "willkührlichen Zeichen."

147. "Bloßen Zeichen"; "Wahrzeichen." The quotations and references summarizing Benjamin can be found in II:141, 147, 153, 154.

148. 1827:338. "Der Mensch und sein ganzes Leben und Thun [erhält] eine viel edlere und erhabenere Bedeutung"

149. 1827:338. "Innere geistige Selbständigkeit und Freiheit"; "passiver Reflex der empfangenen äußern Eindrücke"; "wie uns die heilige Schrift lehrt, das ebenbildliche

Geschöpf einer unendlichen, über allen Naturzwang erhabenen, absolut freien Intelligenz [. . .] ein lebendiger Spiegel der Gottheit."

150. The 1857 edition contains an explicated discussion of an "Ebenbild—Spiegelbild" (pp. 548–549) dynamic but with particular emphasis on the autonomy of humanity and God in relationship to the question of good.

151. 1827:338/1857:549. "*Als Ebenbild der Gottheit ist* das intellektuelle Erkennen *des Menschen* ein endliches creatürliches Nachbilden der unendlichen Ideen Gottes." The italicized sections are from the second edition.

152. 1827:338. "In sofern ist der Mensch mit seiner idealen Gedankenwelt ein creatürliches Abbild der Gottheit, welche von Ewigkeit die Idee der Schöpfung in sich trägt. [. . .] Das Wort ist der Übergang von der innern Ideal—zur äußern Realwelt, das Sprechen ein Hinausbilden und außer sich Stellen des innern Gedankens; da nämlich die reine Geistigkeit des Denkens sich beschränkt, und in dem Wort ein äußeres Abbild von sich erzeugt."

153. A reasonable objection to Benjamin's thesis might concern the notion of time in the divine world, offering God an opportunity to think apart from action. Seen however from the perspective of his remarks on time and his profound awareness of the eternity of the divine, the separation of thought and existence would have no meaning, for Him, in the divine world. We can recognize this in the citation in the text below, which speculates on the existence of a thought that is unknown to God. II:141.

154. 1827:338. "Ist das Sprechen gewissermassen das Bild des unendlichen Schaffens, oder das Hervorbringen der ewigen urbildlichen Idee als ein Daseyn außer Gott."

155. ref 315. "Ein Dasein, welches ganz ohne Beziehung zur Sprache wäre, ist eine Idee; aber diese Idee läßt sich auch im Bezirk der Ideen, deren Umkreis diejenige Gottes bezeichnet, nicht fruchtbar machen." II:141.

156. The father represents thinking, the son speaking, and the holy spirit realizing, "wirken" or "wesenhaft machen." 1827:339.

157. 1827:339. "Untrennbar vom Denken und stets bei dem Denken. Denn das Denken selber ist nichts anders, als ein inneres geistiges potentiales Reden, und die Gedanken sind gleichsam geistige potentiale Worte."

158. 1827:340. "Alle Gestalten der irdischen Dinge sind also Abbildungen und Ausdrücke geistiger Kräfte und intellektueller Ideen, und alle Formen liegen selbst auf höhere Weise in den geistigen und intellektuellen Principien; jedes Wesen trägt daher in seiner Gestalt die Signatur an sich, die seine inneren Eigenschaften unmittelbar ausdrückt."

159. Compare Scholem jIII:36 and the section on microlinguistic speculation in this chapter. Scholem, in contrast to Benjamin, develops the notion of the written form as opposed to its audible pronunciation.

160. 1827:340. "Alle Formen in der äußern Natur sind lauter göttliche Schriftzüge, die ganze sichtbare Natur ist die eingegrabene Schrift Gottes oder das äußere schriftliche offenbarte Wort, das mündliche hingegen ist blos innerlich im Geiste vernehmbar."

161. 1827:341. "So wie das Wort der Ursprache ein reiner Abdruck des Gedankens ist, und das Wort ursprünglich selber eine magische Kraft hat, so war auch die Urschrift des Menschen, wie jegliches Wort und jegliche That der figurirte Ausdruck des magischen Wortes, und darum selber magisch in ihren Wirkungen. Die Urschrift bestand daher eben so wenig aus willkührlichen Zeichen, als die Ursprache aus willkührlichen Tönen."

162. 1827:341. "eine Nachahmung Gottes, [. . .] des göttlichen Redens und Schreibens" by which "die Gottheit ist der einzige, unendliche, allmächtige Redner, in dem ewig fortdauernden Akte der Schöpfungs-Sprache, womit sie immer aufs neue die Schöpfung hervorbringt." The messianic implications of the return of language to creation did not go unnoticed by Molitor. Indeed, a distinct conflict between the messianic and an "enlightenment" notion of history is detectable in Christoph Schulte's article on Scholem and Molitor. Rather than a conversion of the Jews or a secularization of redemption in enlightenment fashion, Molitor believed that the "Geschichte, auch Weltgeschichte, ist und bleibt im Kern die Heilsgeschichte des auserwählten Volkes," explains Schulte. Although one can rest assured that the reversal of both Catholic and Enlightenment dogma here would have appealed to Scholem and Benjamin, it remains to be seen if the notion of a *Heilsgeschichte* can truly express a Judaic-messianic conception of history. See Schulte, "'Die Buchstaben haben . . . '" p. 162.

163. 1827:342. "Daß die Buchstaben Abdrücke göttlicher Kräfte sind, daß Gott durch die Magie der Buchstaben Himmel und Erde erschaffen, und derjenige, welcher die Versetzung der Buchstaben verstehe, Wunder zu wirken im Stande wäre."

164. 1827:342. "Abbildliche Reste jener alten heiligen Ursprache und Schrift."

165. 1827:343. "So wie nun der eigenthümliche Bau der ebräischen Sprache auf eine innere Verwandtschaft mit der Ursprache hindeutet, so beurkundet auch die Gestalt der ebräischen Quadratschrift eine höhere Abkunft. Die ursprünglich wahren Schriftgestalten können nämlich keine willkührliche Zeichen, sie mußten die plastischen Ausdrücke der Töne und Sprachaktionen selber gewesen sein." These architectonic observations on the form and shape of Hebrew letters, which were to play such a major role in mystical speculation in Jewish linguistics, particularly in relation to the printed word, appears not to have made much of an impression on Benjamin at this stage. What is even more surprising is the fact that it also forms a very small part of Scholem's late analysis of language. For a discussion of a semiotic conception of divine language that reflects the visual but not syntactic, as opposed to a semantic conception, see Dan, "The Name of God, the Name of the Rose," pp. 229, 231–234, 247f.

166. 1827:346. "Die Spuren ihres Ursprungs."

4. GERSHOM SCHOLEM AND THE NAME OF GOD

1. This essay appeared in a poor translation in 1972 as "The Name of God and the Linguistic Theory of the Kabbala." I have consulted this version for my own

translations here, yet do not cite it each time, as my own translations often depart radically from this version.

2. That Benjamin was never truly able to understand the Hebrew language is surely a great loss to this and future generations of Hebrew speakers.

3. This is also the opinion of Biale, *Gershom Scholem*, pp. 80–81.

4. "Instinktiv"; "tiefste Intution." See Scholem's description in his 1964 essay on Benjamin in *Walter Benjamin und sein Engel*, pp. 29, 34, respectively.

5. In this respect, the purpose of this chapter is a philosophical study of the concepts behind Benjamin's essay and the influence they were to exercise upon Scholem into his mature years. Needless to say, it cannot, at the same time, be a linguistic history of the Kabbalah, which took Scholem himself over fifty years to construct. Should this essay serve as an explication of the early (and perhaps for some researchers even cryptic) influences, it would meet the intention of the author.

6. Scholem actually maintains here that a long letter sent to Benjamin around November 10, 1916, which contained some of his reflections on mathematics and language, was incorporated by Benjamin into later versions of this essay. If correct, it suggests further intellectual cooperation in Benjamin's early essay. See freund:47–48.

7. tag II:500. "Ich überlege ernstlich die Möglichkeit einer Dissertation über ein Gebiet der jüdischen Sprachtheorie. Wenn ich einige Zeit mich in das Studium des Sohar versenken könnte—wenn es zu diesem Buch nur so etwas wie einen Index gäbe, irgendwo!—wäre das vielleicht eine ziemlich einfache Aufgabe, mit schöner Disposition."

8. von berlin: 134. "Sprachtheorie der Kabbala"; "war jugendlicher Überschwang, wenn nicht gar Hochmut. Als ich an die Sache ernstlich heranging, mußte ich bald erkennen, daß ich viel zu wenig wußte, um dieses Thema wissenschaftlich verantwortungsvoll abzuhandeln, und besser systematischer und vor allem bescheidener anfangen sollte. In der Tat habe ich die Arbeit über die Sprachtheorie der Kabbala, vor der ich 1920 resignierte, genau fünfzig Jahre später geschrieben."

9. Scholem gives the following translation: "Der Anfang [oder auch: das Wesen] seines Wortes ist Wahrheit." Psalms 119:160. The English translation above is slightly augmented to match Scholem's.

10. jIII:7."Wahrheit war in dem zuerst vom Judentum konstituierten Sinn das Wort Gottes, das akustisch = sprachlich vernehmbar war."

11. In Scholem's dissertation on *Sefer Bahir* he explores its linguistic mysticism in some detail. On acoustic expression, see §32 on the importance of the sounds of His words (Exodus 20:18, Deuteronomy 4:12), in which his voice was expressed in a single word. Scholem cites a long history concerning this tradition, beginning with *Midrash Tanchuma*. See Scholem, *Das Buch Bahir*, p. 35.

12. Deuteronomy 4:12: "And the Lord YHVH spoke to you out of the midst of fire: you heard the voice of the words, but saw no form; only a voice."

13. See Exodus 20:3–5.

14. jIII:7–8. "Daß die Sprache, das Medium, in dem sich das geistige Leben des Menschen vollzieht, eine Innenseite hat, einen Aspekt, der in den Beziehungen der

Kommunikation zwischen den Wesen nicht restlos aufgeht. Der Mensch teilt sich mit, sucht sich dem andern verständlich zu machen, aber in all diesen Versuchen schwingt etwas, was nicht nur Zeichen, Kommunikation, Bedeutung und Ausdruck ist. Der Laut, auf den alle Sprache gebaut ist, die Stimme, die sie gestaltet, aus ihrem Lautmaterial aushämmert, ist für diese Ansicht schon *prima facie* mehr, als je in die Verständigung eingeht."

15. In §54 of *Das Buch Bahir* on creation, Scholem translates the content of divine creation based on the expression of the "Inhalt" of God's name. See p. 55.

16. jIII:8. "Der symbolische Charakter der Sprache, der diese Dimension bestimmt."

17. "Eine Metapher aber ist das Wort 'Sprache' in solchem Gebrauche durchaus nicht. Denn es ist eine volle inhaltliche Erkenntnis, daß wir uns nicht vorstellen können, daß sein geistiges Wesen nicht im Ausdruck mitteilt." II:141.

18. jIII:8. "Daß aber sich hier in der Sprache etwas mitteilt, was weit über die Sphäre hinausreicht, die Ausdruck und Gestaltung gestattet; daß ein Ausdrucksloses, das sich nur in Symbolen zeigt, in allem Ausdruck mitschwingt, ihm zugrunde liegt und [. . .] durch die Ritzen der Ausdruckswelt hindurchscheint. [. . .] (So war W. Benjamin lange ein reiner Sprachmystiker)." Compare Scholem's initial remarks to the discussion of language and symbol in Benjamin's early essay: "Sprache ist in jedem Falle nicht allein Mitteilung des Mitteilbaren, sondern zugleich Symbol des Nicht-Mitteilbaren. Diese symbolische Seite der Sprache hängt mit ihrer Beziehung zum Zeichen zusammen, aber erstreckt sich zum Beispiel in gewisser Beziehung auch über Name und Urteil. Diese haben nicht allein eine mitteilende, sondern höchstwahrscheinlich auch eine mit ihr eng verbundene symbolische Funktion." II:156.

19. A determination whether Benjamin's ideas are truly mystical requires a valid notion of what mysticism is. Should one seek the curtaining off of rationalism from esoteric speculation, then it would only be possible to view his linguistic study in the context of the latter. But in terms of the characteristic and pursuits of mystics that one finds in the Kabbalah, Benjamin's mysticism appears rather inconclusive.

20. jIII:9. "Was nicht auf Mitteilung eines Mitteilbaren ausgerichtet ist, sondern vielmehr [. . .] auf Mitteilung eines Nicht-Mitteilbaren, das ausdruckslos in ihr [die Symbolik] lebt und selbst wenn es Ausdruck hätte, so jedenfalls keine Bedeutung, keinen mitteilbaren *Sinn*."

21. jIII:9. "Um [. . .] die Sprache als Offenbarung zu finden."

22. jIII:9. "In die gesprochene Sprache hinein sich die Sprache der Götter oder Gottes verflicht und sich aus solcher Verflechtung heraus aufdecken ließe."

23. jIII:9. On the influence of Hamann on Benjamin (in relation to Scholem), see chapter 3.

24. jIII:10–11. "(1) Die Auffassung, daß Schöpfung und Offenbarung beide vornehmlich und wesentlich Selbstdarstellungen Gottes sind, in die daher, der unendlichen Natur der Gottheit entsprechend, Momente des Göttlichen eingegangen sind, die im Endlichen und Bestimmten alles Erschaffenen sich nur in

Symbolen mitteilen können. Damit hängt unmittelbar die weitere Auffassung zusammen, daß das Wesen der Welt Sprache sei. (2) Die zentrale Stellung des Namens Gottes als des metaphysischen Ursprungs aller Sprache und die Auffassung der Sprache als Auseinanderlegung und Entfaltung dieses Namens, wie sie vornehmlich in den Dokumenten der Offenbarung, aber auch in aller Sprache überhaupt vorliegt. Die Sprache Gottes, die sich in den Namen Gottes kristallisiert und letzten Endes in dem *einen* Namen, der ihr Zentrum ist, liegt aller gesprochenen Sprache zugrunde, in der sie sich reflektiert und symbolisch erscheint. (3) Die dialektische Beziehung von Magie und Mystik in der Theorie der Namen Gottes nicht weniger als in der überschwänglichen Macht, die dem reinen menschlichen Wort zuerkannt wird."

25. The unfolding of the name takes place in revelation, existing at the same time in language itself.

26. In his *Trauerspiel* (1925) work, Benjamin distinguishes allegory and symbolism. I:336–409. Scholem, however, does not appear to take on Benjamin's later categorical distinctions after the debate on the meaning of metaphor. Later in life, he seems to use the term *symbolism* more generally in his research into the Kabbalah and apparently independent of Benjamin's late formulations.

27. jIII:31. "Grundlage jeder Sprache."

28. jIII:11. The reference is to Exodus 3:3–5.

29. jIII:13. "Daß zwischen ihm und seinem Träger eine enge und wesensmäßige Beziehung besteht."

30. Scholem was able to explore the nonsyntactic meaning of the divine name in *Das Buch Bahir*, §76, where God's countenance (or face) is interpreted as His name. §§79–81 moves into a discussion of the *shem ha-meforash*. See *Das Buch Bahir*, pp. 77–82.

31. jIII:14. "Das Sinnliche des Wortes vollauskostenden Sprechenden darstellt."

32. jIII:14. "Praktikablen Magie"; "ungeheuren Gewalt"; "Inbegriff des Heiligen [. . .] des durchaus Unantastbaren,"; "eine innerweltliche, in der Schöpfung wirkende Konfiguration der Macht, ja der Allmacht Gottes."

33. His analysis of violence, which although drawn from the "ungeheuren Gewalt" of the divine realm, is to remain slightly candid in regard to linguistic power, as compared to Scholem.

34. jIII:14. "Himmel und Erde sind vergänglich, aber 'Dein großer Name lebt und besteht in Ewigkeit.'" See also Blau, *Das altjüdische Zauberwesen*, pp. 119–120.

35. jIII:15. "Der Name, in dem Gott sich selber benennt und unter dem er anrufbar ist, sich aus der akustischen Späre zurückzieht und *unaussprechbar* wird."

36. jIII:15–16. "Gerade diese Unaussprechbarkeit, in der der Name Gottes zwar *angesprochen*, aber nicht mehr *ausgesprochen* werden kann, hat ihn für das Gefühl der Juden mit jener unerschöpflichen Tiefe ausgestattet, von der noch ein so radikaler Repräsentant des theistischen Rationalismus wie Hermann Cohen [. . .] zeugt."

37. jIII:16. The reference is to Cohen, *Jüdische Schriften*, 1:63.

38. "Bekanntgegeben"; "ausdrücklich erklärt"; "ausgesprochen"; "absondert" and "vorborgen." On the *shem ha-meforash* and its relationship to the Tetragrammaton. See A. Marmorstein, *The Old Rabbinic Doctrine of God*, 1:20–23; also *Sefer Bahir*, §81.

39. jIII:17. On the idea of language in the rabbinic period, particularly with regard to *Maaseh Merkabah*, see the study by Janowitz, *The Poetics of Ascent*, especially introduction and appendix.

40. We have, for example, in Scholem's edition of *Sefer Bahir*, §63, speculation on the various letters of the name of God. Scholem, pp. 64–69, 77–83.

41. jIII:18–19. The idea that the name sealed and sanctified creation is also to be found in pre-Christian apocalyptic texts and in the Greater Hechalot.

42. The former would be better associated with intention rather than Benjamin's notion of the creating word. II:150.

43. jIII:19. "Wenn [. . .] vom Namen Gottes als dem *agens* der Schöpfung die Rede ist, so liegt dem offenkundig noch die magische Auffassung von der Macht des Namens zu Grunde, die sich wieder durchgesetzt hat. Der Name ist eine Konzentration göttlicher Kraft, und je nach der verschiedenen Zusammensetzung dieser hier konzentrierten Kräfte können solche Namen verschiedene Funktionen erfüllen. Das schöpferische *Wort* Gottes, das Himmel und Erde hervorruft, von dem der Schöpfungsbericht der Genesis, aber auch der Hymnus der Psalmisten zeugt—"durch Jahwes Wort sind die Himmel entstanden" (PS 33:6)—, ist für die biblischen Autoren noch keineswegs der Name Gottes selber."

44. jIII:19. "das etwas mitteilt, zu einem Namen, der nichts mitteilt als sich selber."

45. II:142. "Jede Sprache teilt sich selbst mit."

46. *Pirkei Rabbi Elieser*, chapter 3.

47. jIII:20. "Gott ebensosehr selbst darstellt, manifestiert, als auch sich seiner Schöpfung mitteilt, die im Medium dieser Sprache selber ins Dasein tritt."

48. jIII:20. "Die Buchstaben der göttlichen Sprache sind es, durch deren Kombination alles geschaffen ist. Diese Buchstaben sind aber die der hebräischen Sprache als der Ursprache und Sprache der Offenbarung."

49. The Talmud reports certain sages who had even mastered the powers of language, Bezalel being one who is to have known the combinations of the letters that enacted creation. jIII:20.

50. jIII:20–21. "Die schöperische Kraft, die den Worten und Namen innewohnt, das unmittelbar Wirkende an ihnen, mit anderen Worten: ihre Magie, ist damit auf die Grundelemente zurückgeführt, in denen sich für den Mystiker Laut und Schriftbild decken."

51. Moshe Idel suggests, alternatively, that the contradiction posed by a physical interpretation of creation is to rule out a materialist understanding by the mystics. See his essay, "Reification of Language in Jewish Mysticism," p. 45f.

52. jIII:21. "Daß im Bezirk dieses Denkens der göttliche Anhauch, der den Menschen nach der Erzählung der Genesis zum lebenden Wesen macht, in ihm das Sprachvermögen öffnet, wird durch eine Äußerung von nicht geringem Gewicht

bezeugt. Die, sozusagen offizielle aramäische Übersetzung der Tora, die im syna-
gogalen Gottesdienst gebraucht wurde, der *Targum Onkelos,* gibt Gen. 2:7 'Der
Mensch wurde zu einer lebendigen Seele' mit 'Der Mensch wurde zu einem
sprechenden Geist' wieder. Das, was das lebendige Wesen des Menschen ausmacht,
ist eben die Sprache. Damit aber verband sich für spekulativ gerichtete Geister bald
die Frage, ob nicht in dem Anhauch Gottes selber dies sprachliche Element schon
enthalten sein mußte."

53. tag II:384. "So übersetzt auch der Targum Onkelos und Jer. I das *nefesh chai*
von 1. Mo. 2, 7 mit *ruach memalela,* sprechender Geist."

54. jIII:22. Air or the pneuma of the senses is here identified with the second
sefirah, the first being God's pneuma or *ruach elohim.* See also Scholem, *Die Jüdische Mystik.* For a German translation of *Sefer Yetzirah,* which would have also
been available to Benjamin had he sought in it a second version of creation, see
Lazarus Goldschmidt, *Sepher Jesirah. Das Buch der Schöpfung,* (Darmstadt: Wissenschaftliche Buchgesellschaft, 1969).

55. jIII:24. "Das Alphabet ist der Ursprung der Sprache und der Ursprung des
Seins zugleich. 'So findet sich denn, daß alle Schöpfung und alle Rede durch einen
Namen entsteht.'"

56. jIII:25–26. "Alles Wirkliche jenseits des Pneumas Gottes enthält also
Sprachelemente, und es ist offensichtlich die Meinung des Autors, daß alles Er-
schaffene ein sprachliches Wesen hat, das in irgendeiner Kombination jener
Grundbuchstaben besteht. Darüber hinaus ordnet er den einzelnen Buchstaben
nicht nur feste Funktionen zu, sondern auch die Objekte, wie Planeten und Zodi-
akalzeichen am Himmel, die Wochentage und Monate im Jahr und die Hauptor-
gane im menschlichen Körper."

57. jIII:26. "Sind auch in ihrem sprachlichen Wesen deutlich aufeinander
bezogen."

58. jIII:26. "Sprachgeist"; "der heiligen Sprache zum für uns faßbaren Ausdruck gestaltet hat."

59. jIII:27. Although the *Bahir* is not dealt with at any length in Scholem's
essay, a large portion is concerned with letter mysticism (for example, paragraphs
11a, 20, 21, 54, 58, 63, 76, 83, 95). This might partly explain Scholem's choice for his
first study of the Kabbalah, but it does not explain its absence in the late essay.

60. jIII:28. "Die ganze Torah aus Namen Gottes besteht, und zwar in der Art,
daß die Wörter, die wir darin lesen, auch auf ganz andere Weise abgeteilt werden
können, und zwar in (esoterische) Namen." The insert here of the word *esoteric* is
Scholem's.

61. jIII:28. "Als Geschichte und Gebote."

62. jIII:29. "Substanz des verehrungswürdigen Namens." This translation is
Scholem's.

63. jIII:29fn. "Ein einziger heiliger mystischer Name." *Zohar* (chapters 3.36a)
in Scholem.

64. jIII:30. "Kraft und Machtfülle Gottes." Although not to be mistaken for
pure esoteric mysticism, this dimension of linguistic theory is equally not "einem

rationalen Verständnis der möglichen kommunikativen und gesellschaftlichen Funktionen eines Names." jIII:30. Thus such theory is neither confined to strictly mystical texts nor a concept of name that could be reduced to a "bourgeois" functionality, as Benjamin was to term it.

65. Scholem stresses the fact that the Zohar contains surprising little on language, considering the importance of linguistic speculation in Judaism. It does however refer to a precursor to emanation as a linguistic event, "denn der innerste Gedanke wird zu einer noch ganz verborgenen, lautlosen Stimme, und diese, aus der alle Sprache geboren wird, wird zum noch unartikulierten Ton." jIII:56.

66. jIII:50. "Die Tora ist also ein lebendiges Gewand und Gewebe, ein *textus* im genauesten Verstand, in den als eine Art Grund- und Leitmotiv das Tetragramm auf verborgene Weise, manchmal auch direkt eingewebt ist und jedenfalls in allen möglichen Metamorphoses und Variationen wiederkehrt."

67. jIII:51. "Das Wort Gottes, das in alle Welten gelang, ist zwar unendlich bedeutungsschwanger, hat aber keine feste Bedeutung. Selber bedeutungslos, ist es das Deutbare schlechthin."

68. See zur kab:63. In *Tikkenei Zohar* (ca. 1300), a mystical reading is contained within the core of the Torah. The word of God, therefore, yields mystical speculation. See jIII:52 and zur kab:91–92, 271.

69. jIII:48, my emphasis. "In der menschlichen Sprache haben wir einen *Abglanz*, eine Reflektion der göttlichen Sprache, die in der Offenbarung miteinander koinzidieren. Friedrich Schlegel, der große Kopf der Frühromantik, pflegte zu sagen, die Philosophen sollten Grammatiker sein. Von den Mystikern läßt sich das nicht sagen, denn die Sprache Gottes, das 'innere Wort', mit dem diese zu tun haben, hat keine Gramatik. Sie besteht aus Namen, die hier mehr sind als Ideen. In der Sprache des Menschen den Namen wiederzufinden, das ist im Grunde das Anliegen, das hinter der kabbalistischen Auffassung von der Natur des Gebets steht."

70. "Wahre Abglanz."

71. jIII:33. "Zeichen, die 'aus ihren Ursachen herkommen', das heißt, die auf die vorborgenen Ursachen hinweisen, aus denen sie, als Signaturen in allen Dingen, entstammen."

72. jIII:34. "In der Welt Gottes gibt es noch keine Verdinglichung, und die *dibb'rim* oder *devarim* sind hier offenkundig noch die Worte als die gestaltenden Kräfte aller Dinge."

73. jIII:34. "In sich versunkenes, sprachloses Denken."

74. jIII:35. "Anfang der Rede"; "es ist noch nicht selbst Sprache, sondern ihr Ursprung und Anfang."

75. jIII:35. "Jedes Sprechen ist in der geistigen Welt zugleich ein Schreiben, und jede Schrift ist potentielle Rede, die bestimmt ist, lautbar zu werden."

76. jIII:35. "Die Schrift, dem Philologen nur ein sekundäres und zudem höchst unbrauchbares Abbild der wirklichen Sprache, ist dem Kabbalisten der wahre Hort ihrer Geheimnisse. Das phonographische Prinzip einer natürlichen Umsetzung von Sprache in Schrift und umgekehrt von Schrift in Sprache wirkt in der Kabbala in der Vorstellung, daß die heiligen Buchstaben des Alphabets selber jene

Lineamente und Signaturen sind, die der moderne Phonetiker auf seiner Platte suchen würde. Das schaffende Wort Gottes prägt sich legitim eben in jenen heiligen Linien aus. Jenseits der Sprache liegt die sprachlose Reflexion, die das reine Denken ist, das sich selber denkt, man möchte sagen, der stumme Tiefsinn, in dem das Namenlose nistet." The quotation is originally from Scholem, *Ursprung und Anfänge der Kabbala*, p. 244.

77. Whether mystics were inclined to speak in the symbolism of light, the content of their speculation was to grow interchangeable as both light and linguistic symbolism were brought together in a theory of emanation. See Scholem jIII:32–33.

78. jIII:37. "Als sinnbildlicher Ausdruck eines der unendlichen Aspekte von Gottes Machtfülle."

79. jIII:38. "Urpunkt der Sprache."

80. jIII:39. "Einheit der sich aus der Urwurzel verzweigenden Sprachbewegung, die im Uräther, der Aura, die Gott umgibt, entsteht."

81. jIII:39. "Indifferenzpunkt alles Sprechen."

82. jIII:39. "Die magische Macht des Sprechenden ist die Macht dessen, der sich an die Wurzel dieser Sprachbewegung zu versetzen weiß und damit alle Sprache und Wesensäußerung umfaßt und ihre Wirkungen zu durchdringen vermag."

83. jIII:42. Abulafia advocated this as necessary secrecy.

84. jIII:44. "Nur im jetzigen Äon ist in der uns lesbar gewordenen Form der Torah das Tetragramm an die Stelle dieses Urnamens getreten, aber in der messianischen Zeit, die das Ende dieses Äons einleitet, wird es durch den Ursprünglichen Namen wieder verdrängt werden."

85. jIII:44–45. "Am Ende des Weltprozesses aber kehren alle Dinge im 'großen Jubeljahr' zu ihrem Ursprung in der dritten Sefira *Bina* zurück, und alle Emanationen und Welten unter ihr verschwinden. Der wahre Name Gottes, der sich aber auch in diesem Stand der Rückkehr aller Dinge in Gottes Schoß erhalten wird, ist eben dieser Urname, eine Offenbarung des göttlichen Wesens, die an sich selbst, nicht an irgend etwas außerhalb von ihm gerichtet ist."

86. jIII:45. "Symbolisch sichtbar."

87. jIII:46. "Metaphorischer Ausdruck allgemein theologischer Vorstellungen"; "Kondensationen, Zusammenballungen der Austrahlungen Gottes"; "metaphysischen Sphäre" in which "das Optische und das Akustische koinzidieren."

88. tag I:472. "*Grundgesetz der mystischen Sprachauffassung*: Alle Sprache besteht aus Gottesnamen."

89. tag II:212. "Das Prinzip der kabbalistischen Sprachtheorie ist: Alle Sprache besteht aus Gottesnamen."

90. According to Scholem, this tradition of proper names originates from a well-read but anonymous commentary on the Merkabah vision of Ezekiel, suggesting Moses Zinfa as the possible author. jIII:46–47. But we are also aware of Scholem's own fascination with the meaning of proper names, reading his own name with imbued messianic meaning as both *shalom*, peace, and *shalem*, to make whole. (A larger discussion on this theme is to follow in the final section of chapter 6.) We also know to what degree Scholem shared this rather intense interest

with Benjamin though his essay "Walter Benjamin und Sein Engel" (1972) and "Die Geheimen Namen Walter Benjamins" (1978). On this point, see also Agamben, "Lingua e storia."

91. Scholem's emphasis. jIII:47. "'Der Name ist also etwas anderes als das Wesen und ist weder Substanz noch Attribut und nichts, was konkrete Wirklichkeit hat, während der Körper sowohl Substanz wie Attribut ist, sowie etwas, das konkrete Realität hat. Der Name tritt hier zum Wesen hinzu, die göttlichen Namen aber sind das Wesen selber und sie sind Potenzen der Gottheit und ihre Substanz ist die Substanz des 'Licht des Lebens' [eine der höchsten Sefiroth]. Aber wenn man es mit den Eigennamen der Menschen ganz genau nehmen will, wird man finden, daß auch sie und die Wesen [die sie bezeichnen] eines sind, so daß der Name nicht vom Wesen getrennt und unterschieden werden kann noch das Wesen vom Namen, denn der Name hängt direkt mit dem Wesen zusammen.'"

92. In order not to drive the reader into total confusion (which the discussion of these very categories in Aristotle's metaphysics has been known to do), I have borrowed the term *essence* from Scholem's translation of Ha'Kohen here to represent Benjamin's *geistige Wesen* (what I have previously termed the "substance of intellect/spirit") so as not to confuse it with *Substanz*.

93. Scholars of the Kabbalah such as Joseph Dan have often wondered why Scholem was to spend the greater part (roughly ten years) of his early carrier on the Kohen brothers. If their linguistic writings could be interpreted along the index of genesic linguistic notions, which Scholem and Benjamin were to assemble, it might offer some clues as to the reasons for this profound interest.

94. jIII:53. "'Von sich selbst zu sich selbst', in der sich jene Freude des *Ein-sof* über sich selber ausdrückt, damit zugleich aber auch schon die geheime Potenzialität allen Ausdrucks."

95. jIII:53. "Urgewand."

96. jIII:53. "Vorborgene Signatur in Gott."

97. jIII:53. "Urkraft aller Sprachbewegung."

98. jIII:54. "Mystischer Gottesnamen, die durch gewisse weitere Kombinationen der ersten Elemente gebildet werden."

99. jIII:54. "Die Namen aller Dinge und aller menschlichen Wesen," meaning "die Welt der Sprache und der Namen überhaupt."

100. jIII:55. "Die ursprüngliche, paradiesische Sprache des Menschen hatte noch diesen Charakter des Sakralen, das heißt, sie war noch unmittelbar und unverstellt mit dem Wesen der Dinge, die sie ausdrücken wollte, verbunden. In dieser Sprache war noch das Echo der göttlichen vorhanden, denn im Anhauch des göttlichen Pneuma setzte sich die Sprachbewegung des Schöpfers in die des Geschöpfes um."

101. jIII:55. "Von vornherein gar nicht zu profanem Gebrauch bestimmt gewesen sei. Die Generation, die den Turm von Babel erbauen wollte, mißbrauchte diese echte sakrale Sprache magisch, um mit Hilfe der Kenntnis der reinen Namen aller Dinge die Schöpfertätigkeit Gottes bis zu einem gewissen Grade nachzuahmen, sich einen 'Namen' zu erschleichen, der für jede Gelegenheit anwendbar sein

würde. Die Sprachverwirrung bestand im weitgehenden Verlust dieser Sprache aus dem Gedächtnis, so daß sich die Betreffenden die Benennungen der Einzeldinge neu ersinnen und erfinden mußten. [. . .] Auch die heilige Sprache ist seitdem mit Profanem vermischt, so wie in den profanen Sprachen noch hier und da Elemente oder Residua der heiligen stecken."

102. Scholem however cites Jechiel Michel Epstein, *Kizzur shnei luchot ha-brit.* jIII:55–56, note 63.

103. See, for example, Scholem's thoughts on language upon arrival in Scholem, *On the Possibility of Jewish Mysticism in Our Time,* pp. 27–30.

104. At the same time that this mystical orientation was to contradict so much of the effect of Maimonides, particularly the movement directly following his death, Abulafia presented his interpretation as revealing the esoteric dimension which always existed in Maimonides teaching, however much hidden. See jIII:57.

105. jIII:58. "Schöpfung, Offenbarung und Prophetie sind für Abulafia Phänomene der Sprachwelt: die Schöpfung als ein Akt des göttlichen Schreibens, in welchem die Schrift die Materie der Schöpfung gestaltet; Offenbarung und Prophetie als Akte, in denen das göttliche Wort sich nicht nur einmal, sondern letzten Endes immer wiederholbar in die menschliche Sprache eingießt und ihr, wenigstens potentiell, den unendlichen Reichtum unermeßlicher Einsicht in den Zusammenhang der Dinge verleiht."

106. Just as in the teaching of the *sh'mittoh,* word combinations that have no meaning in this world will develop a meaning in the next. Future meanings exist within words and will be exposed when this level of limited knowledge is surpassed, whether through individual enlightenment or through messianic transition. jIII:67. See Lipiner, *Ideologie fun Yidishn Alef-Beis* (Yiddish), pp. 107–155; Silver, *A History of Messianic Speculation in Israel,* p. 146.

107. jIII:58. "Schöpfung als Akt des göttlichen Schreibens, in dem Gott seine Sprache den Dingen einverleibt, sie als seine Signaturen in ihnen hinterläßt."

108. jIII:60. "Jeder der Himmelssphären des ptolemäischen Weltbilds entsprach nämlich hier eine ihr innewohnende Intelligenz, die eine geistige Wirkung des göttlichen Schöpferwillens war."

109. jIII:64. "'Wissenschaft der höheren, innerlichen Logik.'"

110. jIII:60–61. "Was in der Sprache der Philosophen die Vernunftanlage im Menschen hieß, konnte also auch als Sprachvermögen verstanden werden."

111. jIII:61. "'Die Ursache der Prophetie liegt in der Rede, die von Gott durch das Medium der vollkommenen Sprache, die alle siebzig Sprachen umfaßt, zu den Propheten gelangt.'"

112. Aside from the later experiments with drugs and the transcendental pursuit that such experimentation implies, there is little evidence of a direct interest in mystical practice, despite a theoretical interest in ritual. In this respect, Buck-Morss, in her book *The Dialectics of Seeing,* wonders if Benjamin's prayed. But to truly answer this question one would have to define the meaning of prayer. Would it be, in Benjamin's case, the expression of *geistige Wesen,* for example? Would it be considered communicative or, alternatively, symbolic action?

113. jIII:62. "So sind bei Gott die Herzen die Schreibtafeln und die Seelen wie die Tinte, und die Rede, die zu ihnen von ihm kommt, die zugleich die Erkenntnis ist, ist wie die Form der Buchstaben, die auf den Bundestafeln von beiden Seiten eingeschrieben waren."

114. jIII:63. "Alle erschaffenen Dinge haben Realität nur soweit sie in irgendeiner Art an diesem 'großen Namen' Anteil haben."

115. jIII:63. "Erkenntnisakt, auch wenn diese Erkenntnis uns noch verschlossen, nicht dechiffrierbar ist." This is undoubtedly a reference to Scholem's interpretation of Kafka, where the law always appears in codes that are indecipherable to Josef K. Scholem sees in Kafka an idea of revelation that is always postponed.

116. Abulafia shared Benjamin's position on the ability of divine matter to be conveyed through translation and in profane languages but ultimately Hebrew is considered the original, divine language. Moshe Idel reinforces Scholem's interpretation of the relationship of divine messages to divine language: "'According to the Kabbalah, the divine speech is only attainable by means of the Holy language, although its existence is ascertainable by means of any language.'" Mafteah ha-Hokmot, Ms. Moscow 133, fol.16b. See Idel, *Language, Torah, and Hermeneutics in Abraham Abulafia*, pp. 14–27, especially p. 22.

117. jIII:65. "Da alle Sprachen durch Korruption aus der sakralen Ursprache entstanden sind, in der sich unmittelbar die Welt der Namen auseinanderlegt, hängen sie noch mittelbar mit ihr zusammen."

118. jIII:66. "Unrestituierten Natur." The divine name bears its secrets for a purpose. Since God hid his name, Abulafia deemed it unwise to reveal how it was that He came to this conclusion. In his estimation, the combination YHVH was merely a "Notbehelf." Behind it stood an original name. jIII:41–43.

119. jIII:67–68. "Er verhält sich aber aller praktikablen Magie und Theurige gegenüber gänzlich abweisend."

120. jIII:68. "Magie als das nicht-Kommunizierbare, und doch aus den Worten Ausstrahlende ist für ihn existent."

121. jIII:68. "Aus der Versenkung in den Namen Gottes, das Zentrum aller Schöpfung, erwächst ihm die Kraft, 'das Wirken der Magier zunichte zu machen.'"

122. II:213. "Magie zu liquidieren."

123. "Der Name Gottes ist der 'wesentliche Name', der der Ursprung aller Sprache ist. Jeder andere Name, unter dem Gott benannt oder angerufen werden kann, steht mit einer bestimmten Aktivität in Zusammenhang, wie die Etymologie solcher biblischen Namen ausweist; nur dieser eine Name bedingt keinerlei Rückbesinnung auf eine Aktivität. Dieser Name hat für die Kabbalisten keinen 'Sinn' im gewöhnlichen Verstande, keine konkrete Bedeutung. Das Bedeutungslose des Namens Gottes weist auf seine Stellung im Zentrum der Offenbarung hin, der er zugrunde liegt. Hinter aller Offenbarung eines Sinnes in der Sprache und, wie es die Kabbalisten sahen, durch die Tora, steht dies über den Sinn hinausragende, ihn erst ermöglichende Element, das ohne Sinn zu haben allem anderen Sinn verleiht. Was aus Schöpfung und Offenbarung zu uns spricht, das Wort Gottes, ist unendlich

deutbar und reflektiert sich in unserer Sprache. Seine Strahlen oder Laute, die wir auffangen, sind nicht sosehr Mitteilungen als Anrufe. Was Bedeutung hat, Sinn und Form, ist nicht dies Wort selber, sondern die *Tradition* von diesem Worte, seine Vermittlung und Reflexion in der Zeit. Diese Tradition, die ihre eigene Dialektik hat, verwandelt sich und geht eventuell auch in ein leises und verhauchendes Flüstern über, und es mag Zeiten geben, wie die unsere, wo sie nicht mehr überliefert werden kann und wo diese Tradition verstummt. Das ist dann die große Krise der Sprache, in der wir stehen, die wir auch den letzten Zipfel jenes Geheimnisses, das einmal in ihr wohnte, nicht mehr zu fassen bekommen. [. . .] Nur die Dichter, [haben] eine Antwort, die die Verzweiflung der meisten Mystiker an der Sprache nicht teilen und die eines mit den Meistern der Kabbala verbindet, auch wo sie deren theologische Formulierung als noch zu vordergründig verwerfen: der Glaube an die Sprache als ein, wie immer dialektisch aufgerissenes, Absolutum, der Glaube an das hörbar gewordene Geheimnis in der Sprache." jIII:69–70.

124. The importance Jewish speculation was to attribute to the form of the letters, their crowns, and acoustic notation find neither a place explicitly in Benjamin's analysis nor in Scholem's late survey where they would surely belong. This absence may point still further to the sheer loyalty expressed by Scholem to the early ideas. See Joseph Dan's important contribution to the mysticism of the shape of the letters in "The Language of the Mystics in Medieval Germany," pp. 12–13.

125. These remarks are related to the section in chapter 2 devoted to Scholem's late political and theological reflections, which I have termed "critical anarchism."

5. PROPHETIC JUSTICE

1. II:173. "Der Charakter nämlich wird gewöhnlich in einen ethischen, wie das Schicksal in einen religiösen Zusammenhang eingestellt."

2. The argument, following the section on *Trauerspiel* and tragedy in chapter 1, concerns the idea of attributing sin rather than challenging the notion of sin altogether, as we shall see in this section.

3. The relevance of Kierkegaard to Benjamin can be seen in the final section on his essay on language (II:153). The editors cite Kierkegaard's *Kritik der Gegenwart* (II:936) as Benjamin himself lists Kierkegaard as number 463 in his tally of books read. Benjamin, *Gesammelte Schriften*, VII:437

4. See, for example, GB I:151, where he mentions reading *The Concept of Anxiety* and GB I: 56 regarding an exchange of letters with his close companion Heinle on original sin. See also GB I:163, 168.

5. See GB I:452

6. ba:18. "Die neue Ethik setzt die Dogmatik voraus und mit ihr die Erbsünde, und erklärt nun aus ihr die Sünde des Einzelnen."

7. ba:100. "Der Begriff Sünde und Schuld setzt eben den Einzelnen als den Einzelnen. Es ist von keinerlei Verhältnis zur ganzen Welt, zu all dem Vergangenen die Rede. Nur davon ist die Rede, daß er schuldig ist, und doch soll er durch das

Schicksal werden, mithin durch alles das, davon nicht die Rede ist, und er soll dadurch etwas werden, was den Begriff Schicksal gerade aufhebt, und dies soll er werden durch das Schicksal."

8. Only very recently has the Church been capable of repudiating the principle without a systematic or serious attempt to evaluate the suffering it has caused for centuries.

9. Since this undertaking seeks to move beyond dogma and places truth as its highest goal, it may perhaps even justify the term *metaphysics.*

10. ba:29. "Die Erzählung der Genesis von der ersten Sünde ist sonderlich in unsrer Zeit ziemlich unachtsam als ein Mythus betrachtet worden. [. . .] Wenn der Verstand auf das Mythische verfällt, so kommt selten etwas anderes als Geschwätz heraus. Jene Erzählung ist die einzige dialektisch-folgerichtige Auffassung. Ihr gesamter Gehalt sammelt sich eigentlich in dem Satze: *Die Sünde ist durch eine Sünde in die Welt gekommen.*"

11. "Offenbarte Wahrheit"; Discovered is rendered here from *aufgefunden.* See chapter 3 for a discussion of whether Benjamin indeed puts forward what amounts to mystical speculation despite his disclaimer to the contrary and Scholem's reply in chapter 4.

12. The notion of idle talk was also to capture Scholem's concern with a new political direction in his farewell letter to politics. See "Abschied" (B I:463) and the discussion in chapter 2.

13. ba:26. "Adam ist der erste Mensch, er ist zu gleicher Zeit er selbst und das Geschlecht."

14. ba:27. "Sündigkeit als ihre Folge bedingende."

15. ba:27. "einen Anfang außerhalb seiner selbst."

16. ba:35. "Die Erzählung der Genesis gibt nun auch die richtige Erklärung der Unschuld. Unschuld *ist* Unwissenheit. Sie ist keineswegs das reine Sein des Unmittelbaren, sondern sie ist Unwissenheit."

17. ba:39. This dialectical transition is considered by Kierkegaard to be that which breaks "alle katholischen Phantastereien von Verdienst."

18. ba:39. "Der Einzige, der unschuldig über die Sünde Leid getragen hat."

19. ba:36. "Er trug über sie Leid nicht als über ein Schicksal, in das er sich finden mußte, sondern trug Leid als der, welcher es frei erwählte der ganzen Welt Sünde zu tragen und für sie die Strafe zu leiden."

20. II:154. "Gut und böse nämlich stehen als unbenennbar, als namenlos außerhalb der Namensprache. [. . .] Denn—noch einmal soll das gesagt werden—Geschwätz war die Frage nach dem Gut und Böse in der Welt nach der Schöpfung. Der Baum der Erkenntnis stand nicht wegen der Aufschlüsse über Gut und Böse [. . .] sondern als Wahrzeichen des Gerichts über den Fragenden."

21. ba:106. "Der Jude nimmt seine Zuflucht zum Opfer, aber es hilft ihm nichts, denn was eigentlich helfen soll, wäre, daß das Angstverhältnis zur Schuld aufgehoben und ein wirkliches Verhältnis gesetzt würde."

22. It is interesting to what degree Kierkegaard's solution to the "Jewish question" is similar to that of the young Hegelian Bruno Bauer in his call for the Jews

to first adopt Christianity before giving up religion altogether. Bauer's "Jewish" program is, in this respect, perhaps only half as ridiculous as Marx's reply, attempting to make use of anti-Semitic myths on behalf of the Jews against the Christian atheistic socialists.

23. ref:310. "Dem Dogma," Benjamin writes, "von der natürlichen Schuld des Menschenlebens, von der Urschuld, deren prinzipielle Unlösbarkeit die Lehre, und deren gelegentliche Lösung den Kultus des Heidentums bildet, stellt der Genius die Vision von der natürlichen Unschuld des Menschen entgegen." II:178.

24. GB I:392. "Wichtige Gegensätze gegen den christlichen Religionsbegriff."

25. See also the observations of Wohlfarth, "On Some Jewish Motifs in Benjamin," on the notion of "natural" innocence.

26. II:176. "Der Schuldzusammenhang ist ganz uneigentlich zeitlich, nach Art und Maß ganz verschieden von der Zeit der Erlösung."

27. See the discussion in chapter 1 on Rosenzweig's *Nächstenliebe*.

28. "Es gibt also einen Begriff des Schicksals [. . .] welcher vollkommen unabhängig von dem des Charakters ist und seine Begründung in einer ganz andern Sphäre sucht." II:176.

29. ref:307 (modified). "Eine Ordnung aber, deren einzig konstitutive Begriffe Unglück und Schuld sind und innerhalb deren es keine denkbare Straße der Befreiung gibt [. . .] —eine solche Ordnung kann nicht religiös sein, so sehr auch der mißverstandene Schuldbegriff darauf zu verweisen scheint. Es gilt also ein anderes Gebiet zu suchen, in welchem einzig und allein Unglück und Schuld gelten, eine Waage, auf der Seligkeit und Unschuld zu leicht befunden werden und nach oben schweben. Diese Waage ist die Waage des Rechts." II:174.

30. "An der Fixierung der besonderen Art der Zeit des Schicksals hängt die vollendete Durchleuchtung dieser Dinge." II:176.

31. II:174.

32. II:174. "Ordnung des Rechts, welche den Sieg über die Dämonen inaugurierte."

33. See the section on judgment in chapter 3.

34. II:154. "Ursprungs des Rechts."

35. Benjamin, "Notizen zu einer Arbeit über die Kategorie der Gerechtigkeit." tag I:401–402. As with pieces such as the "Metaphysics of Youth" and "The Journal," Scholem received either a typewritten copy from Benjamin to read or was given Benjamin's notebook for safekeeping or transcription. See the "Anmerkungen" in *Gesammelte Schriften*, II:915–949, VI:625–638, VII:527–531, and Schweppenhäuser, "Benjamin über Gerechtigkeit.

36. A copy of the letter is reproduced in briefe I:125–8

37. tag I:382–402. See also the description of the meeting with some discrepancy in freund:33.

38. Scholem returns to this evening in August in his book on Benjamin: "Benjamin sprach schon damals in diesem Zusammenhang von dem Unterschied zwischen Recht und Gerechtigkeit, wobei das Recht eine nur in der Welt der Mythos begründbare Ordnung sei. Er hat diesen Gedanken dann vier Jahre später in

seinem Aufsatz *Zur Kritik der Gewalt* näher ausgeführt." freund:45. On the discussion of myth, see Scholem's understanding in tag I:389 and note 39, this chapter, as well as the discussion in chapter 6 on judgment and violence.

39. tag I:386. "Wir haben während unseres ganzen Zusammenseins ungeheuer viel über das Judentum gesprochen: einmal über das Nach-Palästina-Gehen und den 'Ackerbau Zionismus', über Achad Haam und die 'Gerechtigkeit', am meisten aber über Buber von dem nach diesen vier Tagen so gut wie nichts mehr übriggeblieben ist. [. . .] Schon hier ist klar, wie nahe Benjamin Achad Haam steht, was nachher noch an einem zentralsten Punkte deutlich werden wird, der Auffassung der Rolle der 'Gerechtigkeit' im Judentum."

40. See the discussion in chapter 2 entitled "Zion: Anarchist Praxis or Metaphor?"

41. The discussion of the "sanctifying of the name" and role this concept was to play in Jewish martyrdom was an ever recurring theme in Jewish circles. Take, for example, Hugo Bermann's essay entitled "Kiddush Haschem" in the influential anthology *Vom Judentum*, published by the Bar-Kochba circle in Prague (1913). The influence of this collection is often mentioned in the first years of Scholem's journal entries. Benjamin returns to this book in a letter to Scholem from 1920–21. See freund:133–134.

42. "Außerordentlich nahe"; "vom geistigen Zentrum."

43. "'Ackerbau *kann* goijisch sein.'"

44. On his understanding of Benjamin's conception of myth, Scholem recorded the following entry that same evening: "Er ließ *nur* den Mythos als 'die Welt' gelten, sagte, er wisse selbst nocht nicht, was der Zweck der Philosophie sei, da der 'Sinn der Welt' nicht erst aufgefunden zu werden brauche, sondern im Mythos schon da sei. Der Mythos sei alles, alles andere (Mathematik und Philosophie) sei nur eine Verdunkelung in ihm selber, ein Schein." tag I:389–390. A late summary of this discussion can be found in freund:44 with, again, a slightly different recollection.

45. tag I:391. "Benjamins Geist kreist und wird noch lange kreisen um den Mythos, an den er von den verschiedensten Seiten heran will. Von der Geschichte, wo er von der Romantik ausgeht, von der Dichtung, wo er von Hölderlin ausgeht, von der Religion, wo er vom Judentum ausgeht, und vom Recht aus. 'Wenn ich einmal meine Philosophie haben werde'—sagte er zu mir—'so wird es irgendwie eine Philosophie des Judentums sein.'" Scholem reproduces this journal entry in freund:45.

46. tag I:391. "Aber all das, was er hier sagte, werde ich in Berlin noch einmal mit ihm besprechen müssen."

47. tag I:392. "Über all das, was wir in unseren ausführlichen Gesprächen zu zweien oder dreien behandelt haben, könnte ich mehr als den ganzen Winter nachdenken: das ganze Leben lang den Zionismus neu aufbauen. Denn ich darf mich doch nicht belügen: Wenn ich wirklich mit Benjamin gehe, müßte ich ungeheuer revidieren." This statement appears to contradict the later recollection of these meetings, which appeared only in the Hebrew version of Scholem's autobiography

in full: "Gewiß spielte gerade meine leidenschaftliche Bindung an das Jüdische in deren Entwicklung eine zentrale Rolle. Benjamin hat diese Bindung, so paradox das bei seiner ziemlich totalen Unwissenheit in jüdischen Dingen scheinen möchte, niemals in Frage gestellt. Er war weit davon entfernt, mich von diesen Neigungen abbringen zu wollen, fand sie im Gegenteil sehr interessant, ja tendierte dazu, mich darin noch, wenn man so sagen dürfte, zu bestärken, da ich seine Adresse für alle Fragen aus diesem Gebiet wurde." The record from the period reveals a perspective on Scholem that is far more active in the formation of his earliest views. See von berlin:75.

48. tag I:401. "Abends mit Benjamin gemeinsame Lektüre von Achad Haam 'Al shetei haseipim.'"

49. tag I:401. Benjamin, "Notizen zu einer Arbeit über die Kategorie der Gerechtigkeit."

50. German permits the term *goods* in the singular, *das Gut*, or in the plural, *die Güter*, as it does the term for an ethical good, *das Gute*, and its plural (in regard to those who are good), *die Guten*, not to speak of the word *die Güte* for "kindness" or "goodness." However, there are also many examples of *das Gut* and *das Gute* being used interchangeably. In an attempt to maintain the reflective play on words here but, at the same time, to carve out the definitive meanings in each word, I have created a term for material goods in the singular, "good (m)," as well as a term for an ethical good, "good (e)." What this may lack in style, it may hopefully make up for in clarity.

51. This is the renowned phrase of Pierre-Joseph Proudhon. See his *Système des contradictions économiques*, pp. 158–255, especially p. 212.

52. As we have seen in the fragment. II:204. See the discussion on nihilism in chapter 2.

53. Some argue thirty-six hidden righteous individuals, others argue for more. We will return to the figure of justice in the last section of chapter 6, "The Righteous, the Pious, the Scholar." See also "Drei Typen jüdischer Frömmigkeit" (1973) in jIV and Scholem, "Die 36 verborgenen Gerechten."

54. If Benjamin here enters upon the ground Rosenzweig cultivates several years later in his *Star of Redemption* with the category of *das All*, he was to do so with much foresight. This may support Stephene Mosès's claim that Benjamin precedes Rosenzweig. See his article "Walter Benjamin and Franz Rosenzweig," p. 228.

55. This statement is unfortunately followed by a sentence that has yet to be deciphered, which, in its proximity to Christian terminology, raises many questions. To juxtapose temptation and redemption, one does not necessary need the trinity, especially if we are to read this independent of a dogma. Was this merely a harmless example or was Benjamin trying to reveal (or hide) something with an overt Christian reference? Kambas suggests a proximity to Christian anarchism of *Das Ziel*, which perhaps might correspond to the praise of Tolstoy and the early Christians in "Das Leben der Studenten." See II:79–80 and Kambas, "Walter Benjamin liest Georges Sorel." On the other hand, it may also hide the Judaic discussion, being deemed too overtly "Jewish" for a discourse on justice.

56. The correlation of these terms is not self-evident. The first term, *ius*, could be defined as right or law. It takes place in the civil arena and is clearly concerned with worldly affairs. Its opposite is *fas*, from which we have the word fate. Divine command and divine right is expressed in *fas*, as is destiny. The term is used, however, for that which is allowed, which is right and lawful and thus establishes the very sphere *ius* requires in order for there to be authority in human law. *Fas* thus appears to be better linked to the Greek term *themis* than *dike* (if we are to understand by Benjamin's list a repeated divine-profane tension in each ancient language). *Themis* is that which is laid down or established not by fixed statute but by customary right, law formed by custom. It has a divine component that offers sanctity and penitence as *themis* can also be used to refer to the decrees of gods, oracles, or ordinances handed down by kings. Custom and usage is expressed as *dike*, even a moral path, a way to right, justice, or judgment. It can be distinguished from *themis* in that it is used to refer to proceedings instituted to determine legal rights and thus has the connotation of trial and those things related to a worldly lawsuit: plea, atonement, consequence of an action, and penalty. The last categories of *mishpat* and *tzedek* we shall return to a bit later.

57. In contrast to the published version, Hermann Schweppenhäuser has noted that the main text is divided from the remarks on time and two further citations (which I have not included) by a double dividing line, indicating that the text probably ended with the list of terms. I have included the paragraph on time because of its immanent connection to Scholem, as we shall see. See Schweppenhäuser, "Benjamin über Gerechtigkeit."

58. It appears to be related to this fragment in the sixth volume of the complete works: "Die historischen Zahlen sind Namen/ Reihe der historischen Zahlen/ Das Problem der historischen Zeit muß in Korrelation zu dem des historischen Raumes (Geschichte auf dem *Schauplatz*) gefaßt werden." Fragment 62, Benjamin, *Gesammelte Schriften*, VI:90, 682. See also freund:45.

59. tag I:390. "Über einer sehr schwierigen Bemerkung verbrachten wir einen ganzen Nachmittag: die Reihe der Jahre ist wohl zählbar, aber nicht numerierbar. Was uns auf Ablauf, Zahlenreihe und vor allem als letzten Ausgangspunkt auf die Richtung führte. Gibt es eine Richtung ohne Ablauf? 'Richtung ist das verschiedene Maß zweier Geraden'. [. . .] Die Zeit ist wohl ein Ablauf, aber ist die Zeit gerichtet? Denn es ist doch eine durchaus metaphysische Behauptung, daß die Zeit gleichsam eine Gerade sei."

60. An example of this might be a range of sequential dates such as 1936, 1919, 1871, 1848, 1789, 1776, 1648 that exist in a countable but non-numerical political continuum.

61. tag I:392. "Zu lesen ist Baader: *Theorie des Opfers*. Verschiedener Sinn des Opfers und der Übertretung in Mythologie und Judentum. Dort wird die Gemeinde Gottes unmittelbar, die der einzelnen wird getötet, im Judentum nur der einzelne, *die "Umkehr" hebt an.* Im mythologischen Heidentum ist das Höchste das Recht, im Judentum die Gerechtigkeit. Äußerst wichtig ist, daß im Hebräischen *mishpat* und *zedaka* ganz verschiedene Stämme sind. *Mishpat* kann sich

nicht offenbaren (Jesaija 58), sondern nur seine *zedaka*. Recht und Gerechtigkeit sind zwei vollkommen verschiedene Dinge. *Das Wesen des Judentums ist die Gerechtigkeit.* Eine göttliche Kategorie. Das Christentums hat den *Raum*, der das Judentum ist, noch einmal schaffen wollen durch die drei Koordinaten Glaube, Liebe, Hoffnung; durchdringt das Judentum wie ein Punkt den Raum durchdringt, bleibt immer auf niederer Dimensionstufe. Im Judentum glaubt man nicht, sondern ist gerecht. In diesem Sinne ist die jüdische '*Tat*' als das Raumerfüllende zu nehmen." The later report of this period in his book on Benjamin gives a somewhat different account of events: "Bei einem Gespräch über die Schriften Franz von Baaders, das wir in der Schweiz hatten [. . .] versuchten wir uns auszumalen, wie das Niveau einer Hörerschaft gewesen sein müsse, welche Vorlesungen dieses Geistesfluges und dieser Tiefe zu folgen imstande war. Ich hattte damals gerade Baaders *Vorlesungen über die Theorie des Opfers nach Jacob Böhme* gelesen und brachte das zur Sprache. Baader imponierte Benjamin mehr als Schelling, von dem er in seiner freistudentischen Periode [. . .] nur die *Vorlesungen über die Methode des akademischen Studiums* gelesen hatte." freund:32–33. Perhaps the most interesting aspect of this discrepancy is the degree to which the memory of influence becomes completely intertwined.

62. Modern scholars would likely dispute the idea of a biblical distinction between *mishpat* and *tzedek*. Most appears to be at odds with each other on the question. See Cox, "Sedaqa and Mispat"; Bosco, "La nozione di 'Giustizia' nell'antico testamento"; "Recht und Gerechtigkeit" in *Jüdisches Lexikon*, vol. 4/1 (Berlin: 1930), pp. 1275–1277; Hermann Cohen, "Liebe und Gerechtigkeit," "die Nächstenliebe im Talmud," in *Jüdische Schriften* vols. 2–3, (Berlin: 1924); B. Johnson, "Mispat"; Schmid, *Gerechtigkeit als Weltordnung*.

63. Being the editor in chief of Benjamin's *Gesammelte Schriften*, along with Adorno, one has to wonder why Scholem failed to discover this text among the other early texts of Benjamin also found in his journals—the sole source for most of what we have come to know as Benjamin's early writings. One can hardly imagine that it consisted of pure oversight, not only because of his fastidious attention to detail but for the very fact that he reviewed his own journals at least twice: once for copies of lost manuscripts of Benjamin's writings and a second time to write his biographical and autobiographical studies *From Berlin to Jerusalem* and *Walter Benjamin: The Story of a Friendship*. It also seems highly unlikely that Scholem would simply forget this text, being that he himself wrote a direct and hitherto unpublished commentary to it, one of the few texts of its kind that reveals such an intimate tie to Benjamin's early work ("Theses on the Concept of Justice"). He also makes direct reference to it in freund:93.

64. See the discussion in chapter 3 on judgment.

65. In a discussion on the ten commandments Scholem read aloud his "Aufzeichnung über den Begriff der Gerechtigkeit als 'Handeln in Aufschub' vor, die bei Benjamin ein starkes Echo fanden." To the question posed—why he did not maintain religious observance—Scholem replied that he "müsse den anarchischen Suspens aufrechterhalten." freund:93.

66. Scholem arc. 1599/277.34 "Thesen über den Begriff der Gerechtigkeit" (hand).

67. Ambiguous handwriting. Seeing that the verb in this sentence takes the accusative, it appears that Scholem placed a German ending on the Latin word *excitare*, meaning "to rouse, incite, kindle, wake."

68. While distributive justice is concerned with the distribution of goods and the problem of inequality (i.e., a man who takes more than his share), it does not present a conception of absolute right, nor does remedial or corrective justice, perhaps the closest to *ius*, bear a messianic link to divine judgment. See book 5 of the *Nicomachean Ethics* and Ernst Tugendhat, "Gerechtigkeit," in *Vorlesungen über Ethik*, pp. 364–392.

69. The more "recent" treatments of Kant, Schleiermacher, and Fichte may also have contributed to the general framework of the discussion but not in any singular or uniform way.

70. The enthusiasm of the young Scholem lead several scholars to trace a possible link between Benjamin's and Humboldt's linguistics with little success. We are therefore unable to treat Scholem's phrase in briefe II:526 as a reference to these sources.

71. Scholem makes the following comment in his journals on the distributive idea, touching on the difference between a socialist and anarchist program: "Die Gütergemeinschaft des kommunistischen Lebens ist keine juristische, wie sie etwa das Recht des Zeitalters kennt. Sie bedeutet die Besitzlosigkeit aller am Geld meßbaren und mechanischen Güter. Des 'Lichtes' kann man nicht *min hahefker* als herrenlosem Gut anteilhaftig sein, mit Bialik zu reden, denn das Licht ist kein Gut. Der praktische Anspruch meines Kameraden erstreckt sich aber auf die Güter, die die kommunistische Gemeinschaft negiert. Die kommunistische Gemeinschaft ist nicht demokratisch, das *Vertrauen* in die Stufe jedes Kameraden richtet eine ganz andere Ordnung auf, eine anarchische natürlich." tag II:374.

72. tag II: 211. "Walter Benjamin definiert Gerechtigkeit als das Streben, die Welt zum höchsten Gut zu machen, Ein altjüdisches Wort lautet: *tzadikim yashkinu shekhina ba-arez*."

73. For a qualification of the term, see the section "Violence and the Politics of Pure Means" in chapter 6.

74. The discussion of the second part reflects a more mature author. The ideas are more refined, suggesting a period of reflection, and there are several points of which Scholem could not have been aware when transcribing Benjamin's "Notes to a Study on the Category of Justice" (1916). These include his own text on Jonah (1919) and Benjamin's "Critique of Violence" (1921), which are both represented in the second part. In this regard, the latter part may well be an attempt to summarize their political theology at a later period. M. Löwy believes the later date: "La curieuse datation de ce Texte ("Thesen über den Begriff der Gerechtigkeit"—"1919 und 1925"— rend impossible de savoir s'il a été écrit avant ou après l'essai "Zur Kritik der Gewalt" de Benjamin (1921), avec lequel il present

des analogies évidentes (mais aussi des différences indéniables)." *Esoterica-Metaphisica*, p. 6.

75. Cf. GB II: 475, 510. The editors of Benjamin's *Gesammelte Schriften* believe that a reference to "Scholems Notizen über Gerechtigkeit" (*Gesammelte Schriften* VI:60) in notes that Benjamin wrote on "objektive Verlogenheit" suggests that he already possessed one of Scholem's texts on justice at a much earlier date. In addition to reading aloud to Benjamin a version of his notes on justice (freund: 93, 181), Scholem comments that he gave Benjamin a copy of the Jonah text in 1920–1921. The editors believe that Benjamin's notes are no earlier than 1922–1923. See *Gesammelte Schriften*, VI:671.

76. The second part of "Thesen über den Begriff der Gerechtigkeit" ("Theses on the Concept of Justice") was written after Scholem was well acquainted with Benjamin's ideas from the *Kritik der Gewalt* ("Critique of Violence"), first formulated in a letter to Scholem dated January 1921. See letter 94 in briefe I:251 as well as the conclusion of the previous chapter.

77. Specifically theses 1, 8, 9, and 11 of the text "Über Jona und den Begriff der Gerechtigkeit" ("On Jonah and the Concept of Justice") reemerge in the second part of the "Thesen über den Begriff der Gerechtigkeit" ("Theses on the Concept of Justice") with slight modification. For all intensive purposes they are reformulated versions of the same ideas.

78. "Die Lehre vom 'Gerechten' in der jüdischen Mystik" first appeared in the *Eranos Jahrbuch* 27 (1958) and was published thereafter in *Von der mystischen Gestalt der Gottheit*. See the last section of chapter 6.

79. "Schlüssel zum Verständnis der prophetischen Idee." Scholem Archive 40 1599/277.36. Now published in tag II:522–532.

80. tag II:523. "Unendlichkeit des göttlichen Wortes."

81. tag II:523. "Die Ordnung des Gerechten."

82. tag II:531. "Das grössere Problem, eben das des göttlichen Aufschubes, inauguriert wird."

83. The story of Jonah is given immense importance on Yom Kippur, where it is read as the Haftorah portion in the final *minkhah* (evening) prayers.

84. Jonah 3.

85. "Wandelt das Recht zur Gerechtigkeit." So far Scholem has interpreted *mishpat* as law (or judgment) and *tzedek* as justice, but here it appears in the inverse. The Jerusalem Bible also translates the sentence in the same way: "For the Lord will not cast off his people, nor will he forsake his inheritance. But judgment shall return to righteousness: and all the upright in heart shall follow it." Psalms 94:14–15.

86. Scholem writes, "Die Setzung der Sprache ist der Spruch der Gerechtigkeit [. . .] Das Buch Jonas schliesst mit einer Frage." The word *Sprache* is crossed out in the manuscript and replaced by *Frage* thus pointing to the proximity of the concept of language to the idea of the question in Scholem's thinking on prophecy.

87. tag II:525. "Beide Bücher sind selbst Fragen, beide geben keine Antwort, sondern die Frage selbst ist die Lösung. Jona schliesst mit einer Frage, der Frage,

durch die Geschichte ins Leben gerufen wird gegenüber dem Recht der Natur.—Hiob ist als Ganzes eine Frage, die in jener einzelnen "Wo warst Du [. . .] (Kap.38), der kosmogonischen Fragen, permanent wird."

88. tag II:526. "Das heisst ihre Antwort muss wesensmässig wieder eine Frage sein."

89. tag II:525 "Der Prophet versteht den Prophetismus nicht; er treibt letzten Endes Politik."

90. tag II:361. "Politik ist Weissagung über das Imaginäre. Über die Zeit, die nicht Vergangenheit, Gegenwart noch Zukunft ist. Das ist die ungeheure Ironie der prophetischen Politik, denn ihre Politik ist die göttliche Ironie. Die Theokratie negiert die Idee der Politik überhaupt."

91. tag II:526. "Erwiderung, Umkehr, der Frage nämlich, die ein neues Vorzeichen bekommt und so gleichsam zurückkehrt."

92. It is possible that Scholem wanted this to read "das mystische Recht." The adjective is a handwritten addition to the typed manuscript.

93. tag II:526. "Jona steht auf dem Standpunkt des Rechtes, von dem aus er ja auch im Recht ist, Gott auf dem der Gerechtigkeit; Gott leugnet das Recht in der Geschichte. In der Bekehrung wird das Recht überwunden und das Urteil nicht vollstreckt. [. . .] Denn dies und nichts Anderes bedeutet Gerechtigkeit im tiefsten Sinne: dass zwar geurteilt werden darf, aber die Exekutive davon völlig unterschieden bleibt. Die eindeutige Beziehung des richterlichen Urteils auf die Exekutive, die eigentliche Rechtsordnung, wird aufgehoben im Aufschub der Exekutive."

94. See II:200–201 and the discussion on "Violence and the Politics of Pure Means" in chapter 6.

95. "In weitestem Umfange eben das ganze Judentum." The first thesis is nearly identical to theses 3 and 4 in the second part of the "Theses on the Concept of Justice," save for a few minor changes and a footnote of considerable interest.

96. tag II:527. "Tod als Bewegung"

97. II:199. This is discussed in more detail in the second section of chapter 6.

98. tag II:527. "Das in dieser Ordnung erfüllte Leben ist das Gericht; die Idee des Jüngsten Gerichtes ist die absolute Setzung einer zeitlichen Ordnung, deren reines Leben Tod ist."

99. tag II:527. "Tod als Bewegung [. . .] in die andere Welt."

100. tag II:360. "Der Tod des Gerechten ist der letzte, absolute Aufschub, in dem die Distanz umschlägt und die Treue auf Gott übergeht. Der Tod des Gerechten ist das mediale Prinzip seines und damit des Lebens."

101. "Religiösen Topographie."

102. Psalms 73:28.

103. tag II:527. "Das *Sein* der Gerechtigkeit."

104. tag II:527. "Neutralisiert und anihiliert."

105. tag II:528. "Gerechtigkeit als Tat"; "der zur Handlung gewordene Aufschub."

106. tag II:528. "Dieses Urteil darf nicht vollstreckt werden; denn der Arme untersteht Gott." As well as a formulation on justice, we have in this statement a reference to Scholem's revolutionary ideas drawn from the emergence of Bolshevism.

Take, for example, his description of the debate with Benjamin on the dictatorship of the impoverished, which he tended to support at the time: "Jedenfalls hatten wir Auseinandersetzungen über die Diktatur, bei denen ich der Radikalere war und den Gedanken der Diktatur, den Benjamin damals noch vollkommen verwarf, verteidigte, soweit es sich um eine 'Diktatur der Armut' handeln würde, die für mich nicht *eo ipso* mit der 'Diktatur des Proletariats' identisch war." freund:100–101.

107. II:191. See chapter 6 on violence and the discussion of a "culture of the heart" that concludes the second section.

108. tag II:528. "Annihilation des Urteils, Gerechtigkeit ist die Liebe der Vollstreckung."

109. tag II:528. "Die Wohltat, zum Beispiel das Almosen als diejenige Leistung, auf die Arme im Namen Gottes, nicht mehr im Namen des Rechtes, Anspruch haben, (S. R. Hirsch), ist Aufschub einer Exekutive durch eine andere."

110. tag II:528. "Im Aufschubhandeln errettet vom Tode."

111. See the discussion on mythical violence in II:200 and the discussion in chapter 6 on this subject.

112. tag II:337–338. "Die Thora kennt die Todesstrafe. Im talmudischen Recht wird dies zu einem der größten Triumphe der Gerechtigkeit: die Möglichkeit, die Todesstrafe, d.h. das Todesurteil über einen Menschen auszusprechen, ist gegeben, aber die Exekution nicht. Diese Grundidee wird realisiert in der Zeugniserschwerung bei den Dingen, auf die Todesstrafe steht. Dies führt ganz tief in das Wesen des talmudischen Judentums hinein. Ein Gerichtshof, der in siebzig Jahren ein Todesurteil vollstreckt hatte, wurde der mörderische genannt. [Mishna Makkot 1,10] Die Gerechtigkeit erlaubt zu urteilen, aber nicht, das Todesurteil zu vollstrecken, und eben darum wird rückwirkend *praktisch* das Urteil selbst durch Erschwerungen unmöglich gemacht. Aber die Idee ist eben immer die: das Urteil ist möglich, die Vollstreckung ist (Menschen) nicht möglich. Das Gottesurteil kann definiert werden als das Urteil, das seine eigene Vollstreckung ist. *Darum* ist das Gottesurteil immer irgendwie im Sinne des Geschehens ein Ereignis: ein absolutes Ereignis, das sich auf der phänomenologischen Schicht absoluter Erfahrung abspielt. Also: das menschliche Gerichtsurteil ist seiner Vollstreckung transzendent, jedoch notwendig mit ihr verbunden im *Recht*, darf daher in gewissen Fällen nicht vollstreckt *werden*, die Idee der Gerechtigkeit füllt diesen Abgrund zwischen Urteil und Exekution aus. Im Gottesurteil aber *ist* das Urteil die Vollstreckung. Das Gottesurteil ist Medium der Geschichte."

113. tag II:529. "Das Urteil ist möglich, die Vollstreckung ist nicht möglich. Das menschliche Gerichtsurteil ist seiner Vollstreckung transzendent. Gerechtigkeit füllt den Abgrund zwischen ihnen aus."

114. tag II:529. "Symbolische Tat."

115. tag II:358. "Sie ist Exekution jeden göttlichen Urteils (Benjamin)."

116. tag II:529. "Die bedeutende Tat ist die mythische und untersteht dem Schicksal"; "Gerechtigkeit eliminiert das Schicksal."

117. "Die elimination des Schicksals aus den Handlungen."

118. For the tasks of the "Kultur des Herzens" which has given humanity the "reine Mittel" of action, see Benjamin's "Kritik der Gewalt" (II:191) and the discussion of a politics of pure means in chapter 6.

119. "Jessja 65:19–24 bedeutet nicht nur die Elimination des Schicksals in der messianischen Zeit, sondern gibt zugleich den Methodos dieser Elimination an in der Idee des Aufschubes."

120. tag II: 359. "Denn in Wahrheit gibt es ja dann gar keinen Sünder, und es bezieht sich dies ironisch eben auf das messianische Zentrum der Gerechtigkeit, denn in der messianischen Zeit ist 'all dein Volk Gerechte.'" Scholem's citation is from Isaiah 60:21. He also cites Isaiah 65:19–24 here as the source of his speculations. The formulation is nearly identical.

121. "Kann nicht angewandt werden." Here one is able to detect the embryo of what Scholem was to formulate as "religious anarchism." I have attempted to qualify the notion of "religious" in this phrase in chapter 2 in the discussion of critical anarchism.

122. tag II:529. "Ist das Recht Gottes, das noch nicht Gerechtigkeit ist, vielmehr dazu sich wandelt, in dem unendlichen Aufschub der Tradition. Offenbarung und messianische Zeit sind in ihr unzertrennlich verbunden." Elsewhere, he substitutes "tradition" for "oral teachings." tag II:358.

123. Psalms 94:14–15. It is often remarked how the words *tzedek* and *mishpat* are identical in the Torah (see the conclusion of chapter 5 and notes) yet this difference in itself forms a key aspect of Scholem's linguistic analysis. He sees this as Jonah's error, of mistakenly substituting one for the other. For "was identisch ist, verwandelt sich nicht," Scholem claims, "und was sich verwandelt, ist nicht identisch." tag II:530–531.

124. tag II:529–530. "Es ist klar, er verwechselt die ewige und die nichtewige Gegenwart. Er soll in Ninive über die ewige Gegenwart weissagen, aber er selbst betrachtet diese Weissagung als eine über die andere."

125. tag II:529. "Grenzbegriff," nor a "mechanische-unendliche, annäherungsfähige regulative Idee."

126. tag II:530. "Ordnung der Welt (tikkuno schel olam) und das messianische Reich die Welt der Ordnung (olam hatikkun)."

127. "Thus says the Lord, Keep judgment, and do justice ('shimru mishpat va'asu tz'dakah) for my salvation is near to come, and my righteousness (tzedakti) to be revealed." Isaiah 56:1.

128. tag II:530. "Gleichwie die kommende Welt besteht, besteht die kommende Gerechtigkeit. Dieses Kommen ist ihre Entfaltung, z'dakah wird nicht, sondern offenbart, enfaltet sich (Jessaja 56:1). Ihr Kommen ist nur das Durchbrechen des strahlenden Mediums durch eine Verdunkelung. Darum auch ist der Zadik, der Gerechte (im Chassidismus etwa) nur 'mithgaleh.' Keiner kann Zadik werden, er kann es nur sein. Der 'verborgene Gerechte' aber ist die Kategorie, in der der Prophetismus den Begriff der Überlieferung entfaltete. Sie ist das lebendige Erbe

des Prophetismus in der Mitte des jüdischen Volkes. Der Mitmensch ist der verborgene Gerechte; er überliefert die namenlosen Dinge."

129. tag II:529. "Ethisch-differenten Handlungen."

6. JUDGMENT, VIOLENCE, AND REDEMPTION

1. An atmosphere of resignation with "nihilistische(n) Züge(n)" (Scholem's description of Benjamin) is best captured in freund:69–72. Scholem's own letters to Werner Kraft from this period also testify to his own immersion in their "grand chalet" at the edge of the abyss in small Swiss town during the First World War.

2. See the fourth section, on revolutionary nihilism, in chapter 2.

3. Scholem's descriptions of the evenings he spent the Benjamin's testifies to this. See freund:69–70, 76.

4. B I:125. "In meinem Leben habe ich noch keine so menschlich ergreifenden und wahren politischen Schriftstücke gesehen wie die Dokumente der maximalistischen [Bolschewistischen] Revolution."

5. tag II:79. "Das *erste* Offizielle Schriftstück der Weltgeschichte, das jeder anständige Mensch unterschreiben kann."

6. tag II:423–424. "Je deutlicher mir selber die Erkenntnis wurde, daß die Theokratie die einzig geordnete Gemeinschaftsform und also Staatsform der Menschen ist, desto schärfer ergeben sich die Kriterien für den Begriff als auch für den Wert der Revolutionen. Ich gelte als sehr bolschewistenfreundlich, und so außerordentlich unsinnig diese Meinung auch ist, ist schon irgendwo etwas daran: nämlich insoweit, als ich allein im Bolschewismus, d. h. also derjenigen Idee, die als das einzige Medium der Aufrichtung des messianischen Reiches die bedingungslose Diktatur der Armut ansieht, eine konsequente revolutionäre Intensität finde, was die heutige Historie angeht. Ich verneine dieses Heute überhaupt, in dem Moment aber, wo ich überhaupt ja dazu sage, scheint mir jedoch der Bolschewismus die unentrinnbare Konsequenz zu sein. Ich habe aber heute, da die Theokratie noch nicht errichtet ist, nicht den bolschewistischen, sondern (was man sehr mit Unrecht verwechselt) den anarchistischen Methodos. Der Anarchismus (nicht der Sozialismus) ist die, wenn man es so bezeichnen darf, einzig denkbare ideale Vorstufe des Gottesstaates, das heißt nicht, daß Anarchie als Zustand erstrebt werden soll, sondern daß die theokratische Einstellung gegen jede nicht ewige Gegenwart Anarchismus heißt. Ich bin also, wenn man so will, zu links für diese heutige Revolution."

7. tag II:556–558.

8. "Der Bolschewismus" (tag II:556–558). All citations are from these pages.

9. Take, for example, the prophecy of Isaiah 9 concerning the rewards of the suffering righteous.

10. It is interesting to note here how Scholem totally overlooks the very basis of Bolshevik teachings, which ultimately rests on a notion of progress.

11. Isaiah 10:27.

12. We see this idea reemerge in the "Kritik der Gewalt" (II:187). A discussion will follow in this section.

13. II:191–192. "Reine Mittel"; "Kultur des Herzens."

14. To suggest, however, that the "Critique of Violence" is a metaphysical work and not a political one is not to imply, first and foremost, that the essay simply fails to deliver concrete political goals and therefore resorts to the form of an abstract treatise.

15. Such an orientation to the problem is perhaps the most interesting aspect of the study by Derrida. See the expanded German edition of the lecture he first delivered in English in Derrida, *Gesetzeskraft*. (The English is "Force de loi/Force of law").

16. For this reason a German discussion of *Gewalt* is not automatically required to define the relationship between the ethical good and juridical law. The term *Recht* covers both the true and actual definition of what is good and, in this sense, Benjamin begins the discussion with categories no less determined by Hegel than other more general sources of jurisprudence.

17. II:180. Here the question turns to a negative determination of the natural and the need for it to be distinguished from a philosophy of justice.

18. Such a principle of Gewalt might be expressed as follows: Where there is energy, there is motion.

19. For an initial definition of positive and natural law, I have consulted the *Deutsches Staats-Wörterbuch,* where natural law is defined in contrast to positive law as "das Recht, welches durch die Vernunft erkannt und auf die menschliche Natur begründet wird, im Gegensatz zu dem Recht, welches von einem bestimmten Staate anerkannt und zur Geltung gebracht wird." *Deutsches Staats-Wörterbuch*, "Gegensätze innerhalb des Rechtsbegriffs."

20. ref 278 (modidied). "ein Naturprodukt, gleichsam ein Rohstoff, dessen Verwendung keiner Problematik unterliegt, es sei denn, daß man die Gewalt zu ungerechten Zwecken mißbrauche." II:180.

21. Benjamin's reference here is thought to be, however, to Spinoza's *Theologisch-Politischer Traktat,* chapter 16: "Über die Grundlagen des Staates, über das Natürliche und das bürgerliche Recht des einzelnen und über das Recht der höchsten Gewalten." See II:945.

22. He is referring, more precisely, to Social Darwinism. For a critique, see the introduction and first chapter of Kropotkin's *Mutual Aid.*

23. ref 278. "Gerechte Zwecke können durch berechtigte Mittel erreicht, berechtigte Mittel an gerechte Zwecke gewendet werden." II:180.

24. ref 287. "Im Gegensatz zum Recht, welches in der nach Ort und Zeit fixierten 'Entscheidung' eine metaphysische Kategorie anerkennt, durch die es Anspruch auf Kritik erhebt, trifft die Betrachtung des Polizeiinstituts auf nichts Wesenhaftes." II:189.

25. The anarchist flavor of this statement is not to be overlooked: "Wenn sie [die Polizei] nicht ohne jegliche Beziehung auf Rechtszwecke den Bürger als eine brutale Belästigung durch das von Verordnungen geregelte Leben begleitet oder ihn schlechtweg überwacht." II:189.

26. Benjamin cites here Erich Unger's *Politik und Metaphysik*. Yet with respect to both Unger and Sorel, Benjamin's own views appear to overlap only tangentially. Manfred Voigts's recent redaction of Unger's lectures (which Benjamin apparently attended) did not convince this author of a more profound connection. See Unger, *Von Expressionismus zum Mythos des Hebrärtums*. On Benjamin and Unger, see pp. xvi, 61–75.

27. ref 287. "Das 'Recht' der Polizei bezeichnet im Grunde den Punkt, an welchem der Staat, sei es aus Ohnmacht, sei es wegen der immanenten Zusammenhänge jeder Rechtsordnung, seine empirischen Zwecke, die er um jeden Preis zu erreichen wünscht, nicht mehr durch die Rechtsordnung sich garantieren kann." II:189.

28. ref 295 (modified). "Rechtsetzung ist Machtsetzung und insofern ein Akt von unmittelbarer Manifestation der Gewalt." II:198.

29. ref:296. "Unter dem Gesichtspunkt der Gewalt, welche das Recht allein garantieren kann, gibt es keine Gleichheit, sondern bestenfalls gleich große Gewalten." II:198.

30. Even contractual agreements are based on a potential Gewalt, says Benjamin. Law-forming Gewalt does not need to be present in every moment of a contract to prove that it is represented in it. It may appear as the origin of a contract, at the end, or merely as a potential, but it is always present. In the case that a contract is broken, there is a guarantee of the right of the application of Gewalt: the initiation and termination of contractual relationships are based on Gewalt or the threat thereof: "Wie der Ausgang, so verweist auch der Ursprung jeden Vertrages auf Gewalt" (II:190). Should a legal institution lose its precarious connection to Gewalt, it is in danger of collapsing. In the context of the uproar taking place in 1920–1921, the German parliament failed to understand the meaning of law-forming Gewalt, he writes. It is for this reason that they had no idea to which ends Gewalt is appropriate and therefore conclude every arrangement in compromise. II:191.

31. On the strike as a means of nonviolence, see Sharp, *The Politics of Non-Violent Action*.

32. ref 282. "Und in diesem Sinne bildet nach der Anschauung der Arbeiterschaft, welche der des Staates entgegengesetzt ist, das Streikrecht das Recht, Gewalt zur Durchsetzung gewisser Zwecke anzuwenden." II:184.

33. II:185. In addition to a kind of metaphysical analysis of the various forms of sanctioned and unsanctioned Gewalt, the empirical events of the day could have easily formed the impetus for a discussion of what is "historically recognized" Gewalt. II:181. From this perspective the discussion of the general strike, as well as the notion of the strike itself, cannot be separated from the series of general strikes that gripped Berlin in 1919 to 1920. From the general strikes of the SPD to those called by Independent Socialists and the Spartacus, to the general strike that "saved the republic" (Crook) from the Kapp Putsch, Berlin was overwhelmed by the idea of the general strike at this time. Even someone completely isolated from world

events (as Benjamin was) would have been forced to sit upright and take notice. On the history of the general strike in this period, see Crook, *The General Strike*, pp. 496–527; on the Kappists, see Ryder, *The German Revolution of 1918*, pp. 237–255.

34. ref 282. "Als Gewalt nämlich ist, wiewohl dies auf den ersten Blick paradox scheint, dennoch auch ein Verhalten, das in Ausübung eines Rechtes eingenommen wird, unter gewissen Bedingungen zu bezeichnen." II:184.

35. II:185. The arbitrary nature of thieving Gewalt and the legal conventions of war are based on the same technical contradiction as the right to strike.

36. ref 283. "Ursprünglichen und urbildlichen." II:186.

37. ref 283. "Naturzwecke gerichtete Gewalt [. . .] der Einzelperson." II:186.

38. These two forms of strike are contradictory. The political strike is a parliamentarian strike, formed out of political opposition. Rather than the violence of the revolutionary general strike, it is the political strike in the form of doctor's blockades and the strikes of other professional classes that has shown the greatest expression of unethical practice, where Gewalt turns to unscrupulous violence, says Benjamin. II:195.

39. ref 291. "Aufgabe der Vernichtung der Staatsgewalt." II:194.

40. ref: 292. "Gänzlich veränderte Arbeit, eine nicht staatlich erzwungene [. . .] ein Umsturz, den diese Art des Streikes nicht sowohl veranlaßt als vielmehr vollzieht. Daher denn auch die erste dieser Unternehmungen rechtsetzend, die zweite dagegen anarchistisch ist." II:194.

41. For a Nazi anthology of Sorel's anti-Semitic and anti-intellectual quotes, see Sorel, *Der Falsche Sieg*. Quite to the contrary, Benjamin even argues for Sorel's ethical integrity. He claims that Sorel was well aware of the violence to which the revolution would be susceptible: "Dieser tiefen, sittlichen und echt revolutionären Konzeption kann auch keine Erwägung gegenübertreten, die wegen seiner möglichen katastrophalen Folgen einen solchen Generalstreik als Gewalt brandmarken möchte" (II:195). Kambas has shown how Benjamin became more critical toward Sorel in the late 1930s. See Kambas, "Walter Benjamin liest Georges Sorel," pp. 267–268.

42. ref 292. "Nach dem Gesetz ihrer Mittel." II:195.

43. "Den tiefsten Sinn in der Unbestimmtheit der Rechtsdrohung wird erst die spätere Betrachtung der Sphäre des Schicksals, aus der sie stammt, erschließen. Ein wertvoller Hinweis auf sie liegt im Bereich der Strafen. Unter ihnen hat, seitdem die Geltung des positiven Rechts in Frage gezogen wurde, die Todesstrafe mehr als alles andere die Kritik herausgefordert." II:188.

44. ref: 286 (modified). "Ist nämlich Gewalt, schicksalhaft gekrönte Gewalt, dessen Ursprung, so liegt die Vermutung nicht fern, daß in der höchsten Gewalt, in der über Leben und Tod, wo sie in der Rechtsordnung auftritt, deren Ursprünge repräsentativ in das Bestehende hineinragen und in ihm sich furchtbar manifestieren." II:188.

45. ref 286. "Den Rechtsbruch zu strafen, sondern das neue Recht zu statuieren." Here the discussion returns to the notion of Gewalt as law forming at the

same time that it is law maintaining. The power of this new law is manifested in the law-forming/state-maintaining relationship between law and fate, which would otherwise appear to have little to do with one another. II:188.

46. See the section on the justice of prophecy in chapter 5.

47. ref 295. "Gerechtigkeit ist das Prinzip aller göttlichen Zwecksetzung, Macht das Prinzip aller mythischen Rechtsetzung." II:198.

48. ref 284. "Militarismus ist der Zwang zur allgemeinen Anwendung von Gewalt als Mittel zu Zwecken des Staates." II:186.

49. Several personal antics retold by Scholem helped to achieve this goal. For instance, staying up all night drinking coffee with Benjamin before the day of his medical examination (freund:27). Scholem's own performance of psychosis at the military barracks in Alleinstein (briefe I: 77–91, von berlin:108) and the collective plan, which they achieved, to move to Switzerland as "invalids," all to avoid the draft.

50. ref 284 (modified). "Kindischen Anarchismus [. . .] daß man keinerlei Zwang der Person gegenüber anerkennt, und erklärt 'Erlaubt ist was gefällt'"; "sittlich-historisch" (II:187). Benjamin's own categorical imperative can been seen here as a minor critique. If the integrity of another is guaranteed not to be used as a means, it does not exhaust the possibility of the use of the self or another to maintain a general principle. This may therefore revert the main clause of the categorical imperative to the justification of the reduction of the individual to a means. On this point, see Figal and Folkers, ed. *Zur Theorie der Gewalt und Gewaltlosigkeit*, pp. 9, 30–57.

51. Benjamin, "Notizen zu einer Arbeit über die Kategorie der Gerechtigkeit. tag I:401. See the second section of chapter 5.

52. II:187. "Handle so, daß Du die Menschheit sowohl in Deiner Person als in der Person eines jeden anderen jederzeit zugleich als Zweck, niemals bloß als Mittel brauchest."

53. II:187. "Darstellung und Erhaltung einer schicksalhaften Ordnung"; "gestaltlosen 'Freiheit'"; "höhere Ordnung der Freiheit."

54. In a letter to Bernd Kampffmeyer, which in turn was forwarded to the anarchist historian Max Nettlau, Benjamin writes that in a text he was working on at the time, concerning the "Abbau der Gewalt," "elimination of Gewalt," he seeks to take an anarchist's perspective into consideration. See GB II:100f.

55. ref: 288. "Bezeichnenderweise hat der Verfall der Parlamente von dem Ideal einer gewaltlosen Schlichtung politischer Konflikte vielleicht ebensoviele Geister abwendig gemacht, wie der Krieg ihm zugeführt hat. Den Pazifisten stehen die Bolschewisten und Syndikalisten gegenüber. Sie haben eine vernichtende und im ganzen treffende Kritik an den heutigen Parlamenten geübt." II:191.

56. The *Blätter für religiösen Sozialismus* (Berlin: 1920–1927) was a largely Protestant, social democratic journal edited by Carl Mennicke, with contributions by Paul Tillich and Martin Buber, among others. Mennicke, in discussion with Tillich on the use of violence and the Kapp putsch, asked the author of the text, a legal scholar by the name of Herbert Vorwerk, to prepare a juridical analysis of the right to violence. The article, "Das Recht zur Gewaltanwendung," appeared in the September 1920 edition of the journal (Jg. 1, Nr. 4). This incidentally makes the

date of April 1920 (which the editors of the *Gesammelte Schriften* gave to Benjamin's "Critique of Violence") rather improbable. For the comments of the editors, see Benjamin, *Gesammelte Schriften*, VI:691.

57. Benjamin, *Gesammelte Schriften*, VI:107. "Diese Anschauung, deren sachliche Unmöglichkeit dem Referenten so sehr ausgemacht scheint, daß er sich nicht einmal ihre logische Möglichkeit als eines eigentümlichen Standpunktes klar macht, sondern sie eine inkonsequent einseitige Anwendung des ethischen Anarchismus nennt, muß vertreten werden wo einerseits zwar (im Gegensatz zu A) kein prinzipieller Widerspruch zwischen Gewalt und Sittlichkeit, andrerseits aber (im Gegensatz zu C) ein prinzipieller Widerspruch zwischen Sittlichkeit und Staat (bezw. Recht) erblickt wird. Die Darlegung dieses Standpunkts gehört zu den Aufgaben meiner Moralphilosophie, in deren Zusammenhang der Terminus Anarchismus sehr wohl für eine Theorie gebraucht werden darf, welche das sittliche Recht nicht der Gewalt als solcher, sondern allein jeder menschlichen Institution, Gemeinschaft oder Individualität abspricht, welche sich ein Monopol auf sie zuspricht oder das Recht auf sie auch nur prinzipiell und allgemein in irgend einer Perspektive sich selbst einräumt, anstatt sie als eine Gabe der göttlichen Macht, als *Machtvollkommenheit* im einzelnen Falle zu verehren."

58. ref 289. "Gewaltlose Einigung findet sich überall, wo die Kultur des Herzens den Menschen reine Mittel der Übereinkunft an die Hand gegeben hat. Den rechtmäßigen und rechtswidrigen Mitteln aller Art, die doch samt und sonders Gewalt sind, dürfen nämlich als reine Mittel die gewaltlosen gegenübergestellt werden." II:191.

59. "'Was dir selber verhaßt ist, das füge auch deinem Nächsten nicht zu—darin ist die ganze Lehre Enthalten.'" See Ahad Haam, *Am Scheidewege*, p. 99.

60. b. Sabbat fol. 31b.

61. II:191. "Herzenshöflichkeit, Neigung, Friedensliebe, Vertrauen."

62. If it is not implicit in the notion of a nonthreatening Gewalt, it is certainly the case that even in utopian social relations between individuals one would never be blind to the Gewalt of distopic relations. Therefore, fear alone is enough to show an implicit Gewalt in an ideal society as well.

63. ref 289. "In der sachlichsten Beziehung menschlicher Konflikte auf Güter eröffnet sich das Gebiet der reinen Mittel." II:192.

64. ref 289. "Daß es eine in dem Grade gewaltlose Sphäre menschlicher Übereinkunft gibt, daß sie der Gewalt vollständig unzugänglich ist: die eigentliche Sphäre der 'Verständigung', die Sprache." II:192.

65. "Denn im Verbot des Betruges schränkt das Recht den Gebrauch völlig gewaltloser Mittel ein, weil diese reaktiv Gewalt erzeugen könnten." II:192.

66. ref 291. "friedlichen Umgang zwischen Privatpersonen." II:193.

67. ref 293(modified). "Da dennoch jede Vorstellung einer irgendwie denkbaren Lösung menschlicher Aufgaben, ganz zu geschweigen einer Erlösung aus dem Bannkreis aller bisherigen weltgeschichtlichen Daseinslagen, unter völliger und prinzipieller Ausschaltung jedweder Gewalt unvollziehbar bleibt, so

nötigt sich die Frage nach andern Arten der Gewalt auf, als alle Rechtstheorie ins Auge faßt." II:196.

68. "Schicksalsmäßiger Gewalt."

69. ref 293. "Unentscheidbarkeit aller Rechtsprobleme." II:196.

70. ref 294. "Entscheidet doch über Berechtigung von Mitteln und Gerechtigkeit von Zwecken niemals die Vernunft, sondern schicksalhafte Gewalt über jene, über diese aber Gott." II:196.

71. "Allgemeingültig."

72. ref 294. "Die mythische Gewalt in ihrer urbildlichen Form ist bloße Manifestation der Götter. Nicht Mittel ihrer Zwecke, kaum Manifestation ihres Willens, am ersten Manifestation ihres Daseins." II:197.

73. References to Greek myth under the context of the "orient" are to be found in several places in Benjamin's early writing. See, for example, the discussion of "Geist des Orients" in *Über das Mittelalter* (II:132) and the discussion in chapter 1.

74. ref 294. "Wie wenig solche göttliche Gewalt im antiken Sinne die rechterhaltende der Strafe war, zeigen die Heroensagen, in denen der Held, wie z. B. Prometheus, mit würdigem Mute das Schicksal herausfordert, wechselnden Glückes mit ihm kämpft und von der Sage nicht ohne Hoffnung gelassen wird, ein neues Recht dereinst den Menschen zu bringen." II:197.

75. ref 297 (modified). "Weit entfernt, eine reinere Sphäre zu eröffnen, zeigt die mythische Manifestation der unmittelbaren Gewalt sich im tiefsten mit aller Rechtgewalt identisch und macht die Ahnung von deren Problematik zur Gewißheit von der Verderblichkeit ihrer geschichtlichen Funktion, deren Vernichtung damit zur Aufgabe wird. Gerade diese Aufgabe legt in letzter Instanz noch einmal die Frage nach einer reinen unmittelbaren Gewalt vor, welche der mythischen Einhalt zu gebieten vermöchte. Wie in allen Bereichen dem Mythos Gott, so tritt der mythischen Gewalt die göttliche entgegen." II:199.

76. At this moment the mythical form of law enters into the picture as the only form of the symbolic divine that humanity will be able to encounter in the profane: "Denn nur die mythische, nicht die göttliche, wird sich als solche mit Gewißheit erkennen lassen, es sei denn in unvergleichlichen Wirkungen, weil die entsühnende Kraft der Gewalt für Menschen nicht zutage liegt. Vom neuem stehen der reinen göttlichen Gewalt alle ewigen Formen frei, die der Mythos mit dem Recht bastardierte" (II:203). Thus the mythic enters history as messianic means, opening up a new historical age within the already existing history. Gewalt, in the introduction of this age, can never be mythical Gewalt, never law-maintaining myth—the "die verwaltete Gewalt" (II:203)—but rather the "höchste Manifestation reiner Gewalt durch den Menschen" (II:202). From this Benjamin concludes that it is critical to decide where true "revolutionäre Gewalt" is possible (II:202) and when such violence can be applied in the introduction of the world to come.

77. II:199. "Ihr Eintritt ist im Sinne des Rechts nicht Zufall, sondern Schicksal."

78. ref 297. "Denn mit dem bloßen Leben hört die Herrschaft des Rechtes über den Lebendigen auf." II:200.

79. ref 297. "Die mythische Gewalt ist Blutgewalt über das bloße Leben um ihrer selbst, die göttliche reine Gewalt über alles Leben um des Lebendigen willen." II:200.

80. See Numbers 16:30–33 where Korah fails to heed the prophecy of Moses. See also II:946.

81. ref 297. "Ein tiefer Zusammenhang zwischen dem unblutigen und entsühnenden Charakter dieser Gewalt." II:199.

82. Benjamin's concept of *das bloße Leben* serves as the basis of Agamben's compelling study on the individual in relation to the power of the state. See his *Homo sacher*. His movement into the French thinkers, particularly Foucault, may however inadvertently lead away from the unique theological dimension of this idea.

83. ref 297. "Diese göttliche Gewalt bezeugt sich nicht durch die religiöse Überlieferung allein, vielmehr findet sie mindestens in einer geheiligten Manifestation sich auch im gegenwärtigen Leben vor." II:200.

84. ref 297(modified). "Daß Gott selber unmittelbar Erscheinungsformen in Wundern ausübt, sondern durch jene Momente des unblutigen, schlagenden, entsühnenden Vollzuges." II:200.

85. ref 297. "Endlich durch die Abwesenheit jeder Rechtsetzung." II:200.

86. See the first section in chapter 5.

87. "Heiligkeit des Lebens."

88. II:201. See also the section on prophetic justice in chapter 5.

89. ref 299. "Nochnichtsein des gerechten Menschen."

90. ref 299. "So heilig der Mensch ist (oder auch dasjenige Leben in ihm, welches identisch in Erdenleben, Tod und Fortleben liegt), so wenig sind es seine Zustände, so wenig ist es sein leibliches, durch Mitmenschen verletzliches Leben." II:201.

91. ref 299. "Ursprung des Dogmas von der Heiligkeit des Lebens"; "daß, was hier heilig gesprochen wird, dem alten mythischen Denken nach der gezeichnete Träger der Verschuldung ist: das bloße Leben." II:202.

92. ref 300. "Auf der Durchbrechung dieses Umlaufs im Banne der mythischen Rechtsformen, auf der Entsetzung des Rechts samt den Gewalten, auf die es angewiesen ist wie sie auf jenes, zuletzt also Staatsgewalt, begründet sich ein neues geschichtliches Zeitalter." II:202.

93. The link from the Last Judgment to eternal, continuous judgment can also be made by the attribute that God tallies, i.e., forms judgment on human action.

94. Scholem writes that both he and Benjamin were so confirmed in their belief in God that the subject of His existence never once came up in their discussions. freund:33. See also Scholem, "Interview with Irving Howe"; and jjc:35.

95. See II:197–200 and the discussion in "Violence and Myth" in this chapter.

96. II:154. "Mythische(r) Ursprung des Rechts." See also II:197.

97. "Schicksalslos"

98. Scholem here uses the term *Verwandelung*, calling on the meaning of the transformation of law to justice, which he interprets in Psalm 94:14–15 in the phrase "ki al tzedek yashuv mishpat."

99. "'Nur ein ganz klein wenig anders.'" Scholem again quotes Maimonides here without citing him.

100. II:175. "Dämonische Schicksal."

101. "Weltzeitalter"; "Katastrophale"; "des schicksalslosen Lebens dargestellt."

102. "Unmetaphorischen Gegenstand(es) des gerechten Lebens."

103. Scholem, *Von der mystischen Gestalt der Gottheit* (henceforth ges). This version is mildly edited, and I have made use of the original version where necessary. Citations from the English translation, *On the Mystical Shape of the Godhead,* will appear with the abbreviation mys.

104. tag II:359. "Die Thora spricht vom göttlichen Gerechten, die Prophetie vom verborgenen Gerechten und die Tradition begründet jenen Begriff des Gerechten, der beide umfaßt. Offenbarung und messianische Zeit sind in der mündlichen Lehre unzerreißbar verbunden."

105. ges:82/mys:88.

106. "Gerechtigkeit und ihre Träger"; "Gottes Gerechtigkeit."

107. "Die Lehre vom 'Gerechten,'" p. 237. I also found helpful Jacobs, "The Concept of Hasid."

108. "Religiösen Gesellschaft."

109. For an analysis of the treatment of the righteous and the pious as synonymous in late Kabbalah, see section 4 of ges:272. In a later "monopolization" of the term *chasid*, the movement of Israel Baal Shem was to loosen the distinction further with the notion of a "chassidischen Zaddik." See ges:274–275.

110. ges:84. "Moralische und religiöse Macht."

111. Closer to God in the sense of Psalms 73:28: "The nearness of God is my good."

112. "Tugendhaft kann nur Erfüllung des Geforderten, gerecht nur Gewährleistung des Existenten (durch Forderungen *vielleicht nicht* mehr zu bestimmenden, dennoch natürlich nicht eines beliebigen) sein." Benjamin, "Notizen zu einer Arbeit über die Kategorie der Gerechtigkeit," tag I:401–402.

113. mys:90. "Der Fromme tut nicht das Verlangte und Geforderte, sondern das Ungeforderte, und auch wo er einer Forderung des Gesetzes nachzukommen sucht, tut er es mit solchem Radikalismus des Überschwangs und der Subtilität, daß sich ihm in der Vollziehung des nüchtern Gebotenen eine ganze Welt offenbart, für die ein Leben gerade ausreichen würde, ein Gebot richtig zu erfüllen." ges:85. The published English version, drawing from the Hebrew manuscript, replaces the word *subtlety* with *exaggeration.*

114. mys:90. "Er ist der radikale Jude, der, indem er seiner Bestimmung zu folgen sucht, ins Extrem geht. Dieser Extremismus, der vom Wesen des Frommen ebenso unabtrennbar ist, wie er dem Typus des Gerechten ganz fremd ist, kann die verschiedensten Formen annehmen. [. . .] Er verlangt von anderen nichts und von sich alles, und es ist eben diese Radikalität, die ihn von der ausgeglichenen Figur des Gerechten abhebt, der einem jeden gibt, was ihm zukommt. In diesem nie im Ausgewogenen bleibenden Extremismus lebt ein anarchisches Element." ges:85.

115. Scholem articulates a neutralization thesis here such that Chasidism was to overtake the euphoric dimensions of Sabbatian messianism: "In der Geschichte der späteren Kabbala treten immer wieder, besonders im Verfolg der großen messianischen Erschütterung von 1666, Gruppen von *Chassidim* auf, die sich solchem natürlichen Enthusiasmus und Extremismus verschrieben und von der radikalen Verfolgung solchen Weges auch charismatische Gaben erhofft haben dürften." ges:113.

116. mys:90. "Etwas Absurdes und oft auch im bürgerlichen Sinn Anstößiges an sich." ges:86.

117. The radical nature of the chasid led Scholem to formulate a derivative of the neutralization thesis: radicalism and the theory of paradox, not to speak of the "Forderung .. 'gefährlich zu leben,' die der ursprünglichen Gestalt des *Zaddik* im Chassidismus ihren hervorstechendsten Zug liefert," came to logical fruition in Sabbatianism. See ges:119–121.

118. mys:92. "Eliminierung des Elements des Gerichts"; "Der Gerechte ist nicht mehr der gerechte Richter, und auch Gott als Richter stellt in der Welt der Kabbala einen ganz anderen Aspekt der Gottheit dar denn Gott als der Gerechte. Das Recht und die Gerechtigkeit, oder Gott als Träger dieser Gerechtigkeit, sind zwei verschiedene Seiten an Gott. Das Neue in dieser Auffasung tritt gerade da hervor, wo nicht von irdischen Gerechten, sondern von Gerechten als einem Aspekt der Gottheit die Rede ist, als einem Symbol eines Status in Gott." ges:87. The italicized section was not retained in the Hebrew edition. This is therefore Scholem's original meaning.

119. "*Din* und *Mischpat* sind von *Zaddik* und *Zedek* geschieden." Scholem's relationship to these categories continues to remain somewhat ambiguous in the later years. While the first two German versions bear this sentence, the Hebrew version attributes the distinction to "Kabbalistic symbolism." What remains unsettled in the early political theology is here rediscovered in the Kabbalah. See mys:284 n.13.

120. Psalms 73:28.

121. ges:97. "Der Gerechte, das ist der Hauptaspekt seiner Betrachtungen, ist der Herr des Lebendigen, wenn er als mystisches Symbol verstanden wird." Psalms 42:3: "My soul thirst for God, for the living God."

122. mys:105. "'Denn darum werden die Gerechten so genannt, weil sie alle inneren Dinge an ihren Ort im Inneren und alles Äußere an seinen Ort im Äußeren stellen, und nichts tritt aus den ihm gesetzten Grenzen, und darum heißen sie Gerechte.' Hier haben wir die erste wichtige neue Bestimmung des Sinnes der Idealfigur des Gerechten, wie sie auch die Ethik der Kabbala beherrscht. Der Gerechte stellt alles in der Welt an die ihm zukommende Stelle. Die Einfachheit dieser Definition sollte uns nicht über die geradezu messianische Implikation und die utopische Sprengkraft täuschen, die ihr innewohnt. Denn eine Welt, in der alles an seinem richtigen Orte steht, wäre im Sinne des Judentums eine erlöste Welt. Die Dialektik des Gerechten mündet in die des Messianischen ein." ges:99–100.

123. Scholem also presents Bachya ben Asher, who claimed that the completely righteous embody within themselves all the goodness of the world in their "nearness" to God. Psalms 73:28. At the same time, he expects of the righteous person a perfect self-control in the face of the ways of evil. ges:111.

124. Should Gikatilla have much to do with this or with the dialectic as Scholem claims is a question that deserves attention in its own right. It lies however beyond the framework of this study.

125. "Die Ruhe des Organischen in seiner Bewegung."

126. The sentence actually reads "Das Nervensystem hingegen ist die unmittelbare Ruhe des Organischen in seiner Bewegung." G. W. F. Hegel, *Phänomenologie des Geistes* (Berlin, 1832), p. 245. See tag I:389.

127. See Benjamin in tag I:401–402.

128. mys:110. "Das Wesen des Gerechten besteht im Sinne dieser Symbolik des Lebendigen und Leben erhaltenden also in der Herstellung der Harmonie oder des Friedens, Begriffen, die in dem hebräischen Wort *Schalom* ja ineinanderfließen. Bedeutet doch *Schalom*, genau verstanden, stets einen Zustand der Vollständigkeit oder Integrität, in dem sich etwas befindet, und erst von da aus Friede." ges:105.

129. The terms *jung Juden* could also be an allusion to the young anarchist-Zionist group to which Scholem belonged, the Jung Juda.

130. tag I:115–116. "Ich will auch die Namen nicht ändern, die mir als natürliche Folgen meiner Beschäftigung über die Lippen kamen, ungerufen und doch willkommen, [. . .] Verkünder der Erlösung." "Wer von uns jungen Juden hat wohl nicht den gleichen Königstraum gehabt und sich als Jesus gesehen und Messias der Bedrückten. [. . .] Ich habe den Erlösertraum so recht gedacht als möglich."

131. tag I:120–121. "Der Weg der Einfältigen ist der Weg der Erlösung. Und der Träumer—den sein Name schon als den Erwarteten kennzeichnete: Scholem, der Vollkommene—rüstete sich für sein Werk und begann gewaltig zu schmieden an den Waffen des Wissens."

132. Four months after these initial thoughts, and a slight bout with suicidal ideation, he realizes that he has indeed not been chosen for this task. See chapter 2 on Scholem's theological politics and tag I:158 for the discussion of suicide. Elsewhere, in an unpublished fragment, he writes: "Die zionistische Verzweiflung führt *niemals* zum Selbstmord, der ihren Ordnungen entgegengesetzt ist." "Die zionistische Verzweiflung" June 19, 1920, Scholem arc. 40 1599/277.47, last line. Unless an addressee for this text can be found, its tone of ironclad conviction appears to be addressed to himself.

133. mys:129. "'Kinder der künftigen Welt.'"

134. mys:129. "Wir sind Possenreißer. Ist jemand traurig, so suchen wir ihn aufzuheitern, und sehen wir Leute streiten, so suchen wir Frieden zwischen ihnen zu stiften." ges:123.

135. mys:129. "Sie sitzen nicht zu Haus und denken an ihr eigenes Heil. Sie arbeiten auf dem Marktplatz, wie er selbst zu tun liebte. Ihre Kraft zur Gottesgemeinschaft, wie er es sieht, bewährt sich in der Aufgabe, die Materie zu durchdringen und sie zum Geistigen zu erheben." ges:123.

136. This description of the just in the eyes of the Baal Shem is perhaps the best explanation that I have encountered as to why the Marx brothers should probably be counted among the hidden righteous.

137. mys:129. "Der Gerechte betritt die soziale Sphäre ursprünglich, um sie zu vergeistigen, um das aktive Leben auf seine kontemplativen Wurzeln zurück-zuführen. Während er dies tut, wird er selbst verwandelt. Der wahre Freund Gottes wird zum wahren Freund der Menschen, und unmerklich verschiebt sich der Akzent." ges:124.

138. ges:125/mys:131.

139. mys:139. "Die chassidischen Autoren haben sehr wohl verstanden, daß die Beziehung des Gerechten zu seinen Mitmenschen eine eigene Dialektik hat. [. . .] Indem er seine Mitmenschen zu erheben sucht, wird er selbst erhoben, und je mehr er seine Funktion als das Zentrum der Gemeinde erfüllt, desto mehr wächst seine eigene Statur." ges:133–134.

140. ges:132. "Konstruktiven Sinn"; "Denn es handelt sich nun nicht mehr um Verrat, Abfall und dämonische Verstrickung ins Böse hinein, sondern um die Erfül-lung einer für den Bestand der Gesellschaft selber wesentlichen Aufgabe." mys:138.

BIBLIOGRAPHY

Adorno, Theodor W. "Charakteristik Walter Benjamins." In *Walter Benjamin, Sprache und Geschichte*. Leipzig: Reclam, 1992.

———— *Über Walter Benjamin*. Frankfurt: Suhrkamp, 1992.

Agamben, Giorgio. *Homo sacer: il potere sovrano e la nuda vita*. Torino: Einaudi, 1995.

———— "Lingua e storia. Categorie linguistiche e categorie storiche nel pensiero di Benjamin" In *Walter Benjamin. Tempo, storia, linguagio*, pp. 65–82. Roma: Editori Riuniti, 1983.

———— "Walter Benjamin und das Dämonische. Glück und Geschichtliche Erlösung in Denken Benjamins." In Uwe Steiner, ed., *Walter Benjamin. 1892–1940, zum 100. Geburtstag*. New York: Peter Lang, 1992.

Agudas Jisroel. *Berichte und Materialen*. Frankfurt: Büro der Agudas Jisroel, 1912.

Ahad Haam. *Am Scheidewege*. 2 vols. Berlin: Jüdischer Verlag, 1901.

Alter, Robert. *Necessary Angels: Tradition and Modernity in Kafka, Benjamin, and Scholem*. Cambridge: Harvard University Press, 1991.

Baader, Franz von. *Vorlesung über eine künftige Theorie des Opfers oder des Kultus*. Münster: 1836.

Bakunin, Michail. *Oevres complètes de Bakounine*. Vol. 1. Paris: Éditions Champ Libre, 1975.

———— *Staatlichkeit und Anarchie*. Frankfurt: Ullstein, 1972.

Bar-Kochba Kreis. *Vom Judentum*. Prague, 1913.

Benjamin, Andrew, ed. *The Problem of Modernity: Adorno and Benjamin*. London: Routledge, 1989.

Benjamin, Andrew and Peter Osborne, eds., *Walter Benjamin's Philosophy: Destruction and Experience*. London: Routledge, 1994.

Benjamin, Walter. *Briefe*. Ed. Gershom Scholem and Theodor W. Adorno. 2 vols. Frankfurt: Suhrkamp, 1978.

——— *Gesammelte Briefe*. Ed. Christoph Gödde and Henri Lonitz. Vols. 1–2. Frankfurt: Suhrkamp, 1995–1997.

——— *Gesammelte Schriften*. Ed. Rolf Tiedemann and Hermann Schweppenhäuser. 7 vols. Frankfurt: Suhrkamp, 1995.

——— *Reflections*. New York: Schoken, 1976

——— *Selected Writings*. Vol. 1. Cambridge: Belknap, 1996.

——— *Sprache und Geschichte. Philosophische Essays*. Stuttgart: Reclam, 1992.

Benjamin, Walter and Gershom Scholem. *Briefwechsel: 1933–1940*. Frankfurt: Suhrkamp, 1985.

Berman, Marshall. *The Experience of Modernity: All That Is Solid Melts Into Air*. New York: Simon and Schuster, 1982.

Biale, David. *Gershom Scholem: Kabbalah and Counter-History*. Cambridge: Harvard University Press, 1979.

——— "Theology, Language, and History." In H. Bloom, ed., *Gershom Scholem*, pp. 47–76. New York: Chelsea House, 1987.

Bialik, Chaim Nachman. *Essays*. Berlin: Jüdischer Verlag, 1925.

Blau, Ludwig. *Das altjüdische Zauberwesen*. Budapest, 1898.

Bloch, Ernst. *Geist der Utopie*. 1st ed. Faksimile der Ausgabe von 1918. Frankfurt: Suhrkamp, 1971.

——— *Gesammelte Schriften: Geist der Utopie*. 2d ed. Vol. 2. Frankfurt: Suhrkamp, 1985.

Blumeburg, Hans. *Matthäuspassion*. Frankfurt: Suhrkamp, 1988.

Böhler, Dietrich. "Walter Benjamin in seinen Briefen." *Neue Rundschau* 79, no. 4 (1967): 664–673.

Böhme, Jakob. *Sämtliche Schriften: "Mysterium Magnum."* Vol. 7. Stuttgart: F. Frommanns, 1955–1961.

Bolz, Norbert and Richard Faber, ed. *Antike und Moderne: Zu Walter Benjamins Passagens*. Würzburg: Königshausen and Neumann, 1986.

Bookchin, Murray. *The Spanish Anarchists*. New York: Harper Colophon, 1979.

Bosco, N. "La nozione di 'Giustizia' nell'antico testamento." *Filosofia* 17, no. 4 (October 1966): 475–495.

Bröcker, Michael. *Die Grundlosigkeit der Wahrheit. Zum Verhältnis von Sprache, Geschichte und Theologie bei Walter Benjamin*. Würzburg: Könighausen und Neumann, 1993.

Brodersen, Momme. *Spinne im eigenen Netz*. Bühl-Moos: Elster, 1990.

Buber, Martin. *Daniel. Gesprache von der Verwirklichung*. Leipzig: Insel-Verlag, 1913.

——— *Drei Reden über das Judentum*. Frankfurt: Rütten and Loening, 1911.

——— *Der heilige Weg*. Frankfurt: Rütten and Loening, 1920.

Buck-Morss, Susan. *The Dialectics of Seeing: Walter Benjamin and the Arcades Project*. Cambridge: MIT Press, 1989.

———— *The Origins of Negative Dialectics.* New York: Free Press, 1977.

Bullock, Marcus. *Romanticism and Marxism: The Philosophical Development of Literary Theory and Literary History in Walter Benjamin and Friedrich Schlegel.* New York: Peter Lang, 1987.

Cohen, Hermann. *Jüdische Schriften.* Vols. 1–3. Berlin: C. A. Schwetschke, 1924.

———— *Kants Theorie der Erfahrung.* Berlin: Ferd. Dummler, 1871.

———— *Religion der Vernunft aus den Quellen des Judentums: Eine jüdische Religionsphilosophie.* Wiesbaden: Fourier, 1995 [1928].

Cohen, M. S. *The Shiur Qomah: Liturgy and Theurgy in Pre-Kabbalistic Jewish Mysticism.* Atlanta: Scholars, 1983.

Cohn, Norman, *The Pursuit of the Millennium.* Oxford: Oxford University Press, 1970.

Consigli, Paolo. "Ricomporre l'infranto. Walter Benjamin e il messianiesimo ebraico." *Aut aut,* no. 211–212 (1986): 151–174.

Cox, D. "Sedaqa and Mispat: The Concept of Righteousness in Later Wisdom." *Studii Biblici Franciscani* 27 (Jerusalem 1977): 33–50

Crook, Wilfrid Harris. *The General Strike.* Chapel Hill: University of North Carolina Press, 1931.

Dan, Joseph. *Ancient Jewish Mysticism.* Tel Aviv: Gefen, 1990.

———— *Gershom Scholem and the Mystical Dimension of Jewish History.* New York: New York University Press, 1986.

———— "Gershom Scholem: Between History and Historiosophy." In Joseph Dan, ed., *Binah: Studies in Jewish Thought,* pp. 219–249. Vol. 2. New York: Praeger, 1989.

———— *Jewish Mysticism and Jewish Ethics.* New Jersey: Jason Aronson, 1996.

———— "Jewish Studies After Gershom Scholem." *EJ Yearbook* (1985):138–145.

———— "The Language of the Mystics in Medieval Germany." In Karl Grözinger and Joseph Dan, eds., *Mysticism, Magic, and Kabbalah in Askenazi Judaism.* Berlin: Walter de Gruyter, 1995.

———— "The Name of God, the Name of the Rose, and the Concept of Language in Jewish Mysticism." In *Medieval Encounters,* no. 3 (1996): 228–248.

———— *The Sacred Cherub Circle.* Tübigen: Mohr Siebeck, 1999.

Dan, Joseph, ed., *The Early Kabbalah.* New York: Paulist, 1987.

Derrida, Jacques. "Force de loi. Le 'fondement mystique de l'autorité'/Force of Law: The Mystical Foundation of Authority." *Cardozo Law Review* 11 (1990): 919–1045.

———— *Gesetzekraft: Der "mystische Grund der Autorität."* Frankfurt: Suhrkamp, 1996.

DeLuca, Pina. "Esperienza mistica e città. Walter Benjamin e Gershom Scholem." *Filosofia e Teologia,* no. 3 (1988): 177–186.

De Man, Paul. *The Resistance to Theory.* Minneapolis: University of Minneapolis, 1986.

Deutsches Staats-Wörterbuch: Gegensätze innerhalb des Rechtsbegriffs. Vol. 8. Stuttgart and Leipzig, 1864.

Dornseiff, Franz. *Das Alphabet in Mystik und Magie.* Leipzig: B. G. Teubner, 1925.

Düttmann, Alexander García. "Tradition and Destruction. Benjamin's Politics of Language." In Andrew Benjamin and Peter Osborne, eds., *Walter Benjamin's Philosophy: Destruction and Experience,* pp. 155–182. London: Routledge, 1994.

Eagleton, Terry. *The Ideology of the Aesthetic.* Oxford: Blackwell, 1990.

Eliasberg, Alexander. *Jüdisches Theater.* München: Müller, 1919.

Erlich, Bruce. "The Aesthetic of True Naming: On the Judaic Tradition of Wittgenstein, Lukács, and Walter Benjamin." In R. Haller, ed., *Ästhetik. Akten des 8. internationalen Wittgenstein-Symposiums,* pp. 203–207. Part 1. Wien: 1984.

Fadini, Ubaldo. "Esperienze della modernità: C. Schmitt e Walter Benjmain." *La Politica,* no. 3–4 (1985): 43–58.

———— "Tra nature e storia. A proposito del fragmento 'teologico-politico' di Walter Benjamin." *Paradigmi* 1 (1983): 161–175.

Fähnders, Walter. *Anarchismus und Literatur. Ein vergessenes Kapitel deutscher Literaturgeschichte zwischen 1890 und 1910.* Stuttgart: J. B. Metzler, 1987.

Fenvis, Peter. "The Genesis of Judgement." In David S. Ferris, ed., *Walter Benjamin: Theoretical Questions.* Stanford: Stanford University Press, 1996.

Fiekau, Wolfgang. "Loss of Experience and Experience of Loss: Remarks on the Problem of the Lost Revolution in the Work of Benjamin and His Fellow Combatants." *New German Critique,* no. 39 (1986): 169–187.

Figal, Günter. "Vom Sinn der Geschichte. Zur Erörterung der politischen Theologie bei Carl Schmitt und Walter Benjamin." In E. Angehrn, H. Fink-Eitel, eds., *Dialektischer Negativismus. Michael Theunissen zum 60. Geburtstag,* pp. 252–269. Frankfurt: Suhrkamp, 1992.

Figal, Günter and H. Folkers, eds. *Zur Theorie der Gewalt und Gewaltlosigkeit bei Walter Benjamin.* Heidelberg: Fest, 1979.

Fiorato, Pierfrancesco "Unendliche Aufgabe und System der Wahrheit. Die Auseinandersetzung des jungen Walter Benjamin mit der Philosophie Hermann Cohens." In Reinhard Brandt and Franz Orlik, ed., *Philosophisches Denken — Politisches Wirken. Hermann-Cohen-Kolloquium* 1992, pp. 163–178. Hildesheim: Georg Olms, 1993.

Fischer, Max. *Heinrich Heine: Der deutsche Jude.*Stuttgart: J. G. Cotta, 1916.

Fuchs, Gotthard and Hans Hermann Henriz, ed. *Zeitgewinn. Messianisches Denken nach Franz Rosenzweig.* Frankfurt: Josef Kneckt, 1987.

Fuld, Werner. *Walter Benjamin. Zwischen den Stühlen. Eine Biographie.* München: Hanser, 1979.

Garber, Klaus. *Rezeption und Rettung. Drei Studien zu Walter Benjamin.* Tübingen: Niemeyer, 1987.

———— *Zum Bilde Walter Benjamins. Studien—Porträts—Kritiken.* München: W. Fink, 1992.

Garetto, Andrea, *Mito e verità nell'opera di Walter Benjamin dagli scritti giovanili a Ursprung des deutschen Trauerspiels.* Torino: Università degli studi di Torino, Facoltà di Lettere e Filosofia, 1997.

Goethe, Johann Wolfgang. *Die Wahlverwandtschaften.* Mainz: Mainzer Presse, 1939.

Goldschmidt, Lazarus. *Sepher Jesirah. Das Buch der Schöpfung.* Darmstadt: Wissenschaft.

Greblo, Edoardo. "Eternità e storia. Tragedia, lingua e redenzione in Franz Rosenzweig e Walter Benjamin." *Filosofia politica* 3, (1989): 117–135.

Habermas, Jürgen. *Philosophical-Political Profiles.* Cambridge: MIT Press, 1983.

——— *Der philosophische Diskurs der Moderne. Zwölf Vorlesungen.* Frankfurt: Suhrkamp, 1985.

Hamacher, Werner. "Affirmative, Strike: Benjamin's 'Critique of Violence.'" In Andrew Benjamin and Peter Osborne, eds., *Walter Benjamin's Philosophy: Destruction and Experience*, pp. 155–182. London: Routledge, 1994.

Hamann, Johann Georg. *Schriften.* Roth ed. Berlin, 1821.

Hamburger, Michael. *A Proliferation of Prophets: Essays on German Writers from Nietzsche to Brecht.* Manchester: Carcanet, 1983.

Handelman, Susan A. *Fragments of Redemption: Jewish Thought and Literary Theory in Benjamin, Scholem, and Levinas.* Bloomington: Indiana University Press, 1991.

Haney, Vera. "Fortschrittsdenken oder Erlöserglaube. Zur Aktualität der geschichtspolitischen Auffassungen Walter Benjamins." *Wissenschaftliche Zeitschrift der Universität Jena* 38 (1989): 801–04.

Hartung, Günter. "Walter Benjamins Antikriegsschriften" *Weimarer Beiträge* 32 (1986): 404–419.

Hering, Christoph. "Messianic time and Materialist progress." *Journal of the British Society for Phenomenology* 16 (1985): 146–166.

Hillach, Ansgar. "Man muß die Aura feiern, wenn sie fällt. Überlegungen zu Walter Benjamins anarchistischem Konservatismus." In Richard Faber, ed., *Konservatismus in Geschichte und Gegenwart*, pp. 167–182. Würzburg: Königshausen and Neumann, 1991.

Hirsch, Samson Raphael. *Neunzehn Briefe über Judentum.* Frankfurt: Kauffmann, 1911.

Hirsch, Samson Raphael, ed. and trans. *Der Pentateuch: Die Genesis.* Part 1. Frankfurt: Kauffmann, 1911.

Hortain, Ulrich. "Zeit und Geschichte bei Franz Rosenzweig und Walter Benjamin." In W. Schmied-Kowarzik, ed., *Der Philosoph Franz Rosenzweig (1886–1929). Internationaler Kongreß*, pp. 815–827. Kassel, 1986; Freiburg: Alber, 1988.

Idel, Moshe. *A. Abulafia, G. Scholem, and W. Benjamin on Language.* In Jens Mattern, ed., *Judisches Denken in einer Welt ohne Gott. Festschrift für Stephane Moses.* Berlin: b Vorwerk 8, 2000.

——— *Language, Torah, and Hermeneutics in Abraham Abulafia.* Albany: State University of New York Press, 1989.

——— "Reification of Language in Jewish Mysticism." In Steven T. Katz, ed., *Mysticism and Language.* Oxford: Oxford University Press, 1992.

Jacobs, L. "The Concept of Hasid in the Biblical and Rabbinic Literatures." *Journal of Jewish Studies* 9, no. 3–4 (1957): 143–154.

Janowitz, Naomi. *The Poetics of Ascent: Theories of Language in a Rabbinic Ascent Text.* Albany: State University of New York Press, 1989.

Jay, Martin. *The Dialectical Imagination.* Berkeley: University of California Press, 1996.

Jay, Martin. *Permanent Exiles: Essays on the Intellectual Migration from Germany to America.* New York: Columbia University Press, 1986.

Jennings, Michael. W. *Dialectical Images: Walter Benjamin's Theory of Literary Criticism.* Ithaca: Cornell University Press, 1987.

The Jerusalem Bible. [Hebrew-English] Jerusalem: Koren, 1992.

Jerzewski, Roland. *Zwischen anarchistischer Fronde und revolutionärer Disziplin. Zum Engagement-Begriff bei Walter Benjamin und Paul Nizan.* Stuttgart: Verlag für Wissen und Forschung, 1991.

Johnson, B. "Mispat." *Theologisches Wörterbuch zum Alten Testament,* pp. 93–107. Vol. 5. Berlin,1986.

Jüdisches Lexicon. "Rect und Gerechtigkeit." Vol. 4/1. Berlin, 1930.

Kafka, Gustav. *Zur Kritik der politischen Theologie.* Paderborn: Schönigh, 1973.

Kainz, Howard. *Democracy and the "Kingom of God."* Dordrecht: Kluwer, 1993.

Kambas, Chryssolula. "Walter Benjamin liest Georges Sorel: 'Reflexions sur la violence.'" In Michael Opitz and Erbmut Wizisla, ed., *'Aber ein Strum weht vom Paradiese her' Texte zu Walter Benjamin,* pp. 250–269. Leipzig: Reclam, 1992.

Kather, Regine. *"Über Sprache überhaupt und über die Sprache des Menschen'. Die Sprachphilosophie Walter Benjamins."* Frankfurt: Peter Lang, 1989.

Katz, Jacob. *Messianismus und Zionismus: Zur jüdischen Sozialgeschichte,* Frankfurt: Jüdischer Verlag, 1993.

Katz, Steven, ed. *Mysticism and Language.* Oxford: Oxford University Press, 1992.

Keller, Ernst. *Der junge Lukács. Antibürger und wesentliches Leben. Literatur- und Kulturkritik 1902–1915.* Frankfurt: Sendler, 1984.

Kierkegaard, Søren. *Gesammelte Werke: Der Begriff Angst.* Vol. 11/12. Düsseldorf: Diederichs, 1965.

Kittsteiner, Heinz Dieter. "Walter Benjamins Historismus." In Norbert Bolz and Bernd Witte, eds., *Passagen. Walter Benjamins Urgeschichte des 19. Jahrhunderts,* pp. 163–197. München: Fink, 1984.

Konitzer, Werner. *Sprachkrise und Verbildlichung.* Würzburg: Königshausen und Neumann, 1995.

Kraft, Werner. *Eines schönen Tages.* Marbach: Schillerges, 1996.

——— *Erlesenes im Gesicht.* Bonn: Heusch, 1985.

——— *Kleinigkeiten.* Bonn: Heusch, 1985.

Kropotkin, Peter. *Mutual Aid: A Factor of Evolution.* Montreal: Black Rose, 1992.

Landauer, Gustav. *Die Revolution.* Berlin: Karin Kramer, 1977.

Levi, I. "Sefer Zerubabbel." *Revue des études juives* 68 (1915): 129–160.

Liebes, Yehuda. *Studies in Jewish Myth and Jewish Messianism.* Albany: State University of New York Press, 1993.

Lipiner, Elias. *Ideologie fun Yidishn Alef-Beis.* [Yiddish] Buenos Aires: YIVO, 1967.

Löwy, Michael. "L'anarchisme messianique de Walter Benjamin." *Les Temps Modernes,* no. 447 (1983): 772–794.

——— "Benjamins Marxismus." *Das Argument* 34 (1992): 557–562.

——— "Esoterica—Metaphisica: les papiers inédits du jeune Gershom Scholem."
Unpublished ms.
——— "Franz Rosenzweig et Walter Benjamin. Messianisme et révolution."
Traces, no. 6 (1983): 94–97.
——— *On Changing the World: Essays in Political Philosophy from Karl Marx to
Walter Benjamin*. New Jersey: Atlantic Highlands, 1992.
——— *Redemption and Utopia: Jewish Libertarian Thought in Central Europe*.
London: Athlone, 1992.
Luther, Andreas. "Variationen über die Endzeit. Bloch contra Benjamin." *Bloch-
Almanach* 4 (1984): 57–73.
Maccoby, Hyam, ed. *Judaism on Trial: Jewish-Christian Disputations in the Middle
Ages,* London: Associated University Presses, 1982.
Maimonides, Moses. *The Guide of the Perplexed*. Trans. Shlomo Pines. Chicago:
University of Chicago, 1963.
Markener, Reinhard and Thomas Weber, eds. *Literatur über Walter Benjamin:
Kommentierte Bibliographie 1983–1992*. Hamburg: Argument, 1993.
Marmorstein, A. *The Old Rabbinic Doctrine of God*. 2 vols. Oxford: Oxford Uni-
versity Press, 1927.
Masuzawa, Tomoko. "Tracing the Figure of Redemption: Walter Benjamin's Phys-
iognomy of Modernity." *MLN* 100 (1985): 514–536.
Mattenklott, Gert. "Mythologie Messianismus Macht." In E. Goodman-Thau and
W. Schmied-Konarzik, eds., *Messianismus. Zwischen Mythos und Macht*. Berlin:
Akademie, 1994.
Meier, Heinrich. *Carl Schmitt, Leo Strauss und das Begriff des Politischen*. Stuttgart:
Metzler, 1988.
——— *Die Lehre Carl Schmitts*. Stuttgart: Metzler, 1994.
Menke, Bettine. *Sprachfiguren. Name, Allegorie, Bild nach Benjamin,* München:
Fink, 1991.
Mendes-Flohr, Paul. *Divided Passions*. Detroit: Wayne State University Press, 1991.
Mendes-Flohr, Paul, ed. *Gershom Scholem. The Man and His Work*. Albany: State
University of New York Press, 1994.
——— *The Philosophy of Franz Rosenzweig*. Hanover: University Press of New
England Press, 1988.
Menninghaus, Winfried. "Das Ausdruckslose" In Uwe Steiner, ed., *Walter Ben-
jamin. 1882–1940*, pp. 33–76. Berlin: Peter Lang, 1992.
——— *Walter Benjamins Theorie der Sprachmagie*. Frankfurt: Suhrkamp, 1980.
Mitsuki, Michio. "Nihon ni okeru Walter Benjamin. Honyaku to Kenkyûbunken."
[Walter Benjamin in Japan: Translations and reseach] In *Doitsu bungaku*, no.
88 (1992): 194–231.
Molitor, Franz-Joseph. *Philosophie der Geschichte oder über die Tradition*. 4 vols.
Vol. 1. Münster, 1827–1857; Frankfurt 1827. Vol. 1, 2d ed., 1857.
Mosès, Stéphane. "Benjamin's Metaphors of Origin." In Timothy Bahti and Sibley
Fries, ed., *Jewish Writers, German Literature*. Ann Arbor: University of Michi-
gan Press, 1995.

—— Der Engel der Geschichte: Franz Rosenzweig, Walter Benjamin, Gershom Scholem. Frankfurt: Jüdischer Verlag, 1994.

—— "The Theological-Political Model of History in the Thought of Walter Benjamin." History and Memory, no. 2 (1989): 5–33.

—— "Walter Benjamin and Franz Rosenzweig." In Gary Smith, ed., Walter Benjmain: Philosophy, History, Aesthetics, pp. 228–246. Chicago: University of Chicago Press, 1989.

Müller, Maler Friedrich. Adams erstes Erwachen und erste seelige Nächte. Mannheim, 1779.

Münster, Arno. Utopie, Messianismus und Apokalypse in Frühwerk von Ernst Bloch. Frankfurt: Suhrkamp, 1982.

Nettlau, Max. Geschichte der Anarchie. 4 vols. Vaduz: Topos, 1981.

—— Michael Bakunin: eine biographische Skizze, mit Auszügen aus seinen Schriften und Nachwort von Gustav Landauer. Berlin: Verlag von Paul Pawlowitsch, 1901.

Neusner, Jacob. Genesis Rabbah: The Judaic Commentary to the Book of Genesis. Atlanta: Scholars, 1988.

Neusner, Jacob. Genesis and Judaism: the Perspective of Genesis Rabbah. Atlanta: Scholars, 1985.

Nieraad, Jürgen. "Walter Benjamins Glück im Untergang. Zum Verhältnis von Messianischem und Profanem." German Quarterly 63 (1990): 222–232.

Nietzshe, Friedreich. Briefwechsel mit Franz Overbeck. Leipzig: Insel-Verlag, 1916.

—— Werke in drei Bänden. Vol. 1. Köln: Könemann, 1994.

Opitz, Michael and Erdmust Wizisla, eds. 'Aber ein Strum weht vom Paradiese her' Texte zu Walter Benjamin. Leipzig: Reclam, 1992.

Pangritz, Andreas. "Il «volto messianico» della società senza classi. Il materialismo d'ispiranzione teologica di Walter Benjmain" Protestantesimo 46 (1991): 175–186.

Pasqualucci, Paolo. "Felicità messianica. (Interpretazione del 'Frammento teologico-politico' di Benjamin)." Rivista internazionale di filosofia del diritto, no. 55 (1978): 583–629.

Picker, Marion. "Darstellung als Entsprechung. Die Idee, das Wort 'Glück' in Walter Benjamins 'Theologisch-Politischem Fragment.'" In Thomas Bedorf., ed., Undarstellbares im Dialog: Facetten einer deutsch-französischen Auseinandersetzung, pp. 228–246. Amsterdam: Rodopi, 1997.

Proudhon, Pierre-Joseph, "Système des contradictions économiques, ou philosophie de la misère." In Oeuvres complètes. Vol. 1/2. Paris: Riviere, 1959.

Rabinbach, Anson. "Between Enlightenment and Apocalypse: Benjamin, Bloch, and Modern German Jewish Messianism." New German Critique, no. 34 (1985): 78–124.

Rose, Gillian. Judaism and Modernity: Philosophical Essays. Oxford: Blackwell, 1994.

Rosenzweig, Franz. Der Stern der Erlösung. Frankfurt: Suhrkamp, 1993.

Rürup, Reinhard, ed. Jüdische Geschichte in Berlin. Berlin: Hentrich, 1995.

Ryder, A. J. The German Revolution of 1918. Cambridge: Cambridge University Press, 1967.

Sarachek, Joseph. *The Doctrine of the Messiah in Medieval Jewish Literature.* New York: Hermon, 1968.

Saperstein, Marc, ed. *Essential Papers on Messianic Movements.* New York: New York University Press, 1992.

Schäfer, Peter and Gary Smith, eds. *Gershom Scholem. Zwischen den Disziplinen.* Frankfurt: Suhrkamp, 1995.

Schmid, Hans Heinrich. *Gerechtigkeit als Weltordnung. Hintergrund und Geschichte des alttestamentlichen Gerechtigkeitsbegriffes.* Tübingen: J. C. B. Mohr, 1968.

Schmied-Kowarzik, Wolfdietrich, ed. *Der Philosoph Franz Rosenzweig.* 2 vols. Freiburg: Alber, 1988.

Schmitt, Carl. *Politische Theologie.* Berlin: Dunker und Humblot, 1990.

———— *Römischer Katholizismus und politische Form.* Stuttgart: Klett-Cotta, 1984.

Scholem, Gershom. *Briefe.* Vol. 1 (1914–1947) ed. Itta Shedletzky; vol. 2 (1948–1970) ed. Thomas Sparr; vol. 3 (1971–1982) ed. Itta Shedletzky. München: C. H. Beck, 1995.

———— *Briefe an Werner Kraft.* Frankfurt: Suhrkamp, 1986.

———— *Das Buch Bahir.* Darmstadt: Wissenschaftliche Buchgesellschaft, 1970 [Leipzig, 1923].

———— *From Belin to Jerusalem.* New York: Schocken, 1980.

———— "Interview with Irving Howe." *Present Tense* (Autumn 1980): 53–57.

———— "Ist die Verständigung mit den Arabern gescheitert?" *Jüdische Rundschau,* no. 91, November 20, 1928.

———— *Judaica.* Vols. 1-6. Frankfurt: Suhrkamp, 1984–1997.

———— *Die jüdische Mystik in ihren Haupströmungen.* Frankfurt: Suhrkamp, 1980 [1941]

———— "Kabbala." *Encyclopaedia Judaica.* Berlin: Eschkol, 1932.

———— *Kabbalah.* New York: Meridian, 1978.

———— "Eine kabbalistische Erklärung der Prophetie als Selbstbegegnung." *Monatsschrift für die Geschichte und Wissenschaft des Judentums* 74, no. 38 (1930): 285–290.

———— "Die Lehre vom 'Gerechten' in der jüdischen Mystik." *Eranos Jahrbuch* 27 (1958).

———— *Major Trends in Jewish Mysticism.* New York: Schocken, 1974.

———— *The Messianic Idea in Judaism and Other Essays on Jewish Spirituality.* New York: Schocken, 1971.

———— "The Name of God and the Linguistic Theory of the Kabbala." *Diogenes,* no. 79 (Fall 1972): 59–81; no. 80 (Winter 1972): 164–192.

———— *1987–1982 Commemorative Exhibition on the Fifth Anniversary of His Death.* Jerusalem: Jewish National and University Library, 1988.

———— *Od Davar. Explications and Implications. Writings on Jewish Heritage and Renaissance.* Vols. 1-2. Tel Aviv: Am Oved, 1992 [Hebrew].

———— *On Jews and Judaism in Crisis.* New York: Schocken, 1976.

———— "On Our Language: A Confession." *History and Memory* 2, no. 6 (Winter 1990).

—————— *On the Kabbalah and Its Symbolism.* New York: Schocken, 1969.

—————— *On the Mystical Shape of the Godhead.* New York: Schocken, 1976.

—————— *On the Possibility of Jewish Mysticism in Our Time and Other Essays.* Philadelphia: Jewish Publication Society, 1997.

—————— "Reflections on the Possibility of Jewish Mysticism in Our Time." *Ariel,* no. 26 (Spring 1970).

—————— *Sabbatai Sevi: The Mystical Messiah.* New Jersey: Princeton University Press, 1973.

—————— "Die 36 verborgenen Gerechten. *"Der jüdischen Tradition in Theater-Wahrheit und Wirklichkeit.* Zürich, 1962.

—————— *Tagebücher, nebst Aufsätzen und Entwürfen bis 1923.* Vol. 1/1, 1913–1917, ed. Karlfried Gründer and Friedrich Niewöhner. Frankfurt: Jüdischer Verlag, 1995; vol. 2/2, 1917–1923, with Karl E. Grözinger. Frankfurt: Jüdischer Verlag, 2000.

—————— *Über einige Grundbegriffe des Judentums.* Frankfurt: Suhrkamp, 1970.

—————— "Eine unbekannte mystische Schrift des Mose de Leon." *Monatsschrift für die Geschichte und Wissenschaft des Judentums* 71, no. 35 (1927): 109–123.

—————— *Ursprung und Anfänge der Kabbala.* Berlin: de Gruyter, 1962.

—————— *Von Berlin nach Jerusalem.* Trans. Michael Brocke and Andrea Schatz. Frankfurt: Jüdischer Verlag, 1994.

—————— *Von der mystischen Gestalt der Gottheit. Studien zu Grundbegriffen der Kabbala.* Frankfurt: Suhrkamp, 1991.

—————— *Walter Benjamin. Die Geschichte einer Freundschaft.* Frankfurt: Suhrkamp, 1990.

—————— *Walter Benjamin: The Story of a Friendship.* New York: Schocken, 1981.

—————— *Walter Benjamin und sein Engel.* Frankfurt: Suhrkamp, 1992.

—————— "Zionism: Dialectic of Continuity and Rebellion: Interview with Gershom G. Scholem, April/July 1970." In Ehud Ben-Ezer, ed., *Unease in Zion.* New York: Quadrangle/New York Times, 1974.

—————— "Zur Frage des Parlaments."*Jüdische Rundschau,* no. 11, February 8, 1929.

—————— "Zur Geschichte der Anfänge der christlichen Kabbala." In *Essays Presented to Leo Baeck on the Occasion of His Eightieth Birthday.* London: East and West, 1952.

—————— *Zur Kabbala und ihrer Symbolik.* Frankfurt: Suhrkamp, 1973.

Scholem, Gershom, ed. *Zohar: The Book of Splendor, Basic Readings from the Kabbalah.* New York: Schocken, 1963.

Schulte, Christoph. "'Die Buchstaben haben . . . ihre Wurzeln oben.' Scholem und Molitor." In Eveline Goodman-Thau, Gert Mattenklott, Christoph Schulte, eds., *Kabbala und Romantik.* Tübigen: Max Niemeyer, 1994.

—————— "Messias und Identität. Zum Messianismus im Werk einiger deutsche-jüdischcer Denker." In E. Goodman-Thau and M. Daxner, eds., *Bruch und Kontinuität.* Berlin: Akademie, 1994.

Schweid, Eliezer. "Jewish Messianism: Metamorphoses of an Idea." In M. Saperstein, ed., *Essential Papers on Messianic Movements.* New York: New York University Press, 1992.

Schweppenhäuser, Hermann. "Walter Benjamin über Gerechtigkeit." *Frankfurter Adorno Blätter IV* (1996): 43–51

Sharp, Gene. *The Politics of Non-Violent Action*. Boston: Sargent, 1973.

Silver, Abba Hillel. *A History of Messianic Speculation in Israel*. New York: Macmillan, 1927.

Silver, Daniel. *Maimonidean Criticism and the Maimonidean Controversy, 1180–1240*. Leiden: Brill, 1965.

Simon, Ernst, *Entscheidung zum Judentum*, Frankfurt: Suhrkamp, 1980.

Smith, Gary, "'Das Jüdische versteht sich von selbst.' Walter Benjamins frühe Auseinandersetzung mit dem Judentum" *Deutsche Vierteljahrsschrift für Literaturewissenschaft und Geistesgeschichte* 65 (1991): 318–334.

Smith, Gary, ed. *Benjamin. Philosophy, Aesthetics, History*. Chicago: University of Chicago Press, 1989.

——— *On Walter Benjamin. Critical Essays and Recollections*. Cambridge: MIT Press, 1989.

Soosten, Joachim von. "Ethischer Skeptizismus und revolutionärer Aktualismus. Die theologischen Wurzeln des Zeitbegriffs in Walter Benjamins Thesen 'Über den Begriff der Geschichte' und dessen politisch-ethische Implikationen." *Zeitschrift für evangelische Ethik* 32 (1988): 36–46.

Sorel, Georges. *Der Falsche Sieg*. Berlin: Dunker und Humblot, 1944.

——— *Reflections on Violence*. London: Collier, 1970.

——— *Scritti politici e filosofici*. Torino: Einaudi, 1975.

Speth, Rudolf. *Wahrheit und Ästhetik*. Würzburg: Könighausen und Neumann, 1991.

Steinheim, S. L. *Die Offenbarung nach dem Lehrbegriffe der Synogogue*. New York: New York Times, 1980 [Frankfurt, 1835].

Strauß, Eduard. *Errinnerungen*. Leipzig: Deuticke, 1906.

——— *Judentum und Zionismus*. Frankfurt: Kauffmann, 1919.

Susman, Margarete. *"Das Nah- und Fernsein des Fremden:" Essays und Breife*. Frankfurt: Jüdischer Verlag, 1992.

Tagliacozzo, Tamara. "Walter Benjamin: un tentativo di teoria della conoscenza in alcuni frammenti degli anni 1917–1921." In Guido Coccoli and Caterina Marrone, ed., *Simbolo metafora linguaggi*. Rome: Gutenberg, 1998.

Taubes, Jacob. *Ad Carl Schmitt. Gegenstrebige Fügung*. Berlin: Merve, 1987.

——— *Die Politische Theologie des Paulus*. München: Wilhelm Fink, 1995.

——— "Walter Benjamin—ein moderner Marcionit? Scholems Benjamin-Interpretation religionsgeschichtlich überprüft." In Norbert Bolz and Richard Faber, eds., *Antike und Moderne. Zu Walter Benjamins Passagen*. Würzburg: Könighaus and Neumann, 1986.

Taubes, Jacob, ed., *Religionstheorie und Politische Theologie: Theokratie*. Vol. 3. München: Wilhelm Fink, 1987.

Tiedemann, Rolf. *Dialektik im Stillstand. Verusuche zum Spätwerk Walter Benjamins*. Frankfurt: Suhrkamp, 1983.

Trabitzsch, Michael. *Walter Benjamin: Moderne, Messianismus, Politik. Über die Liebe zum Gegenstand*. Berlin: Verlag d. Beeken, 1985.

Traverso, Enzo. "Il materialismo messianico di Walter Benjamin." *Il ponte*, no. 2 (1990): 47–70.

Tugendhat, Ernst. *Vorlesungen über Ethik*. Frankfurt: Suhrkamp, 1993.

Unger, Erich. *Von Expressionismus zum Mythos des Hebrärtums: Schriften 1909–1931*. Würzburg: Könighaus und Neumann, 1992.

——— *Politik und Metaphysik*. Berlin: David, 1921.

Unger, Rudolf. *Hamanns Sprachtheorie im Zusammenhange seiner Denkens*. München: C. H. Beck, 1905.

Urbach, E. E., R. J. Zwi Werblowsky, and Ch. Wirszubsky, eds. *Studies in Mysticism and Religion: Presented to G. G. Scholem*. Jerusalem: Magnes, 1967.

Venturi, Franco. *Roots of Revolution*. Oxford: Oxford University Press, 1977.

Volwerk, Herbert. "Das Recht zur Gewaltanwendung." *Blätter für religiösen Sozialismus* 1, no. 4 (September 1920).

Werblowsky, R. J. Zwi. "Tradition in 'säkularer' Kultur." In Peter Schaefer and Gary Smith, eds., *Gershom Scholem. Zwischen den Disziplinen*, pp.70–80. Frankfurt: Suhrkamp, 1995.

Wilde, Oscar. "The Soul of Man Under Socialism." *The Works of Oscar Wilde*. Vol. 8. New York: AMS, 1972.

Witte, Bernd. "Bilder der Endzeit. Zu einem authentischen Text der 'Berliner Kindheit' von Walter Benjamin." *Deutsche Vierteljahrsschrift für Literaturwissenschaft und Geistesgeschichte* 58 (1984): 570–592.

——— *Walter Benjamin: mit Selbstzeugnissen und Bilddokumenten*. Reinbek bei Hamburg: Rowohlt, 1985.

——— "'Wie Welt allseitiger und integraler Aktualität.' Die Säkularisierung jüdischer Motive in Walter Benjamins Denken." *Der Deutschunterricht* 37 (1985): 26–37.

Wohlfarth, Irving. "Et Cetera? The Historian As Chiffonnier." *New German Critique*, no. 39 (Fall 1986): 147–168.

——— "'Haarschaf and der Grenze zwischen Religion und Nihilismus.' Zum Motiv des Zimzum bei Gershom Scholem." In P. Schäfer and G. Smith, eds., *Gershom Scholem. Zwischen den Disziplinen*. Frankfurt: Suhrkamp, 1995.

——— "Immer radikal, niemals konsequent." In Norbert W. Bolz and Richard Faber, eds., *Antike und Moderne: Walter Benjamin's Passagen*. Würzburg: Könighauusen und Neumann, 1986.

——— "No-Man's-Land: On Walter Benjamin's 'Destructive Character.'" In Andrew Benjamin and Peter Osborne, eds., *Walter Benjamin's Philosophy: Destruction and Experience*, pp. 155–182. London: Routledge, 1994.

——— "On Some Jewish Motifs in Benjamin." In Andrew Benjamin, ed., *The Problem of Modernity: Adorno and Benjamin*, 157–215. London: Routledge, 1989.

——— "Resentment Begins at Home: Nietzsche, Benjamin, and the University." In Gary Smith, ed., *On Walter Benjamin*, pp. 224–259. Cambridge: MIT Press, 1988.

——— "Walter Benjamin's 'Image of Interpretation.'" *New German Critique*, no. 17 (Spring 1979): 70–98.

———— "'Was nie geschrieben wurde, lesen'. Walter Benjamin's Theorie des Lesens." In Uwe Steiner, ed., *Walter Benjamin. 1882–1940*, pp. 297–344. New York: Peter Lang, 1992.

———— "Die Willkür der Zeichen. Zu einem sprachphilosophischen Grundmotiv Walter Benjamins." In Christoph Türche, ed., *Perspektiven Kritischer Theorie. Eine Sammlung zu Hermann Schweppenhäusers 60. Geburtstag*, pp. 124–173. Lüneburg: zu Klampen, 1988.

Wolin, Richard. *Walter Benjamin: An Aesthetic of Redemption*. New York: Columbia University Press, 1982.

Wunsche, A, ed. *Der Midrasch: Bereschit Rabba*. Leipzig: Otto Schulze, 1881.

———— *Kleine Midraschim zur jüdischen Ethik, Buchstaben- und Zahlen Symbolik*. Vols. 1–4. Leipzig, 1907–1909.

Wyneken, Gustav. *Der Kampf für die Jugend*. Jena: Diederichs, 1919.

———— *Die neue Jugend: Ihr Kampf um Freiheit und Wahrheit*. München: Steinicke, 1914.

———— *Schule und Jugendkultur*. Jena: Diederichs, 1914.

INDEX